STRANGE
STORIES

STRANGE
STORIES

and other Explorations in Victorian Fiction

Robert Lee Wolff

Gambit INCORPORATED
Boston 1971

FIRST PRINTING

Copyright © 1971 by Robert Lee Wolff
All rights reserved including the right to reproduce this book or parts
thereof in any form
Library of Congress Catalog Card Number: 70–144338
ISBN Number: 0–87645–047–8
Printed in the United States of America

To
Howard Mumford Jones

PREFACE

All three essays in this volume deal with Victorian fiction, and none would have been written had the author not succumbed long ago to the agreeable vice of collecting nineteenth-century English novels. The first essay is partly confessional and partly intended as a demonstration that the pleasures of the chase can inspire the hunter to reflect intelligently on his quarry. The mere possession and contemplation of certain novels with certain associations, I argue, and hope I show, can help to dispel the heavy mists that separate us from the Victorian world, a civilization close to us in time, but often remote from us in attitudes and feelings. The second essay tries to demonstrate that the reading of neglected novels can illuminate in unexpected ways the lives, and indeed the times, of the novelists. Exploring the irrational and the neurotic as revealed in two works of fiction, it attempts to produce a new understanding of two important Victorian writers who were not primarily novelists but each of whom expressed in a novel truths about themselves that they could hardly tell in any other way. And from the two novels and the two writers it rashly proceeds to make some tentative suggestions about the nature of the society as a whole. The third essay deals with three occult novels and several short occult tales by a prominent, popular, and prolific novelist that have received very little critical attention. It seeks to relate his fiction not only to his voluminous reading but also to his own long and hitherto unexplored career as a practicing occultist and investigator of allegedly supernatural phenomena. It emphasizes in fact that, although he was virtually alone among English writers in the depth of his interest in and knowledge of such subjects as alchemy, clairvoyance, spiritualism, and magic, he had in Goethe and Schiller, in Balzac and Victor Hugo forerunners and contemporaries who shared not only his preoccupations but many of his views.

Of course any one of the three essays can be read by itself.
But they are linked together in many ways. One of the five key
novels in the first essay is Le Fanu's *Uncle Silas,* just as surely
a tale of the supernatural as Bulwer's *Strange Story,* which
gives its title to the third essay. In the second essay will be
found not only a summary account of the revival of mesmerism
in England, which brought to Harriet Martineau a cure for
illness and a deep conviction that mesmeric theories were true,
but an examination of the close relationship between mesmerism and the strange influence exerted by Thomas Lake Harris,
the American religious leader, over Laurence Oliphant. In the
essay on Bulwer we return to mesmerism and allied phenomena
both in his fiction and in his life. In the second essay we shall
find that it was Bulwer who suggested to Miss Martineau that
she try mesmerism, and in the third we shall find that it was
Miss Martineau who provided Bulwer with a "key" to his
puzzling novel *Zanoni,* which he thereafter ordered to be
printed with the novel. Mesmerism and its relationship to psychotherapy, then, play a major rôle in both these essays. And
as for Bulwer, he is not only the central figure of the third essay
and a *deus ex machina* in the second, but we find him also in
the first, providing direct inspiration for Harrison Ainsworth,
whose *Rookwood* is another of the five key novels there discussed. And a third of the five, *Peter Ibbetson,* reveals its author as preoccupied with dreams and dream-life and no less
original in his treatment of them than Bulwer himself. If after
examining this book and my previous work on George Mac-
Donald any reader should conclude that I have a marked interest in the peculiar, I could only agree with him.

Of the three essays, portions of the first and a shorter version
of the second have at various times formed the subject of
papers presented before audiences at Yale, the University of
Texas, the Massachusetts Historical Society, The Club of Odd
Volumes, the "Harvard Victorians," and—most helpfully to
the writer—a psychoanalysts' study group in Boston presided
over by Dr. Grete Bibring. But the present versions are quite

different. Nor was either essay previously published. The third essay has never been tried out on anybody, but comes to the publisher hot off the typewriter, and perhaps none the worse for that.

Though the novels and manuscripts discussed in these essays are all in the author's collection, the book could not have been written without the resources of the Harvard College Library, where it is a great privilege to work, and those of the Boston Athenaeum, where I often found books that Harvard did not possess. To the staffs of both libraries and to my friends Mr. and Mrs. S. D. Warren, to whom I owe not only my Athenaeum reader's ticket but much bourbon, moral support, and willingness to listen, go my heartiest thanks. Friends and colleagues who have helped include John Clive, Henry Hatfield, Jr., Howard Mumford Jones, Gregory Rochlin, Zeph Stewart, B. J. Whiting, and Isidore Twersky. My friend and secretary, Mrs. Elizabeth Flavin, has typed and retyped the manuscript effectively and uncomplainingly, and has shown some satisfactory and unmistakable signs of a growing addiction to alchemy and Rosicrucianism.

Lady Browning (Daphne du Maurier) has kindly granted permission for the quotation in print of my unpublished letters of George du Maurier, and the Hon. David Lytton Cobbold has done the same for an unpublished letter of the first Lord Lytton and for the various unpublished materials in the Lytton Manuscripts now in the Hertfordshire County Record Office. I am indebted also to the County Archivist, Mr. Peter Walne, and to his kind and courteous assistants.

CONTENTS

Preface   vii

List of Illustrations   xiii

I

Some Pleasures of the Chase   1

Notes   61

II

The Novel and The Neurosis: Two Victorian
     Case Histories   69

Notes   130

III

Strange Stories: The Occult Fiction of
     Sir Edward Bulwer-Lytton   143

     1   Bulwer as a Literary Man: His
         Early Use of the Occult   145

     2   *Zanoni* (1842): a Commentary   159

     3   *Zanoni* (1842): Interpretations   202

     4   The Years Between: Bulwer as
         a Practicing Occultist (1842–1862)   233

     5   *A Strange Story* (1862): a Commentary   265

     6   *A Strange Story* (1862): Interpretations   288

     7   *The Coming Race* (1871): Climax
         and Epilogue   323

Notes   334

Index   367

LIST OF ILLUSTRATIONS

Novels in boards and presentation copies of cloth-bound three deckers 6

Four "Yellowbacks" 7

Hajji Baba, Photo the Suliote, Beggar My Neighbour, George Donnington, The Manchester Man, Scarsdale, and *Ribblesdale* 16

Geoffrey Hamyln, Robbery Under Arms, Policy and Passion, and *The Frozen Pirate* 17

The Tower of London, book issue and part issue 28

Ainsworth's holograph letter in *the* copy of *Rookwood* 29

Ghost Stories and *the* copy of *Uncle Silas* 34

First edition front cover of *Gabriel Denver* 35

Inscribed copy of *The Dwale Bluth* and *the* copy of *Gabriel Denver* 44

The copy of *Robert Elsmere* 45

An original George du Maurier drawing for *Punch* 52

A George du Maurier drawing from *Trilby* in *Harper's* 53

Letters by George du Maurier about *Peter Ibbetson* and *Trilby* 56

The copy of *Peter Ibbetson* and first English edition of *Trilby* 57

Presentation copies of *Deerbrook* and *The Hour and the Man,* and some first editions of Harriet Martineau's other works 75

Harriet Martineau's holograph letter concerning mesmerism 89

Altiora Peto, Traits and Travesties, Piccadilly, and

Masollam   119
Original drawing of Bulwer by Daniel Maclise for
Fraser's Magazine   147
Some first editions of Bulwer's works, and *Zanoni,
A Strange Story,* and *The Coming Race*   155
Bulwer's letter to M. E. Braddon concerning *A
Strange Story*   305

I

SOME PLEASURES OF THE CHASE

A scholar will often ask a book collector what use he thinks he can possibly be to scholarship. And even if the scholar politely refrains from asking the question out loud, the collector knows or thinks he knows that the question is there, trembling, waiting to be asked. When it has been answered, usually lamely, defensively, the scholar often follows it with a second one, equivalent to the question that young men out on the town allegedly used to ask especially attractive ladies of easy virtue: how did you ever get into this sort of life? When a collector himself *is* a professional scholar the result is a mild but agreeable sort of schizophrenia. How did I, one asks oneself from time to time, ever become a collector, and what possible use to scholarship can my collecting be? After thirty-odd years of collecting—and scholarship—perhaps it is time to face up to these two questions in print. The first, of course, I can try to answer directly. The answer to the second, I can only hope, will gradually emerge of itself.

I

I began to collect Victorian fiction back in the 1930s when as an undergraduate at Harvard I heard the rumor that one of the most formidable members of the History Department had been recommending—and only half in fun—that his graduate students pay more attention to the boys' books of the English writer G. A. Henty (1830–1902). Henty wrote about ancient Egypt (*The Cat of Bubastis*) and about the Boer War (*With*

Roberts to Pretoria) and also about virtually everything that
had ever happened during all the millennia in between: more
than a hundred books. Remembering some of them with pleasure from my childhood, I began in a desultory way to search
for Henty in the bookshops of Boston. At first I bought reprints, but they were often grubby and mean. Then I saw my
first first edition: *With Buller to Natal*, published in New York
by Scribner's, but uniform with the gaily blocked and deco-
rated Blackie English issue. I began to discard my reprints and
to replace them with first editions. Collecting fever had me in
its grip. The gold and glitter of the Blackie spines sped the
virus through my system. After a few months I stumbled upon
my first three-volume novel, Henty's *Dorothy's Double*. I
winced at the price, which was three dollars, but I bought it.
Never since have I seen another copy for sale.

My temperature rose. I told my father of my illness. Thinking to assuage it, he gave me a copy of Michael Sadleir's
Excursions in Victorian Bibliography, with its fine short essays
on some major minor Victorian novelists, and bibliographies
of their books. I was done for. By Christmas my father was
wincing too, since I had found a copy of the first edition of
Wilkie Collins' *Moonstone* in original cloth and was asking
that it be my Christmas present. I kept adding Hentys, but the
wish for Henty had become a yearning for nineteenth-century
English fiction in general. This was to be my quarry, but how
was I to recognize it and hunt it successfully?

By now I had learned that early in the nineteenth century
publishers stopped putting the novels they issued into their own
leather bindings. Instead they sent them out bound in paper
boards with printed paper labels on the spines, usually in
three volumes (a "three-decker"), but sometimes in four, five,
two, or even one. The purchaser usually declined to keep
them in his library in so fragile or drab a form, and had them
rebound. In original boards they had mostly disappeared, and
those that I could find were usually dirty, frayed, and broken.
This made the search for good copies hard, but not impossible.

By the 1830s publishers' cloth had often replaced the boards-and-labels binding, and cloth remained standard from then on. But these cloth-bound novels, often very handsome when issued, seemed even harder to find in decent condition.

Why? Because the ordinary three-volume novel cost thirty-one shillings and sixpence, or about eight nineteenth-century dollars, perhaps forty dollars of today's purchasing power. Then as now, very few people would spend forty dollars to own a novel. So the publishers had to assume that the circulating libraries would buy up most of their output of every title. And the libraries would put their own disfiguring paper labels in or (worse) on the volumes. After being labeled and passing through the hands of many borrowers, surviving Victorian novels in cloth seemed even less appealing than those in boards. If one could find a copy of a cloth-bound novel that had never been in a circulating library, this meant either that somebody had originally paid the equivalent of forty dollars for it, or that the author himself had obtained it from the publishers to give to a friend, often inscribing it first. Such presentation copies are rare, but among fine surviving copies of a Victorian novel—themselves such rarities—not so very uncommon. The chase took on new excitement.

Since the success of a novel depended upon the willingness of the libraries to buy up the first thousand copies or so upon publication, the publishers had to cater to the libraries' prudery, exaggerated even for the Victorian age. If the author submitted a manuscript that seemed to defy the rules even slightly, the publisher would not take it. Once in a while a storm rose over a novel that had already been printed, and it would be quickly withdrawn from circulation. You will not easily find a copy now of Mortimer Collins' *Sweet Anne Page*: it was suppressed as scandalous because of a few rather prolonged embraces between an engaged couple, and a tickling match between two young ladies who were undressing for the night—one of them, admittedly, was the young wife of a Bishop. To obtain *Sweet Anne Page* took me years of prurient searching.

Above, two examples of novels in boards: William Godwin's *Mande-ville* ((1817) and Captain Frederick Marryat's *Jacob Faithful* (1834); *below,* presentation copies of cloth-bound three-deckers: George Mac-Donald's *Alec Forbes of Howglen* (1865) with an inscription to John Ruskin, and George Gissing's *The Nether World* (1888) with an in-scription "From 7K to Smallbrook Cottage." Gissing was living at 7K Cornwall Mansions, and his brother Algernon at Smallbrook Cottage.

Four "Yellowbacks": *left*, two with "daring" covers to catch the eye at railway stations; *right*, Mayne Reid's two Yellowback first editions.

The other famous Victorian practice of publishing certain novels in shilling monthly paper parts also gravely affected the authors whose books appeared in this form. It was chiefly the recognized popular novelists—Dickens, Thackeray, Ainsworth, sometimes Trollope or Charles Lever—whose fiction came out in parts, Dickens always in greenish-blue wrappers, Thackeray in yellow, each part with two illustrations. Over a period of twenty or even twenty-four months, the buyer would collect the parts and then send the complete set to be bound up as a book. The binder would throw away the advertisements for bloater paste and brass bedsteads, for macassar oil or Enos Fruit Salts that had adorned each part issue. Even those novelists who usually appeared in parts did not always do so: *Esmond* was published as a three-decker; so was *Great Expectations*. But for *Vanity Fair*, for *Pendennis*, for *The Newcomes*, Thackeray sat up late at night scribbling away with a wet towel around his head while the printer's boy waited impatiently in the passageway outside the study door to seize the completed copy of the installment and rush it off to meet the inexorable deadline. Thackeray himself complained that his fiction would have been better had he been able to produce it all of a piece. So one gradually discovered the intimate relationship between publishing practices and the content and quality of Victorian novels.

In the sixties and seventies part publication gave way to the kind of magazine serialization we still have today. I quickly learned to want the original periodicals, with their splendid woodcut illustrations by such artists as Arthur Hughes or Charles Keene or George du Maurier, illustrations that often were not reprinted when the novel came out in book form. And the magazines usually had special Christmas numbers, devoted to short stories, again frequently to be found in no other place. The Christmas (and sometimes Easter) Annuals had succeeded the Regency and early Victorian Gift Books of the twenties and thirties, with their bindings of leather or vellum or heavily gilded cloth and their elegant steel engravings, often containing a story by some favorite author which was never re-published and remained unlisted even in the most complete of bibliographies. Finally there were the cheap reprints—"yellow-backs," as they were called from the lurid paper boards in which they were bound—sold in the railway stations to be read on trains, sometimes luring the prospective buyer much the way modern paperback fiction tries to do, but far more dec-orously. Among the reprints lurks an occasional yellow-back first edition: Captain Mayne Reid, for example, published at least two books for the first time in this form.

The three-volume form continued to hold sway into the 1890s, but gave way gradually to the one-volume novel. The last three-decker appeared in 1897. Conan Doyle, Rider Hag-gard, and many other novelists began their careers in the three-volume period (*The White Company, Dawn*) but published most of their fiction in one volume.[1] The wide variety of physical forms in which the novels appeared, and the physical attraction of triplets on the shelf gave me increasing pleasure as I accumulated examples and learned more about what I was doing. When I could afford it, I began to buy autograph letters by authors about their books, and even an occasional original manuscript. Marriage, children, World War II pro-vided brief periods of remission. But the disease always returned and raged yet more furiously. My sufferings continue and increase. Reluctant at first to buy books by the greatest authors of the period, because they were both very well known and very expensive, I concentrated in the early years of my col-lecting upon the lesser authors. Among them I found many surprises and delights.

Gradually I worked out my own rules: insisting on decent condition, I would buy any English novel published during the reign of Queen Victoria, and any other novel by the same author, even though it might have appeared before 1837 or after 1901. It has been estimated that there were about 42,000 novels published in the great Queen's reign. If so, I now have between twenty and twenty-five per cent of the total. Many of my

runs of the most prolific authors—and novelists often wrote
fifty novels or more (Mrs. Oliphant, one of my favorites,
wrote more than one hundred)—are complete or nearing completion. As a whole, the collection provides a mirror of Victorian life, and offers extraordinary opportunities to the
student of Victorian social history as well as the student of
literature. As I have bought each novel, I have made for it a
catalogue slip with a bibliographical description of the book,
guided by Sadleir's practices in the catalogue he issued of his
own collection in 1951, but including some comment on the
story itself. Although not yet published, this catalogue has
already proved useful to me and to others. The collection has
provided many adventures in fields of learning happily far
removed from my own professional interests. Twice before,
I have ventured to publish some findings that seemed to me
new and interesting that sprang directly from the collection.
An article on Henry Kingsley in 1959 was followed by a book
about George MacDonald in 1961.[2] The essays in this present
volume are a mere foretaste of what I have in store for the
hapless reader.

2

The Victorian novelists took for their province the whole
surface of the globe. If one began in India, let us say, one
could easily travel westward around the world in Victorian
novels. In Captain Meadows Taylor's sensational *Confessions
of a Thug* (1839), for example, there speaks a captured member
of that sinister religious association that murdered countless
travelers as a religious duty, as well as for plunder and for
pleasure. At intervals Taylor followed the *Thug* with a series
of five other novels, planned to introduce the English reader to
the complex and strange new world of the huge Indian sub-
continent at five different periods in its history. Meadows

Taylor spent a lifetime in the service of the Nizam of Hyderabad, learned several of the Indian languages, married a part-
Indian woman, traveled widely, and wrote well. I have all his
novels; some (including the *Thug*) are the copies he presented
to his father with long loving inscriptions, and this despite
the fact that Taylor senior had rather unfeelingly sent his
son out to India at the age of twelve to make his own way.

Long before Kipling, dozens of other writers tried their
hands at an Indian tale. In 1826, for example, the novel *Pandurang Hari* appeared in London. Celebrated in its own day,
it purported to be the autobiography of a Hindu—and most
convincingly—but was actually written in England by a certain Cyrus Redding from notes sent to him by W. B. Hockley,
another Englishman living in India. Almost half a century later,
in 1872, when Sir Bartle Frere wanted to reprint the novel,
he reported that Meadows Taylor could trace only a few copies
in private hands, one of which was borrowed to serve as the
basis for his text. I have *Pandurang Hari*, and Hockley's later
novels as well. The Sepoy Mutiny of 1857 produced a whole
crop of novels, one of the most arresting being *The Dilemma*
by General George Chesney, an able army officer who tried
to explain as dispassionately as possible not only what had happened but how it could have happened. My collection includes
The Dilemma and Chesney's other works of fiction, among
them one that urges the adoption of the General's ideas for
reforming the Indian army. Here too is his celebrated pamphlet,
The Battle of Dorking (1871), that warned against a German
invasion of England after the Franco-Prussian War, together
with some of the many pamphlet responses pro and con to
which it gave rise.

In *Oakfield; or, Fellowship in the East* (1853) Matthew
Arnold's younger brother, William Delafield Arnold, writing
as "Punjabee" four years before the Mutiny itself, had given
an unforgettable picture of the cynicism and coarseness of
his fellow officers in India, indicting by implication at least
the whole British occupation for its contemptuous and philis-

tine attitude toward the Indians. Though *Oakfield* is a very important and almost forgotten Indian novel, it is also more than that, since it speaks movingly and convincingly to a modern reader about the crisis of conscience of Arnold's generation. J. W. Kaye, later to become the historian of British India, published anonymously as a youth in Calcutta a revealing and entertaining Indian novel, called *The Story of Basil Bouverie* (1842). But—so a signed note in Kaye's hand in my copy reveals—only fifty copies were printed, and of these the author himself retained all but two or three in his own hands. In the 1880s and 1890s a prolific and far less profound novelist, Bertha M. Croker, then immensely popular, now forgotten, wrote many novels about India, as she did about her native Ireland. I have many of them, and with them her correspondence with her publisher, in which she shows proper pride in the comparisons that the reviewers were making between her fiction and that of the young Rudyard Kipling.[3]

Moving westward from India, one finds oneself immediately deep in the novels of Persia: with his *Hajji Baba* (1824)—still well-known if not very often read—and his other books, both fiction and nonfiction, James Morier began a genuine cult of Persia among English novel readers. He was ably seconded, among others, by the Scot James Baillie Fraser, whose *Kuzzilbash* (1828) deals with the dervishes on the Persian-Turkish border, and most of whose other novels are set in this region that he knew so well at first hand. Morier's and Fraser's novels are all in the collection, and so are many others about the Near East and the Balkans, including *Photo the Suliote* (1857) by Morier's brother David, a serious novel about the Albanians, Greeks, and Turks in the 1820s. When an English publisher in 1951 wanted to print an abridged version, he had to borrow the British Museum copy. My copy of the first edition was presented by Morier to Edward Lear, on Corfu in 1857, and laid in to it are a series of little notes from Morier to Lear, inviting him to dinner in a delightful mixture of Greek, French, German, Italian, and English. Here in Greece and Turkey the fiction approaches my own proper professional field of study of eastern and southeastern Europe, and I particularly enjoy finding novels I have never heard of before.

Thus *Beggar My Neighbour* (1882) by E. D. Gerard proved to be a gripping tale of rural life in eastern Poland, complete with profligate and spendthrift nobles, poverty-stricken peasants, priests, and Jewish moneylenders. E. D. Gerard in turn proved to be a pen name for two sisters, Emily and Dorothea Gerard, both of whom had married officers in the Austro-Hungarian army, Emily a Magyar and Dorothea a Pole, and lived for many years in eastern Europe. In addition to the several novels that they wrote together as E. D. Gerard, each wrote fiction independently, Dorothea indeed producing more than fifty novels, most of them about eastern Europe. They are hard to find, and so I am still a long way from completing my Gerard collection; but each time I find one I also find it well worth reading. The world of eastern Europe, though geographically much closer to England than the Middle East or India, was far less well known to English readers. The Gerard sisters did not venture over the Russian border, but there were plenty of novelists who did, both before and after the Crimean War. In 1845, for example, a man called Hennigsen who had probably been a British agent in Russia wrote a fictional exposé of serfdom, *The White Slave*. Among many others I would single out *George Donnington; or, In the Bear's Grip* (1885), which I ordered from a catalogue, thinking it was perhaps a story of hunting grizzlies in the Rockies, but which proved to be the tale of a young English businessman who becomes involved in a Russian spy network when he goes to Odessa for his firm. It is a serious study of secret police methods, and was an altogether unexpected find.

In the tamer world of western Europe, the novels of France and Italy are thick upon the ground; but there are fewer about Germany, except about English tourists there, and still fewer about Spain, despite the English love affair with that country that can be followed in the pages of George Borrow or of

Richard Ford's magnificent guidebook. About Portugal I have only one novel, *The Prime Minister* (1845), but it is the second novel of William H. G. Kingston, who later wrote literally hundreds of tales for boys. The Prime Minister is Pombal, the eighteenth-century Portuguese enlightened despot. Kingston had lived in Portugal for many years, learned the language, and done his homework.[4]

As for the British isles, one finds of course novels set in every county from Cornwall to East Anglia and the northern tip of Scotland, while the novels of Ireland form an especially large and exciting group only beginning to be studied. Here the well-known jostles against the less well known and the still totally unknown. Mrs. Gaskell's novels of Lancashire's industrial cities—*Mary Barton* (1848) and *North and South* (1855), for example—have always had readers since they first appeared, and have deservedly won increasing admiration in recent years. But few now know Mrs. G. Linnaeus Banks's novel, *The Manchester Man* (1876), the story of the career of a self-made cloth manufacturer, and at the same time a chronicle of the city's fortunes in the early nineteenth century. From eyewitnesses and family documents Mrs. Banks drew a lively picture of the so-called Peterloo Massacre of 1819, when troops fired on the population. All of Mrs. Banks's Lancashire novels are well worth reading, and so hard to find that I actually own the original complete author's manuscripts of two that I have never been able to find in book form. James Kay-Shuttleworth, a leader in the field of education in nineteenth-century England, also wrote two north-country novels, relegated by his biographer to a footnote and utterly forgotten today, but well worth rediscovering. In the first, *Scarsdale* (1860), we find ourselves in the early days of industrialization, and witness the spoiling of the Lancashire and Yorkshire countryside by the smoke and waste of the first factories, while local craftsmen thrown out of work by the new machines grow desperate, arm themselves, and attack the proprietors. In *Ribblesdale* (1874) we are brought face to face with the subtler clash between the ancient landholding gentry and the new commercial rich now establishing themselves in the county. Since Kay-Shuttleworth, as he tells us himself, could see the virtues of both classes, he produced a remarkably subtle work of delicate social shadings, with no crude black-and-white judgments.

One could go on region by region and topic by topic across the length and breadth of England: if Charles and Henry Kingsley made the Devon coast peculiarly their own, and introduced their contemporaries and a few loyal present-day devotees to the storms and shipwrecks of the region, the virtually unknown Anna Eliza Bray, who lived for almost a century, wrote ten novels of Devonshire history that would still command attention if they could be found and read. Good fortune has brought me most of them, many with her inscriptions to members of her family. As for Ireland, the brothers Banim (who wrote as "The O'Hara Family"), William Carleton, Gerald Griffin, and others have slowly been acquiring again the fame that once was theirs,[5] while Lever, Lover, and Le Fanu have never disappeared from view. But there are literally hundreds of other novelists of Ireland and many hundreds of Irish novels waiting in obscurity. Have you read the novels of Lady Emily Lawless, of Fanny Gallaher, of Mary Laffan Hartley, of half a hundred others? They are on my shelves, and deserve rediscovery.

Pioneering days in Australia were very like those in the United States, and yet the contrasts were so striking that Australian novels will always have a special interest for Americans. The natives are there, but they are primitive black fellows instead of red Indians; the wild animals are there, but they are kangaroos or Tasmanian devils. There is a gold rush, the opening of new lands, the springing up of new cities, dangerous explorations across deserts, banditry, vigilantism; but though we recognize them all, we seem to be viewing our own West through distorting spectacles. Australians themselves have in recent years rediscovered some of their own early

Above, Hajji Baba, Photo the Suliote, Beggar My Neighbour, and *George Donnington; below, The Manchester Man, Scarsdale,* and *Ribblesdale.*

Above, Geoffry Hamlyn with an inscription from Henry Kingsley to the wife of his brother Charles. She disliked him intensely. *Below, Robbery Under Arms, Policy and Passion,* and *The Frozen Pirate.*

fiction. Charles Kingsley's scapegrace brother Henry, after
five years as a remittance man in Australia, produced in 1859
The Recollections of Geoffry Hamlyn, full of action, but
presenting a land altogether inhabited by English gentry who
have transplanted to the bush all the amenities of Devonshire
country life. Marcus Clarke, a newspaperman who had settled
in Australia and intended to write a novel about it, thought
Geoffry Hamlyn so good that he postponed his own effort for
fifteen years. But in 1874 he did produce *His Natural Life*, a
grim story of the penal colonies that gave the reader of Henry
Kingsley a more balanced view. Fourteen years later still, T. A.
Brown, writing under the pseudonym of Rolf Boldrewood,
published his *Robbery under Arms* (1888), the story of Captain Starlight, the daring bush ranger–bandit. These three
novels are the most celebrated of those dealing with Australia, but, as so often, not necessarily the best.

Today not even the Australians remember Mrs. Campbell
Praed, born in 1851, the daughter of a Queensland politician,
who married, moved back to England, and lived unhappily
ever after. In her fiction she returned repeatedly to the scenes
of her youth. *Policy and Passion* (1881) sensationally attacked
the leading political figures of Queensland without much
effort to disguise them. *Mrs. Tregaskiss* (1896) portrayed the
agony of a sensitive and cultivated woman forced to live out
her life on a distant station (ranch, in American) with no
social or cultural opportunities: a kind of Australian *Main
Street* a generation before Sinclair Lewis. These and Mrs.
Praed's other Australian novels ought to be better known:
most are in the collection, but some continue to elude me.

3

There is no way of conveying in a single essay the *density*
of a collection that includes so many thousands of novels and

other fiction. Here are the novels of school and college life,
of which there are many as good as *Tom Brown* but still
unread; novels of the sea and of the merchant service, where
I share the deep affection of King George V and of Swinburne (did they have anything else in common, or have I anything else in common with them?) for the works of W. Clark
Russell. He wrote more than ninety novels. The publicity they
gave to the conditions of the fo'csle actually led to an improvement in the quality of the food served to the men before the
mast. But my favorite is *The Frozen Pirate* (1887), in which
an eighteenth-century ruffian who has survived for a century or
so in a state of deep-freeze (cryogenically?) is discovered in
the cabin of his ship, stuck in the ice off Cape Horn, and
thawed out with surprising results. Although I had read this
yarn as a child, I could not obtain a first edition of it for
more than thirty years, but I have one now, thank heavens.[6]
And here are the novels of military life, of sport in the hunting field and on the racetrack, novels of the stage and of the
artists' studios, of London Bohemia and the London underworld, novels of crime and detection, novels of the clergy and
of theological and social problems: all the classifications one
can think of, and a rich selection of examples. In the pages
that follow we shall be making a closer acquaintance with a
few of them.

Even with well-known authors, such as Wilkie Collins, their
lesser-known novels often have surprises in store: *The Moonstone* and *The Woman in White*, and to a lesser extent *Armadale* and *No Name*, have always had devotees. But, except for
a few modern students, *Man and Wife*, for instance, written at
the height of Collins' powers in 1870, has had very little attention. Yet it is an extraordinarily vivid story of a gentle, highborn lady trapped by a moment's indiscretion in Scotland into
marriage with a smooth and vicious athlete. Collins was aiming
first at the Scots marriage laws just approved by a Royal
Commission, which sanctioned marriage by mere consent:
no witnesses, no ceremony, not even consummation was neces-

sary for a legal marriage. His second target was the cult of sport and muscular Christianity generally so puffed by Charles Kingsley and others, which annoyed the frail, fat, gouty Wilkie Collins beyond endurance: he decided that all athletes were surely stupid, and quite likely to be villainous as well. Sport, he maintained, led to rioting, excess, the blunting of all moral sensibilities, and the complete stultification of a university education. This may not be the greatest of all nineteenth-century novels, but it is a remarkable protest against certain fashionable attitudes, which is no doubt why it went unread even in its own day.

My copy of the first edition is inscribed "To Mrs. George Graves. Wilkie Collins," which may not seem remarkable until one realizes that Mrs. Graves, so formally addressed in 1870, had met Wilkie Collins somewhat unconventionally fourteen years before. He and some friends, walking home late one night through North London, heard the piercing scream of a "young and very beautiful woman dressed in flowing white robes that shone in the moon light," who rushed out of a villa and "seemed to float rather than to run" toward them, and "paused . . . in an attitude of supplication and terror." He pursued her, and discovered that she had been kept a prisoner under hypnotic influence by a wicked man (not her husband, although she had one). Collins took her as his mistress, and with them lived a little girl, her child by her husband. The dramatic first appearance of Caroline Graves—and Wilkie did usually call her by her first name—inspired *The Woman in White*. Although Caroline left Collins briefly and got married to somebody else, and although during her absence Collins had four children by another woman, Caroline came back to him, and their ménage went on as before. My copy of *Poor Miss Finch*—his novel about a lady who turns blue because of an overdose of silver nitrate—is also inscribed to her. And to the little girl, Lizzie, who loved Collins dearly and grew up to be his secretary and the wife of his solicitor, H. P. Bartley,

Collins inscribed two of the other novels in my collection. My copy of *Blind Love*, Collins' last novel, left unfinished at his death, has in it a note in Lizzie Graves Bartley's own hand that reads, "In memory of my dear Wilkie Collins, godfather, generous benefactor, and friend, the last work on which we were engaged." So these inscriptions take one into the heart of one of the most celebrated irregular households of Victorian literary London, where Collins, who suffered horribly from arthritis of the eyes, would dope himself steadily with laudanum, and have a few jolly men friends in of an evening to cheer him up.

My copy of Collins' *New Magdalen* (1873)—one of the very first Victorian novels to present a reformed prostitute as a heroine—is inscribed to Georgina Hogarth, Dickens' sister-in-law, who stayed on in the Dickens household after the scandal caused by Dickens' separation from her sister Catherine, and who took care of the younger Dickens children, never marrying. From the *New Magdalen* Collins made a successful play. My copy is the prompt copy which belonged to Ada Cavendish, the leading lady, and in it is a letter from Collins inviting Palgrave Simpson to play the male lead. *The Evil Genius* (1886) Collins dedicated to the famous pre-Raphaelite painter Holman Hunt, and my copy is the dedication copy, presented to Hunt by Collins. Other novels by Collins in the collection have inscriptions to other close friends; the unpublished and unused letters to Harper and Brothers about the serial appearance of *Man and Wife* in this country are also there, and so are about a hundred other letters and a drawing made by Collins in the earlier days when he thought of following his father's career and becoming a painter. The Collins collection, then, which includes all his books in first edition, is an exciting one because of the many intimate personal relationships that one thinks of when one examines it.[7]

Indeed, perhaps the greatest pleasure of collecting Victorian fiction, aside from that of reading it, is finding and acquiring such association copies. And among my association copies, there is one super-category reserved for books that I can call *the* copy. Let me illustrate what I mean. In his parody of Alexander Woollcott, who adored coincidence, Wolcott Gibbs has him report how Rebecca West, prowling among the *bouquinistes* along the banks of the Seine, had found a copy in fine condition of the East Chicago Vice and Crime Commission's Report for 1906: and on the title page, scrawled in a childish hand so faint as to be barely legible, appeared the inscription: "To my little friend William Lyon Phelps on his third birthday," and the signature "Harpo Marx." Would anybody deny that Rebecca West had stumbled upon *the* copy—not just *a* copy—of the Commission's Report? If I had a copy of the first edition of *Wuthering Heights* (as, alas, I have not) in its original boards, inscribed "To Charlotte, Anne, and Branwell, with happy memories of Gondal and all my love: Emily," would I not be justified in responding to the next friend who asked me whether I had a copy of *Wuthering Heights*, "Not just *a* copy: *the* copy"?

The copy is usually but not always a first edition; it is usually but not always a copy inscribed by the author; it may be the dedication copy—that inscribed to the book's dedicatee; but it is not necessarily any of these. *The* copy is one that so compellingly evokes for its owner the author of the book, the circumstances under which it was written, its impact on its time and on readers since its appearance, its *meaning*, in the largest sense of that term, that the owner smugly says: this is it, *the* copy. In the nature of things, this cannot happen very often to any collector. But it has happened at least five times to me. These five discoveries of *the* copy have prompted the five brief essays that follow, which I offer as a practical illustration of the joys and uses of collecting. The five novels are *Rookwood* by W. Harrison Ainsworth, *Uncle Silas* by J. Sheridan Le Fanu, *Gabriel Denver* by Oliver Madox Brown, *Robert Elsmere* by Mrs. Humphry Ward, and *Peter Ibbetson* by George du Maurier. Each of the five in its own way is a very important novel: four of them were best-sellers when they came out and influential long after their publication. All are highly readable today. Yet their authors and their authors' purposes could hardly vary more widely. And they appeared at considerable intervals during the nineteenth century: *Rookwood* in 1834; *Uncle Silas* in 1864; *Gabriel Denver* in 1873; *Robert Elsmere* in 1888; and *Peter Ibbetson* in 1892.

4

In 1824, at the age of nineteen, dashing and well-to-do, Harrison Ainsworth had come from Manchester to London to study the law, which he soon abandoned for journalism and literature. He had written for *Fraser's Magazine* and published a few short stories when, in his late twenties, he set to work on his first novel, *Rookwood*. Influenced by the enormous success of Bulwer's *Paul Clifford*, which had appeared in 1830, with an imaginary highwayman as hero, and *Eugene Aram*, which had appeared in 1832, retelling in fiction the story of a true historic murder and enlisting the reader's sympathy for the murderer, Ainsworth now made the notorious eighteenth-century highwayman Dick Turpin a subsidiary character in *Rookwood*. Then, in a day and a night, he imagined and wrote of Turpin's flight from London to York on his mare, Black Bess—a hundred pages of narrative that simply swept the public off its feet. In real life, Turpin had never made such a ride, nor had Ainsworth really intended Turpin to be his hero: this made no difference:

Well do I remember [Ainsworth wrote later] the fever into which I was thrown during the time of composition. My pen literally galloped over the pages. So thoroughly did I identify myself with the flying highwayman that, once started, I could not stop.

Into his novel Ainsworth introduced four songs written in underworld slang, and they too simply delighted his readers. One of them had a rousing chorus at the end of each stanza, that went "Nix my doll, pals, fake away," meaning "Never mind, friends, just keep on stealing."

Fashion had been made. After an interval of five years, Ainsworth in 1839 followed *Rookwood* with *Jack Sheppard*, about another historic highwayman, very clever at escaping, but hanged at last: there was nothing wrong with the moral, but the press, which had hailed *Rookwood*, now quite inconsistently launched a moral counteroffensive against *Jack Sheppard* like that with which Bulwer's enemies had greeted *Eugene Aram*: what could be expected of the young if they read novels that actually glorified highwaymen and jailbirds and murderers? Crime would multiply. And in fact, in 1840, a valet who rejoiced in the name of B. F. Courvoisier murdered his master, Lord William Russell, and—so the Sheriff of London and Middlesex declared—confessed that the idea of the murder had come to him from reading a copy of *Jack Sheppard* borrowed from the valet of the Duke of Bedford. The press attacks became louder and more strident: it was urged that *Jack Sheppard* be publicly burned by the hangman.

But of course public taste had its way. The vogue of the "Newgate" novel—as the new genre was called after the famous prison, where some of the most affecting scenes usually took place, and after the Newgate Calendar of crime—ran fast and furious, and all the sermonizing only made the books more popular. *Jack Sheppard* was adapted for the stage, and the "Nix my doll, pals" poem originally in *Rookwood* was now set to music, inserted into the *Jack Sheppard* play, and sung to wild applause every night.

Jerry Juniper's Chant

In a box of the stone jug [cell of the jail] I was born
Of a hempen widow the kid forlorn,
                          fake away

And my father as I've heard say,   fake away,
Was a merchant of capers [dancing master] gay
Who cut his last fling [was hanged] with great applause
           Nix my dolly, pals, fake away.
        . . . .
And ne'er was there seen such a dashing prig
With my strummel [hair] faked in the newest
           twig [style], fake away,
With my fawnied flams and my onions [rings on my
           hands and seals] gay, fake away,
My thimble of ridge and my driz kemesa [keme*say*] [gold
           watch and laced shirt]
All my togs were so niblike and splash,
           Nix my dolly, pals, fake away.
All my togs were so niblike and splash
Readily the queer screens I could then smash [I could
           pass counterfeit banknotes], fake away,
But my nuttiest blowen [favorite mistress], one
           fine day, fake away,
To the beaks did her fancy man betray
And thus I was bowled out at last,
           Nix my dolly, pals, fake away.
And thus I was bowled out at last,
And into the jug for a lag was cast, fake away,
But I slipped my darbies [handcuffs] one morn
           in May, fake away,
And gave to the dubsman [turnkey] a holiday
And here I am, pals, merry and free,
A regular rollicking romany,
           Nix my dolly, pals, fake away.

"Nix my dolly travelled everywhere," said the contemporary wit, Theodore Martin:

> . . . it made the patter of thieves and burglars familiar in our mouths as household words. It deafened us in the streets where it was popular with organ grinders and German bands. It clanged at midday from the steeple of St. Giles, the Edinburgh Cathedral. That such a subject for cathedral chimes and in Scotland too could ever have been chosen will scarcely be believed. But my astonished ears often heard it.

It was whistled by every dirty guttersnipe, and chanted in drawing-rooms by fair lips, little knowing the meaning of the words they sang.

With W. E. Aytoun, Martin even wrote a poem called "On Hearing 'Nix My Dolly Pals, Fake Away' Played on the Bells of St. Giles Cathedral 14th May, 1840," that dramatically tells how a street urchin was corrupted for life by hearing the bells play the tune: "Lightly ye came upon my infant ears," it says, and "from that day/It passed not from my soul, that glorious 'fake away.'" He goes to the bad of course:

> Freely I lived on love, and gin, and swipes:
>   My togs were rigged in very spicy style;
> No fob could stay my penetrating snipes;
>   The prince of Buzgloaks I, the knowing file!
> Fawnies or fogles, tickers, onions gay,
> All were the same to me, at all I faked away.

And concludes:

> Cathedral steeples, pointing to the skies
>   Shake their old sides to the prevailing mirth
> And bear aloft the strains that daily rise
>   From the full bosom of the joy-struck earth
> No more cold penitential hymns they play,
> But spire to steeple winks, and chuckles "Fake away!"

The young Charles Dickens, having scored in 1837 with *Pickwick,* turned to the Newgate theme in 1838 with his second real novel, and gave the public *Oliver Twist,* in which the criminals were not heroes, it is true, but still fascinating. But *Jack Sheppard* at once outsold *Oliver Twist.* The young W. M. Thackeray satirized the whole new fashion in *Catherine,* running serially in *Fraser's Magazine.* And as late as the February, 1847, part-issue of *Vanity Fair,* Thackeray included a brief and delicious parody of the Newgate vogue which he later took out of the novel:

Horrible night! It was pitch dark, pitch dark; no moon. No, no. No moon. Not a star. Not a little, feeble, twinkling, solitary star. There had been one at early evening, but he showed his face, shuddering, for a moment in the black heaven, and then retreated back. One, two, three! It is the signal that Black Vizard had agreed upon. 'Mofy! Is that your snum?' said a voice from the area. 'I'll gully the dag and bimbole the clicky in a snuffkin.' 'Nuffle your clod, and beladle your glumbanions,' said Vizard, with a dreadful oath. 'This way, men: if they screak, out with your snickers and slick! Look to the pewter room, Blowser. You, Mark, to the old gaff's mopus-box, and I,' added he in a lower but more horrible voice, 'I will look to Amelia!'

So from 1834 on into the 1840s the Newgate novel took command of the public imagination. And in it all *Rookwood* had played a most important part.

Now *Rookwood* appeared first in the usual three-volume form, without illustrations. I have a nice copy of the first edition, with a presentation inscription by Ainsworth to a newspaper publisher acquaintance, and a letter requesting him to review it. But this is not *the* copy. After it had run through three editions, the author and publisher in 1836 turned to the illustrator George Cruikshank for engravings to illustrate a fourth edition, to be substantially rewritten. Cruikshank was then forty-three: he had illustrated Dickens' *Sketches by Boz* (which preceeded *Pickwick*), but he had not yet reached the height of his powers. The collaboration between him and Ainsworth proved a very fruitful one: he did the illustrations for several of Ainsworth's later and most famous novels, such as *The Tower of London*, which appeared first in parts and then in book form with extraordinarily fine engravings. I have a nice set of the parts and a copy of the book in cloth signed by Cruikshank, but these, again, are not *the* copies. Later on, the collaboration broke up, when Cruikshank, who was always an eccentric, convinced himself that it was *he* who had originated *The Tower of London* and also *Oliver Twist*. But while it lasted the Ainsworth-Cruikshank collaboration produced some of the finest and most typical illustrated novels of

Ainsworth: *The Tower of London*: *above,* book issue signed by Cruik-shank; *below,* part issue.

Ainsworth: a passage from the letter in *the* copy of *Rookwood*.

the nineteenth century. And *that* all began with *Rookwood* too.

Now the received version of the early relationship between author and artist is that Ainsworth and his publisher, Macrone, were dissatisfied with Cruikshank's work and had grave doubts as to its success: the standard accounts say this. This is because the only available letter Ainsworth wrote on the subject—one dated March 8, 1836—to Macrone, did object to some of Cruikshank's preliminary designs for the book as "sketchy," and expressed the fear that Cruikshank would "put us off—badly." And it is this that brings us to *the* copy of *Rookwood*: not a copy of the first edition, but of the first edition with the Cruikshank plates: not even a very fine copy —*but* having inserted at front and back two further long holograph letters from Ainsworth to publisher, Macrone, dated March 30 and April 12, 1836, unpublished, unconsulted, hitherto unknown. In the first Ainsworth says:

> My dear Macrone . . . Cruikshank's etchings are exquisite. He has succeeded to a miracle! Nothing can be more charming than the frontispiece unless it is the vault and nothing can surpass the vault unless it be the gipsy scene. I am abundantly satisfied with the designs. . . . Beware how you meddle with what is already so good, and do not let George alter one of the chimneys or gables or that delicious dovecot spire. I do not see *how* it can be improved.

There follow many detailed comments and a few suggestions —Could George make Titus a little fatter . . . Sybil's face would look better if smaller I think—and at the end, "I really cannot express how much pleased with George's sketches— they beat his 'Boz' hollow. Let him go on and prosper." And about two weeks later in the second letter, "I am in rapture with George's handiwork. The sketches delight me vastly and I am quite sure that the Public will be equally delighted."

So here in my copy of the first illustrated edition of *Rook-wood* is the first and hitherto unknown evidence of the true enthusiasm which one of the century's prominent novelists in the first flush of his youth and popularity, felt for the work of his collaborator, one of the century's most prominent artists. Ainsworth here says that Cruikshank's sketches for *Rookwood* beat his *Boz* hollow. For me this thrillingly evokes the thirties—and the literary scene just before the accession of Queen Victoria, at the beginning of the intertwined careers of Ainsworth, Cruikshank, and Dickens. That is why I venture to say that for me this is *the* copy.[8]

5

Next, *Uncle Silas*: by common consent, Joseph Sheridan Le Fanu, descendant both of the Sheridans and of a Huguenot family long domiciled in Ireland, ranks as the chief master of the horror story in the nineteenth century. He also tried his hand successfully at Irish historical fiction, edited the *Dublin University Magazine*, and lived in a fine house in Merrion Square with Sheridan family portraits on the walls. Algernon Charles Swinburne, Henry James, E. F. Benson, M. R. James, Dorothy Sayers, Elizabeth Bowen, V. S. Pritchett, virtually every English writer who has himself tried his hand at ghost stories, and every critic who has developed any fondness for the genre, has joined in a chorus of approval for Le Fanu. How does he do it? Why can't we do it? The machinery is convincing, the apparitions genuine. Many readers still admire *Green Tea*, in which a clergyman is haunted and eventually hounded to death by a grim monkey; or *Carmilla*, a vampire story that I am sure inspired Bram Stoker when he wrote *Dracula* in the nineties; or the episode of the hand of glory that appears, disembodied, in an inserted tale in one of Le Fanu's novels, plump and white and horrid on the pillow of the doomed.

M. R. James, Provost of Eton, authority on medieval manuscripts, and probably the best twentieth-century English writer of ghost stories, searched the pages of forgotten Victorian magazines and by 1923 had rescued enough unpublished Le Fanu short stories for a fine new anthology. Le Fanu's own first collection appeared in 1851, *Ghost Stories and Tales of Mystery*. It is a very rare book, and I have the copy that belonged to M. R. James himself: *almost the* copy, perhaps since it links the two masters of the art.

But the novels are more important. Le Fanu wrote a dozen or so in the sixties and early seventies that are generally regarded as his best work. In decent original condition they are really infuriatingly scarce. It took me about thirty years to complete my collection. Critics disagree as to the best of these. Some prefer *The House by the Churchyard*, set in the eighteenth century, with its fantastic scene of a trepanning operation performed by an elegantly dressed and thoroughly drunken brain surgeon, in the flickering light of a lantern, after a duel. Supposedly this was one of the four books in the library of James Joyce's father. At any rate, James Joyce loved it, and references to it stud *Finnegan's Wake*: at one point it even appears in Dutch as *De oud huis bij de Kerkegaard*. I don't say that you can understand *Finnegan* if you have read Le Fanu's novel, but I would maintain that you cannot understand it if you have not. Other critics prefer *Wylder's Hand*, in which the dark deed is finally revealed because the right arm of the victim emerges erect from the swamp like the withered limb of a tree.

But most vote for *Uncle Silas*. "The best," says E. F. Benson, "a masterpiece of alarm . . . there is no pause in the relentless drip, drip, drip of ominous and menacing incident." *Uncle Silas* is set in a gloomy region of Derbyshire in a house with fluted pillars and doorways, and balustraded summit, and (of course) a "stained and moss-grown front," reached through "the florid tracery of an iron gate, standing between tall fluted piers, of white stone all grass-grown and ivy-bound, with

great cornices surmounted with shields and supporters, the
... bearings washed by the rains of Derbyshire for many a
generation, almost smooth by this time, and looking bleached
and phantasmal...." Needless to say, nothing good happens
behind these gates, glimpsed at first in blinding moonlight;
and quite the most repellent character in the house itself is
Madame de la Rougierre, the loathsome French governess.

Here let me turn directly to Swinburne's reaction to *Uncle
Silas*, written in June 1866, in a letter to a close friend who
had loaned him the novel: Swinburne, that tiny, wiry, vivid
man, with a shock of flaming red hair and such a violent sensitivity to alcohol that two glasses of wine turned him into a
screaming drunk, who like as not would tear off all his clothes
and caper and skip around the dining table, howling obsceni-
ties until he was forcibly restrained; Swinburne, who com-
bined the richest poetic talent of his generation and brilliant
critical insight, with a perverse fascination for cruelty, who
openly professed himself a disciple of the Marquis de Sade,
and who once—in an evening I have often tried vainly to
imagine—read aloud some of his purplest new poems to Henry
Adams, of all people, at the house of Monckton Milnes. Well,
here is what Swinburne wrote about *Uncle Silas*:

> I thought I was too old to dream of books but I have not
> yet ceased to dream of Uncle Silas. The vigour of effect
> is wonderful. I only wish the edges were a little smoothed
> off (not as to the "criminal" or terrific side of course) but
> as regards the construction of incident and character. Even
> Uncle Silas would be more terrible and admirable if we saw
> him better. I don't know if I am intelligible when I say that
> he would be more ghastly if he were less ghostly.... One
> other cavil: Mme. de la Rougierre (I hardly like yet to write
> her name) is too ugly to be tragic. There is too much repe-
> tition of "wet grin," "rotten teeth," bigness and baldness of
> head.... A little more evolution of character and less repe-
> tition of effect would have made the book truly great. But

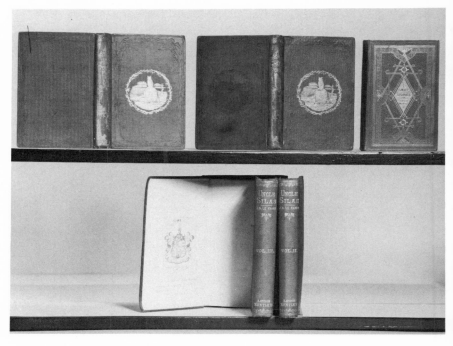

Le Fanu: *above, Ghost Stories* in three variant bindings, including an unrecorded one, in which the design on the back cover repeats in blind-stamping the gilt-stamping on the front cover. *Below, the* copy of *Uncle Silas,* showing the Nanteos book-plate.

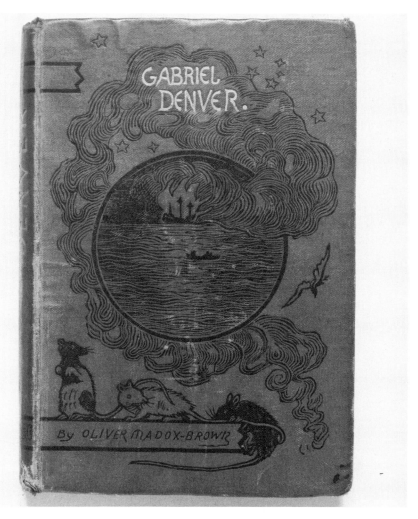

Oliver Madox Brown: front cover of the first edition of *Gabriel Denver*.

certainly the author may claim the praise given by [Victor]
Hugo to Baudelaire—that of having invented "un frisson
nouveau."

Of all the many pages of Le Fanu criticism, I think these
few sentences come closest to the mark: Le Fanu had faults,
but despite them he certainly invented and patented the new
kind of shudder. Now the friend to whom Swinburne was
writing the letter was a young, talented, musical, dissolute
Welsh squire named George Powell, whose family house was
called Nant-Eos (Nightingale's Brook, in Welsh), a beautiful
Georgian place set in splendid grounds about four miles from
Aberystwyth. Unlike most Victorian gentlemen, who borrowed their novels from circulating libraries, often in great
boxes of a hundred at a time, and then returned them of
course, George Powell's father—whom George cordially disliked—and *his* father before him *bought* their novels and then
loaned them to friends, even ordering from their printers a
special label, which they often pasted in under their armorial
bookplates, reminding borrowers to be sure to return the
books.

Within the last decade the Nant-Eos novels have been dis-
persed: first and last, from several dealers I bought at intervals more than two hundred of them, mostly dating from
the sixties and seventies; and I count myself lucky to have
got them because they are usually in fine condition. When
the flurry had subsided and I was sure there would be no
more for sale, suddenly, all by itself in the summer of 1967,
there was offered to me a fine copy of the first edition of
Uncle Silas, the only such copy to my knowledge that has
come on the market since World War II. It was the only
Le Fanu novel that I lacked; of course I ordered it, completing my collection, and when it came it had the bookplate
of Powell of Nant-Eos. I rushed off to the Lang edition of
Swinburne letters: sure enough—it *was* young Powell of
Nant-Eos who had loaned the book to Swinburne. And so I

had not just *a* copy, but what to me was *the* copy, the very volumes that had elicited from Swinburne the letter to Powell that constitutes for me the wisest and best balanced criticism of the greatest of the Victorian ghost stories.[9]

6

Next, *Gabriel Denver*. It was published on November 5, 1873, in a single volume, by Smith and Elder, who had complained that it was too short for the usual three-volume form. It was, however, a striking book to see, in mustard-colored cloth with an extraordinary black-and-gold cover design showing, in a central medallion, a ship afire in the background, while in the foreground a lifeboat floats on the waves. The smoke from the conflagration has burst out of the medallion and coils itself across the whole of the front cover, enveloping the stars of the Southern Cross, which stud its upper portion and surround the lettering of the title; an albatross flies alongside, and atop the scroll at the lower edge, on which the author's name appears, there moves a realistic procession of three rats. The foremost stands erect on his hind legs, his long naked tail coiling over the back of the second, who is crouching; his tail is being frantically bitten by the third, who is clambering onto the scroll from below. As a piece of design, the cover of *Gabriel Denver* is unlike any other Victorian book cover known to me, and little wonder: it was the work of Ford Madox Brown, the distinguished painter who was so closely allied with the pre-Raphaelites, though he refused to become one of the brethren. His most celebrated painting has always been *The Last of England*, now in the Fitzwilliam Museum in Cambridge, but his entire *oeuvre* is now enjoying a new wave of appreciation.

It was the only book cover he ever designed; but the author

was his own son, and only eighteen years old; so the circumstances were indeed unusual. Son of Ford Madox Brown's
second marriage, with two elder half-sisters by the first, Oliver
Madox Brown had been a precocious delight to his family
since earliest childhood. The elder sister, Catherine, married
Francis (or Franz) Hueffer and in due course became the
mother of Ford Madox Hueffer, who would later call himself
Ford Madox Ford and, before he became celebrated as a
novelist, would write articles and books on the pre-Raphaelites, including the only full-length study yet attempted of his
grandfather's life and work (1896). The younger of Oliver's
two elder half-sisters was Lucy, of whom more later. Born
in 1855, Oliver, at the age of five, whipping-top in hand, had
been painted by his father as *The English Boy*. He himself
neglected his school work for painting: at fourteen he exhibited his picture of *Chiron Receiving the Infant Jason from
the Slave*, and he contributed two illustrations to the edition
of Byron that William Michael Rossetti was editing. All the
rest were done by Ford Madox Brown. At sixteen Oliver exhibited and promptly sold a water colour of *Prospero and
Miranda*, and the next year his water-color illustration of a
dramatic scene in George Eliot's *Silas Marner* aroused much
admiration. But by that time he was seventeen and had abandoned art for literature.

Even in his childhood, he had written sonnets, many of
which are not preserved. But now, during the winter when
he turned seventeen, he was spending most of his time—without telling his family about it—writing a novel that he had
long been planning: *The Black Swan*. Its protagonist, the Australian Gabriel Denver, has married without loving her the
only available woman, Dorothy, who did indeed love him,
and who had the money he needed to free himself from a
heavy burden of debt. When he learns of a legacy that he
must go to England to claim, Denver takes passage for himself and Dorothy aboard the *Black Swan*. On the ship he falls
instantly in love with a young girl, Laura, who, with an old

female servant, is the only other passenger. When the servant dies and Laura is left alone, the love affair between her and Denver intensifies. Dorothy is desperately jealous: at first Denver pays her hardly any attention, but soon he comes to hate her. When Dorothy screams her reproaches at her husband, he is tempted to throw her overboard. But the ship soon bursts into flame: Dorothy has put the torch to its cargo of turpentine, and the only survivors, floating in the lifeboat we have already seen, are Gabriel, Dorothy, and Laura. Dorothy drinks sea water, and dies, cursing Laura and Gabriel with her last breath. A ship rescues the other two and Dorothy's corpse. But the lovers are doomed. Laura is too weak to survive, and before the crew of the rescue ship can bury her at sea, the desperate Gabriel has seized her dead body in his arms and leaped overboard.

The elements themselves—though never explicitly—have throughout reflected the torments of love and hate experienced by the man and the two women. The destroying fire symbolizes both the burning love between Denver and Laura and Dorothy's burning jealousy. When the crew of the rescue vessel has buried Dorothy at sea, the skies cloud over, and the hurricane that then begins symbolizes Dorothy's final curse and portends Laura's imminent death and the lovers' final tragedy. Denver has a dream premonitory of his eventual fate: he is back in Australia, and in his wanderings he finds that the lock of hair Laura has given him has turned to dead, dried leaves; in his despair he is about to leap from a cliff, but instead wakes to find himself aboard the ship, which is already afire. He will indeed leap to his death, however, and Laura's body in his arms will be as dead as the lock of hair that symbolized her in his dream.

Brown wrote effortlessly and with a thoroughly professional knowledge of the ship and the sea around her. His imagery is usually spare and often striking, as when, during the hurricane, the rescue ship is guided by "just the corner of a sail set, and inflated like the hood of a cobra." His de-

scription of the behavior of the ship's rats when they discover
the fire, before Denver knows of it, reflects his deep interest
in natural history, and his long observation of his own pet
rats:

> One stood up in the manner so characteristic of its kind,
> no matter what danger they may be flying from, rubbing
> its neck and whiskers carefully with its wet paws; then it
> deliberately inspected the end of its tail, and disappeared
> after the . . . others . . . their keen teeth and fierce little eyes
> glistening as they caught the light. . . .

Oliver's father had read this passage carefully and would draw
the rats to the life.

One of the few modern scholars to have read the novel
compares it to the writings of Hawthorne and of Poe; but
Melville or Conrad would perhaps be nearer the mark. In
any case the reader is convinced that a married man who had
never loved before would be smitten by his first wild love
as Gabriel is smitten; that an inexperienced girl like Laura
would find it impossible not to return so desperate and concentrated a passion; and that a neglected and mistreated wife
might indeed be driven so mad by jealousy that she would
try to destroy a ship and all its people in the hope of killing
the guilty couple. Had *The Black Swan* appeared as the work
of a mature and experienced novelist, it would have been an
arresting novel. As the first effort of a seventeen-year-old
writer, it is quite unbelievable.

Before they would publish it, Smith, Elder forced Oliver
Madox Brown to make many changes against his will. To
satisfy contemporary prudery, Dorothy could not be Gabriel
Denver's wife: she became now instead merely his fiancée, a
jealous spinster cousin, Deborah. Nor could the tragic ending be accepted: Deborah still dies, but she deserves her fate
—after all she has burned the ship—but Gabriel and Laura
survive to live happily ever after. Lengthened, weakened, and
given a new title, *Gabriel Denver* was delayed so that it

might catch the Christmas trade in 1873. "Hideous, . . . but not without some power . . . coarse . . . disagreeable . . ." said the *Athenaeum*. But—

> every now and then . . . we are startled by some observation which seems to indicate a frightful knowledge born of almost personal experience. . . . "Hunger endured for a while becomes strangely soporific, and paralysing on the nerves, and this lack of energy which it causes is one of the chief reasons why people starve so easily in the midst of great cities. There is even some slight pleasure to be obtained from it, for a starving man sees visions like an opium-eater's."

The *Saturday Review* was much more condescending. But a critic worth more than these, Dante Gabriel Rossetti himself, wrote to Oliver that he had been

> much astonished and impressed by it. I really believe it must be the most robust literary effort of any imaginative kind that anyone has produced at the age at which you wrote it . . . though I am uncertain as to the exact time of life at which the Brontë girls wrote their first books. . . . I fully expected your story to suffer by changes. Still . . . I think you have managed so well that the strength of the situation is maintained. . . . The literary quality of the work is surprisingly accomplished and even. However, the last hundred pages or so do not seem to me . . . quite so finished in execution as the rest [and little wonder, since Brown had not wanted to write this portion at all]. There seems to me no question that you may reach any degree of success in the future. . . .

Yet Smith, Elder, who had given Oliver fifty pounds for his book, reported that they had sold only three hundred copies. Nothing daunted, he began a new major novel, set in Devonshire, in which the deadly nightshade, or belladonna, plays a crucial part. The west-country name for this plant is "the dwale bluth," and this was the title he gave his story. But before it could be completed, and only a year after *Gabriel Denver* had appeared, Oliver Madox Brown died (November

5, 1874), after a severe illness, aged only nineteen. It was a horrible blow to his family.

Some months before, in March 1874, his half-sister Lucy Madox Brown, a painter in her own right, had been married to William Michael Rossetti (1829–1919), already forty-five and the only "square" pre-Raphaelite—never much of a painter, but an assiduous scholar and critic, and for almost half a century between 1845 and 1894 an employee of the excise office, where he rose to be Assistant Secretary before retirement. In William Michael there burned the true Rossetti fire; but it was often banked, sometimes oddly enough by Gabriel, who suppressed William Michael's republican and anticlerical *Democratic Sonnet*s in 1881 as likely to cause trouble. With Gabriel, George Meredith, and Swinburne, William Michael had set up housekeeping in Cheyne Walk in 1862, in a brief and unsuccessful experiment. The memoirist of the Brotherhood, his publications of later years have alone made possible serious modern studies of Gabriel and Christina. Now, only a few months after his marriage to Lucy Madox Brown, William Michael, with Oliver's other brother-in-law Hueffer, undertook the compilation of a posthumous collection of Oliver's writings. It appeared in two volumes, dated 1876 but published in December 1875, as *The Dwale Bluth . . . and Other Literary Remains of Oliver Madox Brown*, with a prefatory account of his life. In Volume II, William Michael and Hueffer published *The Black Swan* for the first time as originally written. Ironically enough, then, we owe to Oliver's premature death our knowledge of the first and best draft of his most important work.

The Dwale Bluth is a very scarce book. My copy of it is inscribed on the front free endpaper of Volume I, "Algernon Charles Swinburne Esq. with best wishes from the Author's Father. Dec—18—75." This is of course a splendid inscription from Oliver's grieving father, the great painter, to the even greater poet, the intimate friend of so many of the Brotherhood. But I would not claim it as *the* copy. This claim I would reserve for my copy of *Gabriel Denver,* which, though inferior to *The Black Swan,* nonetheless first brought before the public the tragic tale of Denver, Laura, and Dorothy. And if *The Dwale Bluth* is scarce, *Gabriel Denver* seems virtually to have disappeared: probably most of the three hundred copies sold vanished into circulating libraries, while the balance of those published were pulped. In any case, by 1883, only ten years after publication, it was already called "a rarity difficult to obtain." My copy shows some signs of wear, but on the verso of the front free endpaper it is inscribed "W. M. Rossetti from the Author, 1873."

From the eighteen-year-old author to the man who in a few months would be his brother-in-law, and in a year would be undertaking the melancholy task of collecting his literary remains, this brief inscription for me evokes the deeply interwoven lives of the whole pre-Raphaelite brotherhood and their friends and companions. *Gabriel Denver* is almost the only novel written by one so close to the movement. *The Dwale Bluth* represents the first of the long series of tributes that William Michael would eventually pay to those who died before him. The words of presentation linking the youngest, the most precocious, perhaps the most promising of these men—and certainly the one to die most prematurely—to his sister's future husband and the pre-Raphaelites' future chronicler makes this copy of *Gabriel Denver the* copy.[10]

7

Next, *Robert Elsmere.* I suppose that no subject preoccupied the Victorians as much as religion, not money or love or even fox-hunting. And their fiction reflects it: there are novels upon novels about the pull of Rome and the Oxford movement, and the counterpull of evangelical Protestantism, novels on the Church of England itself, high, low, and broad, and

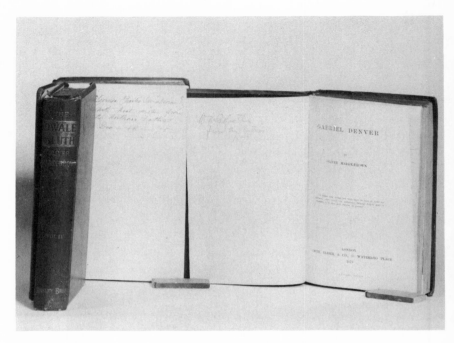

Oliver Madox Brown: my inscribed copy of *The Dwale Bluth* and *the* copy of *Gabriel Denver*.

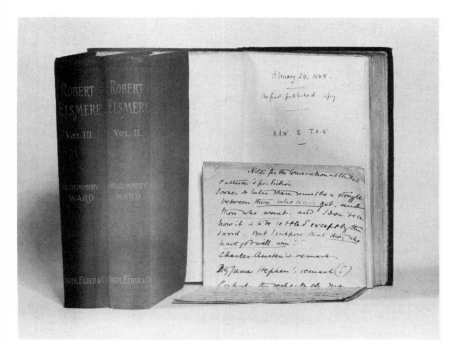

Mrs. Humphry Ward: *the* copy of *Robert Elsmere*.

on the Dissenters, novels that slang the Jesuits and sensationally expose the dangers of their plots against English security and womanhood, novels that satirize the unctuousness
and hypocrisy of the lower-middle-class Low-Church or nonconformist do-gooder preacher, and novels that deal with
everything and everybody churchly in between. The novels
do more than portray: as always, they reflect the problems
of the society. No problem came nearer the surface than the
problem of faith: not only what to believe but how to believe and even, most important, whether to believe. "Never,"
says Marguerite Maison, "has any age in history produced
such a detailed literature of lost faith, or so many men and
women of religious temperament standing outside organized
religion." In novels, the problem of doubt was tackled from
all points of view. *Robert Elsmere* is both the best and the
most celebrated.

Mrs. Humphry Ward was born Mary Augusta Arnold,
daughter of Thomas Arnold, a brother of Matthew (and of
William Delafield Arnold, who wrote *Oakfield*), and thus a
granddaughter of Dr. Arnold of Rugby. One of Lytton
Strachey's four *Eminent Victorians*, Dr. Arnold fiercely opposed the "Oxford malignants," as he called them, who had
introduced the corruption of Catholicism into the proper
Church of England. And so, perhaps naturally, young Tom
Arnold was converted to Catholicism in his youth: it happened in Tasmania, where he had married a girl of Huguenot
ancestry, and as a result of the conversion he had to leave
his post as Inspector of Schools. In fact, in those days he could
get no decent post as a Catholic. Several times in his later
life he began to have doubts about his faith, and re-entered
the Church of England only to be offered a splendid post
of just the right sort to keep his family from starvation; but
each time it happened he would promptly relapse into Catholicism and lose all chance of preferment. It has its comic
side, but it must have been frightful for his family, including
his daughter.

Resentful of his Catholic faith, which all his family deplored, the girl grew up in the Oxford of the sixties that was just then coping also with the new German scholarship in history and interpretation of the Scriptures. An excellent scholar herself and a friend of the leading scholars, she was soon doing research on the early Visigothic churchmen of Spain for a learned encyclopedia. Married in 1872 at twenty-one to T. Humphry Ward, a fellow and tutor of Brasenose, she had two children, and on a pitifully small income managed her household and wrote constantly, reviews and articles, taking her own religious stand as far from her father's as possible: denial of miracle, free criticism of scripture, Christ only a great human teacher. In 1881 after listening to a sermon by a conservative clergyman, who attacked as sinners all those who held unorthodox views, she published a pamphlet in response, called *Unbelief and Sin*. This was the germ of *Robert Elsmere*, which she wrote after her husband had joined the staff of *The Times* and the family had moved to London.

Robert Elsmere, the hero, is a balanced, manly, and exemplary clergyman—frank, genial, open-hearted, good at games, not at all the usual doubter of life or fiction, but happy, prosperous, and secure in his Surrey rectory, a contented husband and father. Then comes *doubt*, engendered like Mrs. Ward's own by the study of history, and impervious to his resolute determination to crush it, and indeed to everything else. Deep depression overwhelms him until he can finally affirm his modernized belief in Christ as a teacher only, a man and not a miracle-worker. But Elsmere's new inward peace is not communicable to his pious wife; he winds up as the founder of a new brotherhood of social workers, and dies of overwork in the cause of the poor. Mrs. Ward is really quite humorless (one thinks of the Beerbohm cartoon in which she begs her dear Uncle Matthew Arnold to "be serious"), and the character study of Elsmere, so convincing as long as the doubts were wracking him, becomes far less so when his creator turns his story into propaganda for her own creed. "One fears," Henry James wrote her later, with an irony she missed, that Elsmere "may suffer a sunstroke ... from the high oblique light of your admiration for him."

Still, a remarkable novel, and from the moment of its appearance in 1888, after endless hours and days of uninterrupted and furious writing (she worked herself "nearly to death," says her daughter Janet, later Mrs. G. M. Trevelyan), it gradually gathered momentum, as the public found out what it was about. It was not easy reading. Mr. Gladstone wrote his daughter that "Mamma and I are each of us still desperately engaged in a death-grapple with Robert Elsmere ... the labour and effort of reading it is six times that of the ordinary novel ... while one could no more stop in it than in reading Thucydides" (!). To Mrs. Ward he remonstrated that *he* believed in the old faith, and that "if you sweep away miracles you sweep away the Resurrection," and *this* he could not bear. He thought her "substitute for Christianity" was "the most visionary of all human dreams."

And soon, though remaining on good terms personally with Mrs. Ward, Gladstone wrote a hostile review of *Robert Elsmere* in *The 19th Century*. His Tory opponents congratulated Mrs. Ward: at last—after two years when he had been able to think of nothing but home rule for Ireland—she had given him something new to get excited about! Thousands of copies were now sold, and nothing else discussed. Thomas Henry Huxley, Mandell Creighton, Hippolyte Taine, all contributed their verdicts. Mrs. Ward herself began to work on a project in social work like Elsmere's New Brotherhood. Thirty thousand copies had quickly been sold in England.

In the United States, William Roscoe Thayer reported,

No book since *Uncle Tom's Cabin* [36 years earlier] has had so sudden and wide a diffusion among all classes of readers; and I believe that no other book of equal seriousness ever had so quick a hearing. I have seen it in the hands of nursery-maids and of shop-girls behind the counter; of frivolous young women, who read every novel that is talked about; of business men, professors, students, and even schoolboys. The newspapers and periodicals are still discussing it, and perhaps the best sign of all, it has been preached against by the foremost clergymen of all denominations.

Publishers rushed to pirate it (this was before the copyright act) and 200,000 copies were printed, of which only one-fourth were authorized. A Buffalo bookshop advertised it at ten cents a copy; in Boston, Jordan Marsh went down to four cents and the queue extended across the street, while the Maine Balsam Fir Company was giving a copy free to each purchaser of a cake of Balsam Fir Soap. Encouraged, somebody over here wrote a "continuation" called *Robert Elsmere's Daughter,* and advertised it, suggesting that it was by Mrs. Ward, who had never heard of it. The resultant scandal in the U.S. led directly to the passage of the Copyright Bill in 1891.

My copy is inscribed "February 24, 1888. The first published copy. M. A. W. to T. H. W."—that is, from Mary Augusta Ward to T. Humphry Ward, from the hard-working, bluestocking, intellectual woman of affairs to her much-loved, greatly loving and admiring, and, one suspects, long-suffering husband. There can never have been a dedication copy of *Robert Elsmere,* since Mrs. Ward dedicated it to two friends both of whom had died long since. With my copy are several holograph manuscript leaves outlining the major dramatic confrontation scene, a kind of preliminary scenario. *The* copy? I think so.[11]

8

And last: *Peter Ibbetson.* Pick up a number of *Punch*—
any number from the year 1863 on through the sixties, seventies, eighties, and into the nineties—and you will find in just
about every issue a drawing that makes a gently humorous
comment on some aspect of the English social scene. Often
the *joke* seems ponderous today rather than pungent, but the
drawing itself is almost always charming: the ladies, even
the socially ambitious Mrs. Ponsonby de Tomkyns, are lovely
to look at, and to study their clothes, or the way they do
their hair as the decades pass, is to give yourself a brief history of Victorian fashions. The men are often handsome, often
more stupid than their wives, and bewildered by the social
maneuvering that is moving them both upward as they de-
terminedly climb their way out of the middle classes; the
foreign musicians are properly hairy; the children are all innocence—but how innocent are they really? As the three little
girls play together, the first says, "*My* Papa's house has a
conservatory," the second, "*My* Papa's house has a billiard-
room," and the third, "*My* Papa's house has a mortgage."
The artist responsible for this worldly drawing, who recorded
for all time the transformation of society from mid-Victorian
days to the nineties, was George Louis Palmella Busson du
Maurier, half French, half English, largely educated in France,
completely at home in both countries and in both languages.
He loved to tease the English on their miserable efforts to
speak French: one drawing shows the proud English traveler
in a French butcher shop ordering a *kilometer* of sausage.

He drew not only the weekly contribution for *Punch* but
illustrations to many of the best contemporary novels: Mrs.
Gaskell's *Wives and Daughters*, the first illustrated edition of
Henry Esmond. Happily married and the father of five chil-

dren, he was a loving, even a doting family man. Among his elders it was Thackeray, who died just as du Maurier's own career was beginning, whom he most admired—Thackeray, near whose initials on the *Punch* staff table du Maurier carved his own, Thackeray, who had begun as a draughtsman and ended as a writer. Thackeray's career was one of the chief determining influences on du Maurier's ambitions. A severe eye disease in youth had left du Maurier nearly blind in one eye and always fearful of an attack in the other, and this also acted as a spur to his trying his hand—aged fifty-seven—at fiction. He attempted to give the plot of a novel to his friend Henry James while they were out for a walk in Hampstead; but James politely refused, and du Maurier later went to work on it himself.

In the five years left him to live, du Maurier produced three novels: *Peter Ibbetson* (1892), *Trilby* (1894), and *The Martian* (1895), the last of which appeared posthumously. All three contain large chunks of autobiography. *Trilby*, of course, is especially famous for the scenes of the *vie de bohème* enjoyed by the young artists Taffy, the Laird, and Little Billee in Paris, and for the idyllic passion of the gentle Billee for Trilby, the beautiful model, who falls under the satanic influence of Svengali the impresario and is transformed by hypnotism into an opera singer. This was the plot that Henry James declined, although it appealed to him, because he felt he knew too little about music.

Trilby was published first in *Harper's Magazine*, with du Maurier's own illustrations. When the third number appeared there was trouble: du Maurier had introduced an artist whom he called Joe Sibley, and whom he described as always in debt, genial, and the most irresistible friend in the world so long as his friendship lasted: then enmity replaced it at once. Sometimes Sibley would try to punch his ex-friend's head, but always he went on through life saying funny things about the ex-friend; "But when he met another joker face to face, even an inferior joker—with a rougher wit, a coarser thrust,

George du Maurier: an original drawing for *Punch*.

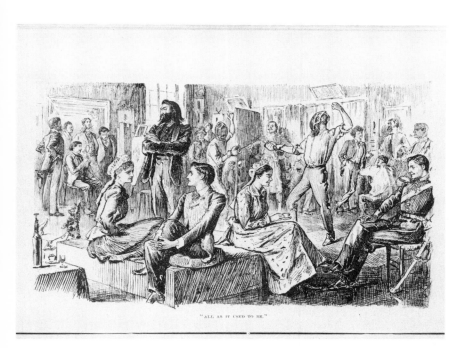

"ALL AS IT USED TO BE."

George du Maurier: drawing from the first publication of *Trilby* in *Harper's*, later suppressed because Whistler recognized himself as Joe Sibley, leaning against the doorpost to the right of the large fencer's elbow.

a louder laugh, a tougher hide, he would just collapse like a pricked bladder." James A. McNeill Whistler recognized himself in Sibley (the very sound of the name is sibilant and whistling) and really there was no doubt: du Maurier had actually drawn Whistler to the life in some of the illustrations. Whistler sued *Harper's,* and forced them to apologize, and to withdraw the offending passage and the drawing with the most recognizable portrait. So the collector must have not only the three-volume first English edition of *Trilby*—which was issued without illustrations and is very hard to find in decent condition—but a set of *Harper's* for 1894, preferably in original wrappers, with the pictures, including the Whistler passage and drawing, *and* the first American edition in book form which contained all the original illustrations but that one. I have all these, but best of all perhaps, I have some fine original and unpublished letters of du Maurier about the book: As it was appearing in *Harper's,* after three numbers he wrote in one of these letters to his English publisher, "Are you still inclined toward the English *Trilby?* And if so, isn't it time to talk about it? . . . I fancy *Trilby* is going to be a go." (And this was indeed an understatement.) In another letter in my possession, written to an American friend who had asked him if the Laird in *Trilby* was a self-portrait, he writes:

> No I am not the Laird. I have pretty much effaced myself. . . . The quartier latin life is however pretty much autobiographical, and the pleasure in reminiscing and writing was great, for it was a happy time when I and T. R. Lamont and T. Armstrong now art director at South Kensington shared a studio together in the rue Notre Dame des Petits Champs in the way I have tried to describe. Indeed, the Laird is a kind of portrait of T. R. Lamont, the only real attempt at portraiture in the book.

Perhaps one could argue that my assemblage of first editions in all possible forms (and there are several others I have not mentioned) with these and other letters of mine might together constitute *the* copy of *Trilby;* but I am not going to do so. Nor will I try to describe the wild mad success of *Trilby*; du Maurier's delightful original drawings for both *Trilby* and *Peter Ibbetson* were sold (as he writes in one of the letters I have) "to a New York enthusiast, c'est toujours ça." Indeed they were . . . his name was J. P. Morgan, and there they are still in the Morgan Library.

No, it's *Peter Ibbetson* for which I make my claim, the tale of the handsome young Apollo of an architect, brought up in France, working in England, who kills his uncle and guardian, a coarse vulgarian. The uncle has spread abroad the rumor that he had been Peter's mother's lover and was himself Peter's father. Confined in an asylum for the criminally insane, the hero encounters in his dreams the beautiful Duchess of Towers, whom he had known as a child in France; they discover that each is dreaming the same dream simultaneously and that they can lead a common dream life together, and so they do for many years. The idea is strikingly original, and alone would have made the first-person narrative of *Peter Ibbetson* memorable. Less than three years after *Peter Ibbetson*, Kipling used the idea of the double dream life in his *Brushwood Boy*.

But in the end what lingers in the memory longest is the enchanting detail of the idyllic childhood of the boy and girl in Passy in the 1840s, remembered from du Maurier's own childhood, brimmingly affectionate for the French schoolmaster, the postman, the cook, for the park and the lake of Auteuil, and for the crooked streets and tumbledown houses of the medieval city that Paris still was then, as well as for the delights of suburb and countryside. Drawn with the artist's pencil, kindly, loving, nostalgic—this is what really distinguishes *Peter Ibbetson*, as much as its extraordinary invention of the love affair conducted in joint dreams. Of course, it is saccharine for the modern taste; but one cannot deny its artistry and sincerity: really, it is du Maurier's best book.

With my copy goes an unpublished letter from du Maurier to F. W. H. Myers, the President of the Society for Psychical Research, who was struck, like all other readers, by the idea

George du Maurier: letters about *Peter Ibbetson* and *Trilby*.

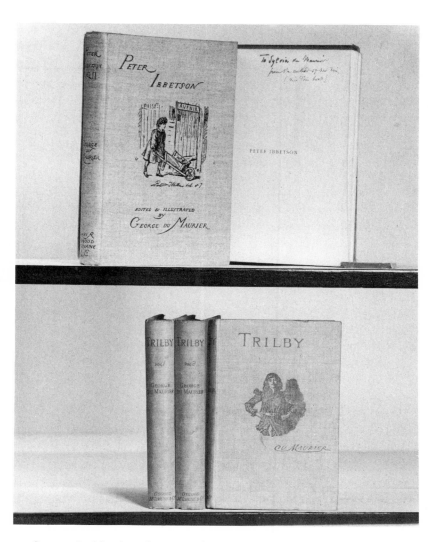

George du Maurier: *the* copy of *Peter Ibbetson* and the first English edition of *Trilby*.

of joint simultaneous dreaming (and no wonder). Du Maurier
writes:

> Naturally I had no pretension to anything like scientific
> purpose in writing Peter Ibbetson. . . . Some day . . . I will
> tell you how near I have been to realizing such dreams in
> sleep (of course without a conscious companion: *that*, so
> far as I know or believe is utterly out of the question). I
> am only speaking of the realizing of pure personal reminis-
> cence (with or without companions who are utterly inno-
> cent of any such partnership)—and, more often than not, of
> quite definite reminiscence of scenes that I cannot remember
> when awake, but which recur again and again in dreams
> with a singular consistency of detail.

Though I think this is a splendid letter, I am not basing my
claim to *the* copy upon it, but upon an inscription in the copy
itself.

This copy of the first edition is worn and shabby; one of
its spines is even missing, but on the half-title of Volume I
is the inscription "To Sylvia du Maurier from the author of
her being (and this book)." Agreeable though this is (in late
Victorian families children often made a joke of the solemn
rôle of their fathers, and teased them as the authors of their
being), is there anything really particular about it? To me
there is.

Sylvia du Maurier was a homely child who had become a
beautiful woman: tall, stately, with a magnificent figure, hair,
and eyes, exactly the kind of woman her father loved to portray in his drawings and writings both. She married a struggling barrister named Arthur Llewellyn Davies, and they had
three little boys. In the late nineties, after the death of George
du Maurier, the Davieses lived in Paddington and the children
went for outings in Kensington Gardens. Here they regularly
began in their early childhood to encounter a small man with
an enormous St. Bernard dog, called Porthos after the dog
in *Peter Ibbetson*, their grandfather's novel. They became
friends, and the man began very early to tell them stories—

stories in which they themselves had somehow actually taken part. This storyteller was J. M. Barrie, and from his stories to the Davies boys eventually emerged the entire cycle of Peter Pan: first the book called *The Little White Bird,* and later the famous play of *Peter Pan* himself—a notable contribution to the childhood memories of the next two generations of English and Americans alike: Peter and Wendy, Tinker Bell, Captain Hook, and with them all an uneasy feeling, which some of us had even as children and I believe that all of us post-Freudians have in our mature years, that there was something terribly wrong about the Darling household, where Mama, Wendy, and Nana, the enormous female nurse-dog, dominated the scene, and father was a mere cowardly custard; and something perhaps even more wrong about Peter Pan, the supernatural boy who could fly but who never wanted to grow up, and whose role by common consent was always taken by actresses.

However queasy this may make us, we do recognize that Barrie's inventions represent a major landmark in the history of English sentimentality, if not in that of English literature. This copy of du Maurier's novel then is quite literally the presentation copy, not only from father to daughter, but by that token from the father of Peter Ibbetson to the mother of Peter Pan. And so it evokes not only du Maurier and Barrie but the link between them, the beautiful Sylvia du Maurier Davies, with whom Barrie fell in love, if indeed he was capable of adult love. He wrote her hundreds of sentimental letters, addressing her by her second name, Jocelyn. He was the only person who ever used it. Barrie established a possessive hold over her and her children partly because he was very rich and gave lavish presents, and the Davies were relatively poor. When Sylvia's husband died in 1907, wretchedly of cancer, Barrie took full financial responsibility for her and her five sons; when his own very attractive wife demanded to be divorced so she could marry a much younger lover, Barrie acceded (his marriage had never been consummated) and became more and more of an intimate of the Davies household. When Sylvia in turn died of cancer in 1910, Barrie adopted the five boys, whose lives continued to be dogged by tragedy. From the Passy of George du Maurier's *Peter Ibbetson* in the 1840s, to the Kensington Gardens of Barrie's *Peter Pan* in the 1890s, to Sylvia's funeral in Hampstead in 1910 and beyond, the whole story is evoked for me by the few words in this copy of *Peter Ibbetson*, which is why for me it is *the* copy.[12]

How entirely subjective my judgments have been in every case I fully recognize. These are *the* copies for me; but each of them may for anyone else be only *a* copy. When considering the pleasures of the collector, we must not forget—in addition to the pleasures of the chase and the pleasures of discovery—the sheer simple pleasure of disagreement with his fellow collectors.

Notes

1. G. A. Henty, *The Cat of Bubastis* (Edinburgh: Blackie, 1889); *With Roberts to Pretoria* (Edinburgh: Blackie, 1902); *With Buller to Natal* (Edinburgh: Blackie, 1901). The Blackie titles were in fact issued in time for Christmas sales of the year preceding the date on the title-pages. The American editions by Scribner and Welford (later Scribner) came out with the title pages dated a year earlier than the English issues. *Dorothy's Double* (3 vols.; London: Chatto & Windus, 1891). Michael Sadleir, *Excursions in Victorian Bibliography* (London: Chaundy & Cox, 1922). Wilkie Collins, *The Moonstone* (3 vols.; London: Tinsley, 1868). Mortimer Collins, *Sweet Anne Page* (3 vols.; London: Hurst and Blackett, 1868). W. M. Thackeray, *The History of Henry Esmond Esquire* (3 vols.; London: Smith, Elder, 1852). Charles Dickens, *Great Expectations* (3 vols.; London: Chapman & Hall, 1861). Mayne Reid's two "yellowback" first editions are *The Pierced Heart and Other Stories* (London: J. & R. Maxwell, [1884]) and *The Star of Empire* (London: J. & R. Maxwell, [1885]), both posthumous, Reid having died in 1883. A. Conan Doyle, *The White Company* (3 vols.; London: Smith, Elder, 1891); H. Rider Haggard, *Dawn* (3 vols.; London: Hurst & Blackett, 1884). Doyle's *The Refugees* (3 vols.; London: Longmans, 1893) and Haggard's *The Witch's Head* (3 vols.; London: Hurst & Blackett, 1885) and *Colonel Quaritch, V.C.* (3 vols.; London: Longmans, Green, 1888) were the only other novels by these two prolific authors that appeared in three-volume form. The latest three-decker in my collection (or known to me) is Algernon Gissing, *The Scholar of Bygate* (3 vols.; London: Hutchinson, 1897); this is George Gissing's brother, who deserves some critical attention.

2. Sadleir's splendid catalogue is *XIX Century Fiction. A Bibliographical Record Based on His Own Collection* (2

vols.; London: Constable, and Berkeley and Los Angeles:
University of California Press, 1951). In *The Book-Col-
lector*, 14 (1965), pp. 335–347 and 511–522, I wrote a
summary account of my collection as it then stood, explaining that Sadleir had ignored many novelists whom I
have assiduously gathered. His collection contained about
one-third as many novels as mine, while mine includes
perhaps seventy to eighty per cent of his titles. My article
on "Henry Kingsley," *Harvard Library Bulletin*, XIII, 2
(Spring, 1959), pp. 195–226, contains descriptions and
photographs of my collection of his novels as it was then.
The book on George MacDonald is *The Golden Key*
(New Haven: Yale University Press, 1961).

3   Captain Meadows Taylor, *The Confessions of a Thug* (3
vols.; London: Bentley, 1839): see also his autobiography,
Story of My Life (2 vols.; Edinburgh and London: Blackwood, 1877). His other novels in the order of their publication are *Tippoo Sultaun* (3 vols.; London: Bentley,
1840); *Tara* (3 vols.; Edinburgh and London: Blackwood,
1863); *Ralph Darnell* (3 vols.; Edinburgh and London:
Blackwood, 1865); *Seeta* (3 vols.; London: Henry S. King
& Co., 1872); and *A Noble Queen* (3 vols.; London: Kegan
Paul, 1878). *A Noble Queen* is set in the 1590s, *Tara* in
1657, *Ralph Darnell* in 1757, *Tippoo Sultaun* in 1788 and
later years, and *Seeta* at the time of the Mutiny of 1857.
Anon. [W. B. Hockley], *Pandurang Hari; or, Memoirs of
a Hindoo* (3 vols.; London: Whittaker, 1826); reprint, ed.
Sir H. Bartle Frere (2 vols.; London: Henry S. King,
1872); Sadleir (*XIX Century Fiction*, I, p. 175) quotes
the preface as I am doing here. Hockley's *The English in
India* (3 vols.; London: W. Simpkin and R. Marshall, 1828)
is perhaps even scarcer. "The Author of The Battle of
Dorking" [General Sir George Chesney], *The Dilemma*
(3 vols.; Edinburgh and London: Blackwood, 1876);
Chesney's novel on reforming the Indian Army is Anon.,
A True Reformer (3 vols.; Edinburgh and London:
Blackwood, 1873). For *The Battle of Dorking*, reprinted
by Blackwood in 1871 after it appeared in *Blackwood's
Magazine* for May of that year, see Bernard Bergonzi,

"The Battle of Dorking," *Notes and Queries, New Series,*
8 (1961), pp. 346–347, with a list of the later works, and
I. F. Clarke, *The Tale of the Future* (London: The Library
Association, 1961), pp. 23–24, with a shorter and different
list. W. D. Arnold's novel was first published under the
pseudonym "Punjabee," *Oakfield; or, Fellowship in the
East* (2 vols.; London: Longman, and Rugby; Crossley
and Billington, 1853), with a second edition published by
Longmans alone in 1854 under his own name and with a
new, signed preface defending the book against its hostile
critics: the collector must have both editions, and will
have trouble finding either. *The Story of Basil Bouverie*
was published as "by the Author of Peregrine Pultuney"
(3 vols.; Calcutta: Privately Printed by S. Smith & Co.,
1842). I do not expect anybody to believe that my copy
has Anthony Trollope's bookplate, but in fact it has. B.
M. Croker, *Village Tales and Jungle Tragedies* (London:
Chatto & Windus, 1895) was the book that reviewers
praised so highly: on March 22, 1895, she wrote her literary agent, Morris Colles, "I see myself . . . compared to
Mr. Kipling or rather to his *Jungle Book*—but this is ri-
diculous." Perhaps: but I recommend *Village Tales* to anybody who can find it, and also her early *Diana Barrington,
A Romance of Central India* (3 vols.; London: Ward &
Downey, 1888), of which I possess her own copy, as I do
of most of her earliest novels.

4   *Adventures of Hajji Baba of Ispahan* (3 vols.; London:
John Murray, 1824). *The Kuzzilbash: A Tale of Khorassan*
(3 vols.; London: Colburn, 1828), originally published
anonymously. Sadleir had all of Fraser except for *The
Dark Falcon* (4 vols.; London: Bentley, 1844), but my collection includes that novel as well as the others. David R.
Morier, *Photo the Suliote: A Tale of Modern Greece* (3
vols.; London: L. Booth, 1857), inscribed "Corfu. Edward
Lear from the Author, July 10, 1857." In addition to
Morier's notes to Lear the book contains a sheet of paper
in Lear's hand on which he has summarized the plot of the
novel. Abridged by J. W. Bagally and reissued as *A Tale
of Old Yanina* (London: St. Catherine Press, 1951). E. D.

Gerard, *Beggar My Neighbour* (3 vols.; Edinburgh and London: Blackwood, 1882). C. F. Hennigsen's *The White Slave; or, The Russian Peasant Girl* (3 vols., London: Colburn, 1845) appeared anonymously. Charles H. Eden, *George Donnington, or, In the Bear's Grip* (3 vols.; London: Chapman & Hall, 1885). William H. G. Kingston, *The Prime Minister: An Historical Romance* (3 vols.; London: Bentley, 1845).

5 Mrs. Gaskell's *Mary Barton: A Tale of Manchester Life* (2 vols.; London: Chapman & Hall, 1848) was published anonymously; *North and South* (2 vols.; London: Chapman & Hall, 1855) as "by the Author of 'Mary Barton,' 'Ruth,' 'Cranford,' &c." Mrs. G. Linnaeus Banks, *The Manchester Man* (3 vols.; London: Hurst & Blackett, 1876). Kay-Suttleworth's *Scarsdale* (3 vols.; London: Smith, Elder, 1860) appeared anonymously; *Ribblesdale* (3 vols.; London: Smith, Elder, 1874) under his own name. On some of the more important Irish novelists see now the excellent critical work of Thomas Flanagan, *The Irish Novelists 1800–1850* (New York: Columbia University Press, 1959). The reader should be warned, however, that he has sometimes omitted titles from ostensibly complete listings of his authors' novels.

6 Henry Kingsley, *The Recollections of Geoffry Hamlyn* (3 vols.; Cambridge: Macmillan, 1859). Marcus Clarke, *His Natural Life* (Melbourne: George Robertson, 1874), republished (3 vols.; London: Bentley, 1875) with a new happy ending, and the title changed in 1878 to *For the Term of His Natural Life*. Rolf Boldrewood, *Robbery under Arms* (3 vols.; London: Remington, 1888), first published serially in the newspaper, *The Sydney Mail*, July 1–August 11, 1883. Mrs. Campbell Praed, *Policy and Passion* (3 vols.; London: Bentley, 1881); *Mrs. Tregaskiss* (3 vols.; London: Chatto & Windus, 1896). W. Clark Russell, *The Frozen Pirate* (2 vols.; London: Sampson Low, Marston, Searle, & Rivington, 1887).

7 Wilkie Collins, *Man and Wife* (3 vols.; London: F. S. Ellis, 1870). The best account of Wilkie Collins, I believe, is Kenneth Robinson, *Wilkie Collins* (London: The Bodley

Head, 1951); on p. 135 he refers to my copy of *Man and Wife*. A later account, Nuel Pharr Davis, *The Life of Wilkie Collins* (Urbana: University of Illinois Press, 1956) is less satisfactory. The quotations in my text are from J. G. Millais, *The Life and Letters of John Everett Millais* (2 vols.; London: Methuen, 1899) as quoted by Robinson, p. 130. *Poor Miss Finch* (3 vols.; London: Bentley, 1872), inscribed "To Mrs. Graves from Wilkie Collins, 1873." *Blind Love* (3 vols.; London: Chatto & Windus, 1890), was completed by Walter Besant after Collins's death and contains a preface by Besant. I have his letter to the publishers about his role in the book. *The New Magdalen* (2 vols.; London: Bentley, 1873); the play is *The New Magdalen. A Dramatic Story* and was published by the author, 90 Gloucester Place, Portman Square. *The Evil Genius* (3 vols.; London: Chatto & Windus, 1886).

8 On Ainsworth, see S. M. Ellis, *William Harrison Ainsworth and His Friends* (2 vols.; London and New York: John Lane, 1911). On the Newgate novel, Keith Hollingsworth, *The Newgate Novel, 1830–1847* (Detroit: Wayne State University Press, 1963). Quotations (in order) from Ellis, I, p. 236; *Rookwood* (3 vols.; London: Bentley, 1834)—the first edition—II, pp. 344–346; Ellis, I, p. 366; Bon Gaultier (i.e., W. E. Aytoun and Theodore Martin), "Illustrations of the Thieves' Literature—No I. Flowers of Hemp; or, The Newgate Garland," *Tait's Edinburgh Magazine*, 8 (April, 1841), pp. 220, 221; Hollingsworth, p. 206; Ellis, I, p. 278; the two unpublished letters from Ainsworth to Macrone in my collection.

9 *Uncle Silas* (3 vols.; London: Bentley, 1864). On Le Fanu, the most detailed and valuable study is the unpublished Harvard Ph.D. thesis of W. C. Lougheed, "Joseph Sheridan Le Fanu: A Critical Biography" (3 vols.; 1962). In print, the study of S. M. Ellis, *Wilkie Collins, Le Fanu and Others* (London: Constable, reprinted 1951) is useful. See also N. Browne, *Sheridan Le Fanu* (London: Collins, 1951). M. R. James's anthology is *Madam Crowl's Ghost and Other Tales of Mystery by Joseph Sheridan Le Fanu* (London: Bell, 1923). For Joyce and *The House by the*

Churchyard, see Herbert Gorman, *James Joyce* (New
York: Farrar and Rinehart, 1939), p. 16; *Finnegan's Wake*
(New York: Viking Press, 1939), pp. 96, 563. E. F. Ben-
son, "Sheridan Le Fanu," *The Spectator,* 146 (February
21, 1931), p. 264. Quotation from *Uncle Silas,* Vol. II, p.
85. The evening at Fryston when Swinburne declaimed
to Henry Adams is often mentioned. See, for example,
James Pope-Hennessy *Monckton Milnes* II, *The Flight of
Youth 1851–1885* (New York: Farrar, Straus & Cudahy
1955), pp. 139ff. Swinburne's letter to George Powell in
C. Y. Lang, ed., *The Swinburne Letters* (New Haven:
Yale University Press, 1959), Vol. I, no. 115, pp. 165–166;
note on George Powell (1842–1882), p. 134, n. 1. At the
same time, Powell loaned Swinburne Le Fanu's *Guy
Deverell* (3 vols.; London: Bentley, 1865), a lesser novel.
In the same letter Swinburne shrewdly characterizes it as
"too hasty. too blurred, too blottesque—the daub of a
clever painter—a brilliant 'pot-boiler.' "

10 *Gabriel Denver* (London: Smith, Elder, 1873). For Oliver
Madox Brown see the brief comment and bibliography in
W. E. Fredeman's indispensable *Pre-Raphaelitism. A Bib-
liocritical Study* (Cambridge, Massachusetts: Harvard University Press, 1965), Section 47, pp. 189–190; Ford Madox
Brown in Section 41, pp. 151–153. The cover of *Gabriel
Denver* is reproduced in Plate VII, opposite p. 154. The
best and fullest account of Oliver Madox Brown is still
John Ingram, *Oliver Madox Brown. A Biographical Sketch
1855–1874* (London: Elliot Stock, 1883). *The Black Swan,*
in *The Dwale Bluth . . . and Other Literary Remains of
Oliver Madox Brown,* ed. W. M. Rossetti and F. Hueffer
(2 vols.; London: Tinsley, 1876), II, pp. 71–247; quotations from pp. 237, 132. Comparison to Poe and Hawthorne, Fredeman, p. 189. I cannot agree with him that "in
part the novel is concerned with diabolical possession."
Reviews in *Athenaeum,* No. 2004 (November 22, 1873),
pp. 658–659; *Saturday Review,* Vol. 37, No. 969 (May 23,
1874), pp. 66–661. *Dante Gabriel Rossetti's* letter published
in Ingram, pp. 83–84. *Gabriel Denver,* a rarity, *ibid.,* p. 90.

11 *Robert Elsmere* (3 vols.; London: Macmillan, 1888). On

Victorian religious fiction generally, see the entertaining book by Marguerite Maison, published in the United States as *The Victorian Vision* (New York: Sheed and Ward, 1961). For the writing and reception of *Robert Elsmere*, see Janet Penrose Trevelyan, *The Life of Mrs. Humphry Ward* (New York: Dodd Mead, 1923). Quotations from Maison, p. 211; Leon Edel, *Henry James, The Treacherous Years: 1895–1901* (Philadelphia and New York: Lippincott, 1969), p. 292; Trevelyan, *Life*, pp. 51, 56, 59, 60; Gladstone's article, *Robert Elsmere and the Battle of Belief*, in *The Nineteenth Century* (May, 1888); *Life*, p. 77.

12 *Peter Ibbetson* (2 vols.; London: Osgood, McIlvaine, 1892). Two thorough books bearing on this section of the essay have appeared since it was originally written: Leonée Ormond, *George du Maurier* (London: Routledge and Kegan Paul, 1969), and Janet Dunbar, *J. M. Barrie, the Man Behind the Image* (Boston: Houghton Mifflin, 1970). Both have full bibliographies. The former contains a fuller account than any previously available of du Maurier's quarrel with Whistler; the latter for the first time prints the texts of surviving letters from Barrie to Sylvia, with Peter Llewellyn-Davies's comments.

II

The Novel and The Neurosis: Two Victorian Case Histories

The English writers of the nineteenth century were enormously articulate about themselves, keeping journals, writing
autobiographies, saving their correspondence. Unaware that
Freud would supply future students with a new set of keys
to the interpretation of character and motivation, they also
often recorded their dreams and their symptoms in a way that
has become all but impossible for their descendants. Under
most circumstances only his psychoanalyst can know about a
twentieth-century man the things the Victorians sometimes
unwittingly told us about themselves. And their fiction too—
in which they were usually still more unguarded—swarms
with clues to character. When read together, the novels and
the biographical material reveal about the author, about his
art, and about his age more than we could have learned in
any other way. For these obvious reasons, nineteenth-century
novelists—Dickens, the Brontës, George Eliot, Henry James,
and many, many others—have of course long attracted psy-
choanalytically minded critics.

But among the Victorians, it was not only novelists who
wrote novels. Sea captains and Prime Ministers, army officers
and educational theorists, civil servants and journalists, car-
dinals and diplomats, men and women of the world all turned
their hands to fiction. These novels their modern biographers
have sometimes wholly overlooked or read with insufficient
attention. This essay deals with what I take to be two such

instances: two neglected novels, each by a prominent neurotic
Victorian not primarily a novelist, and each shedding much
light upon the author's inner life, and perhaps—I would also
tentatively suggest—upon the anxieties of their age.

The two authors, Harriet Martineau and Laurence Oliphant,
were both household names in their own day, and have attracted a great deal of attention since. Harriet Martineau
(1802–1876) was an immensely articulate pamphleteer, who
discovered a way of popularizing social and economic issues
by dealing with them in short fictional tracts: *Illustrations
of Political Economy, Poor Laws and Paupers Illustrated,
Forest and Game Law Tales.* Historian and propagandist, she
wrote a history of the years between 1816 and 1846 in England, works on India and Ireland, on the United States and
on the Near East, on morals and manners. She wrote an anti-
slavery novel about Toussaint L'Ouverture, the black Haitian
revolutionary. A learned and didactic bluestocking, she dealt
vigorously and positively with all the problems of the day.
She began as a devout Unitarian and ended as a disbeliever in
immortality, an enthusiast for science, almost an infidel—
"There is no God," said Douglas Jerrold, "and Harriet is his
Prophet." Unhappy in her later years to see "heathen bar-
barism" triumphant in Europe, regarding English politics and
politicians as "hopeless," and in despair with regard even to
the future of America, she nonetheless proclaimed her certainty of a "renovation...a return to correctness," and retained her confidence in the "law of Progress" and in the
virtue of man.[1]

Laurence Oliphant (1829–1888), more than twenty-five
years younger, was a "traveller, barrister, hunter, philan-
thropist, warrior, filibuster, conspirator, legislator, author,
ploughman and teamster, war correspondent, man about town,
mystic, and heresiarch," to which formidable contemporary
list we would add secret agent and satirist. From his early
twenties on he turned up wherever there was action or danger
—in Nepal, in Canada, in China, in the Crimea and Circassia

(the War Office called upon his special knowledge during
the Crimean War), in Garibaldi's camp, in Montenegro and
Albania, in Japan (where terrorists just missed assassinating
him), in Poland during the revolution of 1863, in Schleswig-
Holstein. He wrote of his travels in a series of lively and popular articles and books. The pet of society, a golden youth, he
poked fun at fashionable folly, notably in *Piccadilly* (1870).
He became a member of Parliament in 1865. From devout
evangelical beginnings, he moved to skepticism, and thence to
a most peculiar and personal form of mysticism. "The world,"
he wrote, "with its bloody wars, its political intrigues, its social evils, its religious cant, its financial frauds, and its glaring
anomalies, assumed in my eyes more and more the aspect of
a gigantic lunatic asylum," where "...a majority...con-
tinue to think...that the invention of new machines and ex-
plosives for the destruction of their fellow-men is a perfectly
good and even laudable pursuit." So he rejected his own
earlier life as "insane," and turned to an investigation of "the
latent forces of nature." His cousin and biographer, the novelist Margaret Oliphant, said of him, "There has been no such
bold satirist, no such cynic philosopher, no adventurer so daring and gay, no religious teacher so absolute and visionary, in
this Victorian age, now beginning to round towards its
end...." And one of Oliphant's friends remembered that, in
talking with him, "You constantly stepped...off perfectly
solid ground into chaos. One moment he would be talking
like a statesman and the next like a half-educated enthusiast...."[2]

In the borderland between religion and psychopathology,
Harriet Martineau and Laurence Oliphant each had a sensational—neurotic—adventure, and both affairs became public
knowledge, and were much discussed and debated at the time
by the protagonists' friends, and ever since by all those who
have been interested in them. Among all their many books,
each wrote one neglected novel which on examination helps
to elucidate the mystery of the author's neurosis. In each case

also, only a familiarity with the neurosis can account for the peculiarities of the novel. The fiction illuminates the life; the life alone makes the fiction intelligible. Harriet Martineau's novel is called *Deerbrook*; it appeared in 1839, when she was thirty-seven years old, five years before she had her adventure, which lasted only a few months in 1844. Laurence Oliphant's novel is called *Masollam*, and it appeared in 1886, when he was fifty-seven, when his adventure had already been going on for more than twenty-five years, and was almost over. Her case is simpler than his and easier to expound, but when examined together the two prove to have much in common. Let us begin with the novel in each case and then proceed to the neurosis.[3] Finally, let us look briefly at the two case histories together, to see whether they may not prompt some more general reflections.

2

In the pretty village of Deerbrook—in handsome adjacent houses—live two prosperous tradesmen, partners in the corn, coal, and timber business: Mr. Grey and Mr. Rowland, each married and with a large family of children. The two lots of children are being educated together by a lame spinster governess, Maria Young. Though Mr. Grey and Mr. Rowland are close friends, their wives are at daggers drawn: Mrs. Rowland is always bitterly critical of the Greys. Two distant relatives of the Greys, young girls, sisters, the Misses Ibbotson, suddenly orphaned and left in poverty, come to live with the Greys. Hester, the elder, is twenty-one, Margaret, the younger, twenty. Both are charming girls, and fit well into the household and the society of the little place. We seem to be launched upon one of those gentle domestic novels, where the crisis will come in Volume III, and will revolve around the question whether the Vicar is actually coming to tea or not. Harriet

Harriet Martineau: *above*, presentation copies of *Deerbrook* and *The Hour and the Man; below*, some first editions of her other works.

Martineau goes to great pains to emphasize the dullness, the provinciality, the quiet of Deerbrook, and the harmless interminable gossip that provides its chief diversion.

Hester Ibbotson, however, has, as she says herself, a "jealous temper, and a jealous temper is a wicked temper"—so much so that she is ready to quarrel with her sister Margaret over which one of them would have been the favorite of their younger brother, if he had lived instead of dying in babyhood: "You and he would have been close friends,—always together—and I should have been left alone. . . . There can never be the same friendship between three as between two." "And why should you have been the one left out?" asked Margaret. . . . "This is all nonsense." Whenever she has a fit like this, Hester feels remorse, and the two sisters swear eternal understanding and companionship afterward.

But Mr. Hope, the eligible bachelor village doctor, soon appears on the scene. Instantly people begin to ask themselves which girl he will prefer. As he comes to call more and more often, Margaret observes that she and her sister talk less about him, and believes that Hope prefers her to Hester. Hester is soon plagued again both by jealousy, and by remorse every time she shows it. Meanwhile, Mrs. Rowland's bachelor brother, Philip Enderby, has also fallen in love with Margaret; and this is soon discovered by the lame governess, Maria Young, of whom he had once been fond.

Though she feels deep pain at the discovery, Maria has long since decided that her role is to be that of benevolent observer:

> I am out of the game, and why should not I look upon its chances? I am quite alone; and why should I not watch for others? Every situation has its privileges and its obligations. —What is it to be alone and to be let alone as I am? It is to be put into a post of observation on others: but the knowledge so gained is anything but a good if it stops at mere knowledge,—if it does not make me feel and act. Women who have what I am not to have,—a home, an intimate, a

perpetual call out of themselves, may go on more safely, perhaps, without any thought for themselves than I but . . . my proper business is to keep an intent eye upon the possible events of other people's lives . . . clearsighted, ready to help.

Though the doctor, Mr. Hope, has fallen in love with Margaret, he realizes that Margaret prefers Enderby. So, when Mrs. Grey goes to work to make a match between Mr. Hope and the older sister, Hester, she more easily convinces Hope that he has committed himself; that proposing to Hester has become a matter of honor; that he will be a cad if he lets her down. Although he knows perfectly well the "guilt of marrying without love," he decides to make "the great mistake of his life." Margaret, whom he loves, herself urges him to propose to Hester. He does so, and is accepted, though all the time he loves Margaret.

Hester confesses to Hope that she had in the past been jealous of her *father's* love for Margaret, thinking it preference; that she is jealous of Margaret's present friendship with Maria Young; and that she is discontented even now as Hope's fiancée. Hope is briefly tempted to end their engagement (she keeps on telling him that she can never make him happy), but he comforts her instead, and they are married. Margaret goes to live with them.

Their domestic situation is obviously impossible. No doubt Hester, carefully drawn from the beginning as preternaturally jealous, senses that her husband really loves Margaret. Soon she is telling Margaret that all married life is wretchedness, and that perfect confidence between husband and wife is unattainable. She sneers at all of Margaret's attachments—even her liking for flowers—but especially at her friendship with Maria Young, until finally even the self-sacrificing Margaret rebels:

> You leave me nothing—nothing but yourself—and you abuse my love for you. You warn me against love—against marriage, —you chill my very soul with terror at it. I have found a friend in Maria, and you poison my comfort in my

friendship, and insult my friend. . . . How ungenerous—
while you have one to cherish and who cherishes you—that
you will have me lonely.

Living with his wife and sister-in-law, Mr. Hope goes right
on loving his sister-in-law. He does pray that she

> will soon be taken from under my shadow . . . for my duty
> there is almost too hard. . . . I cannot even be to her what
> our relation warrants. . . .

When Margaret nearly drowns in a skating accident, Hope
almost gives away his secret, but she is so pure that even
when she hears him saying aloud "Oh God, my Margaret"
as she is being rescued from the icy river, she attributes it
all to his largeness of heart. Unfortunately other listeners—
the usual village gossips—interpret his cry differently. When
Hester insists on quarreling with Margaret, Mr. Hope faints
at Margaret's distress. When Enderby proposes to Margaret
and is accepted, Mr. Hope still feels he cannot live without
her. When Mr. Hope receives a letter from a brother in India,
and for good reason will not read the whole of it to Hester,
she has a renewed outburst of jealousy, crying ". . . call me
your housekeeper at once, for I am not your wife."

Other troubles besides these passions cloud the horizon. Mr.
Hope displeases the local landlord by voting Whig in a parliamentary election, and begins to lose his medical practice as
a result. The primitive villagers are convinced that he dissects
bodies. The fiendish gossip, Mrs. Rowland, spreads rumors:
that the Hopes' marriage is unhappy; that her own brother,
Margaret's lover, Philip Enderby, is really engaged to somebody else. When this fails, Mrs. Rowland tells Philip that Mr.
Hope and Margaret have been in love all along—true for
Hope of course, not true for Margaret.

Grim external adversity: sudden poverty, as Hope's practice
dwindles and Mrs. Rowland wickedly induces a rival doctor
to come to the village; violence, aroused as the villagers sack
Hope's house and armed men rob it; misunderstanding, as Mrs.

Rowland succeeds in temporarily alienating Enderby from Margaret; even an epidemic of the plague, all play their rôle in *Deerbrook,* and make turbid the stream of village life which had at first seemed so calm. But of course, all comes out well in the end. A child helps bring new understanding to the marriage of Hester and Mr. Hope, although at first Hester is jealous of Margaret's affection for the baby. She quickly apologizes, and Margaret once again forgives her. "Happy they," says Harriet Martineau, "whose part it is to endure and to conceal, rather than to inflict, and to strive uselessly to repair." But adversity itself and the struggle to meet it bring maturity to Hester: "This is Life; and to live— to live with the whole soul, and mind, and strength, is enough." Persecution itself has made Hester happier; indeed, when their fortunes are at their lowest ebb, and Hope refuses a legacy in order that his sisters may have the money, Hester approves.

Hope's vigorous efforts among the poor smitten by the plague cause his practice to revive, and even the insidious Mrs. Rowland finally confesses her wickedness, as Hope strives vainly to save her daughter, who has caught the disease. Enderby realizes how he has been deceived and is reconciled with Margaret. Mr. Hope explains Mrs. Rowland's truly incredible malice as "the result of long habits of ill will, of selfish pride, and of low pertinacity about small objects." At the very end, Maria Young, the onlooker, consents to look on at the wedding of Philip Enderby, the man she once loved, with Margaret, her friend.[4]

Those few who have paid any attention at all to *Deerbrook* have concentrated on the external aspects of it. They have pointed out that Harriet Martineau had deliberately set out to write of everyday middle-class life rather than of "high life or low life or ancient life," all three of which in 1839 were still the staple of most fiction; and that in Mr. Hope, she was portraying a man of science striving against obscurantism; and that, no matter how great the power of evil, faith and constancy and suffering for the right bring victory in the end.[5] These points are undeniable.

But is it not just as interesting—and it has hitherto been overlooked—that *Deerbrook* also provides us, in Hester, with a clinical study of jealous possessiveness? Hester is jealous whether there is reason or not. We have seen her jealous even of what she supposes might have proved to be the affections of a brother who had in fact died in babyhood, jealous of her father's memory and of her baby's affections, jealous of everybody to whom her sister pays attention or who pays attention to her sister—so jealous of her husband that until her not wholly credible reformation she finds nothing but disappointment in the marriage she had yearned for.

Now what are we to make of this jealousy of Hester's, or, for that matter, of Margaret's devotion and suffering, Maria Young's detachment, or Mrs. Rowland's viciousness? What do these aspects of feminine character, that make *Deerbrook* such an uneasy, uncomfortable novel, teach us about Harriet Martineau? For help in finding our answers we may turn to her long and celebrated autobiography, in which the very wealth of detail itself bespeaks obsession. This is an important Victorian psychopathological document, a clinical treasure house.[6]

She begins in her very earliest childhood, and—fortunately —spares us nothing. Her wetnurse, she says, was inadequate:

> My bad health during my whole childhood and youth, and even my deafness, was always ascribed by my mother to this. . . . Never was poor mortal cursed with a more beggarly nervous system. The long years of indigestion by day and nightmare terrors are mournful to think of now. —Milk has radically disagreed with me all my life: but when I was a child, it was a thing unheard of for children not to be fed on milk; so, until I was old enough to have tea at breakfast, I went on having a horrid lump at my throat for hours of every morning, and the most terrific oppressions in the night. Sometimes the dim light of the window in the night

seemed to advance till it pressed upon my eyeballs and then the windows would recede to an infinite distance. If I laid my hand under my head on the pillow, the hand seemed to vanish almost to a point, while the head grew as big as a mountain.

Such distortions are hysterical symptoms entirely familiar to psychologists.

She fears the sea as she glimpses it through the holes in a jetty; she fears her own dreams, which she recounts in full; she fears a magic lantern ("to speak the plain truth," she says, "the first apparition always brought on bowel complaint," and ensuing shame); she fears an old lady, fears the police, fears the dancing colors on the wall, thrown by prisms in the lustres of the drawing room. She blames her parents for not discovering her fears, and for not treating her "with a little more of the cheerful tenderness which was in those days thought bad for children." To this straightforward catalogue of hysterical symptoms, she adds an account of her early religiosity: she was constantly planning suicide to escape her unhappiness; full of self-pity, tortured by conscience.

Her nearest sister, Rachel, a year and a half older, had a hat with a velvet button on top, the touch of which gave Harriet a sensation so "rapturous" as to be "monstrous." "When we were little more than infants, Mr. Thomas Watson, son of my father's partner, one day came into the yard, took Rachel up in his arms, gave her some grapes off the vine, and carried her home, across the street, to give her Gay's Fables, bound in red and gold. I stood with a bursting heart, beating my hoop, and hating everybody in the world. I always hated Gay's Fables, and for long could not abide a red book." "My capacity for jealousy," she says, "was something frightful." It was Rachel whom their nurse called "quick and well," while she called Harriet "slow and sure." Harriet assures us that she felt no jealousy about this; the distinction was a true one. But then one of her schoolmates one day

asked me, in a corner, in a mysterious sort of way, whether
I did not perceive that Rachel was the favorite at home,
and treated with manifest partiality. Everybody else, she
said, observed it. This had never distinctly occurred to me.
Rachel was handy and useful, and not paralysed by fear, as
I was; and, very naturally, our busy mother resorted to her
for help, and put trust in her about matters of business, not
noticing the growth of an equally natural habit in Rachel
of quizzing me or snubbing me, as the elder ones did. From
the day of this mischievous speech of my school-fellow, I
was on the watch, and with the usual result to the jealous.
Months, —perhaps a year or two—passed on while I was
brooding over this, without a word to anyone.

Then came a dreadful scene. Harriet exploded and told her
mother, in Rachel's presence, that "everything that Rachel
said and did was right, and everything I said and did was
wrong. Rachel burst into an insulting laugh, and was sharply
bidden to 'be quiet.' " Harriet's mother declared that she was
so displeased that she was not sure she could forgive her. But
nothing was ever said afterward, and "henceforth a scrupulous
impartiality between Rachel and me was shown." Still, says
Harriet, her mother ought to have said " 'My child, I never
dreamed that these terrible thoughts were in your mind. I
am your mother. Why do you not tell me everything that
makes you unhappy?' I believe this would have wrought in a
moment that cure which it took years to effect, amidst reserve
and silence."
Harriet was miserly from the start, and convinced that nobody cared for her: a conviction easily interpreted as reflecting
the difficulty she herself felt in caring for anybody. She had
a friend, a lame girl, and associated deep feelings of guilt with
the friendship. She was not allowed to walk with the girl, for
fear it would make Harriet grow crooked; and she had to tell
her friend of this, and once she briefly abandoned her to play
with some other children. Harriet's own handicaps—deafness
and lack of a sense of taste—she discusses from the first symp-

toms, emphasizing her sufferings and adjuring those who have all their senses not to judge sufferers.

In her young womanhood, Harriet adored her younger brother, James: "Brothers are to sisters what sisters can never be to brothers as objects of engrossing and devoted affection," she reminds herself. In a few lines in her autobiography she deliberately dismisses what she herself calls "the strongest passion I have ever entertained," because her brother and she later quarreled. But she refers to herself as "widowed," at his return to college after a vacation. She was engaged for a while to be married to a friend of her brother, John Worthington, a minister, himself a severe neurotic, but she remembers it in these words:

> I was ill—I was deaf—I was in an entangled state of mind
> ... and many a time did I wish, ... that I had never seen
> him.

Worthington, after a sudden rise in spirits and improvement in health, became completely insane and died. Harriet maintains that her grief was compounded by insults from his family, and that she never understood these until many years later, when she discovered that they had falsely believed her engaged to somebody else all along. Most families would have found it enough that she refused to go to his bedside when summoned, and that even *before he died* she wrote asking his family to return all the letters she had written him, lest they be misused. These things she conveniently forgot in her autobiography, but they are nonetheless true. She was clearly anxious to write him off and forget their engagement even before he was safely dead. This was the only conventional love affair of her life. As she says:

> I am in truth very thankful for not having married at all.
> I have never since been tempted, nor have suffered anything
> at all in relation to that ... which is held to be all-important
> to women, —love and marriage. I can easily conceive how I
> *might* have been tempted, —how some deep springs in my

nature *might* have been touched, then, as earlier; but as a matter of fact, they never were; and I consider the immunity a great blessing. . . . If I had had a husband dependent on me for his happiness, the responsibility would have made me wretched. . . . If my husband had *not* depended on me for his happiness, I should have been jealous.[7]

When we read *Deerbrook*—a novel of 1839—together with the autobiography down to the year 1835, our questions find an answer. The men in the novel have no real interest or character of their own and are there just to keep things going. But three of the women in the novel—the jealous Hester, the submissive Margaret, the detached Maria Young—we may safely regard as different aspects of Harriet Martineau herself. The wild jealousy that Hester feels in the story for her sister Margaret, Harriet herself tells us that she felt in real life for *her* sister Rachel. Even the imagined fear that, *if* a younger brother—who in fact had died—had grown up, he would— like everybody else—have preferred Rachel, reflects Harriet's own fears at home. Sick with the aggressions she cannot hide, prone to inexplicable bursts of bad temper, disillusioned with marriage though ostensibly deeply and passionately in love with her husband, Hester displays a mixture of characteristics all of which Harriet Martineau knew she shared, declared to be her own, and was in *Deerbrook* striving to portray.

Margaret too, long-suffering, submissive, only once complaining against her domineering elder sister, with almost super-human gifts for taking emotional blows calmly and with good sense, is in part Harriet as she wished to be. But more than that: she is also Harriet as Harriet often was. Though Harriet was rebellious against her mother, she nonetheless felt the great need to submit to maternal authority. At twenty-seven, after her career in London was launched, Harriet meekly obeyed her mother's "peremptory order" to return home to Norwich:

> I rather wonder that, being seven and twenty years old, I
> did not assert my independence, and refuse to return, —so

clear as was, to my eyes, the injustice of remanding me to a position of helplessness and dependence, when a career of action and independence was opening before me.... I went home, with some resentment ... in my heart.

And a few years later still, when living in London, although Harriet seethed with the resentment against her mother that had been bottled up for years and had gone on growing in depth and volume, she actually invited her mother to come to live with her. By now Miss Martineau was a literary lion and in great social demand:

> ... my mother, who loved power and had always been in the habit of exercising it, was hurt at ... distinctions shown, and visits paid to me; and I with every desire to be passive, and being in fact wholly passive in the matter, was kept in a state of constant agitation.

She attributes the onset of the illnesses which now began to plague her largely to the vexations inflicted by her mother. But she also refers significantly to the "pleasures" of being ill; and she submitted eagerly to her mother's nursing.[8] The patient, submissive Margaret in *Deerbrook* seems to portray certain aspects of her creator just as decisively as the jealous Hester.

And of course, the third woman, the detached Maria Young, for whom there can never be any marriage or any home of her own, is Harriet too: Maria talks of love—and we have heard her—in a voice exactly like Harriet's. No doubt Maria Young preserves certain characteristics of Harriet's long-suffering, lame childhood friend, toward whom she had felt such attraction and such guilt, and this is probably why lameness was the deformity she chose to inflict on Maria. But deafness is a handicap too, and Harriet was deaf; in the passage of her autobiography in which she has told us why she shrank from marriage even as an engaged girl, she begins with "I was deaf ..." and at the end of the episode, as she narrates it, she rejoices over her immunity to love, and declares that hers was to be the life of action.

And as for the fourth woman in *Deerbrook,* the evil Mrs.
Rowland, of course, as others have said, she *is* there to point a
moral: this is the sort of unhappiness that idleness, small-town
narrow-mindedness, cold-blooded snobbery, and stupidity can
create. But in her behavior, motivated by what Mr. Hope
called "ill will, selfish pride, and low pertinacity about small
objects," does not Mrs. Rowland also portray—if with some
elements of caricature—Harriet Martineau's own mother, the
unfair parent, the one who grudges her daughter her social
success, who insists on her daughter's spending too much
money? This the critics have not suggested. Nor perhaps is it
any wonder that at the end of *Deerbrook* Mrs. Rowland is pun-
ished by the loss of a daughter, who dies of the plague despite
all that Hope can do. "Won't my mother be sorry when I'm
dead?" the author seems to be saying.

Having come so far, we can hardly fail to recognize that
by 1835—still four years before *Deerbrook* appeared—Harriet
Martineau was neurotically ill. It was only after making her
trip to America in the mid-thirties, however, and after writing
the two famous books that it inspired—the analytical *Society
in America* (1837) and the more personal *Retrospect of Western Travel* (1838)—that she turned to the writing of fiction,
perhaps in an effort to relieve some of her aggressive feelings
by saying in a novel what she could otherwise never say at all.
After years of writing "almost entirely about fact," she says,
she "longed inexpressibly for the liberty of fiction." Believing
that plots for novels should come from real life, she was first
attracted by a story told her by her American friend Catherine
Sedgwick:

> It is a story from real life which Miss Sedgwick has offered
> in her piece called 'Old Maids,' in her volume of *Tales and
> Sketches,* not likely to be known in England: —a story of
> two sisters, almost ten years apart in age, the younger of
> whom loves and finally marries the betrothed of the elder.
> Miss Sedgwick told me the real story, with some circum-
> stances of the deepest interest which she, for good reasons,

suppressed, but which I might have used. I should of course have acknowledged the source. But I deferred it, and it is well I did. Mrs. S. Carter Hall relates it as the story of two Irish sisters, and impresses the anecdote by a striking wood-cut, in her 'Ireland:' and Mrs. Browning has it again, in her beautiful 'Bertha in the Lane.' [9]

In this story, so to speak, Margaret would have married Mr. Hope, leaving Hester lovelorn; or, put another way, Harriet herself would have triumphed over Rachel. No wonder it had its attractions. But apparently too many others had written the story already, and so it was abandoned.

After briefly contemplating a novel about Toussaint L'Ouverture, Miss Martineau temporarily shelved that too, and went back to the theme of two sisters, but with a difference. Once again she began with what she believed to be a true episode: a friend of her family "had been cruelly driven, by a match-making lady, to propose to the sister of the woman he loved, —on private information that the elder had lost her heart to him, and that he had shown her enough attention to warrant it." Though the story later proved untrue, it had—as we know—given her the germ of the plot of *Deerbrook*, and her own neurosis gave her the characters.

In the very year of *Deerbrook*'s publication, Miss Martineau took to her bed. Her mother was going blind, and "the irritability caused in her first by my position in society, and next by the wearing trial of her own increasing infirmity, told fearfully upon my already reduced health." Her mother insisted upon going out alone and endangering her life on the London streets. Even after Mrs. Martineau was settled in Liverpool near three of her other children, Miss Martineau tells us that she "rarely slept without starting from a dream that my mother had fallen from a precipice, or over the bannister, or from a cathedral spire; and that it was my fault." As her illness drew on, Miss Martineau herself thought it neurotic—"a tumour was forming of a kind which usually originates in mental suffering. . . ." But the physiological symptoms were genuine.

So she retreated for six months to the house of a married sister (not Rachel), and then to a sickroom in lodgings in Tynemouth near Newcastle. Here for five years she remained an invalid, continuing to write, receiving visitors, reflecting on the contemporary scene, suffering keenly, but enjoying her suffering, assuring everybody that she would never get well, and, as she said, "expecting an early death until it was too late to die early." [10] The general public knew all about her illness. Not only was she a celebrated figure, but as usual she lost no chance to put herself in the limelight, writing a volume of essays on *Life in the Sickroom.*

It was mesmerism that cured Miss Martineau. Invented in Vienna in the 1770s by Franz Anton Mesmer (1735–1815), and based upon his teaching that a superfine fluid surrounded and pervaded all bodies, and that all illness derived from obstacles to its free flow, this treatment consisted in passes made by the mesmerist over the patient, at first with an iron magnet, and then simply with the hands, or even the nose. The force at work was called "animal magnetism." It transmitted a magnetic current from the healer into the patient, removed the obstacles to the free flow of fluid, and cured the illness. Introduced into Paris by Mesmer and his disciples in the 1780s, it became the rage. Many cures indeed took place. They were often accompanied by a convulsion or fit, followed by a deep sleep or hypnotic trance, during which some patients, like sleepwalkers, or *somnambules,* followed commands and could even remember and carry out after they awoke orders given while they slept, although they would have no memory of what had happened during the trance. Such people, Mesmer's follower Puységur maintained, might even prophesy the future. Closely related to the radical politics of the prerevolutionary and revolutionary years, mesmerism was ended by the Revolution, and was revived only in the 1820s, coming to England in 1837. As in Vienna and Paris in the eighteenth century, so in England in the nineteenth; the medical profession generally suspected and feared it, although some doctors, like Dickens's

was touched, we owed it to
Mesmerism to say nothing
for fear of relapse.
There is no fear now.
The disease is so reduced
that I hardly feel it; &
in general health I am
quite well. I have left off
all medicines, sleep & eat
well, — have recovered my
proper figure, — & walk
daily from 3 to 5 miles.
But even these vast facts
are almost lost in others
daily arising. Mesmerism
is true to the whole extent
claimed. We have here in

the house, a somnambule
of our own, — herself quite
unconscious, — & we find
her lucidity now increased
to clairvoyance. — And
I am ~~apparently~~ entering
into the sleeping state,
probably to speak & read
also. But this, time will
show. — I love & respect
my Mesmerist heartily.
I have not a moment
more. — I trust you are
better. God bless you!
Your affec^te
H. Martineau.

Harriet Martineau: her letter announcing that "Mesmerism is true. . . ."

and Thackeray's friend John Elliotson, took the lead in urging
that it be studied, and in publicizing its successes. Once again,
those of a radical bent in politics, already dazed by recent
scientific advances, found it credible and attractive. Among
others, Bulwer—whose interest in such phenomena we shall
soon be reviewing in more detail—urged it upon Miss Martineau.[11] In 1844, her doctor, who was her brother-in-law,
T. M. Greenhow, recognizing that mesmerism was particularly
likely to help hysterical patients, brought an itinerant mesmerist in to see her.

Though he did her some good, his efforts were not nearly
as effective as those of her maid, who had watched the mesmerist making his passes, but had never been trained to do so
herself. Harriet Martineau now obtained instant relief, although the malady lingered, somewhat improved, until a
female professional mesmerist, a Mrs. Wynyard, came to live
in the house. Miss Martineau, who had found it delightful to
submit to the nursing of her mother in her earlier illness, this
time enjoyed—so she said—the subordination of her will to that
of her maid, and most particularly to that of Mrs. Wynyard.
Between June and October 1844 she recovered almost entirely.
Mrs. Wynyard also treated Miss Martineau's landlady's daughter, who, when cured of some kind of eye trouble of hysterical
origin, herself proved to be a *somnambule* and seeress, who
went into trances and even made predictions in which Miss
Martineau fully believed.

On the characteristic and successful efforts that Miss Martineau made to publicize her recovery and to give the maximum
credit to mesmerism, and on the immense amount of public
discussion of her case and the storm of public protest that arose
in opposition to her, we need not linger here. Her autobiography, her *Letters on Mesmerism,* her own correspondence as
examined by her most recent biographer, all tell the story. But
perhaps it may be useful to publish here one of her letters
never printed previously. It adds only one new fact to those
that have long been known. But it has, I think, the merit of

freshness. We get her own view of her own experiences in her own words. She would have bitterly disapproved of its use: she tried her best to prevent any of her correspondence from being preserved.

Tuesday
My dear friend
I have been ashamed & grieved not to have written sooner. Day by day have I tried to do so: but we (my kind mesmerist & I) can get *nothing* done but our main business, —I am out so many hours of the day! —I have wanted to tell you all. But I will send this line meantime: & if I can't tell you my story soon, I will set somebody else to tell you.

I began on the 22d of June, & was *much* better when you were here. Mrs. Reid & I did so long to tell you! But you were going where you wd be questioned, & we must have bound you irksomely, —as *till* we knew that the disease was touched, we owed it to Mesmerism to say nothing, for fear of relapse.

There is no fear now. The disease is so reduced that I hardly feel it; & in general health I am quite well. I have left off all medicines, —sleep & eat well, —have recovered my figure, —& walk daily from 3 to 5 miles. But even these vast facts are almost lost in others daily arising. *Mesmerism is true to the whole extent claimed.* We have here in the house, a somnambule of our own, —herself quite unconscious, —& we find her lucidity now increased to clairvoyance. —And *I* am apparently [word written and later crossed out] entering into the sleeping state, probably to speak & reveal also. —I love & respect my Mesmerist heartily.

I have not a moment more. —I trust you are better. God bless you!

Your affec^te

H. Martineau.[12]

It is noteworthy that at this moment Miss Martineau expected to become a *somnambule* and *clairvoyante*. This she never managed to do, but in 1845 she did arise from her sick-bed, cured by mesmerism, and she did live for thirty-two more years, industriously writing the entire time. Do not her symptoms and her recovery, as she recorded them herself, make *Deerbrook* more interesting and more intelligible? And does not *Deerbrook* help us to understand what happened to her, although it was written so long before the event, and has not a word about mesmerism in it?

3

If *Deerbrook* is an uneasy and uncomfortable novel, Oliphant's *Masollam* is positively fishy. In the fashionable world of political and parliamentary London, and especially in a country house belonging to Mr. Charles Hartwright and his family, there appears a family of Armenians named Masollam: father, mother, and daughter, Amina. Surrounded by mystery, they are armed with proper letters of introduction from a French nobleman named Santalba, an old family friend and business associate of Mr. Hartwright, who urges that he seek the aid of Mr. Masollam in his financial embarrassments. Hartwright himself hopes to solve his problems by marrying his daughter, Florence, to his enormously rich nephew, her first cousin, Sebastian Hartwright.

The appearance and personality of Masollam are extraordinary:

> There was a remarkable alternation of vivacity and deliberation about the movements of Mr. Masollam. His voice seemed pitched in two different keys, the effect of which was, when he changed them, to make one seem a distant echo of the other. . . . When he talked with what I may term his "near" voice, he was generally rapid and vivacious; when he exchanged it for his "far-off" one, he was solemn and impressive. His hair, which had once been raven black, was now streaked with grey, but it was still thick, and fell in a massive wave over his ears, and nearly to his shoulders, giv-

ing him something of a leonine aspect. His brow was over-
hanging and bushy, and his eyes were like revolving lights in
two dark caverns, so fitfully did they seem to emit flashes,
and then lose all expression. Like his voice, they too had a
near and a far-off expression, which could be adjusted to the
required focus like a telescope, growing smaller and smaller
as though in an effort to project the sight beyond the limits
of natural vision. At such times they would ... produce almost the impression of blindness, when suddenly the focus
would change, the pupil expand, and rays flash from them
like lightning from a thunder-cloud, giving an unexpected
and extraordinary brilliancy to a face which seemed
promptly to respond to the summons. The general cast of
countenance, the upper part of which, were it not for the
depth of the eye-sockets, would have been strikingly handsome, was decidedly Semitic; and in repose the general
effect was almost statuesque in its calm fixedness. The
mouth was partially concealed by a heavy moustache and
long iron-grey beard; but the transition from repose to ani-
mation revealed an extraordinary flexibility in those muscles
which had a moment before appeared so rigid, and the
whole character of the countenance was altered as suddenly
as the expression of the eye. It would perhaps be prying too
much into the secrets of nature, or at all events into the
secrets of Mr. Masollam's nature, to inquire whether this
lightening and darkening of the countenance was voluntary
or not. ... Mr. Masollam had the facility of looking very
much older one hour than he did the next. There were
moments when a careful study of his wrinkles, and of his
dull, faded-looking eyes, would lead you to put him down at
eighty if he was a day; and there were others when his flash-
ing glance, expanding nostril, broad smooth brow, and
mobile mouth, would for a moment convince you that you
had been at least five and twenty years out in your ... first
estimate. When he was erect, he stood about six feet in his
stockings, but his attitudes varied with his moods, and he
often drooped suddenly and tottered along with bowed
shoulders and unsteady gait. These rapid contrasts were calculated to arrest the attention of the most casual observer,

and to produce a sensation which was not altogether pleasant when first one made his acquaintance. It was not exactly
mistrust—for both manners were perfectly frank and natural,
—so much as perplexity. He seemed to be two opposite
characters rolled into one, and to be presenting undesignedly
a curious moral and physiological problem for solution,
which had a disagreeable sort of attractiveness about it, for
you almost immediately felt it to be insoluble, and yet it
would not let you rest. He might be the best or the worst of
men. . . . The effect of this peculiarity upon sensitive natures
with whom he was brought into contact, was to produce in
them corresponding alternations of sympathy and antipathy.

In moments of need, his daughter Amina gives him a rather
peculiar kind of massage. He

undid his shirt-collar and bared the upper part of his chest
. . . she . . . pressed both her palms upon his temples. . . . slowly
moved one hand to his forehead, while she placed the other
upon the lower part of the back brain, and again pressed, but
in an opposite direction, with the same firm but gentle force.
. . . Her . . . respiration underwent a remarkable change.
The breathing became deeper, fuller, and more prolonged,
until her lungs seemed to acquire a power of unnatural expansion, while that of her father appeared altogether to
have ceased; his eyes had closed, his whole frame stiffened,
as the gentle heaving of his chest subsided into complete
quiescence; and, except for a faint colour in his cheeks, which
was not the hue of death, he would to the casual observer
have presented all the appearance of a corpse.

Amina holds Masollam's hand between hers, rubs in a special
fluid, waits half an hour, then massages his chest, and he comes
to; and "their breathing was absolutely synchronous." In such
trances, Masollam can "penetrate into regions which are closed
to the common herd"; he can foresee a certain amount of the
future; and he responds almost chemically to the moods and
qualities of other men: for example, he is caused "excruciating
torture" by influences radiating from the greedy nature of Mr.
Charles Hartwright.

Sebastian Hartwright's best friend is Reginald Clareville, heir to a peerage, immensely attractive and successful, and like Sebastian a member of Parliament. But Clareville is disillusioned with politics and determined to give it up. He joins the peculiar house party I have been describing, and falls madly in love with Amina. He concludes that the Masollams are trying to land Sebastian and his millions for Amina instead of Florence. Soon Santalba, the French nobleman, also appears, and establishes an extraordinary influence over Clareville:

> . . . a delightful sense of calm, almost amounting to languor was stealing over him. He could scarcely realise that only a few days before he had been tossed upon the stormy billows of political life. . . . He, who . . . had often read with cynical amusement and incredulity the narratives of conversion which had from time to time been forced upon him by those who professed to be interested in his soul's welfare, had suddenly found himself stirred to the depths by a new and unknown force which would give him no peace, but which had apparently originated in the innermost depths of his own being. . . .

Clareville now determines to embark on

> . . . a course of moral and physical experiment, with the view of testing in his own person the truth of certain conclusions in regard to the nature and extent of the human faculty, and the laws governing the vital forces which control it. . . . He could hardly believe that he was the same man who was so lately spinning around in the social and political whirlpool, making splash enough as he did so, to raise the hopes of his friends and to gratify his own vanity. . . . It had sufficed for the silent watches of one night to tear away what he could only describe to himself as a sort of barrier between an outer and an inner conscience, of the very existence of which he had been hitherto unaware. His old conscience had, so to speak, disappeared. It had been a good workaday sort of conscience—the average conscience of an English gentleman and a man of honour; . . . a conscience very particular indeed about money, especially where gambling debts were

concerned—not perhaps quite so particular about tradesmen,
but even they had not much to complain of; a conscience also
particular about women, especially those whose husbands
were his own personal friends; a conscience that forbade
him under any possible circumstances to tell a lie, except
where a woman was concerned. . . . but its lamp had been
eclipsed in a night by the effulgence of a moral ray that had
shot across his being, revealing to him a code written as
though in letters of fire, and which seemed imperatively
to demand of him the sacrifice of himself, with all his personal aims and ambitions, at the shrine of his fellow-men. . . .

Clareville has the "crude notion" that he ought "to bury
himself in the slums of London, and go to work among its
outcasts," but Amina proposes something very different. She
suggests

> . . . processes of self-preparation for the work to which he
> felt himself called, so foreign to all his instincts, and so
> violently antagonistic to his prejudices, that it needed all
> his love for her, and all the influence of Sebastian, and the
> assurances of his friend that he too had determined actively
> to participate in the same effort, to reconcile him to the
> new departure.

It is Santalba who tells Reginald what the new departure is to
be, though Reginald reserves the right to withdraw from any
experiments that may violate his moral consciousness. What he
must do, he learns to his astonishment, is to "submit to the
absolute guidance and direction of Mr. and Madame Masollam."
Clareville hates and suspects both the Masollams, yet feels he
must obey.[13] Sebastian also consents.

Masollam's first order is that Amina and Clareville give up
their companionship and speak to each other as little as possible,
and that Florence Hartwright and her cousin Sebastian, who
also love each other, do the same. This provides a kind of
"severe moral vivisection" for the two young couples. By this
torture they are stripped of superficiality; first they will find
their true moral natures, and then God. For the desires of the

flesh they are substituting a love "for the world at large as intense as that for any single unit in it."

But in fact a strange and deadly competition is under way between Madame Masollam, on the one hand, and Amina, under the influence of Santalba, on the other, to control Masollam himself. Madame Masollam's chief interest is in money. By securing vast sums, her husband has hoped to reconstruct industrial society upon a cooperative basis; and, once competition has disappeared, to "apply the principle of altruism as a moral law." Thirty years earlier, Santalba had enthusiastically embraced the scheme, and had helped make a great fortune to speed its fulfillment. But now Madame Masollam has lost sight of the ultimate altruistic goal, and wants only the marriage between Sebastian and Amina so that the Hartwright fortunes may fall under her husband's control.

Masollam himself, however, has other plans for Amina. Brutally, he dismisses Clareville, and tells Amina that in fact she is not the Masollams' daughter at all but a Druse princess, rescued from a massacre in her childhood by Santalba, and brought up by the Masollams. Her own mother has been discovered, and is nearby. And Masollam is not even married to his ostensible wife, who has merely been his co-laborer and sufferer for forty years, "but has now abdicated." Masollam tells Amina that alone he is powerless: "that it is only a woman who can feed me with the elements that are necessary to the ultimation of my forces, which need this conjunction to make them operative. . . . Let her who has been hitherto my daughter, henceforth become my queen."

On hearing the news, Amina faints: all her life she has been subject to the hypnotic influences of Masollam; but she has always thought of herself as his daughter, and now she loves Clareville. She has had a "terrible revelation of a love that violated all her pure and maidenly instincts," yet she has been so conditioned to think of herself as an instrument of the divine purpose that she wonders whether she should not make the sacrifice, all the more because she loves somebody else and that makes the sacrifice harder. But Santalba reassures her. Her repugnance is quite right. He too has just discovered that Masollam

> ... has allowed a base and selfish passional force to burst through the barriers which should have been opposed to it, and so to pollute the divine love-currents, the purity of which it was the effort of his former life to protect, that his whole moral consciousness has become perverted, and his powerful organism has been taken possession of by the enemy. . . .

Astonished at how long and how successfully she has been duped, Amina now is spirited away by Santalba. With her own true mother and with Clareville (who leaves them in London), she goes off to Syria to her native village, leaving Masollam in a terrible rage.

Santalba now confronts and defies Masollam, accusing him of betraying his divine commission for gold. In her excitement at this interview, Florence Hartwright has a heart attack, which Santalba tends by "a treatment that differs from any which has yet been recognized by science." But when her father appears and rages at her for her decision not to marry her rich cousin Sebastian (whom Masollam and Santalba have forced her to renounce), she has a relapse. While Santalba is looking after her, the Masollams and Mr. Hartwright succeed in persuading a local doctor that Sebastian is insane, and manage to get him confined in a lunatic asylum. The evidence of madness is in part the following verses, which Sebastian has written:

> Murmurs of innocence, touches of charm
> Songs of sweet lullaby, lulling the calm,
> Mystical movements, thrills of delight,
> Spells of enchantment, perfumes of night;
>
> Tender imaginings, love the bright goal,
> Whispers of angels, stirring the soul.
> Flashes of purity, white and intense,
> Yearnings unearthly lifting the sense;

> Fainting pulsations, spasms of prayer,
> Visions of loveliness, floating in air,
> Ardent aspirings, voices that ring,
> Noble ambitions, hopes that upspring;
>
> Wellings of happiness, sobs of desire,
> Altars of sacrifice, scorchings of fire,
> Bursting of bondages, snapping of cords,
> Cries of sharp agony, clashing of swords;
>
> Healing with ointments, soothing with balm,
> Pants of prostration, wakings to calm,
> Breathings celestial, solemn and deep,
> On the All Mother's breast falling asleep.

The Masollams now intend to use Sebastian as a counter-hostage against Santalba, in order to force him to return Amina and Clareville. But Santalba is not defeated. He explains to Florence, who has almost died for love of Sebastian, that "Had you married your cousin for your own sake, and under your own conditions, having made no sacrifice for him, . . . you would each of you have been victims through life—he to the tie which bound him to a woman whose selfishness would have repelled his love; and you to the pangs of unrequited affection which would finally have altogether alienated you from the man to whom you had been attached. This was what I foresaw; and determined to prevent. . . ." But now that the sacrifice has been made, she may follow her inclination, tell her father that she will marry Sebastian, rescue him from the madhouse, and thwart the Masollams. She of course agrees, and Santalba explains to the puzzled Hartwright that he had not known of the Masollams' change in motives and character: ". . . it rests with you to free yourself from a yoke which you will find worse than slavery. Once allow Masollam to get you thoroughly into his power, and he will hold you and yours with a grip compared to which that of the Old Man of the Sea was mere child's play."

Santalba has let Florence sicken almost to death because "It was only this morning that Florence's internal, or spiritual, or essential, or subtler material conditions—call them what you will—completed the change which will enable her to assimilate as a healing infusion those elements which she can derive as a remedial agent from her cousin. Had she altered her resolution before the change was completed, she would have arrested it, and these same elements would have operated in her as a slow poison. . . ." Hartwright agrees—but says it all sounds like bosh to him.[14] At this first wholly sensible remark that any of the characters has made in two volumes, the marriage between Sebastian and Florence duly takes place.

With the Masollams apparently on the brink of defeat, the scene abruptly shifts to a village in Syria, where Amina's grandfather is a Druse chieftain, Sheikh Mohanna, a student of the occult, an old friend of Santalba. It has been revealed to him that God, the eternal word, is both male and female, a bi-sexual power ruling the universe; and he realizes that the day of deliverance has come, through Amina, not only for himself and their tribe, but for the whole world. At this point the novel has still a whole volume to go before the desperate plots of the Masollams to get Amina back are frustrated. Clareville and Amina, who have separated from each other as part of the ordeal, are reunited. Sebastian Hartwright indeed is Amina's long-lost brother and heir to the Druse Sheikhdom (this was why Santalba knew that Amina and Sebastian must not marry). Married to Florence, who is of course not his cousin at all, his wealth and energy are enlisted on Santalba's side to redeem society and to smash the evil of the Masollams' world-wide organization.

How are we to regard this turgid, prolix, and almost lunatic novel? If we ignore it, as others have done, we shall remain without much light that we would otherwise have on the fantastic story of Laurence Oliphant himself. *Masollam* is not truly fiction but a kind of personal history. The people, events, ideas, delusions, are all real. The lunacy, if such we think it, was Oliphant's own. Yet his biographers have paid *Masollam* almost no attention.

They have barely noticed that Mr. Masollam is a carefully drawn portrait (the best we have, indeed) of Thomas Lake Harris,[15] whom William James once called America's greatest mystic.[16] Born in England in 1823, Harris was brought to Utica, New York, by his parents when he was five years old. At twenty-two he was a Universalist Minister in New York City. Soon he fell under the influence of a still younger man, Andrew Jackson Davis, a self-styled "harmonialist," a spiritualist and utopian socialist with an intricate theology and philosophy of his own that owed much to Swedenborg, and included a theory like Swedenborg's, that the "masculine elements of Father-God and the feminine properties of Mother-Nature meet . . . in the Man's constitution; out of which they unroll progressively, and from which they bloom with an immortal beauty, in spheres beyond the stars." [17] After quarreling with Davis, Harris in 1850 began to have a series of personal revelations, which from the first included the idea of a bisexual god, the "two-in-one," divine love made flesh in the union of the sexes.

By 1854—after his wife had died—Harris had had his first vision of Queen Lily (or Lily Queen) of the Conjugial (sic), his own immortal bride and divine counterpart, with whom he lived during his sleep at night, while during the day he was a hard-working itinerant preacher and writer. Married again, he allegedly lived with his second wife in celibacy. Abandoning Universalism, he became a Swedenborgian of the Christian spiritualist wing of that movement, in opposition to the social and political reforming wing that included the elder Henry James. Preaching as a Swedenborgian minister, though not ordained, Harris received in 1857 direct from the Lord a revelation of the inmost meaning of the Word, and thus in his own view became the prophet—the "pivotal man"—on whom human salvation depended; he was therefore under constant fire from the forces of evil. These fiendish attacks by demons against his body and his soul almost cost him his earthly life.

Just a century after Swedenborg's own description of the

Last Judgment in 1757, the spirit of Swedenborg personally blessed Harris's work in revealing the "Celestial" sense of the Word, where Swedenborg himself had modestly limited himself to the "Spiritual" sense. Harris's *Arcana of Christianity* (1858) created a sensation, describing as it did life on other planets. It also emphasized the importance of breathing: "It is impossible for any man to be internally intromitted into the truths which make up the celestial body of the Word, save through the aura of the Celestial Heavens, which descends and is inhaled in his celestial respiratories," through three stages of breathing, each higher than the last. It is the divine breath that regenerates. Spiritual seeds or " 'fays' . . . cause all natural processes and constitute the inner mechanism of the universal 'nuptial order.' . . . The Eternal Masculinity is the Divine Love. The Eternal Femininity is the Divine Truth. The eternal proceeding of the two in one is the Divine Ability. The mystery of the Divine Nature is typified in the relations of conjugial [sic] love. . . . In [the Lord] the Eternal Masculine and the Eternal Feminine, otherwise the Divine Good and the Divine Truth, are one, for evermore, in the Holy Ghost." [18]

Harris was, then, an originator and practitioner and prophet of a new and original kind of sexual mystical system, far more complex in its ramifications than we can (or need to) show here. Fundamental to it were the bisexual god, the theory of celestial counterparts, and the mysteries of respiration. The Swedenborgians expelled his group. In 1859 the Lord ordered Harris to England.

Though Harris was at first welcomed there by Garth Wilkinson (a friend of the elder Henry James, who named a son after him) and by other Swedenborgians, and though they admired the eloquence of his preaching, they found him not enough of a social and political thinker and far too much of a spiritualist. During his stay in England he determined to found a community, the Brotherhood of the New Life, united by "internal respiration," in which no discord could exist. And in England, too, Harris now became more of a social radical, inveighing against economic and social inequality, against governments and manufacturers, but explaining the origins of social wrongs in terms of his own idiosyncratic history and theology, and in his own peculiar vocabulary. The first crisis in the history of mankind came with the Flood, after which man could no longer perform "simple celestial" breathing, and moral evil caused degradation. The second crisis came with the Incarnation, when Christ (divine and human) restored to man the capacity for internal respiration. The third crisis had come with Harris himself—the pivotal man—who would reinstate good in the universe through man's "open respiration." [19] In 1861 he decided to go back to America and found his new brotherhood there. It was during his stay in England that Harris had met Laurence Oliphant, whose life he profoundly affected, and who was to portray him a quarter of a century later as Mr. Masollam.

Born in 1829 to Sir Anthony Oliphant, then Attorney General of the Cape Colony, and to his beautiful and much younger wife, neé Mary Campbell, the daughter of an army officer, Laurence remained an only child. Both parents came from well-connected families. Both were deeply pious evangelical Protestants, with a besetting sense of sin, and a habit of regularly searching and cross-examining themselves, each other, and their child to keep themselves on the paths of righteousness. Going off to England at the age of eight alone with his mother, who "idolized him," and not seeing his father again for five years, Oliphant was—his cousin and biographer tells us— "something of a hothouse plant, brought up at his mother's feet." The attachment to his mother was deep and lasting. In his young manhood, Oliphant's father took him to a special exhibition in Paris that vividly and horridly depicted in *papier-mâché* figures the dangers of venereal disease. Long afterward Oliphant was to admit to his second wife his regret that he had not heeded the lessons of this exhibition. In fact, he became a rake. The Prince of Wales, with whom Oliphant was on easy terms of personal intimacy, remarked of him, "He sugar-doodles the ladies"; we may safely take the word of so notable a sugar-doodler. After his almost frenzied series of missions and adventures all over the globe, interspersed with an active life in London high society, Oliphant by his early thirties was probably diseased, surely guilt-ridden, nurturing his love for his pure, beautiful, and now-widowed mother, with whom he lived (and whose maid he allegedly seduced), disillusioned with the round of social gaiety and with strong religious impulses.[20]

In 1860 Oliphant met Harris for the first time. Though he continued for another five years his missions abroad and frivolous life in London, his fate was already determined. To understand his state of mind we cannot do better than to reread the passage already quoted from _Masollam_, describing Reginald Clareville at the moment of his meeting with Mr. Masollam as "stirred to the depths by a new and unknown force," and determined to embark on moral and physical experiment. For Clareville is Oliphant's portrait of himself as he was when he first encountered Harris. Like Clareville, he had the initial impulse—"crude" he calls it—to put his efforts into social work. In the novel Clareville is persuaded instead to submit completely to the Masollams. Though a less important figure in the novel, without characteristics of his own notably different from those of Clareville, Sebastian Hartwright (who also submits to Masollam and also lives to regret it) is also a self-portrait of Oliphant: the verses Sebastian writes, which we have quoted, are of course by Oliphant himself, and were intended, like Harris's own voluminous and often unintelligible poetry, to be taken with the utmost seriousness.

Elected to Parliament in 1865 as a Liberal member for the Scottish borough of Stirling, Oliphant delivered a successful maiden speech, but his cynicism and disillusionment grew stronger as the politicians throttled the reform bill he favored. It was in the summer of 1865 that _Piccadilly_ began to appear anonymously as a serial in _Blackwood's Magazine_, but it was not long before everybody in the know was aware that Oliphant was the author. He drew himself as the disillusioned and truly Christian Lord Frank Vanecourt; some other characters were also recognizable: Monckton Milnes, for example, was Lord Dickiefield. And Thomas Lake Harris, back in London on another visit, also appeared briefly and portentously in *Piccadilly* as an unnamed prophet. In its pages, Oliphant quoted some of Harris's verses as the work of "the greatest poet of the age, as yet, alas! unknown to fame," and attributed them to Harris in a footnote. Moreover, the prophet takes Vanecourt's arm in Piccadilly and denounces the godlessness of their contemporaries. It was now that Oliphant decided to submit to Harris's will, as the fictional Reginald Clareville and Sebastian Hartwright decided to submit to Mr. Masollam. And as Masollam imposed ordeals on his neophytes, so Harris forced Oliphant to undergo a severe "moral vivisection." [21]

Had Harris in some way exercised occult hypnotic powers to lure Oliphant? Was Oliphant simply mad? These two theories were popular with his friends. But it is of the utmost importance to note that Harris had also converted Laurence's mother, Lady Oliphant, and that she was permitted to join Harris's community, then established at Amenia, New York, two years before Harris would let Oliphant follow her.[22] By way of initiation, Lady Oliphant had to "go to a lady whose influence upon and relations with Laurence in a former part of his life had given her the deepest pain, to offer her the new light, and to invite her to become a member of the community and abandon all evil ways." [23]

So it may be seen that in real life Harris imposed upon Oliphant and his mother the same kind of forced separation that the fictional Masollam imposed upon the two pairs of lovers in the novel, Clareville and Amina, and Sebastian and Florence. But this was only a part of the systematic process by which Harris broke the wills of his new disciples. Lady Oliphant, delicately reared and unaccustomed to domestic labor, was at the age of fifty-six put to the most menial tasks in Harris's community's kitchen and laundry. Harris required the Oliphants to turn over all their money to him. Their contributions of more than $100,000 provided almost half the funds Harris needed to move his community (which varied between about fifty and about one hundred members) to Brocton on the shores of Lake Erie, and to build there a new settlement for the believers, including a luxurious house for himself. Harris would not let Oliphant resign his seat in Parliament, but neither would he let him speak again; so the brilliant young politician was silenced and humiliated, while the London world wondered what had happened to his promise. And when in 1867 he did come to America, he was allowed to have very little communication with his mother, was forced to sleep in a barn, make his own bed out of a wooden crate, tend the horses, and perform all sorts of other rigorous manual labor. It was no small matter to submit one's will in all things to that of Thomas Lake Harris.

Yet Oliphant accepted it all without questioning. He wrote to his friend Mrs. Cowper (later Cowper-Temple and Lady Mount-Temple, friend of Ruskin, George MacDonald, and many other prominent Victorians) that the separation from his mother "is not very serious, for I can look at her going about her daily avocations out of any window, with a light step and a merry laugh, such as I never saw or heard before. She is perfectly and entirely happy, except when fighting her own evils, but cannot get gossiping without a danger of our states mixing and passing over to Faithful, and the moment is too critical to run any risks right now." [24] Faithful was Harris's name in the cult (Oliphant's was Woodbine), and he was of course intensely sensitive to the "states" or "spheres" (what we might call moods or vibrations) of others, since the demons were out to destroy him.

Like Masollam, Harris oscillated between two voices and two appearances, and needed ministrations such as those provided by Amina in the novel. We now recognize these as deriving from the respiratory theories that Harris had developed from Swedenborg: the simultaneous breathing of Amina and

Masollam reflects the respiratory practices of the Harris sect. Faithful told Woodbine that, if he returned to London and took his seat in Parliament again, the divine protection would be withdrawn, and he might die. Oliphant was convinced indeed that he could not have lived through the session, but that if he were absolutely true to "our use" death would no longer be a possibility. He did not even mind being so completely out of touch that he did not for many months hear of Disraeli's new ministry.

Long afterward, in conversation with his second wife, Oliphant himself explained his actions in terms that are revealing to twentieth-century readers. Harris, he said,

> met me at a moment when I was at the parting of the ways, I had come to realise that pride, vanity, conceit, was the bane of man, his self-sufficiency standing as an impenetrable wall between his God and himself. . . . Being filled with ourselves we cannot be filled by Him. There is no room for Him to enter. . . . Wherever I had turned, success had followed me. . . . How was I to get rid of my foolish conceit influencing every breath I drew? This question was paramount in my mind when I met T. Lake Harris. It turned out that he was better able to bully me than any man I had ever met, and as I needed to be bullied I remained with him until his tyrannies had had the desired effect. . . . I had to be broken in, and Harris was chosen as an effective instrument, for a worse, a more unreasonable tyrant than he came to be I never encountered.[25]

But recognition that Harris was such a tyrant came only after almost two decades. And even after it came, and *Masollam* could be written, Oliphant continued to believe that the actual labor he had performed for Harris had been salutary. And so, in *Masollam*, Clareville and Sebastian, before they rejoin Amina in Syria, take laborers' posts on a Swiss railway line, working with pick and shovel; and Florence becomes a washerwoman and spends "most of her day drubbing people's linen on the stones by the side of the lake." None of the three would

spend any money except what they could earn, and Florence
and Clareville had to support Sebastian for a week when he
was laid up with rheumatism. When they tell her how they
have learned about the misery of the poor by living it, Amina
approves of the effort not only from the social point of view
but also from the mystical:

> by the loving contact you were both maintaining with
> mother earth and that Florence was keeping up on the lake
> bank, you were all purifying your organisms of gross mag-
> netic elements which you had acquired in the fashionable
> world, and which had impeded the growth of pure and
> divine life within you.... the moment I touched you when
> you arrived, I felt that a subtle change had taken place in
> those finer essences which ... were so charged with fashion-
> able filth as to be at times almost intolerable.[26]

In his fiction as in his own life, Laurence Oliphant found the
ordeal of manual labor rewarding and purifying. And there
is no doubt that many members of the Brotherhood found
peace and happiness in the life of hard work and simple and
spontaneous pleasures enjoined by the awe-inspiring founder.

Harris commanded his followers to plant vineyards and to
make and sell wine, as well as other farm produce. They had
a gristmill, a restaurant, which Oliphant ran for a while, and
a hotel. Harris was a shrewd businessman, much of whose
money came from the property of his new converts, each of
whom had to surrender everything he had upon entering the
Brotherhood. But more money was always needed, and it was
largely because Oliphant could still earn substantial sums by
writing that Harris ordered him back to London in 1870. He
reappeared in society with all his old gaiety and charm,
talked freely of his experiences, and disappointed those who
expected to hear that he had broken with Harris. He arranged
for the book publication of *Piccadilly*, and he became a correspondent for *The Times*, covering the Franco-Prussian War.
Harris did not allow him to communicate with his mother
during his absence. "It was bitter," says Margaret Oliphant,

"the highest refinement of cruelty; yet, if any man had the right to exact such a thing, the most severe proof of sincerity." Lady Oliphant fell ill and nearly died. Laurence was summoned back from Paris to see her; and in 1871 they were allowed to settle in Paris together.

Here Oliphant met and fell in love with Alice LeStrange, a beautiful and talented young Englishwoman of gentle birth. Before marrying her, Oliphant converted her to the Harris faith, all of which she adopted whole-heartedly, although she later wrote to Harris himself that

> One only thing has been a terrible pang to me, the giving over of my own judgment in questions of moral judgment to any human authority. It is so absolutely new and incomprehensible an idea to me, that any outer test should supplant, without risk to itself and to me, the inner test of my actions that my conscience affords, that... I decided to shut my eyes and leave the seeing to you—I felt as though I were putting out the one clear light that had been given to me for my guidance; ... as though I had suddenly thrown my own compass overboard ... and with the grim question asking itself over and over again in my heart, whether I were not doing wrong.[27]

But Harris, the original of Masollam, a "man of extraordinary skill and insight, as well as of remorseless purpose and determination, ... put his hand upon the very sources of life, and controlled them." An adept of Harris's theories of earthly and celesial marriage himself, forty-three years old, and perhaps still a syphilitic, Oliphant knew that he must not have sexual relations with Alice after they were married.

> " 'As a man of the world,' " he frankly told his second wife almost twenty years later, " 'and knowing the habits of my comrades, I became convinced that sex sins are the most dangerous sins on earth. ... If one is not the master of powerful passions, one is bound to be their slave. ... Hence, I learned self-control by sleeping with my beloved and beautiful Alice in my arms for twelve years without claiming the

rights of a husband. We lived as a sister and a brother. I am a passionate lover, and so it was difficult, very difficult,' he said, unconsciously clenching both hands as he remembered the struggle, 'but it did not prove to be impossible. I was able to keep my vow, and I shall never regret having made it. . . . when my health failed for a short time, my physician ascribed my break-down to my continence. "I do not believe you," I said . . . but even were it true is it not high time for men to be willing to suffer a little in order to prove that passion can be bridled. . . ." ' " [28]

Furious to learn of Oliphant's intention to marry, Harris ordered the couple to separate; and for months before the wedding took place, Oliphant in Paris prepared Alice in London by a voluminous correspondence not only for a marriage with him that would be only a spiritual relationship, but also for what seem to us the horrors of subjection to "Father" Harris, whom she had never seen, but who was himself in Paris during part of this period. How pathological the relationship was to be we may see by a few brief excerpts:

> If in some things you are my child, in others I have got to become yours, and this is the moment I am longing for, when I can drink in and absorb from you the mysteries of a love which the world knows nothing of yet. . . . I believe that when you come into child-states, and thus become susceptible to the divine influence . . . you will become conscious of deep inner truths . . . and these may be the basis of the new feminine part of the religious structure.
>
> It would do you no harm to go through a little course of this (being considered dull or stupid) as I did . . . when my friends thought I was going to electrify the House and the country—when I was forbidden to open my lips, and finally was set down as a parliamentary failure, it having been the ambition of my life to be a parliamentary success, and I being conscious that I had it in me to be one, if I were only allowed to try.[29]

Perhaps it was Harris who forbade the couple to live together in normal marriage. Certainly he demanded and received all of Alice's property. When he summoned the Oliphants back to Brocton in 1873, he is said to have ordered Alice to be buried at once up to the neck in freshly dug earth to see if she could become fit to live in the Brotherhood. Oliphant he separated from her again, ordering him to go into business in New York, where he became Director of the Direct United States Cable Company. In 1876 Alice wrote that she would like to tell Mrs. Cowper "about the greatest and deepest mystery . . . but I cannot bring myself to trust it to the post. I will only say to you that things more wonderful than any imaginings become the simple realities of everyday experience." In 1875 Harris had moved with a few associates to Santa Rosa, California. He summoned Alice there in 1877. Neither her husband nor her mother-in-law was allowed to go. She could not write to anybody because, as Oliphant himself explained, " . . . she is going through deep spiritual experiences. . . . These require entire isolation. . . . We are all awaiting anxiously a full and apparent manifestation of the Lily Queen [Harris's celestial counterpart, it will be remembered, who lived in Lilistan]. When this takes place I have no doubt all our lives will be changed."

In California Harris began to publish a whole series of new revelations: God's kingdom was to be established on earth; Harris was the shadow of the King, Chrysantheus, whose feminine counerpart Chrysanthea lived in eternity; Christ himself had been masculine-feminine, two-in-one, Christus-Christa and Jesus-Yessa; and Chrysantheus-Chrysanthea revealed respectively the Lord's wisdom and His love. "I am the Bridegroom," Harris wrote in a sermon; "Whosoever dwelleth not in the conjugial dwelleth not in me. I am marriage in its primaries, marriage in its potencies, marriage in its ultimates, and marriage in its eternities. . . . I am Sex. Whoever receiveth me, though he were born impotent, shall receive my potency. . . ." Though the dense clouds of verbiage thrown out by Harris have obscured the vision even of his closest students—what *does* he mean?, they ask—one may nonetheless conjecture with reasonable certainty what Alice's "greatest and deepest mystery" was. The way to find one's celestial counterpart was through the ritual of getting into bed with Lily Queen. Since Lily Queen was "inside of Father," the only way to perform the rite was to get into bed with Harris. Yet Harris feared and hated women, as his maunderings often show, and had general promiscuity been a feature of his cult, disillusionment, scandal, and exposure would presumably have been inevitable. Probably only a chosen few of the women were initiated, but it is virtually certain that Alice Oliphant was one of them.

The evidence, as one would expect, is not conclusive. But after the great quarrel between Oliphant and Harris in 1881, Harris in 1882 maintained that Alice had taken on the image of Lily Queen and had magically molested him during the night. What is more likely than that the mad Harris had, in his own queer language, accused her of doing to him what he had actually done to her? In any case, Alice left Santa Rosa late in 1878 (Oliphant on a visit to California earlier that year had not been allowed to see her), and taught school in two California towns before finally defying Harris and joining Laurence in London in 1880 after a four-year separation.[30]

At this juncture, let us recall the figure of Amina in *Masollam,* suddenly told by the old charlatan whom she has for many years loved as a daughter that he is not her father and insists upon becoming her husband. Can we not, in rereading those passages, see in them a fictional rendering of Harris's behavior toward Alice Oliphant? Had not Harris— "Father," as he was called—seduced her, or at least abandoned the paternal relationship and lured her into his bed through use of the counterpart doctrine? And had she not, like Amina, felt bound to obey, despite her doubts, because of the very habit of obedience, because she had renounced her own will and subjected herself in everything to Harris? Certainly as Laurence Oliphant tried in fiction to portray Harris, and to portray his younger self in the course of becoming an adept, he would have felt compelled to come as near as the libel laws would let him in exposing Harris's behavior with the innocent female. I think we are unlikely ever to know much more about the reasons for Alice Oliphant's leaving Harris than *Masollam* tells us.

But Oliphant himself did not break with Harris in 1878. He had—perhaps through loneliness—established a relationship with his own counterpart, whom he called Alawenie, and who was heralded by a vision of Lily Queen herself. He was disgusted with the crookedness he found in the business world, and he resigned from the Cable Company. Later he told his second wife that Harris "had wished me to use, as it seemed to me dishonourably, the knowledge I gained by occupying an inner place in a certain business centre, in order to make a large sum of money, and was angry when I refused. I had had doubts of him before this, but from this time the scales fell completely from my eyes. Yet in answer to the deepest supplication for guidance I knew how to utter, I was still led to remain under his orders, although the position had grown to be most irksome." This episode seems to refer to 1878 and the end of the Cable Company affair. And it is faithfully mirrored in *Masollam* by the greed that had perverted the aims of the Masollams' movement. As Oliphant said about Harris, "In the beginning I believed Harris to be a great and a good man, and I still think he might have filled a lofty place had he taken the right turn; but he took the wrong one, being blinded, principally, through love of power and love of money." "I had reason to believe," Oliphant wrote elsewhere, that "he had entirely abandoned the early purpose of his life, and was selling for gold and his own private ends the gifts with which God had intrusted him for the service of humanity, thus converting him from a religious reformer into a religious impostor." [31] Precisely the case in *Masollam*.

Although the final break had not yet come, by the end of 1878 Oliphant had independently launched a new project of his own: to persuade the Ottoman government to grant him a twenty-five-year concession in Palestine for the purpose of settling European Jews there and developing the country. He believed that such an enterprise would be a blow against the Russian efforts to dominate the region through their sponsorship of Orthodox Christian pilgrimages, and would therefore be in the interests of England. He also expected to be able to raise large sums of money for the plan, having obtained the backing of Disraeli and Lord Salisbury, to whom he was introduced by the Prince of Wales himself. Oliphant thus takes his place as a kind of proto-Zionist, although there was only a very small element of specifically pro-Jewish sentiment in his thinking. In Constantinople during 1879 he failed to secure the concession despite months of intrigue; but he did write a book on Palestine (*The Land of Gilead*), and he decided to make Palestine his home.

He was also moving swiftly toward heresy from Harris's point of view, since Alawenie was now regularly transmitting messages demanding that she and Oliphant should join "in the unity of place and state" with Lily Queen and Harris, "the four making one." It was in fact a summons to Harris to come to Palestine. This posed a direct threat to Harris's supremacy, and he denounced it. While Oliphant and Alice were on holiday in Egypt, came one of Harris's usual "peremptory and unreasonable" commands, "when," Oliphant records, "suddenly the words came to me, 'It is finished.' Chains, more binding than any physical chains could be, dropped from me as if by magic, and I instantly knew a freedom so unfettered that I seemed as one born again." Oliphant returned to America to "make a settlement" with Harris— i.e., to recover his investment in the Brotherhood—to find that Harris had "failed to grasp the fact that his control over me was at an end." Harris "did not understand that the bondage had been wholly self-imposed, voluntary, that it had been suffered for a given end, to kill my pride."

On his way to California in 1881, Oliphant stopped in Brocton, where he persuaded a good many members of the Brotherhood to secede with him. He had not been allowed

to hear from his mother for years, and had assumed that her
close contact with her dead counterpart, his father, was sustaining her. But he found her ill, and took her with him to
Santa Rosa, perhaps in the hope that Harris could help her.
Soon after their arrival, and a stormy interview with Harris,
Lady Oliphant died. Having lost both his mother and his
spiritual master, Oliphant collapsed. He left his claims against
Harris in the hands of his lawyers, and eventually recovered
a substantial part of his investment, as did the other disillusioned members of the Brocton settlement.

It is only now that we can understand and identify the
character of Santalba in *Masollam*. Just as Reginald Clareville
and Sebastian Hartwright represent different aspects of Oliphant himself in his early phase as a member of the Harris
cult, so Santalba represents Oliphant as the disillusioned de-
fector, the experienced initiate, the leader of the schismatic
wing. It is he who suddenly, out of the blue, makes the discovery that Masollam's high purposes have now been perverted by greed, and he who leads the successful fight against
Masollam's schemes. Even the episode in which the Masollams
have Sebastian declared insane parallels Harris's own behavior
at the time of the break with Oliphant: he proposed to have
Oliphant restrained as "mediumistically insane." [32] But, as in
the novel, Santalba won the struggle.

Listen to him now, as he tells Amina in Syria about his
own delusions:

> ...I...contrived to do violence to my conscience at his
> behest. It was under his orders that I, who am by nature...
> absolutely indifferent to wealth, engaged in those commercial
> speculations.... And though we were careful to adhere to
> the world's standard in such matters, I was conscious of
> repeatedly violating my own higher instincts, and of justi-
> fying that violation by the reflection that I had a selfish pride
> in my own high standard of honour, and that God demanded
> that I should outrage it as a sacrifice to Him.... I regret
> nothing, for our motives were pure...and every spasm of

agony we underwent was ... the blast of a purifying fur-
nace, which was needed to fit us to be the instruments we
seek to be.[33]

Indeed, when Santalba heals Florence Hartwright with "a
treatment that differs from any which has yet been recognized by science," he is performing a ritual Oliphant himself
had devised, not Harris, a ritual that could hardly be described
in a novel, or in print at all, and that would become the center
of Oliphant's own heresy from the Harris faith.

Though the scales had fallen from Oliphant's eyes so far
as his submission to Harris was concerned, he was himself,
alas, madder than ever. And during the seven years of life
that remained to him, he tried to redeem mankind and save
civilization by ideas and practices of his own. For some months
after the rupture with Harris, Oliphant did not know whether
Alice, alone in England, would decide to remain in the Harris
faith. Unwilling to face her, he took a long trip in the American Southwest and to Florida and Cuba before returning
early in 1882 to England, where the loyal Alice in fact became the first initiate into the new Oliphant cult.

By the end of 1882 the Oliphants were settled in Palestine,
with a winter house in Haifa—where, oddly enough, there
was already a small German-American religious colony—and
a summer house on Mount Carmel at Dalieh. There they became the center of a small community of their own, including
some former inmates of Brocton. Visitors were many (including, for example, General Gordon—"Chinese" Gordon—
who formed an instant friendship with Oliphant, which they
explained plausibly enough on the grounds that each was considered "one of the craziest fellows alive"). Both Oliphants
devoted themselves to social work among the Druse moun-
taineers. The entire Near Eastern flavor of *Masollam*, with
its lively and detailed pictures of Druse life, derives of course
from their experiences. The idea of turning Harris into an
Armenian for fictional purposes was under the circumstances
a natural one. But the program of good works among the

natives was intended to prepare them for the new Oliphant message:

> It is by the active and conscientious performance of daily duties . . . pure love, humility, and upright dealing, and purity, that the frame can be prepared for the conscious presence of the other half, and for the descent of Christ as the comforter and bridegroom.

By which it will be seen that the doctrine of counterparts was still very much alive.

> When the body after long trials, has been thus prepared, the next stage can be entered upon, concerning which it is not permitted to write yet.[34]

Yet Laurence and Alice now tried to write about it without really writing about it. Perhaps this helps to account for the extraordinary viscousness and opacity of the prose of their book, *Sympneumata*, which Oliphant allegedly wrote entirely from Alice's dictation, and which in 1885 was published anonymously, as "edited by Laurence Oliphant."[35] "Sympneuma," as they used the word, meant something like the Harris counterpart, but with the additional overtone of simultaneous mutual breathing like that we have already encountered in *Masollam*. The book could not say outright what it seems to mean: that God is to be sought—after self-denial—through sexual sensation aroused here on earth, between men and women, each of whom becomes the other's counterpart, and each bisexual, engaging in "high love" but not procreating children: in short, as Henderson puts it, a "kind of mystical masturbation," rather than sexual intercourse. No doubt Alice and Laurence Oliphant's years of self-imposed marital continence had made them both madder than they had been to start with. It is perfectly possible to read *Sympneumata*, or at least to scan its words, without getting this message: "Last night," wrote Oliphant—incredibly enough —from Balmoral in 1886, "I dined with the Queen and told her about *Sympneumata*. She wants to read it, and I am giving it wherever I find the soil pregnant." Indeed, the Oliphants were deliberately guarded in writing about the details, which "could not yet be told," or about the remedies which were not yet known to science.

But they were apparently less guarded about their behavior. Alice Oliphant imparted the sympneuma and thus the arrival of the counterpart to a number of doubtless surprised and grateful local Arabs by "getting into bed with" them "no matter how degraded or dirty they were," and Laurence did the same for innocent Englishwomen on his visits to England. Alice died suddenly in 1885, and Oliphant, in his *Scientific Religion*, published the next year—the same year as *Masollam* —came a little closer to a definition of his true practices when he said that the training for the great experience was more rigorous than any asceticism, as when two young people in love never engage in the usual marital relation. It is the woman who must attain the "sympneumatic life" first and then lead the man to it. "From first to last he must be a passive instrument in her hands; under her guidance he must crush out of his nature every instinct of animal passion. . . ." Then the two exchange magnetism "by constant and close proximity, by which new electromagnetic forces can be generated. . . ." [36]

In *Masollam*, Santalba, who is the schismatic mature Oliphant, preaches as well as practices sympneumata. To his friend, Amina's father, the Druse Sheikh, he says that if a revelation

propounds a method of grappling with the universal misery of today—if it suggests the discovery and application of forces hitherto unknown in nature, by which moral and physical disease may be attacked in their secret strongholds —let [a man] not be deterred by the sneer of science or the bigotry of theologians from boldly searching out such forces and experimenting with them. They lie literally in the womb of nature, for they are its procreative and its recon-

Laurence Oliphant: *above, Altiora Peto, Traits and Travesties* with a presentation inscription to Margot Tennant, later Lady Asquith; and *Piccadilly*, the front cover of which shows Oliphant as drawn by the celebrated artist, Dicky Doyle; *below, Masollam.*

structive vigors.... let him associate himself devotionally
and interiorly in absolute purity, with one of the opposite
sex, animated by like aspirations and equally desirous with
himself to become receptive to the divine afflatus, regardless
of the tremendous sacrifices which such a determination must
necessarily involve. If, with these precautions taken ... one
of these workers ... receives mental images of methods,
hitherto untried and unknown, for grappling with the universal humanitary need, by the invocation of forces in nature
which have never yet been developed, and if such images
are confirmed by the mental consciousness of the other
worker, they may be safely regarded as revelations ... and
the pair may then formulate them for their own guidance
in such poor and inadequate language as our vocabularies
supply, and may present them to their fellow-creatures in
the form which seems best adapted to the limited scope of
their apprehension.... At this crisis of the world's history,
the human race is brought face to face with two alternatives
—union in impurity, which is infernal; or union in purity,
which is divine. Yet so strangely perverted has the social
moral sense become, that we who seek to prepare it for
the mystery of the sacred nuptials, dare only whisper in
trembling accents the cry which we should shout with joy
—"Behold the bride-groom cometh."

Here in *Masollam* is a clearer description than any in *Sympneumata* or *Scientific Religion* of what Oliphant thought he
and Alice were doing. Indeed it describes the writing of the
books as well as the inspiration.

And a few moments later Santalba adds,

She who was my associate on earth, and who has passed into
higher conditions, is not prevented thereby from co-oper-
ating with me, in many respects far more effectively than
she would otherwise have done ... but this is due to the
fact that during our external union we had by long and
arduous effort and ordeal, arrived at a consummation,
whereby an internal and imperishable tie had been created,
the mystery of which I dare not enter upon now.... The
benign operation of the associate intelligence is to reinforce

by means of a subtle impregnation, the moral aspirations and intellectual faculties of the co-worker on earth. . . . So long as [mystics, scientists, and theologians] refuse to grapple with the problems that are involved in the sex question, and to investigate the nature of the forces which produce depravity . . . will they continue to run riot. . . .[37]

Compared to *Sympneumata* and *Scientific Religion*, *Masollam* gives us a clear statement of the Oliphant doctrines—buried until now in a novel that not even those who have studied him most closely have bothered to read. Alice, now dead, was his counterpart; in fact he rippled constantly with electromagnetic messages from her, and the work went on.

The epilogue may be brief. Scandal had hovered over the Oliphants in Palestine, and caught up with Laurence in England, after he had "tried to push the world on a little faster by placing two or three young couples, who were not married, in tempting proximity in order to teach them the habit of self-control." That is to say, he introduced them to the sympneumata by getting into bed with them. One of the young ladies eventually denounced Oliphant to the National Vigilance Association, and a suit against him for corrupting the morals of a minor was pending at the time of his sudden death in 1888. By then he had impulsively rushed off to America once more, after reading a book called *Male and Female Created He Them* by the spiritualist Rosamond Dale Owen—granddaughter of Robert Owen and daughter of Robert Dale Owen—whom he carried off to England (she was forty-two at the time) and married out of hand. He died of cancer only a few months later. After his death, his widow alone had to face the storm of abuse that descended on her husband's memory. Their marriage was so recent that many probably thought she was Alice Oliphant, the real partner in his experiments. Rosamond Oliphant bravely defended him. But the irony was that she had not approved of his actions. For when Oliphant had told her about his activities with the young couples, she had replied that he had made a mistake by putting too much temptation in their way, and had advised him to "leave the work of God in the hands of God." Laurence, she reports, assented quickly: "As usual," he said, "it is conceit which has misled me; I thought I could improve on God's methods and hurry his work." [38] A better epitaph could hardly be found for him.

4

At first glance one sees only contrasts between Harriet Martineau and Laurence Oliphant. She was a woman, an intellectual, a rationalist, a believer in science and progress, a puritanical moralist, and a skeptic. He was a man, ill-educated, emotional, gullible, nonrational, a libertine, and a mystic. Yet *Deerbrook* and *Masollam* sound similar notes, producing unexpected identical resonances. In *Deerbrook* the male characters fail to convince the reader and scarcely seem to engage the real attention of the author: Hope is a wooden incarnation of science at war with obscurantism, Enderby nothing but a puppet. Only the women are real. And of the four important women in the novel, one (Mrs. Rowland) represents Harriet Martineau's domineering mother—let us remember that when *Deerbrook* was written, Harriet Martineau had not yet met her mesmerist—while the other three (Hester, Margaret, Maria Young) represent different aspects of Miss Martineau's own personality. So in *Masollam* the female characters are unconvincing: Amina has some of the attributes (or at least has undergone some of the experiences) of Alice Oliphant, but remains a shadowy figure; while the sinister Mrs. Masollam, I would suggest, represents no living model, but was introduced in part to make the portrait of Harris less recognizable by giving him a female partner, and in part perhaps to suggest the importance of female assistance for any effort, even a wicked one, to reform the morals of society.

Only the men are real. And of the four important men in the novel (I omit the Druse Sheikh), Masollam represents the domineering Harris, and the other three (Clareville, Sebastian Hartwright, Santalba) represent different aspects of Oliphant's own personality at different stages in his career. So the two novels reveal a certain unexpected and parallel symmetry: the author, split into three characters, struggles against the sinister efforts of a highly powerful and threatening figure of the same sex. The domestic village of Deerbrook is not so remote from the exotic village of the Druses after all.

As with the novels, so with the neuroses. Harriet Martineau tells us that she felt the need to submit, and experienced pleasure—even ecstasy—in submitting, during her earlier ill-nesses, to her mother's care; and, during her later and graver illness, to the mesmeric passes—not so much of her male mes-merist, who was comparatively ineffective—but of her less experienced maid, and finally of her "dearly" loved female mesmerist. Laurence Oliphant, though not laid low upon a sickbed but ostensibly in the full vigor of a frenetically active career, tells us that he was so convinced of the sinfulness of his own pride that he felt the need to be "bullied" and "broken in" by another man, Thomas Lake Harris, who exerted by all accounts a highly mesmeric influence over his followers.

Mesmerism, with its successful cures, especially of hysterics, was of course a crude early form of psychotherapy. And al-though Elliotson and most of Miss Martineau's contemporaries failed to push past the "psychological radio system with one personality acting as a transmitter of mental suggestions to another mind attuned to receive them," James Braid of Man-chester, who invented the word hypnotism, took the impor-tant scientific step of abandoning Mesmer's hypothetical fluid and emphasizing instead suggestion, the link between two imaginations, especially powerful when the patient was in a hypnotic trance. From Braid back across the channel to Dr. Liebault of Nancy in the 1860s, and thence to Bernheim of Nancy and Charcot in Paris passed the hypnotic method of discovering the unconscious cause of symptoms. And, of course, to Charcot's clinic in the 1880s came Freud, who would translate Charcot's and Bernheim's books, including the latter's *Hypnotism, Suggestion, and Psychotherapy.* Freud himself lectured on hypnosis immediately upon his return from Paris, despite its unpopularity among the leaders of the medical profession. And between December 1887 and June 1888, he used hypnotic suggestion as his own preferred method of treatment. Psychoanalysis with its brilliant substitution of "free association" for hypnosis as a method of treatment still lay in the future; hypnosis would be gradually rejected (not finally abandoned until 1896) because it "conceals the important phenomenon of resistance and transference"; but the historic line of progress runs clearly from Mesmer to Freud.[39]

Thus Harriet Martineau was "cured" by her mesmerist and restored to her career. Oliphant's subjection to his mesmeric "bully" lasted—because of Harris's and Oliphant's special attitudes and theories—all but a few of the remaining years of Oliphant's life, and it certainly worked no cure. Oliphant emerged sicker than ever, much weakened physically, and with no detectable trace of what little judgment he had ever manifested, the leader of a schismatic cult, with theories and practices more peculiarly sexually obsessed if possible even than those of Harris's Brotherhood of the New Life, and depending even more upon the flow of magnetic fluids that vividly resembled those of the mesmerists.

Masochism and homosexuality seem clearly to have been present in both cases. Without reference to *Deerbrook,* Miss Martineau's careful modern biographer, Professor Webb, has conjectured that she was "latently homosexual." Elizabeth Barrett Browning, referring specifically only to Miss Martineau's fortitude and logic, once called her "the most manlike woman in the three kingdoms," a comment that we might perhaps construe in a broader context.[40] And, in addition to the charge of corrupting the morals of the young that was pending against Laurence Oliphant when he died, there was also apparently one of homosexuality: in hastening his young couples' discovery of the divine sympneumata through the sense of touch, he had, one gathers, not limited his missionary efforts to the young women. It is true that all the documents upon which the National Vigilance Association had based their case were destroyed when Oliphant died before the charges could be pressed. But the lawyer who collected these materials, B. F. C. Costelloe, was the son-in-law of the student of religious fanaticism Hannah Whitall Smith, and his wife later married Bernard Berenson. Both Mrs. Berenson and her daughter, Ray Costelloe Strachey, in the 1930s gave Dr. George Lawton interviews in which they confirmed the nature of the charges.[41] But one need not postulate any overt homosexual act on the part of either Harriet Martineau or Laurence Oliphant. The evidence provided by the lives and by the novels cannot be treated as clinical evidence, but it seems strong enough to warrant our tentative diagnosis. No doubt the neuroses of both writers retain much of their mystery. But without the fiction they would have remained inexplicable indeed. *Deerbrook* and *Masollam* have helped us. Students of eminent and not-so-eminent Victorians neglect at their peril the occasional novel of the occasional novelist.

As one would of course expect, the illnesses of Miss Martineau and Laurence Oliphant were hardly unique in Victorian England. Other Victorians, their lives and works awaiting study, were fellow sufferers. What about Mrs. Eliza Lynn Linton (1822–1898), successful novelist, whom Walter Savage Landor loved as his own daughter, the enemy of George Eliot, the friend of Swinburne, briefly and unsuccessfully the wife of the radical artist W. J. Linton? She wrote her autobiography in the form of a novel, as if she had been a man (*The Autobiography of Christopher Kirkland*); bitterly attacked all forms of female emancipation in a famous essay, "The Girl of the Period"; constituted herself the defender of the sweet and feminine and innocent young woman; and suffered agonies she herself did not fully understand when her beloved younger

woman companion of many years married and left her. No
modern student has yet read with understanding her tense,
passionate, well-written fiction, with its highly suggestive
clues to her tragedy and the tragedy, perhaps, of other Victorian women. Flourishing at a somewhat later period than
Miss Martineau and without her eminence as a social and economic publicist, but a far better novelist, Mrs. Lynn Linton
had much in common with her.[42]

As for Laurence Oliphant's sexual and religious mystical
fantasies, they too represent only a highly sensational case
of a far more general phenomenon. When in the person of
Sebastian Hartwright, Oliphant speaks poetically of "On the
All Mother's breast falling asleep," he is briefly proclaiming
that femininity of God about which he mumbled at such intolerable length in *Sympneumata* and *Scientific Religion,* and
which his Druse Sheikh announces in *Masollam:* "the Eternal
Word was twofold, masculine and feminine, and the feminine
principle was shown to me that I might understand this."
Oliphant here is of course echoing Harris, whose *Declarations
of the Divine One-Twain* (1882), for example, written in
part as an attack on Oliphant after the apostasy, most vividly
sets forth his doctrine of the Divine Mother, to whose womb
he was returning as the "culmination of private bliss." [43] But
the fantasy of a bisexual God whose feminine characteristics
often almost overwhelm the traditional masculine ones of God
the Father goes back to Swedenborg, and thence to the mystical German cobbler-philosopher Jakob Boehme (1575–1624)
and to many Gnostic writers of late antiquity. It found acceptance among certain Victorians, especially those former
Calvinists and evangelicals who could not accept the harsh
masculinity of the traditional Calvinist God.

So George MacDonald, for example, admirer and follower
of Boehme and Swedenborg (as of Novalis, E. T. A. Haff-
mann, Blake, and Wordsworth) wrote several still-popular
fairy tales for children and adults—*Phantastes* (1858), *At the
Back of the North Wind* (1871), *The Princess and the Goblin*

(1872), *The Princess and Curdie* (1883), *The Wise Woman* (1875)—in which the female divinity appears as a benevolent earth mother, grandmother goddess, nature spirit, or wise woman; and many novels, in which God the Father behaves in a motherly and effeminate way. MacDonald, whose own mother died when he was an infant, and who was brought up by a severe but kindly father, yearned in his childhood for the mother he never had, and yet felt deeply guilty at what he feared might be his disloyalty to his father. The mystic doctrine of the bisexual God provided therapy for him, as it did for Oliphant.[44] Even the muscular Christian Thomas Hughes proclaims at the end of *Tom Brown's School-Days* (1857), the very bible of the cult of masculine strength, that God is motherly and sisterly as well as fatherly and brotherly.[45]

And across the English Channel, where they order these things better, the Swedenborgian divine One-Twain also enjoyed considerable popularity in the nineteenth century. Louis du Tourreil's "fusionist" religion of the 1830s and 1840s would have seemed entirely familiar to Harris or Oliphant. Its androgynous God above was reflected at a lower level by Eve-Adam, a kind of demiurge. Christus-Christa and Jesus-Yessa would have felt entirely at home in this pantheon. And the year 1838 saw the advent of the new deity "Mapah"—whose name was made from the first syllables of the words *maman* and *papa* (and feminists will please observe which came first)—

On the day of the Assumption of the Virgin, the fifteenth of August 1838, and the first day of the year Evadah: Mary is no longer the mother; she is the wife; Jesus Christ is no longer the Son: he is the husband. The old world (compression) is over; the new world (expansion) is beginning. The time is ripe, the sacrifice of love has been consummated, the woman has given birth in her anguish to her well-beloved son. Oh, my Mother, you have appeared to me and said "I was but thy mother. I wish to be thy mother and thine affianced bride. That is why I have died and have

risen again. Mapah salutes you . . . in the name of the great
Evadah. . . . And you, Mary, you Mary-Eve, birth-giving
[*génésiaque*] female union, you Christ-Adam, birth-giving
[*génésiaque*] male union, Mapah proclaims you under the
androgynous name Evadam. . . .

Soon the Mapah—whose real name was Ganneau—had obtained as followers men and women with marked radical and
feminist social views. The adventurous Flora Tristan, disciple
of Fourier, found in him a suitable mystic confirmation of her
own expectation that the Messiah would be a woman. Except
for the preoccupation with the Virgin, perhaps inevitable in
France, there was little here to which Harris, Oliphant, or the
Druse Sheikh could have taken exception. Nor was it lunatics
alone who found Mapah inspiring. In his poetry and his fiction
alike, Victor Hugo sometimes followed the strange Mapah
theology as he did that of other occultists and illuminati. In
his novel *Séraphîta*, Balzac makes the protagonist both male
and female.[46]

The suggestion that the neuroses of Harriet Martineau and
Laurence Oliphant may have been common, may even have
been endemic in the culture of Victorian England, must remain for the moment nothing but a suggestion. "There are
moments," a recent critic notes, however, "when it seems that
homosexuality suppressed, sublimated, practised or preached,
general or specialized, may turn out to be the skeleton in every
great Victorian's closet." But that such neuroses were peculiar
to Victorian England nobody could for a moment suggest.
Norman O. Brown, whose *Life Against Death* has since its
publication in 1959 exerted a profound influence on contemporary anti-intellectuals and mystics, also harks back to
Boehme's proclamation of the androgynous nature of God.
Like Rosamond Dale Owen Oliphant before him, Brown
points to Genesis 1:27: "God created man in his own image.
. . . male and female created he them," and underlines the
cabbalistic interpretation of the passage that has always insisted that this must mean that *God* was *both* male and female.

Citing also Galatians 3:28, "There can be no male and female for ye are all one in Christ Jesus," and summoning Berdyaev, the Taoists, and Rilke to his support, Brown finds even in Freud himself the continuation of this mystic tradition: Freud, he says, "used the myth of the formation of mankind by bisection of an originally bisexual creature to suggest that Eros, in seeking ever wider unification, might be seeking to reinstate a lost condition of primal unity." And in Brown's argument (with which I disagree, but whose importance I cannot gainsay) "psychoanalysis...is only an interpretation of the dreams of mysticism." [47]

In our day of Unisex, when, as Rilke prophesied, man and maid no longer always seek each other as opposites, it would be rash to deny that Oliphant's delusions were flourishing among us still. Masollam's successors tell us daily that fusion with the Cosmos and the Creator, which Oliphant believed could be achieved by sympneumatic means, can be achieved through psychedelic drugs. Allegedly the drugs produce a kind of diffused love for all mankind, of precisely the sort that Masollam strove to bring about in the pages of the novel when he required his two young couples to substitute "for the desires of the flesh...a love for the world at large as intense as that for any single unit in it." And in our contemporary "touch-and-tingle" schools of group therapy and sensitivity training perhaps it would not be farfetched to see contemporary experiments with the sympneumata themselves. All the questions still seem open, all the answers the same.

NOTES

1 The most recent and far the best book about her is R. K.
Webb, *Harriet Martineau, A Radical Victorian* (London:
Heinemann, 1960). In his bibliography, pp. 368ff., he
lists and criticizes all earlier studies. Joseph B. Rivlin,
*Harriet Martineau: A Bibliography of her Separately
Printed Works* (New York Public Library, 1937) is also
excellent. Fuller description of many individual books
and pamphlets can be found in Michael Sadleir, *XIX Century Fiction* (London: Constable, and Berkeley: University of California Press, 1951), Vol. I, pp. 248ff. Webb,
p. 299, for Douglas Jerrold's witticism, and pp. 359–360,
363, 365. The anti-slavery novel is *The Hour and the
Man* (3 vols.; London: Moxon, 1841).

2 There is no single work on Laurence Oliphant as satisfactory as Webb's book on Harriet Martineau. The most
recent study is Philip Henderson, *The Life of Laurence
Oliphant, Traveller, Diplomat, and Mystic* (London: Robert Hale Ltd., 1956). But still indispensable is the learned
book—the fruit of many years' assiduous collecting of
data including personal interviews—by Herbert Schneider
and George W. Lawton, *A Prophet and a Pilgrim, Being
the Incredible History of Thomas Lake Harris and Laurence Oliphant; Their Sexual Mysticisms and Utopian
Communities Amply Documented to Confound the Skeptic* (New York: Columbia University Press, 1942). Only
three years after Oliphant's death, his cousin and friend,
the prolific novelist and historian Margaret Oliphant Wilson Oliphant, produced the sympathetic *Memoir of the
Life of Laurence Oliphant and of Alice Oliphant, his
Wife* (2 vols.; Edinburgh and London: Blackwood, 1891),
quoting in full the texts of many important letters. Oliphant's second wife, Rosamond Dale Owen, published her
own memoirs, many years after Oliphant's death, *My*

Perilous Life in Palestine (London: George Allen & Unwin, 1928), containing the record of several important conversations. Ray Strachey, in *Religious Fanaticism: Extracts from the Papers of Hannah Whitall Smith* (London: Faber & Gwyer, 1928), published the valuable notes about various religious fanatics of her acquaintance made by her grandmother, wife of Robert Pearsall Smith, the evangelist, and mother of Logan Pearsall Smith, the essayist, and of Mrs. Strachey's mother, Mrs. Mary Costelloe, later Mrs. Bernard Berenson. Mrs. Smith knew both Oliphant and Thomas Lake Harris. To her mother's short chapters Mrs. Strachey prefixed a general introduction describing "the curious religious sects and communities of America during the early and middle years of the nineteenth century." While the book hardly offers the last scholarly word on the subject as a whole, it is valuable to us because of its first-hand testimony with regard to Oliphant. Remarkably well-written and concise is the anonymous article "Laurence Oliphant," *Blackwood's Edinburgh Magazine*, 150 (July, 1891), pp. 1–20, reviewing Margaret Oliphant's *Memoir*. The quotations in the text are from this article, p. 3; from Laurence Oliphant, *Episodes in a Life of Adventure* (New York: Harper, 1887), pp. 342–343; from Margaret Oliphant, *Memoir*, Vol. II, p. 374; and from Sir Mounstuart Grant Duff, *Notes from a Diary*, as quoted by Henderson, p. 273. Surprisingly enough, Hugo von Hofmannsthal wrote a very entertaining, very Viennese review of Margaret Oliphant's *Memoir* for the *Moderne Rundschau*, reprinted as "Englisches Leben" in *Prosa*, ed. H. Steiner (Frankfort: H. Fischer, 1950), pp. 58–72.

We must also note here the existence of a novel about Laurence Oliphant, by Haskett Smith, M.A., *For God and Humanity: A Romance of Mount Carmel* (3 vols.; Edinburgh and London: Blackwood, 1891). It is "reverently" dedicated "To the Memory of My Beloved Friend, Laurence Oliphant," and the preface declares that "An attempt has been made, however imperfectly, to portray in the following pages the salient points of his personal principles, and to embody in the character of Cyril Gordon a likeness of him who has gone." But the reader is doomed to disappointment. The celibate, colorless Cyril Gordon is hardly recognizable as a portrait of Oliphant, despite his devotion to self-sacrifice as the initiation into true piety, and despite an occasional merely verbal reminiscence of some of Oliphant's mystic ideas. The novel is largely made up of stilted dialogue about the sights and scenes of the Holy Land, a crudely fictionalized guidebook. Smith, a clergyman of the Church of England, followed the Oliphants to Palestine and joined their cult, but was expelled by the authorities when the natives grew alarmed at his overenthusiastic attempts to convert the Druse girls. Alas, one would never guess it from the pages of *For God and Humanity*. Oliphant also appears as "Harold" in Rosa Emerson, *Among the Chosen* (New York: Henry Holt, 1884), a melodramatic but revealing novel written by an American girl who, with her parents, was for a time a member of Harris's community. Schneider and Lawton have made extensive use of the book.

3   Harriet Martineau, *Deerbrook: A Novel* (3 vols.; London: Edward Moxon, 1839). Laurence Oliphant, *Masollam; A Problem of the Period: A Novel.* (3 vols.; Edinburgh and London: Blackwood, 1886). All references will be to these first editions.

4   *Deerbrook*, Vol. I, pp. 27, 25, 67–68, 222, 227; Vol. II, pp. 131, 165, 113, 216; Vol. III, pp. 141, 190, 286.

5   So Webb, pp. 183–189, summarizing what contemporaries thought about the novel, but carrying his own analysis and criticism not much further than theirs.

6   *Harriet Martineau's Autobiography, with Memorials by Maria Weston Chapman* (3 vols.; London: Smith, Elder, 1877). The first two volumes of this edition are an unchanged reprinting of the first edition of the work issued in 1857. All references will be to the edition of 1877.

7   *Autobiography*, Vol. I, pp. 10, 11, 19, 85 ff., 99, 118, 131–132. Webb, pp. 49–52, provides information about her

relationship with Worthington which is not in the *Auto-biography*, taken from surviving shorthand transcripts made by James Martineau of Harriet's letters to him, when in 1843 he reluctantly obeyed her request to return the originals so that she might destroy them.

8 *Autobiography*, Vol. I, pp. 149, 249, 251.

9 *Autobiography*, Vol. II, pp. 108, 111. Miss (Catherine M.) Sedgwick, *Tales and Sketches* (Philadelphia: Carey, Lea, and Blanchard, 1835), pp. 108–116, tells the story of the two sisters as part of a spirited dialogue on "Old Maids." The elder sister relinquishes her lover to the younger, and goes on toiling as a schoolteacher for the rest of her days. The book is dedicated to Harriet Martineau. Mr. and Mrs. S. C. Hall (see below, n. 12), *Ireland: Its Scenery, Character, &c.*, A New Edition (London: Jeremiah Row, 1846) Vol. I, pp. 29–32, tell the story of a girl called Grace Connell, whose fiancé goes off instead with her younger sister Nell. The tale is full of pathos and self-sacrifice, which is heightened even further in Mrs. Browning's "Bertha in the Lane," a dramatic monologue in which the elder sister speaks from her deathbed, relinquishing her lover to the younger just before dying of the overexposure to the elements she suffered when she fainted on hearing her young man making love to her sister. How the younger girl can possibly survive this magnanimity Mrs. Browning does not tell us. First published in *Poems* (London: Moxon, 1844), the poem can be found more easily in *The Poetical Works of Elizabeth Barrett Browning* (Oxford: Humphrey Milford, 1920), pp. 216–219. It was very popular. Harriet Martineau does not mention a far older—and somewhat different—version of the story, the ballad of "The Twa Sisters," whose lover "courted the eldest wi' brooch and knife,/But he lo'ed the youngest abune his life." The eldest so "much envied her sister fair" that "wi' grief and spite she almost brast," but instead of relinquishing their joint lover, she drowned her younger sister instead. Conveniently in B. E. Stevenson,

The Home Book of Verse (New York: Henry Holt, 1920), Vol. II, pp. 2648ff. My friend Mrs. Elizabeth Flavin called this ballad to my attention.

10 *Autobiography*, Vol. II, pp. 113, 150, 151.

11 Robert Darnton, *Mesmerism and the End of the Enlightenment in France* (Cambridge, Massachusetts: Harvard University Press, 1968) provides a splendid (and sometimes hilarious) scholarly account of mesmerism in its earliest phases and of its intimate connection with radical thought and politics in prerevolutionary France. Of course occult writers from Paracelsus (Theophrastus Bombast von Hohenheim, 1495–1541) on had made pronouncements similar to Mesmer's about the relationship between men and celestial bodies, and the best ways to keep this in balance. And charlatans and scientists alike thought in terms of universal fluids. But Mesmer's treatments came at just the right time and place to catch on. And they often worked. For the revival in England see Webb, pp. 234ff., and the sympathetic account, which he cites and uses, of Dr. Elliotson's career by (John Hargreaves) Harley Williams, *Doctors Differ* (London: Jonathan Cape, 1946), pp. 25–91.

12 The original holograph letter is part of my collection of Harriet Martineau. Though undated, its description of the progress of her cure permits us to assign a date in late September or early October 1844 (see Webb, p. 229). It is written on three pages of a four-page folded leaf. On the otherwise blank fourth page is the following note: "Given to Mr. Morris by Miss Martineau's permission by Mrs. S. C. Hall—to whom it was written—A. M. Hall." Annia Maria Hall (1800–1881), author of several books on Ireland (for example see above, note 9) and many novels and other works of fiction, was the wife of Samuel Carter Hall, editor and publicist, widely believed to have been the original model for Dickens's Mr. Pecksniff in *Martin Chuzzlewit*. The Halls, an oleaginous couple, knew everybody in the Victorian literary world, and deserve a memoir of their own. The mesmerist referred to

is of course Mrs. Wynyard. For Mrs. (Elizabeth) Reid, a close friend of Miss Martineau and a frequent visitor, see Webb, p. 17.

13 *Masollam*, Vol. I, pp. 29–34; 56–58; 125; 235; 257–260; 262, 274.

14 *Masollam*, Vol. II, pp. 25, 30, 40, 78–79, 99, 106, 152, 193, 206–207, 217, 219. Amanda McKittrick Ros herself, proud author of *Fumes of Formation*, would have had to concede that "Pants of prostration" has a splendor beyond praise.

15 The following are the only references to *Masollam* in the literature on Oliphant known to me. In his very rare brief pamphlet (I have used the copy in the Boston Athenaeum), *Personal Reminiscences of Laurence Oliphant: A Note of Warning* (London: Marshall Brothers, n.d. [1891]), Louis Liesching—a boyhood friend of Oliphant's in Ceylon, who remained close to him throughout his life, but clove to his own evangelical faith and deplored his friend's religious eccentricities—says (p. 26), "I gather from passages in 'Masollam' that [Oliphant's] opinion was that the teachings of his master were true, but that he himself had given place to the devil." The anonymous author of the *Blackwood's Magazine* article of 1891 says (p. 19), "Harris certainly did supply some traits for the character of Masollam, but we have good reason to believe that Laurence Oliphant did not intend Masollam to be received either as a caricature or as a likeness of the Brocton prophet." We can better understand this altogether unconvincing disclaimer if we remind ourselves that Blackwood was the publisher of *Masollam*, of Margaret Oliphant's *Memoir*—which had just appeared and which had brought threats of lawsuits from Harris—and of this article itself: no doubt they sought to free themselves from the imputation of libel at least so far as *Masollam* was concerned. Ray Strachey, in *Religious Fanaticism*, refers (p. 138) to *Masollam*, quite properly, as "incredible." But Schneider and Lawton, in their study of Harris and Oliphant, mention the novel only twice (pp. 94, 386)

for the sole purpose of pointing out that Mr. Masollam is
indeed a portrait of Harris; and Henderson (p. 112) has
a single reference to it, quoting a small portion of the
passage we have quoted above *in extenso*, agreeing that
it does portray Harris. Nobody has ever troubled to read
the novel as we have just done, or to work out in any
detail the intimate relationship between it and Oliphant's
own life, as we shall now do.

Oddly enough, Schneider and Lawton have paid far
more attention to Oliphant's other novel, *Altiora Peto*
(2 vols.; Edinburgh and London: Blackwood, 1883), in
which Oliphant took his own family Latin motto (altiora
peto = "I seek for higher things") and made it the given
name of his American heroine. This was something of a
best-seller (though Henry Adams commented that he
simply could not read it), but even the most careful reading provides little if any light on Oliphant's personality,
except for a few general statements on the importance of
unselfishness in love. Similarly, in *Traits and Travesties
Social and Political* (Edinburgh and London: Blackwood,
1882), which includes several satirical sketches on America, among them the celebrated story "Dollie and the
Two Smiths," and "The Autobiography of a Joint Stock
Company (Limited)," both of which reflect Oliphant's
experiences in the world of affairs, one finds nothing
whatever bearing on his inner life. It was into *Masollam*
alone that he poured all he could never say except in
fiction about his extraordinary relationship with Harris
and about his own mystic beliefs.

16 G. W. Lawton, *The Drama of Life After Death* (New
    York: Henry Holt, 1932), p. 510.

17 Andrew Jackson Davis, *The Magic Staff* (New York:
    J. S. Brown & Co., 1857), p. 373, and cited by Schneider
    and Lawton, p. 6.

18 Schneider and Lawton, pp. 7–30 and pp. 32, 33, 34.

19 Schneider and Lawton, p. 55. Harris's theory of three
    crises in human history is another example of mystic
    thinking in terms of triads that goes back to Joachim of
    Fiore (1145–1210), a Calabrian monk who divided uni-

versal history into an age of the Father, with the Old Testament as its revelation, an age of the Son, with the New Testament as its revelation, and a future age of the Holy Ghost, with a third testament yet to be revealed. Comte, Hegel, Marx, and even Hitler have all been associated with such apparently satisfying thinking in threes. See Norman Cohn, *The Pursuit of the Millennium* (Fair Lawn, New Jersey: Basic Books, 1957), pp. 99ff. and 391–392, and Robert Lee Wolff, "The Three Romes," *Myths and Mythmaking*, ed. Harry A. Murray (New York: Braziller, 1960), p. 176.

20 Oliphant left no autobiography like that of Harriet Martineau. But the key facts of his life are well-established and often reported in his own words, not only in his books of travel and *Episodes in a Life of Adventure*, but in the many and revealing letters quoted by Margaret Oliphant, by Schneider and Lawton, and by Henderson. Hannah Whitall Smith and Rosamond Dale Owen Oliphant provide remembered conversations. Finally, as I hope this essay will demonstrate, there is *Piccadilly* and, most important, *Masollam* itself. For the "hothouse plant," Margaret Oliphant, *Memoir*, Vol. I, p. 13. Louis Liesching (p. 6) says that "Oliphant ran considerable risk of being spoilt by a mother whose idol he was." For admissions to his mother that he was more flirtatious than he could confess to her, see *Memoir*, Vol. I, p. 21; for "sugardoodling," Liesching, p. 14; for Lady Oliphant's maid, Schneider and Lawton, p. 113, n. 21; Henderson, p. 132. Schneider and Lawton, pp. 114ff., dsicuss the question of Oliphant's putative venereal disease. It seems entirely probable that he was a syphilitic, although one hesitates at first to credit a story later so assiduously put about by Harris and his defenders. Even Margaret Oliphant (*Memoir*, Vol. II, p. 36) quotes a letter in which Oliphant accused himself of the "most reckless dissipation." The story of the Paris exhibition of venereal diseases is in Rosamond Dale Owen, *My Perilous Life*, p. 23, and quoted in full by Schneider and Lawton, pp. 117–118.

21 *Piccadilly* was not published as a book for five years after

its serial appearance. References here are to the first book edition, acknowledged by its author: Laurence Oliphant, *Piccadilly: A Fragment of Contemporary Biography* (Edinburgh and London: Blackwood, 1870). Harris's verses pp. 84–85, and attribution in footnote, p. 85; Harris's appearance on the scene, pp. 281–283.

22 There is disagreement among the authorities as to which went to America first, mother or son. Margaret Oliphant, *Memoir*, Vol. II, p. 30, has Lady Oliphant arriving a year after Laurence, and so does Ray Strachey, *Religious Fanaticism*, pp. 131–132. But it seems clear that in 1865 Oliphant was allowed to bring his mother to America, and was then forced to return to England without her and wait there two more years before he got permission to cross the Atlantic again. See Henderson, p. 138; Schneider and Lawton, p. 113 and n. 22.

23 *Memoir*, Vol. II, p. 30. It is notable that even Margaret Oliphant, a thoroughly reticent, if not prudish, Victorian, should in 1891, only three years after Laurence's death, have been willing to include in her laudatory biography of him so unmistakable and significant a reference to a mistress.

24 Schneider and Lawton, p. 128; Henderson, p. 148.

25 Owen, *My Perilous Life*, pp. 28, 33. Cf. Schneider and Lawton, pp. 118–119.

26 *Masollam*, Vol. III, pp. 218ff.

27 *Memoir*, Vol. II, p. 31; Schneider and Lawton, pp. 257–258.

28 Owen, *My Perilous Life*, p. 23. Margaret Oliphant, *Memoir*, Vol. II, p. 125, obviously knew about the renunciation. Immediately after recording the wedding in June 1872, she says, "It is impossible to enter into other circumstances of this union, which make it more remarkable still . . . but which belong entirely to the privacies of individual life."

29 Schneider and Lawton, pp. 262–264.

30 *Ibid.*, pp. 275, 278–279, 289, 302 (they admit bafflement); 183ff. and Appendices for the sexual experiences of in-

mates; 326–327 for Harris's accusation of Alice. Henderson, p. 200, assumes that there were sexual relations between Harris and Alice Oliphant.

31 Owen, *My Perilous Life,* pp. 28–29; Schneider and Lawton, p. 338.

32 Schneider and Lawton, pp. 337, 339, 342.

33 *Masollam,* Vol. III, pp. 12–15.

34 Schneider and Lawton, pp. 372, 374.

35 Edinburgh and London: Blackwood, 1885.

36 Schneider and Lawton, pp. 375ff., 382; Henderson, p. 236ff.

37 *Masollam,* Vol. III, pp. 17–20, 26, 28, 30–33.

38 Owen, *My Perilous Life,* pp. 24, 25.

39 (J. H.) Harley Williams, *op. cit.* (note 11 above), pp. 82ff., for Braid and his immediate French followers. Ernest Jones, *The Life and Works of Sigmund Freud* (New York: Basic Books, 1953), Vol. I, pp. 226–244.

40 Webb, p. 51, and footnote 1; p. 233.

41 Henderson, pp. 254–255, and p. 268, n. 1.

42 For the external facts of her life, see the biography by her nephew, George Somes Layard, *Mrs. Lynn Linton: Her Life, Letters and Opinions* (London: Methuen, 1901). My collection includes several important unpublished letters of hers to Landor, unknown to Layard. Her own little *Reminiscences of Dickens, Thackeray, George Eliot,* published posthumously (London: Hodder and Stoughton, 1899) contains her attack on George Eliot, whom she knew when they were both girls and George Eliot was living at John Chapman's. See also Gordon Haight, *George Eliot and John Chapman* (New Haven: Yale University Press, 1940). The initial bond between her and Swinburne was their common affection for Landor, and Mrs. Lynn Linton's disappointment and anger at having been left out of Forster's biography of Landor. Swinburne soothed her, wrote her many letters—for which see the *Letters,* ed. C. Y. Lang (6 vols.; New Haven: Yale University Press, 1959–1962), *passim*—wrote a sonnet to her, and grieved at her death. She dedicated

her novel *Ione* (3 vols.; London: Chatto & Windus, 1883)
to him; see his letter of appreciation, *Letters*, Vol. V, no.
1242. *The Autobiography of Christopher Kirkland* (3
vols.; London: Bentley, 1885) deserves a reading like the
one we have here given *Deerbrook*. "The Girl of the
Period," first published in *The Saturday Review*, March
14, 1868, was later reprinted in *The Girl of the Period
and Other Social Essays* (2 vols.; London: Bentley, 1883).
For some of the reactions it inspired, both serious and
comic, see Sadleir, *XIX Century Fiction*, Vol. I, pp. 210–
211; all these and many others are in my collection. A
later novel, *The One Too Many* (3 vols.; London: Chatto
& Windus, 1894), is dedicated to "...the sweet girls
still left among us who have no part in the new revolt,
but are content to be dutiful, innocent, and sheltered."
See Layard, pp. 191ff., for an account of the relationship
between Miss Beatrice Sichel, later Mrs. Hartley, and
Mrs. Linton. Also in my collection is a copy of *The
World Well Lost* (2 vols.; London: Chatto & Windus,
1878) inscribed to "My dear child Bee Sichel" with a long
affectionate note.

43 Schneider and Lawton, pp. 361–363.

44 *Masollam*, Vol. II, p. 282. For MacDonald see Robert Lee
Wolff, *The Golden Key, A Study of the Fiction of
George MacDonald* (New Haven: Yale University Press,
1961), where these points are argued at length with specific reference to his life and writings.

45 Walter E. Houghton, *The Victorian Frame of Mind*
(New Haven: Yale University Press, 1957), p. 202, n. 24.

46 Auguste Viatte, *Victor Hugo et les Illuminés de son
temps* (Montreal: Les Éditions de l'Arbre, 1942), pp. 82ff.,
for the Mapah; the passage quoted is my translation from
pp. 87–88. For Hugo's use of Mapah eschatology, *passim*.
See also Jules-L. Puech, *La Vie et l'oeuvre de Flore Tristan*
(Paris: Marcel Rivière, 1925). On *Séraphîta* see most recently G. Delattre, "De 'Séraphîta' à 'La Fille aux yeux
d'or,'" *L'Année Balzacienne* (1970), pp. 183–226, and
references in note 76 to "Strange Stories," below.

47 "Clashing Beards and Beardless Boys," *The Times Literary Supplement*, No. 3853 (October 30, 1970), p. 1279. Norman O. Brown, *Life Against Death: The Psychoanalytical Meaning of History* (Modern Library Paperback; New York: Random House, 1959), p. 133.

III

STRANGE STORIES:
THE OCCULT FICTION OF
SIR EDWARD BULWER-LYTTON

1 / *Bulwer as a Literary Man:*
His Early Use of the Occult

Looking back in 1951, twenty years after he had published
the first volume of a biographical and critical study of Edward
Lytton Bulwer, Michael Sadleir remarked wryly that "No
one wanted Bulwer nor ever pretended that he did." So Sadleir, who had learned more about his man than anybody since,
abandoned his project, leaving Bulwer in 1836, aged only
thirty-three. In 1971 the collected editions of Bulwer's writings still crowd the shelves, volume upon volume, more numerous and more varied even than the changing forms of his
aristocratic name, which rang so musically in his own ears.
By their number and variety his books attest to the enormous
popularity and esteem that he enjoyed in his own lifetime.
And by their mere presence—they are always *there*, available,
in the stacks—they bear witness to the neglect into which he
has now fallen. Only an occasional wandering scholar ventures into this airless region of literary interstellar space, and
when he emerges he almost invariably publishes his findings
with a prefatory word of deprecation. Bulwer is neglected,
the scholars say, and, on the whole, he deserves to be. His
style is impossibly baroque, his personality unpleasing, his
fiction third-rate. *But*, on the other hand, there is this or that
about him that deserves to be recalled.

Prolific he certainly was, but no more so than many Victorians who wrote for money. He was politician as well as
writer, spending many years in Parliament and holding high
office. But his friend Disraeli, with whom he had so much in
common for so long a period, reached the very top of the
pole, and wrote better, if fewer, novels than Bulwer. In literary versatility, however, Bulwer was perhaps unmatched. His
plays—especially *The Lady of Lyons* (1838) and *Money*
(1840)—scored great successes, and for decades after their
first performances were produced again and again, forming

part of the repertory of the Victorian drama. In 1911, at the coronation of George V, *Money* was selected—seventy-one years after its opening night—as the play to be given an all-star special performance in honor of the German Emperor and Empress. Bulwer's poetry and his verse translations of Schiller won wide admiration. He wrote history, critical essays, political pamphlets, and what we now would call sociology (*England and the English*, 1833). And in his novel writing he tried all the existing genres, and invented several new ones.

His very first novel, *Pelham* (1828), introduced the earliest dandy-hero of English fiction, and carried fashionable Byronism several steps further than Byron himself. Pelham wore a black coat in the evening, in accordance with his mother's advice: only a distinguished man could look well in one, she assured him. The black coat became the fashion, and we wear it still, but few of us now know or care why. And in *Pelham*'s successors, *Godolphin* (1833), *Ernest Maltravers* (1837), and others, Bulwer continued to set the standards for the contemporary novel of high society. In *Paul Clifford* (1830) he produced the very first of the "Newgate" novels, stimulating Ainsworth and Dickens to imitation, and Thackeray to hostile satire. And in *Paul Clifford*'s successors, *Eugene Aram* (1832) and *Lucretia* (1846), Bulwer gave fictional treatment to actual murders. These and *Night and Morning* (1841) brought fierce storms of abuse upon him: he was making crime too attractive, his enemies charged; but the books also brought him welcome notoriety and still more welcome cash. Novels of crime and its relationship to society still command an eager audience, but Bulwer's are virtually forgotten.

In his series of successful historical romances, Bulwer asserted that he had outdone Scott in historical accuracy by drawing upon the most reliable original sources, which occasional German doctoral candidates have triumphantly identified. But whether the reader found himself in fourteenth-century Italy (*Rienzi*, 1835) or in the England of the Wars

Bulwer: the original drawing by Daniel Maclise, made in 1830 for *Fraser's Magazine*'s famous series called "A Gallery of Illustrious Literary Characters." Each portrait was accompanied by a brief sardonic commentary, usually by William Maginn. "Viewing his face and reviewing his beard," says Maginn, Bulwer the dandy "but looked in the glass and drew from himself."

of the Roses (*The Last of the Barons*, 1843) or of the Norman Conquest (*Harold, the Last of the Saxon Kings*, 1848), he was sure to be exposed to Bulwer's own opinions on the policies and issues of contemporary Victorian England, and on the larger questions of reaction and reform, liberty and despotism, feudalism and progress. Bulwer's political position changed from Benthamite and reforming Whig to Young England Tory Radical, but many of his political convictions did not change: while not unsympathetic to the Chartists, he always feared the mob; he admired reactionaries and romanticized feudal relationships, but conceded the desirability of progress and reluctantly saluted the steam engine he disliked.[1] Later Bulwer wrote a series of popular discursive novels on English middle-class family life (beginning with *The Caxtons*, 1849) which have had little recent critical attention.

One further major category remains—the fiction of the occult, the subject of this study. Here Bulwer did his best work, the work that lay closest to his own heart. No critic has yet explored it in any depth, perhaps because it is difficult, and the exploration leads the student into unfamiliar territory. But the voyage is worth the effort, and one returns from it with a higher esteem for Bulwer than any accorded him since his death. His two most important novels of the occult are *Zanoni* (1842) and *A Strange Story* (1862), while for certain important themes we place with them *The Coming Race* (1871), much shorter, and the last of Bulwer's books to be published during his lifetime. With these belongs also a masterly occult short story, "The Haunters and the Haunted; or, The House and the Brain" (1859). The mere dates of publication suggest that for almost thirty years Bulwer maintained his deep interest in the supernatural. He dealt with it in fiction at long intervals, each time on the basis of new experiences, further reading, and much reflection. But in fact, the record is longer still. Bulwer's active studies of the occult began in the early 1830s, and became increasingly important to him as the years went by. Astrology, alchemy, mesmerism, clairvoyance, hypnotism, spiritualism, and magic: he investigated them all at first hand, and wrote about them all. We shall find the record of his own experiences, so far as it can be recovered, indispensable to our study of his writing.

For the first full-scale fictional expression of his interest in the supernatural, then, Bulwer's readers had to wait until 1842 and the appearance of *Zanoni*. But both *Godolphin* (1833) and *The Last Days of Pompeii* (1834)—perhaps his only novel that is still read—give unmistakable notice of his new preoccupation. Let us look first at these two forerunners. On a visit to Rome, Godolphin, a typically blasé and fashionable Bulwer hero, becomes the pupil of Volktman, a Danish recluse and astrologer, once a sculptor. (Was he perhaps suggested to Bulwer in part by Thorwaldsen?) A "singular and romantic visionary," with a "weird and Gothic" enthusiasm not only for astrology but for subjects "still more shadowy and benighted—the old secrets of the alchemist, and perhaps even...those arcana yet more gloomy and yet rational," Volktman casts for Godolphin an ominous horoscope that predicts not only an early death but an unfortunate conjunction between his star and that of Volktman's young daughter Lucilla, who has already indeed fallen in love with Godolphin. In Godolphin's absence, Volktman tells Lucilla how one may conjure up a vision or dream of an absent person: by fasting, in solitude, and in "intense reverie," one can so well learn to control the imagination that—especially with the aid of a charmed astrological drawing of "the figure of a man asleep on the bosom of an angel"—one may see in sleep the person one summons up. Volktman believes in "magnetism," "sympathy," and the power of trance and rapture to transport a man out of himself, and enable him to see and hear events at a distance and even to converse with the dead.

For two idyllic years after Volktman's death, Lucilla is Godolphin's mistress, but she renounces him and disappears when she learns—by using her father's drawing to summon up a vision of Godolphin during an absence—that his former love is now widowed and that Godolphin wants to marry her. Many years later Lucilla turns up in London as a seeress, a believer and practitioner of her father's doctrine of the power of the trained imagination. To Godolphin's wife, Constance, Lucilla tells of the invisible beings that share the world with us, "Dread Solemn Shadows ... the night is their season as the day is ours; they march in the moonbeams, and are borne upon the wings of the winds." And she shows Constance

> a sort of glass dial marked with various quaint hieroglyphics and the figures of angels, beautifully wrought; but around it were ... many stars and planets ranged in due order. These were lighted from within by some chemical process, and burnt with a clear and lustrous, but silver light. ... the dial turned round, and the stars turned with it, each in a separate motion; and in the midst of the dial were the hands of a clock that moved ... slowly. ... One star burned brighter than the rest; and below it, halfway down the dial, was another, a faint and sickly orb, that ... seemed to perform a much more rapid and irregular course.

These are Godolphin's and Lucilla's stars. When they meet the mechanism will halt. She knows exactly when it will happen, and she and Godolphin will die. Though this seems like madness to Constance, in fact, as Volktman had predicted, and as the astrological dial shows, the fates of Lucilla and Godolphin are inextricably entwined: she summons him to her deathbed, and while he is riding home after her death he is drowned in a sudden flood.

Much of *Godolphin* has nothing to do with the occult: it is a novel of fashionable life and politics and world-weariness, but the mainspring of the action depends upon an astrological prophecy. While its fulfillment may be construed as Godolphin's fit punishment for his abandonment of Lucilla, all that he had done had been ordained in the stars, and his fate was inescapable. The book abounds in references to the Chaldaeans as the earliest and wisest students of the occult.

These Chaldaeans, the power of the imagination, the importance of trance, the possibility of clairvoyance, and the Dread
Shadows—all touched upon only lightly in *Godolphin*—we
shall encounter among the central themes of *Zanoni*. But astrology, the chief occult theme in *Godolphin*, we shall find
explicitly renounced and even scorned in the later novel.

As for *The Last Days of Pompeii*—it is of course in part
a costume piece, and in part an extremely clever attempt to
capitalize in fiction on the contemporary fad for reflection
upon great natural disasters and the lessons that mankind
might learn from them, a theme that inspired a good deal of
painting, philosophy, and literature in the early 1830s. It also
offered Bulwer the chance to comment on the decadence of
late Regency Englishmen while seeming to portray only that
of early imperial Romans. In it he displayed much learning
with regard to Egyptian religion and the mystical cults popular in the Roman world. He made his villain, the wicked
Egyptian, Arbaces, a magician. Rich, a sensualist, Arbaces
thinks that "the cabala of some master soul" might be able
to divert Nature from her course and work miracles. So

he pursued Science across her appointed boundaries, into
the land of perplexity and shadow. From the truths of as-
tronomy he wandered into astrologic fancy. From the secrets of chemistry he passed into the spectral labyrinth of
magic; and he who could be sceptical as to the power of
the gods was credulously superstitious as to the power of
men.

Indeed, Arbaces was known as "Hermes, Lord of the Flaming Belt"—a clear reminiscence of the thrice-greatest (Trismegistus) Hermes, with whose name so much magical writing
is associated. Bulwer adds that Arbaces's writings were later
burned by the Christians at Ephesus: this helps lend veri-
similitude to his characterization. And when in the novel Arbaces visits the Saga (witch) of Vesuvius to obtain some
poison, he wears his flaming belt, "a cincture, seemingly of

fire, that burnt around his waist, clasped in the centre by a plate whereon was engraven some sign...vague and unintelligible, but...not unknown to the Saga." In the course of our reading of *Zanoni* we shall have occasion to refer again to Arbaces and his magic. But here we need note only that Bulwer professes total scepticism as to his wicked arts. In *The Last Days of Pompeii* occult phenomena are treated with flippancy, instead of being solemnly presented as credible, as they had been in *Godolphin* and would be again in *Zanoni*.

One of the themes that we shall find Bulwer dwelling upon in *Zanoni* made its first appearance in a short story first published in 1832, called "The Tale of Kosem Kosamim the Magician," which Bulwer had outlined in his schooldays and later extracted from the unfinished romance out of which *Zanoni* eventually grew. We must therefore regard this little tale as a kind of fragment of *Zanoni* excluded from the novel and given separate publication. In it the magician tells how in his youth he passionately yearned for knowledge: "My mind," he says,

> launched itself into the depth of things—I loved step after step to trace effect to its first cause. Reason was a chain from heaven to earth, and every link led me to aspire to the stars themselves....I knew the secrets of the elements, and could charm them into slumber, or arouse them into war. The mysteries of that dread chemistry which is now among the sciences that sleep [i.e., alchemy] ... the exercise of that high faculty—the Imagining Power...which trained and exercised, can wake the spectres of the dead—and bring visible to the carnal eye the Genii that wall the world... the sleepless science that can make a sage's volume of the stars [i.e., astrology]—these were mine, and yet I murmured—I repined!—what higher mysteries were yet left to learn?

The magician, we can see, already possesses all the powers of Volktman, but he still yearns for the "great arch secret of all,...not knowledge, but the source of knowledge...the

One Great Productive Spirit of all things." He has a vision of Fire, with which he can talk familiarly, and for a time believes it to be the principle he has been seeking. But in the end, the seemingly supreme spirit of fire proves to be Corruption, a demon, the first principle of nature for those who accept nature itself as the First Cause, and do not believe in God. Except for this final Christian moral, "Kosem Kosamim" is thoroughly occult. The wild desire to discover the secrets of the universe we shall learn in *Zanoni* to recognize as an important characteristic of the neophyte in the occult. And the primacy of fire is a thoroughly alchemical notion: fire is both the lofty revealing light of nature, and hell-fire, the consuming principle of evil. We shall not encounter Kosem Kosamim's fire again until *A Strange Story* in 1862, but we know at least that Bulwer had read the alchemists thirty years before that.[2]

Indeed, Bulwer was an extraordinarily cultivated, even a learned, man. Though he might in the pages of a novel carelessly deprecate his hero's classical learning, by which he meant his own, in fact he had an easy working knowledge of Latin and Greek. He liked to give his chapters epigraphs from Aeschylus or Hesiod, and condescendingly supplied translations. Nor in Bulwer's case did the fashionable sprinkling of his pages with French and Italian tags mean—as it did with so many of his contemporary writers on high society—that these tags were all the French and Italian he knew. He lived much in France and Italy, spoke both languages fluently, read his French historians, memoirists, novelists, and scientists, and his Italian poets, notably Ariosto and Tasso. His devotion to Germany and things German was if anything even greater. He dedicated *Ernest Maltravers* "to the German people." We have already noticed and shall often be returning to his translation of Schiller, to which he prefixed a biographical sketch so laudatory that the leading authority on Schiller's influence in England uses it to mark the beginning of what he calls the "religion" of Schiller there. Scholars have frequently pointed out the debt of Bulwer's fiction to Goethe's *Werther* and *Wilhelm Meister*. We shall demonstrate that his debt to Goethe is greater than has been noticed, and in *Zanoni* we shall find clear indication that Novalis too—not heretofore recognized as a source for Bulwer's thinking—also exercised an important influence over him.

Bulwer's study of the occult led him to the Neoplatonists —Iamblichus and Proclus in particular, to the treatises on demons of the eleventh-century Byzantine, Michael Psellus, and to an astonishing variety of other reading in postclassical Greek as well as to the sixteenth- and seventeenth-century Latin writings of certain alchemists (Paracelsus, Cornelius Agrippa, Jean Baptiste Van Helmont, and others), to whom we shall be returning. And throughout the four decades of his interest in the supernatural, he also read as they appeared the latest works on physiology, philosophy, and what passed for psychology, in French, German, and English. Not only Bacon, Newton, Descartes, Locke, Condillac, Hume, Reid, Kant, Schelling, and Hegel, but Lamarck, Laplace, Maine de Biran, Sir Humphrey Davy, Faraday, Darwin, Louis Agassiz —we shall find him citing all these and many others. Yet, characteristically, he wrote

> I do not pretend to be a philosopher; and if I did, I know of no sect of philosophy to which I could unreservedly give a disciple's adhesion. I do not presume to call myself a scholar, but I am and have been for years... a student of life and books.[3]

An erudite author does not necessarily write good novels, and the insistence on a display of erudition in fiction may irritate critics almost beyond endurance, especially when the erudite novelist also writes, as Bulwer did, a deep purple prose, and irritates people for other reasons as well. He irritated them because he was an aristocrat, an extravagant spend-thrift in his youth, a Byronic *poseur* who designed his own peculiar clothes and spoke with his own peculiar brand of

Bulwer: *above*, first editions of some of his important books; *below*, *Zanoni*, *A Strange Story*, and two copies of *The Coming Race*, one with corrections in the author's own hand.

haughtiness, elegance, and snobbishness, because he seemed to think himself better than other men and to be intolerably weary of ordinary life and ordinary people. He irritated them because he put himself into all his books, and whatever he wrote was instantly successful, no matter how inferior the critics insisted it was. He irritated them because he was early made a Baronet for services to literature that they did not believe he had rendered, and because political success came easily. He irritated them—let us admit it—because they were jealous. The clique at *Fraser's Magazine*, and Thackeray in particular, for years found it impossible to stop taking pot shots at Bulwer. His marriage collapsed in 1836 in spectacular fashion, and his obsessed and demented wife for decades thereafter made scandalously embarrassing public scenes, and filled the air and the pages of her own novels with the most libelous portraits of him and unbridled attacks on his alleged behavior. Though far from blameless in the quarrel, he could hardly be said to have deserved the misery it brought him. In some quarters he was hailed as a genius, greater than even Dickens or Thackeray, and in all quarters he was read. Though it is no part of our business to strike a balance as to his character, one should in fairness emphasize his unfailing kindness to young and unknown writers, to whom he regularly gave constructive critical advice, and for whom he opened the doors to publication. Nor can one forget the intimacy he achieved with those very few friends whom he had learned to trust. Sensitive, shy, elusive, peculiar he certainly was, but it is almost a century since he died, and we may now claim the right to examine his fiction as he wrote it.

His occult writings always enjoyed particular popularity, and aroused particular distaste. Almost thirty years after his death, in 1901, Walter Frewen Lord, a critic, remarked of Bulwer that "At first for pleasure, and later for curiosity, and at last for business reasons, he saturated his mind with the love of magic." And, though Lord could hardly have known it, he was echoing, but far more disagreeably, W. E. Aytoun's amusing verses of 1843, only a year after *Zanoni*, in which Bulwer, as one of the "would-be laureates" after the death of Southey, is made to say:

> They throng around me now, those things of air,
>   That from my fancy took their being's stamp:
> There Pelham sits and twirls his glossy hair,
>   There Clifford leads his pals upon the tramp:
>   There pale Zanoni, bending o'er his lamp,
> Roams through the starry wilderness of thought
> Where all is everything, and everything is nought.
>
> Yes, I am he, who sung, how Aram won
>   The gentle ear of pensive Madeline,
> How love and murder hand in hand may run,
>   Cemented by philosophy serene,
>   And kisses bless the spot where gore has been;—
> Who breathed the melting sentiment of crime,
> And for the assassin waked a sympathy sublime.
>
> Yes, I am he who on the Novel shed
>   Obscure philosophy's enchanting light,
> Until the public,' wilder'd as they read,
>   Believed they saw that which was not in sight.
>   Of course, 'twas not for me to put them right;
> For in my inmost heart convinced I am,
> Philosophy's as good as any other flam.

Of course the occult paid, but so did everything else that Bulwer set his hand to. We must gently repudiate the notion that he went in for the occult for business reasons or that philosophy to him was as good as any other flam.

Yet perhaps we shall also find it hard to accept Bulwer's grandson's insistence that his grandfather's attitude toward the occult was

exactly that of the members of the Psychical Research Society of the present day [i.e., 1913] anxious to learn something that would extend the horizon of human knowledge and experience, yet forced to confess that nothing which he had witnessed himself truly justified any definite conclusions.

That was what Bulwer wanted his public to believe, or rather it was one of the things he took pains in his writing to convey to the public. On the other hand, for what it was worth, he also became a Rosicrucian, and Grand Patron of the Order,[4] and made many experiments in company that disinterested scholars would hardly have approved. In this way, as in so many others, Bulwer was ambivalent. He loved to cover his tracks, to enjoy the reputation of being a kind of sorcerer while protesting that in fact there was probably nothing in it. He enjoyed mystification as much as mysticism, and it will be one of our amusements and problems in the pages that follow to try to pin him down.

In 1835, while in the early stages of his occult studies, Bulwer had a dream about a sage who had learned to make and use an elixir of life that rendered him immortal from all human illnesses, though of course he was still vulnerable to violent or murderous assault. In alchemy, the elixir of life is generally regarded as one aspect of the Philosopher's Stone, the ultimate substance so passionately sought, the mysterious, liberating perfect instrument. In 1838 Bulwer published a version of this dream as a fragmentary story called, after its hero, *Zicci*. Later he returned to the theme, changed the protagonist's name, and transformed the fragment into a full-length three-volume novel, *Zanoni*, published in 1842. On the title page of Volume I appears an epigraph: "I cannot make head nor tail on't"—*Le Comte de Gabalis*. *Zanoni*, then, will be a puzzle.[5]

In a bookshop in Covent Garden specializing in "works of Alchemist, Cabalist, and Astrologer"—where the proprietor himself believes "in his Averroes and Paracelsus"—the narrator, a brash young man, hopes to find books about the Rosicrucians, perhaps "written by one of their own order, and confirming ... the pretensions to wisdom and to virtue which Bringaret had arrogated to the successors of the Chaldaean and gymnosophist." He meets an elderly customer, an authority on the subject, with whom he becomes friendly. The old man, a painter who had witnessed the first French Revolution and had suffered, tells him that the Rosicrucians, who are true Christians, "still existed, and still prosecuted, in august secrecy, their profound researches into natural science and occult philosophy," but that they are only "a branch of other fraternities yet more transcendent in the powers they have obtained and yet more illustrious." These are the Platonists, whose sublimest works are in manuscript; and constitute the initiatory learning not only of the Rosicrucians but of the nobler brotherhoods. . . . More solemn and sublime still is the knowledge to be gleaned from the elder Pythagoreans and the immortal masterpieces of Apollonius.

The two also discuss art: the painter far prefers what he calls the "Greek" school, which exalts Nature into the Ideal and thus is "true," to the "Dutch" school, which merely imitates life and thus is "real." And, in answer to a literary query, the painter reads aloud in Greek and in English a passage from Plato and a commentary upon it, to the effect that the human soul ordinarily ascends through four successive stages of enthusiasm or divine inspiration: the musical, the "telestic or mystic," the prophetic, and that which belongs to love. In each case, "that part of the soul which is above intellect is excited to the gods, and thence derives its inspiration." He himself, the painter says, has written a book "with that thesis for its theme . . . a romance, yet not a romance, truth for those who can comprehend it, and an extravagance for those who cannot."

Soon afterward the painter dies and leaves to the narrator the manuscript of his book, entirely in hieroglyphics which must be painstakingly deciphered with a key. After two years' work, the narrator only secures "by way of experiment. . . . the insertion of a few desultory chapters in a periodical." These arouse interest, and, finding that he had in fact been bequeathed two distinct versions, the narrator has now proceeded to prepare for publication the more elaborate and detailed one.[6]

The preface provided readers of *Zanoni* with an explanation of the earlier publication of the fragmentary *Zicci*: which, we are to believe, was the painter's shorter version. *Zanoni*, we learn, will—in accordance with a passage in Plato—show the part of the soul that is higher than intellect mounting successively through divinely inspired stages of enthusiasm: musical, "telestic or mystic," prophetic, and "that which belongs

to love." There is indeed a passage in Plato's *Phaedrus* in which
Socrates, summing up the previous discussion, says that the
"divine madness [*manía*] was subdivided into four kinds,
prophetic [*mantiké*], initiatory [*telestiké*], poetic [*poetiké*],
and erotic [*erotiké*]," of which the last is the best; and this is
the passage that surely lay behind what the painter had read
aloud and announced as the theme of his romance. But—we
note immediately—the order of the four kinds of divine madness, or enthusiasm, differs. Socrates tells us that his third
kind of madness, the poetic, is presided over by the Muses,
which makes it clear enough that this is the same as the
painter's "musical" enthusiasm. But the painter had put it first,
and he had also reversed the Platonic order of the telestic, or
mystical, and the prophetic forms of madness. Nor does the
Phaedrus say anything about the progressive ascension through
the four forms of *manía* of that part of the human soul that
is above intellect.

However, the scholiast Hermias, in commenting upon the
passage in the *Phaedrus*, did put the four kinds of madness in
the order in which we have them in *Zanoni*, and he did include the statement about the soul. His long discussion had
been translated into English by Thomas Taylor (1758–1835),
the celebrated Platonist, in the additional notes to his translation of the Neoplatonist Proclus's commentary on Plato's
Timaeus, and Taylor reprinted it among the additional notes
to his translation of the Neoplatonist Iamblichus's work *On
the Mysteries* (1820). Bulwer knew and used both Proclus and
Iamblichus, as we shall see, and it seems to me in the highest
degree probable that he used Taylor's convenient and recent
translation. The following, then, was in all probability the
very passage in English which Bulwer had found and which the
painter had read aloud to the narrator:

> ... Plato here delivers [i.e., discusses] four kinds of manía,
> by which I mean enthusiasm, and possession or inspiration
> from the Gods, *viz.* the musical, the telestic, the prophetic,
> and the amatory [Note that the order is now the same as

that in *Zanoni*].... Of the rational soul there are two parts, one of which is *dianoia*, the other *opinion*. Again, however, of *dianoia*, one part is said to be the lowest, and is properly *dianoia*, but another part of it is the highest, which said to be the intellect of it.... There is also another thing above this, which is the summit of the whole soul and most allied to *the one*.... Enthusiasm... properly so called, is when this *one* of the soul, which above intellect, is excited to the Gods, and is from thence inspired.... [here is almost the exact wording in *Zanoni*.]

Although there are other *manías*, or enthusiasms, Plato mentions our four because, the "soul being about to ascend is in the first place possessed with the musical mania, afterwards with the telestic, then with the prophetic, and, in the last place, with the amatory mania." Each of these requires the others.

The musical mania... leads to symphony and harmony the agitated and disturbed nature of the parts of the soul.... The telestic mania causes the soul to be perfect and entire ... so that the intellectual part of it may energize... according to the whole of itself and... live intellectually. But the Applliniacal [i.e., prophetic] mania converts and co-excites all the multiplied powers, and the whole of the soul, to the *one* of it.... And the remaining *mania*, the amatory, receiving the soul united, conjoins this *one* of the soul to the Gods, and to intelligible beauty.... This is the order and these are the energies and powers within the soul itself, of these four manias....

This, then, gives us one essential clue to *Zanoni*. A second may be found in the aesthetic rejection of the "real" or "Dutch" school of representation in favor of the "ideal" or "Greek" school. And of course the painter's erudite account of the Rosicrucians and of the even more transcendent schools of secret learned brotherhoods serves to put us on warning that we shall be exploring the occult. This is a region as unfamiliar to most of us as it was to most of Bulwer's readers. Its sages and movements gave him a fine opportunity for the sonorous name-dropping useful in creating a properly mysterious and portentous atmosphere. Wherever that is all he seems to be doing we shall need only a brief identification in a footnote.[7]

But one cannot understand *Zanoni* without a familiar acquaintance with the history and achievements of certain notable personages and groups associated with occult history and practice, and when we encounter these we shall need a fuller clarification. The Rosicrucians, for example, we shall continue to meet throughout *Zanoni*: indeed *Zanoni* is often—though inaccurately—called a "Rosicrucian novel." Who were the Rosicrucians anyway? The question is hard to answer because much of the literature about them has been written by persons claiming to be members of the order, and has been intended at least as much to mystify and confuse the reader as to inform and enlighten him.

The Rosicrucians made positively their first historic appearance in 1614 and 1615 in Germany, with the publication of three small related anonymous treatises. One called for the general reformation of society, and satirized the social and moral evils of the day, largely plagiarizing from a recent Venetian satirical poem by Boccalini. A second, far more important, called "A Report on the Fraternity" (*Fama Fraternitatis*), launched the Rosicrucian myth itself. The *Fama* told the world for the first time of Christian Rosenkreutz, a noble German youth, born in 1378, who made the pilgrimage to Palestine, studied the wisdom of the "sages of Damcar" at Damascus, continued at Fez to acquire knowledge of man's relationship to the universe, and then—having met a hostile reception in Spain—returned to Germany. Here he founded the brotherhood called after his name—largely out of dismay because German savants kept themselves in isolation, and did not communicate to each other their elixirs and other discoveries. The brothers took a vow of chastity, wrought miraculous cures, traveled throughout the world adopting everywhere the dress and customs of the locality, attended an annual reunion, and each selected a disciple to succeed him at his death. Rosenkreutz, the *Fama* said, had lived to the age of one hundred and six, dying in 1484. For one hundred and twenty years thereafter his wonderful tomb had been kept secret. It was discovered in 1604 by the brethren. The *Fama* described the tomb fully, but declined to reveal some of the mystic inscriptions on its walls. Many books were found there, including the works of Paracelsus—not a member of the Brotherhood, but a hero of the struggle to establish the republic of the true sages—and a copy of Rosenkreutz's own life. An altar with a copper plate bore the inscription: "During my lifetime I have singled out for myself as a tomb this summary of the universe," and beneath a copper slab lay the intact corpse of the sage, holding in its hand a small parchment book written in letters of gold. On the slab itself was engraved a long inscription, couched in mystical language, telling how Rosenkreutz had "by divine revelation, by the most lofty instruction, and by tireless zeal, found access to all the mysteries and hidden [occult] things of heaven and of human nature." The *Fama* summoned the sages and rulers of Europe to join the order, not for the "damnable business" of making gold (note the effort to show that this is not just another alchemical society) but in order to see the heavens open and the angels mounting and descending.

The third treatise was full of dark apocalyptic prophecies about the imminent end of the world, the beginning of the Kingdom of the Holy Ghost amid unspeakable sufferings, and the Last Judgment, which depends upon the word of the Rosicrucian Brotherhood, predestined by God for man's salvation. The treatises aroused a tremendous furor, and set off an instant blizzard of pamphlet warfare—almost 1,000 different titles in the years between 1615 and 1618. Physicians particularly feared technological unemployment as the result of the Brotherhood's claim to miraculous healing powers. The authorities in Germany and in France—where the news rapidly spread—were aroused against the supposed Brotherhood.

Recent scholarship has conclusively demonstrated that in fact there never was such a person as Rosenkreutz, and that when the treatises were published there was no Brotherhood either. The authorship of the treatises has been convincingly ascribed to a group of friends, all Lutherans, but all given to mystic speculation and all eager for social change, who lived in Tübingen, and whose leading spirit, Johann Valentin Andreae (1586–1654), all his life vainly dreamed of one project after another for the establishment of a truly Christian commonwealth on earth—not easy to popularize at the best of times and altogether swept away in the turmoil of the Thirty Years' War. By 1620, Andreae himself, afraid of religious persecution, was satirizing and denouncing the Rosicrucian manifestos as a fraud, though he continued to put forth their basic ideas in other forms. There was no secret Order, he said: all true Christians were *ipso facto* members of it. It had been a *ludibrium*, a joke or hoax. It was an effective one.

Certain it is that Andreae alone had written between 1602 and 1604 a fourth treatise, the earliest of all, *The Chemical Marriage (Chymische Hochzeit) of Christian Rosenkreutz*, which, however, was not published until 1616. The word "chemical" puts the reader on notice that he is dealing with alchemical allegory: the "marriage" signifies in part the union between Christ and the individual human soul. In the *Chymische Hochzeit* Rosenkreutz himself tells of his invitation to, travel to, and presence at the mystical marriage of a king. With others, the king is then beheaded. But soon afterwards all are resuscitated by the elect. Whatever may have been Andreae's rôle in the writing of the *Fama* and the other two treatises first published in 1614 and 1615, as the author of the *Chymische Hochzeit* of 1604, he was undoubtedly the inventor of Rosenkreutz, and the date 1604 chosen by the team that wrote the *Fama* for the discovery of the tomb was presumably selected because Andreae—by completing the *Chymische Hochzeit* in that year—had, as it were, discovered the burial place of his invented hero. The name Rosenkreutz was probably suggested by the cross and roses on Andreae's own coat of arms, although there was an earlier mystical alchemical significance attributed to a progress "through the cross to the rose." The symbolism is that, for the true believer, for the friend of God, for the initiate in heavenly wisdom, the burdens of the cross—illness and poverty, real or spiritual, and also affliction of the soul—become the delightful and pleasurable flower of the rose. The hero's name itself, then, is a parable.

Contemporaries of the treatises were reluctant to believe Andreae when he said the Order was a hoax, or the voice of Tommaso Campanella in his prison cell, who knew it was the "phantasm," as he called it. Like many lesser men, Descartes searched for its members in order to apply for admission, but could never find them. At the end of the century, Leibniz too reluctantly decided that there never had been any real Rosicrucians. Others defended the Order's authenticity and antiquity. Michael Maier, the court physician of the Emperor Rudolf II, and an alchemist, wrote in 1617 that the Order were the heirs of the Brahmans, the Egyptians, the mages of Persia, the gymnosophists of Ethiopia, the Pythagoreans, and the sages of Arabia, thus giving them the pedigree that Bulwer's painter claimed for them. In 1618 Heinrich Neuhaus, another pamphleteer, explained that the brothers were so hard to find because they had all moved to India and Tibet. It was such a good story that men were reluctant to disbelieve it, or to accept the allegory for what it was: by the myth of the Order's rules, secrecy, initiation, and remote headquarters, the writers had intended only to appeal to men to follow the inner life and perform pious works. The ordeal of admission signified only that men had to lay aside their vices before they could receive true illumination. So, when the mood passed, Andreae kept assuring whoever would listen that all true Christians were automatically brethren, and that—because it was all a *ludibrium*—nobody who claimed to be a brother could in fact be one.

The myth died away temporarily, but was revived in England by Thomas Vaughan (Eugenius Philalethes), writing in the 1650s during the Commonwealth, and by John Heydon a few years later. Neither claimed to be a member of the Order, but both repeated its message, together with a jumble of other oddments from other occult sources. From England the myth moved back to the continent. By the early eighteenth century the newly forming masonic lodges caught hold of the story. Claiming to have discovered new manuscripts, falsifying their sources, and embroidering them with fantastic new details, they gave the legend new currency. It was not long before there were indeed actual groups claiming to be Brothers of the Rose-Cross. In the last quarter of the eighteenth century in France, with the new rage for occultism, the Freemasons and self-styled Rosicrucians achieved a new prominence. Goethe's poem *Die Geheimnisse* (1784–1786), for example, is thoroughly steeped in Rosicrucian symbolism and imagery—the wrath and death embodied in the cross are tempered by the love repre-sented in the roses wound around it, a love that portends the resurrection and, alchemically, reflects the sun of heaven. It will not be long before we meet the eighteenth-century mystics in the pages of *Zanoni*.[8]

Indeed *Zanoni* takes the reader back to the days of the painter's youth, the time just before the French Revolution—the late 1780s—in Naples. The first book is called "The Musician": we are launched on the "Platonist" design for the novel, and concentrating first upon the soul made enthusiastic by music. The great violinist of the Naples orchestra, Pisani, a genius whose violin seems at times to have a life of its own (was he suggested by Paganini?), has composed an opera—*The Siren*—which cannot be performed (Pisani is eccentric and unpopular); but his lovely and talented daughter Viola, the prima donna of the opera, "a daughter less of the Musician than the Music," successfully contrives to have it staged with-out her father's knowledge, and scores a great success as the heroine.

In her audience is a stranger, Zanoni, recently arrived from

India with a vast fortune. People fear that he has the evil eye.
An octogenarian remembers having seen him seventy years before, seemingly no younger than he is at present, and at that
time someone had seen him sixty years earlier still. The suggestion that he has lived at least one hundred and fifty years is
ridiculed: "the same thing had been said of the quack, Cagliostro, mere fables." Zanoni makes a deep impression upon Viola,
but, to her distress, he is leaving Naples.

We now follow him to Rome and to Paris. In Rome, he
confers with an elderly sage, living as a recluse, whom he has
not seen for years. They talk of the future: man is now standing "as at the death-bed of the Old World," and beholds "the
New Orb, blood-red amidst cloud and vapour, uncertain if a
comet or a sun." The oncoming Revolution threatens mankind:
Zanoni feels deep sadness at the prospect, but the elder sage has
no emotions; he shows nothing but an "icy and proud disdain."
In Paris, Zanoni attends a dinner party of intellectuals: Condorcet, Malesherbes, Champfort, J. S. Bailly, and La Harpe are
all there. They talk of the happy days that lie ahead when
there will be no kings and no priests, no wealth and no poverty,
and when life can be prolonged. Only two of those present fail
to chime in, Zanoni and Cazotte, the novelist. They have met
before, when Cazotte had sought initiation into "the mysterious
order of Martines de Pasqualis." Zanoni had been present at
the time—but only in order to see "how vainly they sought to
revive the ancient marvels of the cabala." A footnote informs
us that of Martines de Pasqually

> little is known, even the country to which he belonged. . . .
> the rites, ceremonies, and nature of the cabalistic order he
> established. Saint-Martin was a disciple of the school, and
> that, at least, is in its favour; for, in spite of his mysticism,
> no man more beneficent, generous, pure, and virtuous than
> Saint-Martin adorned the last century. Above all, no man
> more distinguished himself from the herd of sceptical phi-
> losophers by the gallantry and fervour with which he com-

bated materialism and vindicated the necessity of faith amidst a chaos of unbelief. . . . Cazotte remained a Christian.

In conversation with Zanoni, Cazotte says he has now shaken off the hold of cabalistic influences, but Zanoni reminds him of "certain ceremonies and doctrines," which Cazotte is "thrilled to find so familiar to a stranger." And Zanoni tells Cazotte that, so far from being dead in him, cabalistic influence still "beats in your heart; it kindles in your reason; it will speak in your tongue." Soon, indeed, Cazotte begins to prophesy that the prisons will before long be filled in the name of liberty and brotherhood. Amid their incredulity and growing dismay, he predicts for each of the guests a grim fate: suicide for Condorcet, the scaffold for most of the others, including himself, and, for La Harpe, the sceptic, conversion to Christianity. In a footnote, the reader is referred to La Harpe's posthumous works.[9]

The insertion of historical scenes with footnote references into a novel written to be awesome and mysterious damages the illusion for a modern reader, but the reader of the 1840s did not mind. The prophecy of Cazotte does indeed appear in La Harpe's memoirs—the dinner party actually took place in 1788—and the episode became celebrated in France. In Bulwer's day the story of Cazotte's prophecy experienced a revival: the newly active devotees of clairvoyance cited it as an entirely authenticated historical event. "Who of late years," wrote Bulwer's friend, Dr. John Ashburner, for example, in his book on animal magnetism and spiritualism (1867), "has not read of the prophecy of Cazotte?" And he went on to tell the story—from La Harpe—in all its details.

Scholarly controversy has raged over the question of the prophecy. Did La Harpe invent the story altogether? Probably not. Jacques Cazotte, who was indeed a member of Martines de Pasqually's secret order, and who wrote a delightful and whimsical occult novel called *Le Diable amoureux* (1772), spent much of his time in the 1780s bent over a magician's smoking tripod, prophesying all sorts of things. It was not remarkable, then, in a period generally disposed to believe in everything magic, that La Harpe should have written the story of the prophecy as he did or that it should have gained wide currency.[10] Nor does it much matter here whether or not Cazotte actually did accurately predict the deaths of his fellow *convives* (and, incidentally, of Louis XVI). What matters is that, like Ashburner and other amateurs of the occult, Bulwer knew and believed the story, and that *he wanted to make Zanoni responsible for the prophecy*. It is Zanoni who talks to Cazotte of cabalistic matters all through the evening before the prophecy, and, finally, it is Zanoni who says that cabalistic influence will "speak" in Cazotte's "tongue." And, lo and behold, it does. The scene helps Bulwer establish Zanoni as a magus.

And, we should note, a magus of a particular kind. Zanoni has attended the ceremonies initiating Cazotte into "the order of Martines de Pasqualis," *only to see how vain* was their effort to revive the cabalistic mysteries. Zanoni, then, we are to realize, belonged to an occult school far more ancient and better instructed in the secrets of nature than Martines de Pasqually and his followers.

Though we have learned much since Bulwer's day about Martines de Pasqually, his origins are still uncertain. He was born probably of Spanish parents, who may or may not have been Jews, perhaps in Grenoble, perhaps in Alicante. Though he may have formed secret occult societies in other French cities in the 1750s, it was in Bordeaux soon after 1760 that he founded his "Order of the Knights Elect Cohens of the Universe" (*Ordre des Chevaliers Élus Cöens de l'Univers*), which in its lower echelons was much like other masonic lodges, but which became more and more secret and mysterious as one rose through the eleven grades. At the very top, those who had been through all the initiations reached the eleventh degree of *Réau-Croix. Réau* means a powerful priest, identical with the

"Great Adam," with whom the initiates had to be "reintegrated" by occult ceremonies. The term Réau-Croix is of course sufficiently reminiscent—and no doubt deliberately so —of Rose-Croix to suggest identity with or at least a strong connection between Martines de Pasqually's order and the Rosicrucians. And, indeed, Jean-Baptiste Willermoz, one of Martines's closest collaborators and deputies, at one moment declared that he was both Réau-Croix and Rose-Croix.

At the top level the chief purpose of the Order was theurgy: the working of magic spells that would put the members in touch with spirits of the invisible world. This activity Martines himself referred to simply as *la Chose,* and during its ceremonies spirits were heard and flashes of light seen. These phenomena were known as *passes.* It was hoped that prophets, saints, and angels would manifest themselves, and the ultimate expectation, for which the Order labored mightily—and, it appears, sometimes with success—was the evocation of Christ himself. These efforts were not undertaken with any hope of obtaining power of any sort, or immortality, or even longevity, but only from the members' determination to "reintegrate" themselves—that is, to regain the primal innocence that mankind had lost through Adam's sin. The Cohens led an ascetic life, and were believed able to work miraculous cures. In their theurgy they used astrology, timing their efforts at the equinox and at certain periods of the moon to thwart the lesser demons. Once the sacred circles had been traced on the floor and Martines had spoken the proper words, the spirits would appear in broad daylight. They spoke, taught, enjoined prayer. He and his fellow Cohens saw good and bad angels, Christ and the Devil, talked with the dead, and witnessed diabolical spirits emerging from their own bodies to enter those of the animals we fear most on earth. The good spirits revealed the future and taught how to ward off evil. One spirit dictated one hundred and sixty-six notebooks full of instruction, a few of which survive and are as incomprehensible as anyone could wish. Martines also used a kind of numerology—a theory that ascribed various occult attributes to the different cardinal numbers, familiar to students of occultism generally.

Cabalistic and other Jewish and Christian occult influences have been found in Martines' practices, which had probably not yet received a form that he would have accepted as definitive when, in 1772, he left France to claim an inheritance in Haiti. There he died in 1774. The Order as such did not long survive him, but several of his former disciples, each now a master, founded new lodges or joined existing ones in the various cities of France. Before he went to Haiti, Martines dictated his *Treatise on the Reintegration of Beings,* of which hand-written copies were sent to the Réau-Croix. The book, extremely difficult to interpret, circulated in manuscript until it was printed at last in 1899, from a text whose precise relationship to Martines's original work is not possible to establish.

Louis-Claude de Saint-Martin (1743–1803), Réau-Croix, whom the footnote in *Zanoni* praises as "beneficent, generous, pure, and virtuous," and a champion of the Christian faith, was Martines de Pasqually's most important follower. Gentle and unassuming, modest, and diffidently unwilling to train disciples, he wrote many surviving mystical treatises, of which the *Book of Errors and of Truth* and its *Key,* of the 1770s, aroused both admiration and irritation among contemporaries. ("What truth, and what falsehood," Goethe wrote to the mystical Swiss pastor, Lavater. "From the deepest mysteries of true humanity he passes to the futilities of emptiness and foolishness.") Saint-Martin's obscure and personal vocabulary has always puzzled the uninitiated, while it often conveys to the initiate several simultaneous meanings on different levels. He believed that the Catholic religion had degenerated because of abuse by Emperors, Popes, and heretics; and he argued that even if it were still in a state of perfection, it would be wrong for its agents to proscribe other beliefs: all men had received God's word. But Saint-Martin also attacked the *philosophes.*

And, though a thorough mystic, he opposed magic and

astrology, thus breaking with his master, Martines. He abandoned *la Chose*, and took the "inner path" of meditation and
prayer, clung to the Scriptures, hoped to speed the reign of
Christ, and, instead of rejecting traditional dogmas and rites,
sought to revivify them by finding and proclaiming their
hidden (occult) meanings. Almost alone among the *illuminés*,
he stood against the waves of charlatanry that from various
quarters were sweeping over France in the prerevolutionary
and revolutionary periods. He became a popular and fashionable "elegant theosophist," sought after in the salons of the
nobility, French and Russian, for his personal sweetness as well
as his learning (he read Hebrew and German well, although
—and no wonder—he needed some help with Boehme's language when he translated him into French). Devotee of Pascal, enemy of Voltaire, much attracted by Rousseau's senti-
mentalism, he seems still to deserve Bulwer's painter's praise.
And what Bulwer's painter put into the footnote in *Zanoni*
we can attribute to Bulwer himself. In these passages he is
telling us what kind of occultist he preferred, and what kind
of occultist he intended us to see in Zanoni—no vain cabalist,
no magician. For purposes of heightened mystery, Zanoni
cannot of course belong to anything so recent in historic time
as the Order that Martines de Pasqually founded and Saint-
Martin adorned,[11] any more than he can be a mere Rosicrucian.

After these episodes, interpolated clumsily but with deliberate intent, we return to Naples. Both of Viola's parents die:
her father is buried with his marvelous, almost human, violin.
Alone but for her ignorant and loyal servant, Viola returns to
her singing. Her heart is faithful, after two years, to the
memory of Zanoni, but she also has a fondness for one of her
suitors, a young Englishman named Glyndon. We are at the
end of the first stage, the musical. The second, the telestic, in
which the soul is rendered enthusiastic by mysticism, now begins.

Glyndon, a man of means, is a promising painter and a
pleasure-seeker: "Brave, adventurous, vain, restless, inquisi-

tive, he was ever involved in wild projects and pleasant dangers
—the creature of the impulse and the slave of imagination."
His companion is a literal-minded and sceptical fellow country-
man, Mervale. At his first encounter with Zanoni—now back
in Naples—Glyndon experiences what Zanoni himself calls
"a strange and unaccountable sensation of coldness and awe . . .
your blood curdles, and the heart stands still; the limbs shiver;
the hair bristles; . . . you have a horrible fancy that something
unearthly is at hand. . . ." Zanoni explains the feeling as the
"repugnance and horror with which our more human elements
recoil from something . . . invisible but antipathetic to our
nature; and from a knowledge of which we are happily secured
by the imperfection of our senses." It is not necessarily caused
by spirits, but

> there may be forms of matter as invisible and impalpable to
> us as the animalculae in the air we breathe, in the water
> that plays in yonder basin. Such beings may have passions
> and powers like our own. . . . The monster that lives and
> dies in a drop of water—carnivorous, insatiable, subsisting
> on the creatures minuter than himself—is not less deadly
> in his wrath . . . than the tiger of the desert. There may be
> things around us that would be dangerous and hostile to
> men, if Providence had not placed a wall between them
> and us, merely by different modifications of matter.

When Glyndon eagerly asks if those walls cannot be removed,
Zanoni says perhaps, but it would be mad to try.

Zanoni's qualities are only gradually revealed. He looks like
an Arab, with dark eyes and hair, and delicate small hands.
Perhaps his name is Italian, perhaps it comes from the Chaldaean word for the sun. In company, he is "equable, serene,
and cheerful, ever ready to listen to the talk of others, however idle, or to charm all ears with an inexhaustible fund of
anecdote and worldly experience." He heals the sick. He is
beneficent but not didactic: a confirmed gambler in Naples
gives up his vice and makes friends with an old enemy as the

result of Zanoni's object lessons. Naturally he fascinates Glyndon. After all,

> ...it was...the day for the most egregious credulity and the most mystical superstitions—the day in which magnetism [i.e., mesmeric theories] and magic found converts amongst the disciples of Diderot, —when prophecies were current in every mouth—when...necromancy professed to conjure up the shadows of the dead—when the Crozier and the Book were ridiculed, and Mesmer and Cagliostro believed....[Now] stalked from their graves in the feudal ages all the phantoms that had flitted before the eyes of Paracelsus and Agrippa. Dazzled by the dawn of Revolution, Glyndon was yet more attracted by its strange accompaniments....

Moreover, one of Glyndon's ancestors (a "wise progenitor") had been a philosopher and alchemist, whose books of "Platonic mysticism" Glyndon had examined in his library at home. Glyndon resembles his ancestor's portrait. Though he loves Viola, his love is vague and desultory, because he has "not yet known enough of sorrow to love deeply."

Zanoni, however, warns Glyndon to avoid him: "If I were to predict your fortune by the vain calculations of the astrologer, I should tell you in their despicable jargon that my planet sat darkly in your house of life." [12] It is only Glyndon's immaturity that attracts him to mystery. Zanoni, we observe, is as contemptuous of the astrologers as he is of the cabalists. But of course the warning to Glyndon fails. On the shore near Naples, Glyndon finds Zanoni gathering herbs: Zanoni plucks a "small herb with a pale blue flower," which he puts into his bosom. The action leads to a long mystical disquisition on the science of herbs:

> The deeper knowledge is...lost to the modern philosophy ...the minute study of nature in her lowliest works...the powers that may be extracted from the germ and leaf. The most gifted of the priestcrafts...sought in the meanest

herbs what . . . the Babylonian Sages explored in vain amidst the loftiest stars. . . .

Here as later in *Zanoni* we observe the central importance of botany: at times the magic of the herbalist seems to be the only occult science worthy of praise, as astrology and cabalism and alchemy are apparently scorned. We should duly note the high probability that Bulwer was here thinking of Goethe's deep mystical study of plants. In 1786 Goethe had come to believe that botany offered the best clues to a universal understanding of nature, and soon afterward, in his concept of the primal plant (*Urpflanze*), he produced a mystical botanical equivalent for the alchemical process. The more we learn of the herbalism of Zanoni, the more it reminds us of Goethe.

But while Zanoni was praising the herbalists as the greatest of the scientists we have seen him pluck and cherish one single herb, one with a pale blue flower. Here Bulwer has given us another important clue. This is the *blaue Blume* of Novalis's *Heinrich von Ofterdingen,* the symbol par excellence of the German romantic poets, betokening the spirit of poetry and love, and perhaps the principle of life itself, often, for the romantics, to be found in death. C. G. Jung has made the further suggestion that "the well-known 'blue flower' of the Romantics might well be the last nostalgic perfume of the [medieval alchemical] rose," which itself represented to the alchemist the earthly counterpart to the face of the Sun in the heavens. In any case, when Zanoni, the magus, puts the pale blue flower into his bosom, we who can interpret the action must appreciate even more keenly what we have already learned from his dismay at the oncoming fury of the French Revolution: this is no bloodless sage, but a man who, despite his conquest of the secrets of nature, has preserved a passionate human heart through all the endless ages he has survived. He cares for mankind. He is a romantic. He will fall in love. He may die, and so live.[13]

Having foiled a powerful Neapolitan prince's effort to abduct Viola, and having saved Glyndon's life in the process,

Zanoni is greatly drawn to Viola, who in turn feels for him the homage "not . . . of mistress to lover, of slave to master, but rather of a child to its guardian, of a neophyte of the old religion to her priest." Love for Viola will mean that Zanoni must abandon his detachment, and perhaps he may lose his powers. Love for Zanoni will mean that Viola will have to suffer "an ordeal which few can pass, and which hitherto no woman has survived." This is the ordeal necessary for achieving immortality on earth. It will involve an encounter with "the Haunter of the Threshold." Should she fail, she will of course grow old and die; and Zanoni, still immortal, will be left inconsolable. To avoid this dilemma Zanoni therefore tries to persuade Glyndon and Viola to love each other.

But although Viola would obey Zanoni if he insisted that she marry Glyndon, she is hopelessly attracted to Zanoni himself. As for Glyndon, he has never been sure he wanted to marry Viola, only that he wanted her as his mistress. He resents Zanoni's efforts to bring about their marriage, and, partly inspired by the example of his ancestor, insists instead upon undertaking his apprenticeship in the occult. The laws of Zanoni's brotherhood require that he help all descendants of those who have toiled "even vainly" in the mysteries of the Order. When Glyndon asks if Zanoni is one of the Rosicrucians, who "in an earlier age boasted of secrets of which the Philosopher's Stone was but the least; who considered themselves the heirs of all that the Chaldaeans, the Magi, the Gymnosophists, and the Platonists had taught," Zanoni tells him that magic is only what is beyond the power of the vulgar, and that he himself professes only "that magic taught of old by the priest who ministered to the temple." Though Glyndon yearns for the great secret of immortality, his matter-of-fact friend Mervale repeatedly causes him to doubt Zanoni and to hesitate. Then, on the slopes of Vesuvius, at night, during a sudden eruption, Glyndon has a horrifying encounter with a colossal shadow which causes him to faint. Zanoni appears and saves his life. So now Glyndon declares that

A fiercer desire than that of love burns in my veins—the desire not to resemble but to surpass my kind—the desire to penetrate and to share the secret of your own existence —the desire of a preternatural knowledge and unearthly power.

He abjures love and demands the apprenticeship, which Zanoni cannot refuse to Glyndon's ancestor's descendant.[14]

Its beginning is temporarily delayed by the Neapolitan prince's plot to abduct Viola. Although he has diced with Zanoni for Viola and lost, the prince, who represents sensuality and materialism incarnate, intends to violate the oath he swore upon his ancestral sword to abide by the decision of the dice. He plans also to poison Zanoni at a banquet. When he has tired of Viola, the prince proposes to pass her on to a repulsive—even criminal—French painter, Jean Nicot, a rabid revolutionary and a pupil of David, but I believe intended by Bulwer as a portrait of David. For help in this crisis, Zanoni writes a letter of appeal and explanation to the sage he had visited in Rome, Mejnour, the only other surviving member of their brotherhood. Mejnour had trained the Neapolitan prince's ancestor in the mysteries, and so is bound to warn the prince against going through with his wicked plans. Zanoni tells Mejnour that he has "sought commune with Adon-Ai; but his presence that once inspired such heavenly content with knowledge and so serene a confidence in destiny now only troubles and perplexes me." He has had a vision of the scaffold, with Nicot gibbering at him. After all this time, Zanoni is abandoning the Ideal for the Real. His decision to marry Viola has virtually deprived him of the power to protect her.

Mejnour fails to deter the prince—who has already kidnapped Viola—from his fatal course. At the banquet Zanoni drinks the poisoned cup without suffering any harm, and maneuvers the prince into a duel with an insulted French nobleman, who kills the prince with the very ancestral sword on which he had sworn the violated oath. Zanoni then leaves Naples with Viola, aboard his own vessel. More impatient than ever for his initiation after Zanoni's brilliant performance at the banquet ("Far more intense than the passion of the gamester was the frantic yet sublime desire that mastered the breast of Glyndon"), Glyndon finds that Mejnour instead is to be his tutor.[15]

Mejnour had passed through the ordeal and attained immortality only after having lived a long human life, full of bereavements and troubles; then, all passion spent, he could become the calm and spiritual sage that he now is. But Zanoni had attained immortality as a young man, and is now seeking "to carry the beauty and the passions of youth into the dreary grandeur of earthly immortality." They discuss the advisability of adding new recruits to their order, in view of the grim agonies and fears of would-be postulants who have died. Scarcely once in a thousand years is "one born who can pass through the horrible gates that lead to the world without." Zanoni hesitates to embark on further attempts to enlarge their number—he can hardly bear to think of what he must go through in order to educate Viola—but Mejnour envisions

a mighty and numerous race with a force and power sufficient to permit them to acknowledge to mankind their majestic conquests and dominion—to become the true lords of this planet—invaders perchance of others, —masters of the inimical and malignant tribes by which at this moment we are surrounded, a race that may proceed in their deathless destinies from stage to stage of celestial glory, and rank at last amongst the nearest ministrants and agents gathered around the Throne of Thrones.

Were it not for the portentous supernatural machinery which surrounds us in *Zanoni,* one might be tempted to see here a reference to the British Empire and a prophecy of its future glory, complete with interplanetary travel; but the malignant tribes, I believe, signify rather the tribes of evil spirits. Perhaps, however, Bulwer meant it both ways.[16]

Occult phenomena have been thick on the ground during these episodes. The reader visits Zanoni's secret chamber, where Zanoni has no spirits to wait upon him (as Albertus Magnus or Leonardo da Vinci had had), and no alchemical apparatus. Nor has he books, though once he had read them; now "the only page he read was the wide one of nature." His outside door is wired in such a way as to give the unduly curious an electric shock. Here Zanoni meditates in a trancelike state, and communes with his soul in the words of Marcus Aurelius: "when the soul is lit by its own light, it sees the truth of all things and the truth is centred in itself." Here, too, he communes with Adon-Ai, whom we shall meet later. Zanoni and Mejnour, then, are not astrologers, not alchemists, not Mesmers or Cagliostros. They are herbalists, profound initiates in the more ancient natural lore that seems supernatural only to the ignorant: the supernatural is only natural law as yet undiscovered. Yet both sages clearly have magic powers: Zanoni appears on Vesuvius, where he is not expected; Mejnour vanishes in a thin and fragrant mist when the Neapolitan prince tries to arrest him.

The painter Nicot, who stands for everything that Bulwer hated in politics and art, happily predicts the glorious days in France when inequality shall have been abolished, and Zanoni angrily declares that his very words are a crime: "the first law of nature is inequality." One hopes that disparities in men's physical conditions may be improved, but the "universal equality of intelligence, of mind, of genius, of virtue...." would be a "hopeless prospect for humanity." Here Zanoni voices an idea which Bulwer would later elevate to be the main theme of his novel, *The Coming Race*. The revolutionaries and egalitarians are denying God himself. Nicot is a mere painter, not an artist; an artist abhors the real, seeks the true, goes to nature as his master, and creates rather than merely discovering. And here we hear the echo of the theories of art and creativity voiced by the old painter who had written the manuscript of *Zanoni*.

One chapter, introducing a high-flown "Self-Confessional" in which Viola has written down the details of her spiritual devotion to Zanoni, begins with the following invocation, which (a footnote testily reminds us) is from the pen of the painter, not of his editor:

Venerable Brotherhood, so sacred and so little known, from whose secret and precious archives the materials for this history have been drawn; ye who have retained, from century to century, all that time has spared of the august and venerable science, —thanks to you, if now for the first time, some record of the thoughts and actions of no false and self-styled luminary of your Order are given, however imperfectly, to the world. Many have called themselves of your band; many spurious pretenders have been so-called by the learned ignorance which still, baffled and perplexed, is driven to confess that it knows nothing of your origin, your ceremonies or doctrines, nor even if you still have local habitation on earth. Thanks to you, if I, the only one of my country, in this age, admitted with a profane footstep into your mysterious Academe, have been by you empowered and instructed to adapt to the comprehension of the uninitiated some few of the starry truths which shone on the great Shemaia of the Chaldaean Lore, and gleamed dimly through the darkened knowledge of later disciples, labouring, like Psellus and Iamblichus, to revive the embers of the fire which burned in the *Hamarim* [hearths?] of the East. Though not to us of an aged and hoary world, is vouchsafed the NAME which, so say the earliest oracles of the earth, "rushes into the infinite world, *akoimeto strophalingi*," yet it is ours to trace the reviving truths through each new discovery of the philosopher and chemist. The laws of Attraction, of Electricity, and of the yet more mysterious agency of that Great Principle of Life, which if drawn from the Universe would leave the Universe a Grave, were but the code in which the Theurgy of old sought the guides that led it to a legislation and a science of its own. To rebuild on words the fragments of this history, it seems to me as if, in a solemn trance, I was led through the ruins of a city whose only remains were tombs. From the sarcophagus and the urn I awake the Genius of the extinguished torch, and so closely does its shape resemble Eros that at moments I scarcely know which of you dictate to me—O Love! O Death!

This resounding passage emphasizes for the reader something that he had learned in the preface: the painter who wrote *Zanoni* was an initiate of the Rosicrucians. More than that, he was the only Englishman of his age to be so. And through his brotherhood's commands he can now adapt for the ordinary reader a few of the more ancient truths. These, however, are not Rosicrucian truths, but Chaldaean truths, the "starry truths which shone on the great Shemaia of the Chaldaean Lore"—Shemaia being a cabalistic term that means ordination of the qualified by the laying on of hands, or the proper initiation of a suitable neophyte. In context this is an allusion to the forthcoming initiation of Glyndon. "Starry truths" refers to the traditional Chaldaean (or Babylonian, as we would probably say) comand over the sciences of the stars.

The "earliest oracles of the earth"—which a footnote in the first edition (later omitted) identifies for us as "Excerpta Orac. Chald. ap. Procl."—are in fact the so-called "Chaldaean Oracles," a lost work believed to have been written or collected by a certain Julianos, who lived under Marcus Aurelius (ruled 161–180), the son—so the Byzantines thought—of a Chaldaean philosopher, and a magician who got the Oracles from the gods themselves. It is quite likely that they were in fact originally uttered by a medium in a trance, and were later put into verse by Julianos. In the view of a leading modern authority, their surviving fragments are "bizarre and bombastic . . . obscure and incoherent." They included "prescriptions for a fire and sun cult, and . . . for the magical evocation of gods." Proclus, whom Bulwer cites as his source for the Oracles, was the fifth-century Neoplatonist philosopher (died 485) who did indeed write an extensive commentary on them. That too is lost, although passages survive in the minor writings of the eleventh-century Byzantine man of letters, Michael Psellus (1018–1078), who once called Proclus the "most marvellous" philosopher. Bulwer here names Psellus as one of the "later disciples" who laboured in their "darkened knowledge." The two words Bulwer leaves in Greek—"*akoimeto strophalingi*" (omitted in later editions)—may be translated as "with a restless (or sleepless) whirling." Julianos was the first to call himself a "theurgist," one who acted upon gods or even created them, as contrasted with a "theologist," one who merely talked about them. Theurgy will soon become the subject in *Zanoni*, and Bulwer, in quoting the Chaldaean Oracles, is citing the words of the earliest available theurgical text.

Together with Psellus, Bulwer mentions Iamblichus, the Neoplatonist who died about 330, as the other sage who had some darkened knowledge of the earlier lore. Iamblichus was an Asian and an occultist, and, like the ancients generally, he gave pride of place to learning that he could call "Chaldaean." He too wrote a lost commentary on the Chaldaean Oracles, as well as an extant treatise on the Mysteries in which he rejected the intellect as the instrument that could bring a theurgist into touch with the gods: if that were all, he said, any mere thinking philosopher could establish such contact. What did effect it was the power of the ritual, what Iamblichus called "the efficacy of the unspeakable *acts* performed in the appropriate manner, acts which are beyond all comprehension, and by the potency of the symbols which are comprehended only by the gods." The Emperor Julian the Apostate (361–363), who attempted to revive official paganism, once declared that Iamblichus and "my namesake," the Julianos who set down the Chaldaean Oracles, were his two favorite authors.

Both Iamblichus and Psellus were greatly interested in demons: Iamblichus taught that the myriad spirits exercised great influence on human life, while, seven hundred years later, the devout Christian Psellus classified demons according to their various types, and believed that by magic rites men could communicate with them and so obtain an occasional vision of God. Bulwer is by no means name-dropping in this passage. For anybody about to undertake a description of theurgy with demonic manifestations, as Bulwer was now about to do in *Zanoni*, he was invoking both the earliest and the best later authorities on the subject.

Despite Bulwer's reference to Proclus, the question still remains: where could Bulwer have found the Chaldaean Oracle he quotes? The answer leads us once again to Thomas Taylor, the Platonist, in whose notes to his version of Iamblichus we found the very passage from Hermias's commentary on Plato's *Phaedrus* that Bulwer—without acknowledgment of course—had taken as the painter's inspiration for *Zanoni*. For Taylor, not in a book but in a series of articles in the *Classical Journal*, in 1817 and 1818 had collected and published with great effort, he says, all the Chaldaean Oracles he could find. And Bulwer's was among them. Taylor gave the Greek, from Proclus's commentary on Plato's *Cratylus*, including of course the words *akoimeto strophalingi*, and rendered the couplet: "There is a venerable name with a sleepless revolution, leaping into the worlds, through the rapid reproofs of the Father." As often happened, Taylor had translated awkwardly and even wrongly. Bulwer improved upon his rendering. But I think that here again, and no doubt elsewhere in *Zanoni* also, Bulwer's immediate source lay in Taylor's voluminous translations.

In the present decadent age, the passage in *Zanoni* said, we Rosicrucians can no longer say the divine "Name," as the Chaldaean sages could, but we can observe the scientists—the philosopher and the chemist—gradually making the discoveries that revive the truths the Chaldaeans knew. The laws of Attraction (i.e., magnetism, and, surely, animal magnetism), of Electricity (and, surely, clairvoyance), and of "the yet more mysterious agency of that Great Principle of Life, which if drawn from the Universe would leave the Universe a Grave," which modern science is gradually discovering, were the basis of the "Theurgy of old." The Great Principle which all the alchemists sought, and which they called the *"prima materia"* and Paracelsus named "iliastrum" or "the great mystery" (*mysterium magnum*), here makes its first appearance in Bulwer's work since Kosem Kosamim's fire. In this context it is surely heat which, we shall shortly learn, the Chaldaean survivors, Mejnour and Zanoni, still control. Ancient science did generally hold that animal heat was the key principle of existence, although occasionally an effort was made to modify the theory. But the vital heat—down into the seventeenth century—"formed part of the doctrine of the strongest and longest-lived biological and medical tradition that man has known." So, for Bulwer, modern science has begun to reflect ancient lore with regard to the great principle of life. We shall later find him noting how scientists of the nineteenth century seem to be echoing Van Helmont. His painter concludes with a solemn invocation of both love and death, for his purposes indistinguishable. Indeed, it will be one of *Zanoni*'s lessons that love leads to death, which is the true eternal life, a message that the illuminati of the late eighteenth century embraced so passionately as to become quite morbid.[17]

We are beginning to see how little *Zanoni* is a Rosicrucian novel. Its purported author, the old painter, and its real author, Bulwer himself, were both Rosicrucians. But this is a novel not of their partial wisdom, but of the truer, the ancient, the largely lost wisdom of the Chaldaeans, of which Mejnour and Zanoni are the only surviving adepts. *Zanoni*, then, is more properly a novel of the wisdom that the Rosicrucians did *not* have.

As epigraph to the fourth book, "The Dweller of the Threshold," which will deal with Glyndon's initiation, we find a German couplet from Schiller's "Veiled Image at Saïs." In his translation of Schiller's poems, Bulwer himself rendered these lines, " 'Behind, be what there may,/ I dare the hazard —I will lift the veil—'/ Loud rang his shouting voice—'and I will see!' " Both the choice of poem and the choice of lines is significant. Schiller's verses tell the story of the youthful seeker after truth who comes to Saïs to learn the secret lore of Egypt's priests, and, impatient with the slow progress of their instruction, determines to raise the veil before the great statue of the goddess Isis (not named in the poem). He *will* behold the truth in spite of the goddess's prohibition: no man may lift the veil; in time she will lift it herself. Thus he violates the command, and is found at dawn by the priests, dead before the statue: "Woe—" as Bulwer rendered Schiller's last line—"to him who treads through Guilt to Truth."

The choice of this epigraph signals to us in advance what will be the course of Glyndon's training: he is so eager to learn that he will not wait. He will ignore Mejnour's injunction, laid down before the training begins, that

> The elementary stage of knowledge is to make self and self alone thy study and thy world. . . . thou hast rejected wealth, fame, and the vulgar pomps of power. . . . To perfect thy faculties and concentrate thy emotions is henceforth thy only aim.

Glyndon will manifest the same impatience as the youth at Saïs: will the results be as fatal?

The veiled image of Isis as the repository of all wisdom was a general property of the romantics: in addition to Schiller's poem, there was also Novalis's fairy tale of Hyacinth and Rosebud, in his *Lehrlinge zu Saïs*, where the goddess Isis, discovered after long and arduous pilgrimage by the postulant, Hyacinth, proves, when he lifts her veil, to be Rosebud, the sweet girl he had left behind. In *The Last Days of Pompeii*, Bulwer had already made much use both literal and figurative of Isis and her veil. Nor would it be any accident that Madame Blavatsky, a dedicated Bulwer addict and much given to plagiarism, would in time call her summons to the Theosophists *Isis Unveiled* (1877).[18]

For Glyndon's training, Mejnour has selected a remote castle in the Italian mountains, its surrounding territory infested by brigands, and its chief servitor an ex-bandit. Lectures on the history of the many races that have in times past overrun the region and on the science of the herbalist

("... tears and laughter, vigour and disease, madness and reason, wakefulness and sleep, existence and dissolution [are]
coiled up in those unregarded leaves") serve to initiate Glyndon into a life of contemplation. Mejnour explains that, while
Zanoni still admires beauty and does good deeds, he himself,
altogether contemplative, does not "meddle with the active
life of mankind." To Glyndon's question whether he and
Zanoni are brothers of the Rosy Cross, Mejnour returns the
answer that we have by now been taught to anticipate:

> Do you imagine ... that there were not mystic and solemn
> unions of men seeking the same ends, through the same
> means, before the Arabians of Damus, in 1378, taught to a
> wandering German the secrets which founded the Insti-
> tution of the Rosicrucians? [We recognize Christian Rosen-
> kreutz, but the date is the date of his canonical birth, in
> the *Fama*, not of his training. And the Arabians should be
> those of Damcar. Had Bulwer ever read the *Fama* itself? It
> seems doubtful.] I allow, however, that the Rosicrucians
> formed a sect descended from the greater and earlier school.
> They were wiser than the Alchemists—their masters were
> wiser than they.

Mejnour and Zanoni are the only two remaining brothers
"of the early and primary order." They have

> no arts by which we can put death out of our option or out
> of the will of heaven. These walls may crush me as I stand.
> All that we profess to do is ... to find out the secrets of
> the human frame, to know why the parts ossify and the
> blood stagnates, and to apply continued preventives to the
> effects of time. This is not Magic; it is the art of Medicine
> rightly understood.... The mere art (extracted from the
> juices and simples) which recruits the animal vigour and
> arrests the progress of decay, or that more noble secret
> which I will only hint to thee at present, by which HEAT
> or CALORIC ... being ... the primordial principle of life,
> can be made its principal renovator ... would not suffice
> for safety.

They are, then, not immortal, but through their elixir of life and their power to control and use heat as an agent of renewal they have become immune to disease. And moreover, they know how to "disarm and elude the wrath of men ... turn the swords of our foes against each other ... glide ... invisible to eyes over which we can throw a mist or darkness." They cannot share their secrets, because a tyrant or sensualist who had the secrets would be a demon let loose on earth. So the ordeals that purify the passions must precede knowledge of the secrets. Nature has put "awful guardians and insurmountable barriers between the ambition of vice and the heaven of the loftier science."

Gradually, Glyndon experiences a "strange and ineffable consciousness of power" and feels ready for initiation, but when he rashly enters Mejnour's second chamber, a fragrant chill mist, coiling with moving bodiless apparitions, almost destroys him. Mejnour drags him out just in time. It is too early. But he may begin with trance: "In dreams commences all human knowledge; in dreams hovers over measureless space the first faint bridge between spirit and spirit—this world and the worlds beyond." Focusing his gaze at Mejnour's command upon a star, Glyndon feels a vapor enveloping him.

> A sort of languor next seized his frame.... a tremor shook his limbs ... the star seemed to expand and dilate ... spreading wider and broader it diffused all space—all space seemed swallowed up in it. And at last ... he felt as if something burst within his brain—as if a strong chain were broken; and at that moment a sense of heavenly liberty, of unutterable delight, of freedom from the body, of birdlike lightness, seemed to float him into space itself.

In this truly psychedelic state, Glyndon sees a vision of Viola and Zanoni, and can overhear their conversation: obsessed with her love for Zanoni, Viola has no interest at all in learning how to be immortal or in avoiding old age.

Mejnour now has Glyndon read the works of the "glorious dupes: ... Hermes ... and Albert, and Paracelsus," all of whom

were deceived, all of whom Mejnour had personally known,
all now dead and rotten.[19] This is the book-learning phase of
the initiation, largely a mere exercise. The true learning is not
in books. Though man can see through a microscope the
"creatures on the leaf, no mechanical tube is yet invented to
discover the nobler and more gifted things that hover in the
illimitable air," between whom and man is a "mysterious and
terrible affinity." Some of the beings in space are benign,
some malign. Only immense enthusiasm purified from "all
... desires" will enable Glyndon to penetrate the barrier.
Once he has done so, Mejnour will not be able to protect
him. The

> very elixir that pours a more glorious life into the frame, so
> sharpens the senses that those larvae of the air become ...
> audible and apparent; so that, unless trained by degrees to
> endure the phantoms and subdue their malice, a life thus
> gifted would be the most awful doom man could bring upon
> himself.

That is why, although the elixir is "compounded of the simplest herbs," it is a poison to the unprepared. And among
the "dwellers of the threshold is one ... surpassing in malignity and hatred all her tribe ... whose eyes have paralysed
the bravest, and whose power increases over the spirit precisely in proportion to its fear." It was indeed a postulate
generally accepted by the alchemists that the elixir of life was
at the same time a deadly poison. This idea is intended to be
taken symbolically as well as literally: to achieve rebirth in
a new life one must kill the old life, repress all the old desires
—in effect drink the poison. Mejnour's teaching here is in
the best alchemical tradition, echoed repeatedly in Goethe's
Märchen and *Wilhelm Meister*, and in the poem called *Weissagungen des Bakis*.

Mejnour also trains Glyndon in the ordinary chemistry of
magic that has produced the famous illusions of the past, so
that he may appreciate them at their low value. He teaches
him the chemistry of heat, and the Pythagorean theories of

numbers, with the art of prediction (here there is a lacuna in the ms!). But he pointedly does not teach him the final crucial step in the art; and then he leaves him for a month, with a Bluebeard prohibition: not to enter the room where he had fainted before—to which, however, he is to have the key— and above all not to light naphtha in certain vessels or to open vases on certain shelves. Of course Glyndon finishes his assigned tasks in less than two weeks, and tries to keep his mind off the forbidden room by taking long walks.

One day he stumbles on a local peasant festival with loud music, and a pretty girl asks him to dance with her. Before he knows it, he is caught up in the dance, beguiled by the music and the maiden:

> Oh pupil of Mejnour! Oh would-be Rosicrucian—Platonist
> —Magian—I know not what! I am ashamed of thee! What,
> in the name of Averroes, and Burri, and Agrippa, and
> Hermes, has become of thy austere contemplation? Was it
> for this that thou didst renounce Viola? I don't think thou
> hast the slightest recollection of the elixir or the cabala.
> Take care. What are you about, Sir? Why do you clasp
> that small hand. . . . Why do you— . . . Keep your eyes off
> those slender ancles and that crimson boddice!

But this is what he cannot do. He is, after all, young. He sees the girl (Fillide) again. And of course he violates the prohibition, goes to the forbidden room, lights the forbidden lamps, inhales the vapor from the forbidden vials. The mist surrounds him, the shapes in it float through the window, and

> as his eyes followed them, the casement became darkened
> with some object undistinguishable at the first gaze, but
> which sufficed mysteriously to change into ineffable horror
> the delight he had before experienced . . . a human head
> covered with a dark veil, through which glared with livid
> and demoniac fire eyes that froze the marrow of his bones.

The coiling shapes in the mist, from which he has once before been saved, but one of which will now manifest itself, exactly resemble the hallucinations that were reported almost as a commonplace in alchemists' accounts of tense moments in their experiments: "You can see," said a treatise falsely ascribed to the fourteenth-century Ramon Lull, "certain fugitive spirits condensed in the air in the shape of divers monsters, beasts, and men, which move like the clouds hither and thither." The phantom speaks to Glyndon:

> Thou has entered the immeasurable region. I am the Dweller of the Threshold.... Dost thou fear me? Am I not thy beloved? Is it not for me that thou has rendered up the delights of thy race? Wouldst thou be wise? Mine is the wisdom of the countless ages. Kiss me, my mortal love.

As the Horror crawls toward him, Glyndon faints, and awakes in his bed the next day.

Beside him is a letter from Mejnour contemptuously dismissing him as a pupil. His "desire for knowledge" has been only "petulant presumption," his "thirst for happiness" only "the diseased longing for the unclean and muddied waters of corporeal pleasure." His inhalation of the elixir has attracted to him a "ghastly and remorseless foe," which he himself must exorcise. He must master the Dweller of the Threshold by conquering his own fear: those "livid eyes" haunt, but cannot harm, and are most to be dreaded when they are not to be seen. Mejnour and all the magic equipment have vanished. Glyndon soon stops blaming himself. His mere breath of the elixir has prompted him to return to his painting: on the wall, he sketches with charcoal a picture of the Egyptian Judgment of the Dead by the Living, but, though it is a fine piece of work, the horror reappears to him and says such ghastly (and unmentionable) things that he flees the castle.[20]

We have now completed, I take it, the second portion of the painter's design, the portrayal of the soul rendered enthusiastic by "telestic" or mystical inspiration. And for the first time we can comment intelligently on the term "telestic." It is the technical term used by Proclus for the theurgical practices that led the initiate into magical communication with the beings of the other world. Though Proclus used it in the narrow sense of making and animating magic images, Bulwer has used it more broadly to apply to Glyndon's whole experience—the eagerness, the novitiate, the demon, and the failure. After an interval, the grand design will be resumed.

Glyndon returns to London, where he first appears at the house of his worldly and matter-of-fact friend Mervale, married now to a wife as conventional as he, who is horrified at the sudden and unexpected arrival, which threatens to upset the placid, well-regulated order of her household. In an episode that provides the only real comic relief in *Zanoni*, Glyndon keeps Mervale up late and gets him drunk, sending him staggering to bed:

> At last, Mr. Mervale appeared in the conjugal chamber—not penitent, not apologetic—no, not a bit of it. His eye twinkled, his cheek flushed, his feet reeled; he sang—Mr. Thomas Mervale positively sang!
> "Mr. Mervale! is it possible, sir!.———"
> "Old King Cole was a merry old soul———"
> "Mr. Mervale! sir!—leave me alone, sir!"
> "And a merry old soul was he———"
> "What an example to the servants!"
> "And he called for his pipe, and he called for his bowl!———"
> "If you don't behave youself, sir, I shall call———"
> "Call for his fiddlers three."

Glyndon takes a house of his own, speculates in the money market and makes a fortune, steeps himself in dissipation, but his grim visitations continue. His younger sister, Adela, in delicate health, comes to live with him and tries to cheer him up. He tells her his whole story: when he had left Mejnour's castle, he had traveled with Fillide to try to find Mejnour to exorcise the evil spirit. One night at Genoa, during the carnival, when he and his companions were riotously drinking and talking about the new age of liberty and license that the

French Revolution would spread over the globe, Mejnour had appeared and sardonically predicted that Glyndon, who "pants for the millennium shall behold it! Thou shalt be one of the agents of that era of Light and Reason." Here, then, was the beginning of the next stage of the soul's enthusiasms: from the telestic or mystical inspiration, the theme has moved to prophecy. In the final days of the Revolution, "amidst the wrecks of the Order thou cursest as Oppression," Glyndon will seek the fulfillment of his destiny and find his cure. Thinking to escape the specter by returning to the "orderly and vigorous pursuits" of England, Glyndon has left Fillide in France, but when he tries to paint he cannot. He falls ill, and his distress so depresses Adela that she too has horrible visions, and soon dies of them, though Glyndon recovers. This interpolated horror story completed, Glyndon returns to France.

It is now the height of the Revolution. Glyndon understands "nothing but the song, the enthusiasm, the arms, and the colours that lifted to the sun the glorious lie—'le peuple Français debout contre les tyrans.'" With the help of Nicot and other revolutionaries, Glyndon takes a place in the Convention. He thinks that by so doing he is following Mejnour's advice, and working for humanity to exorcise his specter: but it remains with him; he has misunderstood. His enthusiasm is for the prophecy of freedom, not now to be fulfilled.

During the two years of Glyndon's apprenticeship, failure, and travels, Zanoni and Viola have been living out their idyll on one of the Ionian islands. By involving himself in an earthly passion, Zanoni has weakened his powers so much that he has trouble summoning his familiar and friend Adon-Ai, a splendid young male spirit. Though the name of course means Lord in Hebrew, one wonders whether Bulwer may not also have been thinking of Adonis. Zanoni wants to know how he can arouse in Viola a desire for immortality, and Adon-Ai and he agree that first she must have a child: then she would soon want to obtain immortality for herself and for it. Driven from the island to Venice by plague before the child has been born, Viola seems to be dying, and Zanoni cannot save her or any longer invoke Adon-Ai. Instead he has to accept a cure offered by the dark formless specter. Viola is saved; their child is born safely. Never once is its sex mentioned: it is a beautiful child, but the specter's presence is constant. Zanoni appeals to Mejnour, who summons him to Rome to see if his arts can protect Zanoni and his wife and child against the threatening dangers.

While Zanoni is in Rome consulting Mejnour, Glyndon comes to Venice from revolutionary France. Bitterly he warns Viola against Zanoni as against a sorcerer. Of course she has observed Zanoni's uncanny activities, and now confides her troubles to a priest, "a worthy and pious man, but with little education and less sense," who "would have made no bones of sending Watt to the stake if he had heard him speak of the steam-engine." He urges her to leave Venice to save her child from its father, and in her indecision she goes to Zanoni's private room, where she opens a crystal vase, and smells the elixir:

> ...suddenly her life seemed...to spring, to soar, to float, to dilate, upon the wings of a bird. The room vanished from her eyes. Away—away, over lands, and seas, and space, on the rushing desire, flees the disprisoned mind.

She has a vision in which she sees Zanoni and Mejnour, and can observe them observing her. "This double phantom— herself a phantom—gazing upon a phantom-self, had in it a horror which no words can tell, no length of life forego." She sees herself kneel by her child's cradle, sees the monster, and has a phantasmagoric vision of rushing crowds. When she sees Zanoni looking at her and springing toward her, she wakes, and makes up her mind to take Glyndon's advice and escape with him to France.[21]

The description of the distorting vision that the elixir produces for Viola suggests—as did the equally careful account

of the happier vision that Glyndon had beheld in his first
trance—that Bulwer had some acquaintance with "mind-
expanding" drugs. Certainly Viola has had a convincing "bad
trip." She writes to Zanoni, explaining that she still loves him,
but must go: "It is the faithful mother, not the faithless wife"
who is acting. When Zanoni learns what has happened he refuses to take Mejnour's advice to abandon Viola and the
child. He knows from the "prophetic shadows" that at some
fatal sacrifice to himself he can save both his wife and his
child, and he is determined to do so.

With the opening of the seventh book of *Zanoni*, "The
Reign of Terror," we enter, I believe, the final phase of the
painter's plan: the theme advances from that of the soul made
enthusiastic by prophecy to that of the soul made enthusiastic by love. We are in Paris in July 1794; the Terror is at
its height, and Robespierre, Payan, and Couthon, all of whom
we meet, are drawing up the lists for execution. Even Nicot,
the painter, is now in danger. Glyndon is appalled by the
excesses of the Terror. He is taking care of Viola and her
child, but Fillide is deeply jealous. Nicot wants Glyndon to
assassinate Robespierre, but Glyndon rejects the proposal: he
has already bribed an official to get passports, and will take
Viola and the child and Fillide and Nicot to England with
him; but Nicot is to assuage Fillide's jealousy by pretending
that Viola is not Glyndon's charge but Nicot's own. The
treacherous Nicot tells Fillide instead that Viola is Glyndon's
mistress, and intends to denounce Glyndon to Robespierre.

In Paris, searching vainly for Viola, Zanoni writes to Mejnour that nothing since the opening night of Aeschylus's
Agamemnon (which they had attended together in Athens
more than two thousand years before) had saddened him so
much as the Terror. But he sees everywhere sublime sacrifices,
of a kind that he and Mejnour had made impossible for themselves when they became immortal: "to live forever upon this
earth is to live in nothing diviner than ourselves." Everywhere
is the ghastly Dweller of the Threshold: the revolutionaries,

... these would-be builders of a new world, like the students who have vainly struggled after our supreme science. ... have attempted what is beyond their powers; they have passed from this solid earth of usages and forms into the land of shadow; and its loathsome keeper has seized them as its prey.

In this comment on the Revolution, Bulwer has brought together two of the chief themes of the novel: the idealistic revolutionaries are like the impatient neophytes—determined to create utopia at once, as Glyndon or Schiller's young man at Saïs were determined not to wait but to *know* at once, they have brought death and ruin upon themselves. The grim Dweller of the Threshold has won the victory in both cases. For the interpretation of *Zanoni* this is a crucially important passage.

Working at menial occupations to support herself and her child, Viola reluctantly agrees that they should leave the country with Glyndon; but the vengeful Fillide, sure that Viola is Glyndon's mistress, arranges with Nicot to have Viola and the child denounced. Nicot, villainous, uglier than ever, an atheist, unable even to paint any longer, persuades Robespierre to order the arrest of Glyndon, Viola, and the child. Nicot himself is also arrested. And as the agents hotly pursue Glyndon through Paris, he is met by Zanoni, who hurries him into safe shelter at his house. Meeting for the first time since Zanoni had left Naples with Viola and Glyndon had begun his apprenticeship, they have a final revealing and deeply important conversation.

Bitterly wondering why he had ever wanted the "wild unholy knowledge" of the sages, Glyndon reproaches Zanoni, who reminds him that it was by his own free will, and against Zanoni's advice, that he had embarked on his study with Mejnour. And to Glyndon's sharp accusation that Zanoni is a wizard, Zanoni replies by reminding him of the stanzas in Tasso's *Jerusalem Delivered* in which the ancient sage and enchanter who counsels the champions of the Holy Land explains the differences between black magic and his own holy arts. Zanoni does not quote the stanzas, but a footnote gives the numbers (Canto XLIV, Stanzas xli–xlvii) and recommends Wiffen's translation, parts of which follow:

> Think not my magic wonders wrought by aid
> Of Stygian angels summoned up from Hell;
> Scorned and accurst be those who have essayed
> Her gloomy Dives and Afrits to compel
> By fumes of voices, talisman or spell!—
> But by perception of the secret powers
> Of mineral springs, in nature's inmost cell,
> Of herbs, in curtain of her greenwood bowers,
> And of the moving stars, on mountain-tops and towers.

> For in these caves mid glooms and shadows brown,
> Far from the sun, not always I abide;
> But oft on sacred Carmel's flowery crown,
> And oft on odorous Lebanon reside;
> There without veil I see the planets glide;
> Notice each aspect; chronicle each phase
> Of Mars and Venus; every star beside,
> That, swift or slow, of kind or froward rays,
> Revolves and shines in heaven, is naked to my gaze.

The sage explains that he had once thought his "powers could compass or command/ Knowledge of all above, around, below,/ That sprang to birth from God's creative hand," but that a holy Hermit had taught him to perceive "how little and confined" his thoughts had actually been. Then

> I saw how, like night-owls at rise of sun,
> Our minds with Truth's first rays are stupified;
> Smiled at the futile webs my folly spun;
> Scorned my vain-glory, and renounced my pride;
> But still my genius, as he wished, applied
> To the deep arts and philosophic quest
> In which I joyed before, but purified
> And changed from what I was, with nobler zest;
> Ruled by the Seer on whom implicitly I rest. . . .

Tasso's lines echo the insistence we have heard several times from both Zanoni and Mejnour that they are not magicians, but scientists who study the "secret powers of mineral springs, ... of herbs... and of the... stars," and that they regard as duped and deluded all those who pose as magicians. Tasso in his madhouse, Zanoni goes on to tell Glyndon, found a holy theurgy that summoned not a fiend but an Angel, a God Genius. Indeed Tasso was "deeply versed... for his age, in the mysteries of the nobler Platonism which hints at the secrets of all the starry brotherhoods, from the Chaldaean to the later Rosicrucian." Bulwer's great affection and admiration for Tasso, reflected here in Zanoni's words, finds an instant analogue in Goethe's similar feelings for Tasso, which he passed on to his hero, Wilhelm Meister.

Theurgy of this good sort is sacred, says Zanoni, quoting Iamblichus to the effect that the soul may become elevated by attraction to natures higher than itself. This is "religious magnetism," and this is what Zanoni and Mejnour practice, and what they had hoped to teach Glyndon; but Glyndon's impatience had ruined the effort. Glyndon cannot understand why Mejnour and Zanoni alone survive; and Zanoni explains (again) that the wonder is rather that even two adepts have chosen to survive on earth: the others had preferred to die rather than prolong a life of terrestrial sorrows. And when human desire reasserts itself, as it has done in Zanoni, the powers fade: he cannot even find his wife and child.

Glyndon tells him where they are, and in gratitude Zanoni helps him exorcise the phantom: he puts Glyndon into a happy trance, wherein he sees his own childhood bedroom. Glyndon wakes to find a note from Zanoni, telling him that he will find a boatman on the Seine ready to call for him. He will be protected until the Revolution is over. Thereafter, he will reach England. For many years he will be spared to "muse over the past and to redeem it." And, we are told, "The Englishman obeyed the injunctions... and found their truth." [22]

It is only now that we can realize with certainty that the painter whose manuscript we have been reading—whom the narrator of the introduction had encountered in the occult bookshop, and who had bequeathed him the manuscript— was Glyndon himself grown old. In fact, then, *Zanoni* as a novel is nothing but Glyndon's own memoir of his youthful adventures. Bulwer never tells us this in so many words, and his restraint is highly artistic: he always feared, as we shall see, that his readers would not understand what he was trying to do; and he often yielded to the temptation to overexplain. When we arrive at this point so near the end of *Zanoni*, and find confirmed our suspicion that the old man of the book-shop—who had been and suffered in the French Revolution, and was a good painter, a defender of the Ideal, and an ama-teur deeply versed in the occult—was after all not merely created to give some sort of artificial framework to the mys-tical narrative of *Zanoni*, but that he is Glyndon himself, and *Zanoni* the spiritual autobiography of his youth, we are grate-ful indeed to Bulwer for a consummate piece of craftsman-ship.

In fact, everything now falls into place: once Glyndon had failed to stay the course with Mejnour, he had lost forever the opportunity of initiation into the "older" brotherhood of the Chaldaeans to which Mejnour and Zanoni alone belonged. But he could still gain access to the Rosicrucians, a later and lesser order, with only a partial knowledge of the ancient lore, and this, we realize, he had done. Not only was he a respected authority on Rosicrucianism, able to give the nar-rator a lesson on the subject, when first we met him as the old man in the bookshop; but throughout *Zanoni* itself he has shown a far more intimate acquaintance with the newer order than with the Chaldaeans, whose secrets he had only begun to learn when the impulses of the flesh put an end to his train-ing. Hence, the invocation to the Rosicrucians, which we have quoted above. And hence, I would argue, the misconception still prevalent among critics, even very good critics, who believe that *Zanoni* is a Rosicrucian novel, and that Zanoni and Mejnour were Rosicrucians.[23]

Not at all. We have repeatedly heard them tell Glyndon that they were *not* Rosicrucians but Chaldaeans of "the early and primary order." For the Rosicrucians they always display a mildly patronizing approval, but no more. When the Rosicrucians are praised, it is Glyndon who does it. In this respect—among others—Glyndon resembles his creator. Bulwer was also a Rosicrucian, as we shall see; and Bulwer clearly was also dissatisfied with their access to the true mysteries. For his romance, *Zanoni*, he invented a brotherhood older and more effective, a brotherhood that actually did possess what the Rosicrucians lacked and what Bulwer desperately wanted: occult knowledge and the elixir of life. Incidentally, it was a brotherhood so small that it had only two members: about as exclusive a club as could be imagined.

And of those two members, as the reader will long since have suspected, Zanoni, bereft of most of his supernatural powers, is about to make the supreme sacrifice for love—the climax of the theme that Glyndon (for we may as well call him so at last) had long ago told us was the last and loftiest stage of the soul's ascending enthusiasms, following music, mysticism, and prophecy. Failing to bring about the fall of Robespierre before Viola and the child are due to be executed, he determines to die in their place. In the last moments Adon-Ai tells him that "the human affections that thralled and humbled thee awhile; bring to thee, in the last hours of thy mortality, the sublimest heritage of thy race, the eternity that commences from the grave." A vision shows Zanoni Mejnour, "at work with his numbers and his cabala ... living on ... indifferent whether his knowledge produced weal or woe." Paradoxically, the human passions are redeeming; and when Zanoni substitutes himself for Viola and goes to the scaffold knowing that she will be freed the next day, after Robespierre's fall, he is received into heaven by rank upon rank of rejoicing angels. It is truly the apotheosis described by the *Fama*: the heavens have opened and the angels come and go. Robespierre is seized by the mob, and Viola dies in her prison bed. The smiling child is left alone, but "the fatherless are the care of God." [24]

The reception of *Zanoni* was, of course, not as enthusiastic as Bulwer would have liked. Yet Carlyle, for example, who had always disliked Bulwer and deprecated him as a "poor fribble," now wrote that Mrs. Carlyle had "laid instant hold of it," so that he had not yet had a chance to read it through (July 23, 1842), but that the "few hasty glances and snatches" he had got had convinced him that *Zanoni* would be a "liberating voice for much that lay dumb imprisoned in human souls; that it will shake old deep-set errors looser in their rootings, and thro' such chinks as are possible let in light on dark places very greatly in need of light"—warm praise indeed, and surely welcome, but not conveying much meaning. Anne Thackeray, as different a reader from Carlyle as it is possible to conjure up, later declared that "Zanoni and the catlike spirit of the threshold are as vivid to me as any of the people who used to come to dinner."

For the professional critics, especially those hostile to Bulwer, it was easy and tempting to dismiss *Zanoni* as incomprehensible. He had shown that he expected nothing better by his prefatory epigraph from the *Comte de Gabalis*; "In short, I could make neither head nor tail on't." The *Athenaeum* reviewer seized gleefully upon this: he neither knew nor cared, he said, whether Bulwer was deliberately experimenting, or had studied the occult too long, or was merely trying to puzzle the simple and pique the thinking reader; but whatever the reason, the author had "wandered far beyond common ken and common sympathy" both in subject matter and in manner. Quoting from the preface the dialogue on the "real" and the "true" between the elderly Glyndon and the young devotee of the occult who would later decipher the manuscript, the reviewer maintained that Bulwer, in following the Ideal, had deprived his characters of reality: "There must be coherence, adjustment of parts, climax of interest, even in a mystical and philosophical *extravaganza*, if it be to take rank as a work of art; whereas *Zanoni* is a strange patchwork of things the most discordant...." The earlier portion of the novel is a "reprint of ... 'Zicci,' which ... seemed, to us, but a dull puzzle, imitated, and not skilfully, from Schiller's 'Armenian.' "

What the reviewer calls Schiller's "Armenian" is the mysterious Armenian character in the short story, *The Ghost-Seer*, never completed, and first published in book form in 1788 after earlier partial publication. Nothing that Schiller wrote ever brought him such success at home or abroad. The tale of a Protestant German prince who falls under the influence of a Catholic secret society in Venice reflected the widespread malaise of the 1780s, in which Schiller shared, at the sudden rapid spread of precisely the sort of mystic illuminism that Bulwer was describing in *Zanoni*, but which Zanoni himself detested and combatted. In creating the Armenian, Schiller had been influenced by the recent publication in the *Berlinische Monatsschrift* of the Countess Elisa von der Recke's account of Cagliostro's visit to the Baltic town of Mitau. So if, like the *Athenaeum* reviewer, one is no expert on magicians and is unwilling to accept Bulwer's specific assurances that Zicci-Zanoni is specifically drawn as *not* a Cagliostro, one might to that extent see a superficial resemblance between the Armenian and Bulwer's hero. And it is also true that *Zicci*, like *The Ghost-Seer*, appeared as an incomplete fragment of a tale with occult overtones. But in *Zanoni* Bulwer had succeeded, as Schiller never did, in fitting the fragment into its proper place as part of a balanced and completed novel.

Like all other admirers of Schiller, Bulwer did know and like *The Ghost-Seer*, which as early as 1828 he had called "a successful novel." In his *Life of Schiller*, in 1844, he referred to it as "so well-known in England." Indeed it was. Anne Radcliffe in *The Mysteries of Udolpho* (probably) and in *The Italian* (certainly), M. G. Lewis in *The Monk*, W. R.

Spencer in *Urania, or The Illuminé* (a parody), Scott in *My Aunt Margaret's Mirror*, Coleridge in *Osorio*, and Byron in *Oscar of Alva*, all drew upon it in varying degrees, while Lockhart, De Quincey, and Samuel Rogers also admired it extravagantly. As for Bulwer, *Zicci* and *Zanoni* both include a scene at the gaming tables highly reminiscent of one in Schiller's story. Glyndon's wild eagerness for occult learning is like that of Schiller's prince ("to get into touch with the spirit-world had been his dearest yearning [*Lieblingsschwär-merei*]"). Like Cagliostro and Zanoni, the Armenian is more or less immortal; in *The Ghost-Seer* elemental spirits are mentioned, and the *Comte de Gabalis*; and there are several necromantic experiments; while early in the morning two gondoliers chant verses of Tasso to each other. So if in fact *Zicci-Zanoni* reminded a reviewer of *The Ghost-Seer*, it was no wonder. Yet under scrutiny *The Ghost-Seer*'s possible contributions to Bulwer's novel seem relatively unimportant.

The *Athenaeum* reviewer immediately went on to contrast *Zanoni* with *Zicci*. This time, he said, Bulwer had

> wrought out a mere tale of wonder into one of those super-sublime allegories, in which tinselled truisms figure as new discoveries, and obscurity of meaning passes for elevation of thought. We have a couple of sages—the one contemplative, the other active—who are the last of a brotherhood of mystics; and we have a neophyte whom disappointed love for . . . Viola piques into aspirings after superhuman knowledge [note how thoroughly Glyndon's curiosity is misrepresented]; these, with sundry minor personages, perform multitudinous evolutions, as in a dream-dance, till the measure leads them into the midst of the French Revolution, where "the charm is wound up." We fear the reader may find this description of "Zanoni" as confused as we have found the tale. Let him read it . . . and we will wager that his perceptions will hardly be clearer. A second and more severe perusal may, possibly, make what is mysterious lucid, and what appears to be absurd be relished as original; but we are not sanguine.[25]

On the same day, the *Literary Gazette*, whose reviewer admired the book as much as the *Athenaeum* man disliked it, made equally heavy weather of interpreting it.

> It is wild, it is true. It is rather more of poetry than of prose. It is finely imaginative, and rests on a supernatural foundation. It is . . . neither a novel nor a romance; but a creation of genius, combining things possible and impossible, credible and incredible, the body and the soul, the realities and the dreams of life—in itself a dazzling dream.

Viola is "an impersonation of all that is lovely. . . . the readers of *Zanoni* must feel and confess the spell which she is destined to cast upon them." Refraining from any effort to retell the story for fear of disturbing "the emotions . . . this work" is "so highly calculated to produce," the friendly reviewer nonetheless falls into the usual error of calling Zanoni a Rosicrucian. The novel shows that we are all mortal, that the mortal lot includes suffering; it inculcates the highest principles; its style is "always impressive, often beautiful, and not seldom sublime. . . . In a word, *Zanoni* is an effusion of *Genius*." 26

Writing to his closest confidant, John Forster, just before *Zanoni* was published, Bulwer said with forced Pelhamish humor,

> I don't know whether *you* will like it. But it is wonderful, read in the proper spirit—nothing like it in the language. If you want to spite me, and convince the world of Mr. Pelham's modesty, publish that opinion as fresh from himself.

But his real anxieties emerged in another letter to Forster, still before Forster had seen the book:

> Your anticipations of *Zanoni* from my fond report, are little likely to be gratified. I do not fancy that anyone will see him with the eye of the author. It is not till the last page that its merits as a whole, in conception, can be seen; and even then few will detect them. It shoots too much over the heads of people to hit the popular taste. But it has given

me a vent for what I long wished to symbolise and typify, and so I am grateful to it.[27]

The long unsigned review that appeared in the *Examiner* on the same day as the other two criticisms we have just noted, surely was by Forster, who was the paper's literary editor. It reveals that he had understood a great deal more of the book than the other two critics, but that Bulwer's apprehensions were not altogether unjustified.

This book, wrote Forster, is "less designed to amuse than to set its readers thinking," and "whether its whole drift is or is not perceived, . . . it is . . . eloquent and thoughtful," not a novel, not a romance, but

> in its peculiar combination of the vague figures of a Dream with the stern realities of Life, it takes an original kind of place in prose fiction . . . is full of Platonism of all sorts, good and bad, and tinged throughout with the mystic notions of that later Pythagorean school which Lucian exposed so wittily.

Forster's dig at "bad" Platonism and his reference to Lucian's satire—presumably the hilarious "Philosophies for Sale" and perhaps the more general attack on occult superstition, "The Lover of Lies or the Doubter"—show how little he liked Bulwer's mysticism.

Forster goes on to discuss the contrast between Zanoni's "perpetual youth and enjoyment" and Mejnour's "perpetual age and contemplation." Mejnour he recognizes as the

> passionless abstraction . . . influencing nothing around him, and therefore himself unchanged. The last page closes on him as the first had opened. And so lives on, in its sublime indifference, the Mejnour of the world—the Science that contemplates, in distinction to the Art that enjoys: the science that cares for knowledge only, and never stops to consider how knowledge may be made subservient to happiness.

Forster has understood, too, that in *Zanoni* it is shown that the highest order of intellect and imagination can only act beneficially on earth by union with the spirit of love.... that in the human affections alone are humanity's divinest heritage ... above all, how majestic and beauteous a thing is Death.

Zanoni achieves his real victory when his love and his sacrifice have opened to him "the eternity beyond the grave."

Forster realizes that Mejnour and Zanoni are not Rosicrucians, and appreciates that they are willing to take on Glyndon as a postulant because his ancestor had been a Rosicrucian. Of the three reviews Forster's is the only one that recognizes that Glyndon's failure to pass through his ordeal is one of the major themes of the novel. Forster sees too that fear and lack of faith lie at the roots of Glyndon's failure, and—even more perceptive—he adds that

even in the failure is a success achieved.... his endeavour for the divine, though unsuccessful, has shown him a truth which makes the human more enjoyable. With faith and virtue, the Old and Customary will keep their beauty still: and he to whom it is not permitted to pass as a seraph to the Infinite, may yet find himself able to return to the Familiar as a child.

Paying high tribute to the novel's "richness of thought" and "deep feeling," praising the supernatural passages for their lack of "the commonplace vulgarity of terror," and especially admiring the characterization of Pisani, Forster objects only to Bulwer's "moral and philosophical view of the French Revolution." This, he says, is

both limited and wrong. There was something far more important shown in that World Wonder, than either the virtue that springs from endurance and death, or the absurdity that is found in all notions of equality. It was an imposture—its idea of all men being equal, in the sense of *sans-culottism*— but it resented a much greater and far more serious imposture. And he who does not feel this, as it seems to us, will never think rightly of that Revolution.

Unlike the other reviewers, Forster had actually grappled with the Protean *Zanoni*, recognized its complexity, and leveled at it one serious (as opposed to frivolous) criticism: in his scorn for the doctrine of equality and his hatred for revolutionary bloodshed, Bulwer was too ready to overlook the viciousness of the *ancien régime*.[28]

Bulwer wrote him that

> ... your lengthened criticism is most kind, and holds a flattering medium between the praises of the *Literary Gazette*, which, no doubt, arise from partiality, and the disparagement of the *Athenaeum*. I am probably the only one who can see that my prophecy was right, that you don't very deeply like or thoroughly comprehend its puzzles. How can I expect that there is any man, however friendly, who will see *Zanoni* with the eyes of the author, or agree with him in believing it to be the loftiest conception in English prose fiction! ... you have gone quite as far as would have been judicious, seeing that *Zanoni* will be no favorite with that largest of all asses—the English Public.[29]

Bulwer was indeed thin-skinned, especially if he really thought that the effusions of the *Literary Gazette* (published by Colburn, one of his own publishers: hence, no doubt, the reference to the paper's "partiality") were more of a compliment to *Zanoni* than Forster's sober and solid—and generally favorable—analysis. The review, flattering though it ought to have been, left Bulwer sure that he had not been fully understood. How could he answer Forster and make the multiple meanings and purposes of *Zanoni* clearer to that large ass, the English Public, and how, in particular, could he point out to them what Forster had missed? He took no fewer than three important steps to do these things.

First, in the guise of a review of Georges Duval's four-volume *Souvenirs de la Terreur*, which had just appeared in Paris, Bulwer published a long essay on the Reign of Terror in the July 1842 *Foreign Quarterly Review*, of which Forster himself was editor. Here, within months of Forster's criticism of his position, Bulwer restated his case, saying much that even he would have hesitated to try to express in fiction, and clarifying for himself and, one imagines, for other serious readers of *Zanoni* who might have responded as Forster had, his actual opinions of the cataclysm.

Bulwer shares Duval's disgust for the recent apologists for the Revolution. There must be no effort to excuse or explain away the horrors. But he goes on, and the passage reads almost like an answer to Forster's review of *Zanoni*:

> It is unquestionably true, indeed, that in the vices of the old *régime* we must seek the causes of the revolutionary crimes. To nations yet more than individuals must be referred the awful menace that the sins of the fathers shall be visited upon the sons. But no less true is it to all, whom philosophical re-finements have not besotted, that humanity itself is under-mined if we allow the circumstances that conduce to guilt to steal away our natural horror of the guilt itself. Rigidly speaking, all guilt is but the result of previous circumstance. To neglected education, to vicious example, we may trace the crimes which send the thief to the hulks and the murderer to the gibbet. But we do not therefore hold excused Jack Sheppard and Daniel Good [both noted criminals]....

Bulwer thus disposed of the kind of apologist who in our own day remarks complacently of revolutionary terror that you can't make an omelette without breaking eggs. But of course these things are matters of emphasis: Forster no more excused the Terror than Bulwer favored the cruelties of the *ancien régime*.

The question was far broader than that, and Bulwer pro-duced a thoroughly serious and well-informed sociological analysis of French development from the time of Richelieu to the time of the Revolution, contrasting it with that of Eng-land, where the early establishment of the Parliamentary sys-tem had bound the classes together. In England the aristocracy had few privileges but much power, while in France it was the other way. In England the middle classes as such could participate in government; in France they were excluded. And so on. The peasantry, the Church, the character of the Court, the origins of the Revolution and its course, all passed in sober review. The revolutionary leaders received no kinder treatment than Bulwer had meted out to them in *Zanoni*, but the heightened rhetoric of the mystic novel had given way to the dispassionate and leisurely judgment of the historian. Toward the end Bulwer declares:

> . . . we think it might be satisfactorily shown, that whatever benefit France has derived from the Revolution itself is a wretched recompense for the crimes through which she waded to obtain it. . . . We grant, at once, that if we compare the state of the people and the nature of the laws, in 1785, with their existence in 1842, there is in great and vital respects a considerable improvement; that improvement, however, is not to be ascribed to the Revolution, *but to the spirit that preceded the Revolution, and could have sufficed for all beneficial changes without it.* . . . Popular principles had only to be temperate in order to be permanently successful. . . . the movement had only to abstain from violence in order to have carried reform to the highest point which the liberty and enlightenment of the Age could have desired. . . . the moment . . . Force began—Reform ceased.

The France of 1842, he goes on, has been deprived by the Revolution of all guarantee "either for permanent government or liberal institutions."

> If we compare the real safeguards for liberty, the real strata and foundations for good government possessed now by the French, *with those at their disposal in 1789,* far from having gained, they have incalculably lost. And at this moment no man can foresee whether, ten years hence, France may not again be a democracy without education or a despotism under a conqueror.

Six years before the revolution of 1848 and just ten before the triumph of Louis Napoleon, this was good prophetic writing. If there had been any doubt as to the political message of

Zanoni this well-written and persuasive essay certainly under-
lined Bulwer's meaning. Forster himself called it "brilliant,"
but was not won over to Bulwer's interpretation, which Bulwer cheerfully declined to change.[30]

Having disposed effectively of Forster's adverse political
criticism, Bulwer turned to the aesthetic front and took his
second step. He decided to dedicate *Zanoni* to John Gibson,
R.A., the sculptor; and beginning with the edition of 1845,
some three years after the book's initial publication, all editions appeared with a new "dedicatory epistle" to Gibson,
dated May 1845. Looking about among living Englishmen,
Bulwer wrote, for one

> who, in his life as in his genius, might illustrate the principle
> I have sought to convey; —elevated by the ideal which he
> exalts, and serenely dwelling in a glorious existence with
> the images born of his imagination. . . .

Bulwer had chosen Gibson, who lived in his Roman house,
removed from the "sordid strife" of the ordinary artistic
genius, "amidst all that is loveliest and least perishable in the
Past," while nobly contributing to "the mighty heirlooms of
the Future." Untainted by any wish for gain or by any competition with others, Gibson had lived and labored "as if [he]
had no rivals, but in the Dead—no purchasers, save in judges
of what is best." Canova's pupil, Gibson had his master's
enthusiasm for his art and his freedom from envy, but had
shunned his affectations. He had "equalled the learning of
Winckelmann, and the plastic poetry of Goethe, in the intimate comprehension of the Antique." In each of his works,
Gibson illustrated the three "great and long undetected principles" of Greek art: "simplicity, calm, and concentration."
Yet Gibson also had recognized the greatness of Flaxman,
the modern. "I, Artist in words," reads Bulwer's peroration,

> "dedicate, then, to you, Artist, whose ideas speak in marble,
> this well-loved work of my matured manhood. I love it not
> the less because it has been little understood, and super-

ficially judged by the common herd. It was not meant for them. I love it not the more, because it has found enthusiastic favourers among the Few. My affection for my work is rooted in the solemn and pure delight which it gave me to conceive and to perform.... Your serener existence, uniform and holy, my lot denies—if my heart covets. But our true nature is in our thoughts, not our deeds.... it is in the still, the lonely, and more sacred life ... that I feel there is between us the bond of that most secret sympathy, that magnetic chain—which united the Everlasting Brotherhood, of whose being Zanoni is the type." [31]

All accounts of Gibson's personality and approach toward his art agree with Bulwer's laudatory description; the two may have met during Bulwer's early visit to Rome in 1833, as his grandson suggests, or possibly in London in 1844, when the sculptor came to England to execute a statue of Queen Victoria. In an case, Bulwer would write the epitaph for Gibson's tombstone when he died in 1866.[32] But while Bulwer's admiration for Gibson was no doubt genuine, the dedication of *Zanoni*, as Michael Lloyd has pointed out, was in effect as much a eulogy of himself as of the sculptor.[33] I too, he is saying, follow the precepts that Glyndon as an aged painter transmitted to his young interlocutor, and that Zanoni had transmitted to Glyndon: like Gibson, I am of the Greek school that elevates Nature to the ideal, and thus portrays the *true*, not of the Dutch school that merely copies Nature, and so produces the *real*.

And to be sure that the stupid public, the common herd he so professed to despise, might truly get the point this time, Bulwer dots every I and crosses every T: "I, Artist in words, dedicate, then, to you, Artist ... in marble...." There: they ought to understand that, at least, he seems to be saying. Even Forster, generally sympathetic, had missed the aesthetic lesson of *Zanoni*. The new dedication would make it harder for readers to do so in the future. And, incidentally, they might ponder the lesson when reading *The Last Days of Pompeii*,

for example, which Bulwer had wrought as carefully and deliberately in the idealizing vein as any of Gibson's statues, or
as any of the contemporary paintings of catastrophe—such
as that of Bryulov—that had helped inspire the novel.[34] But—
as Lloyd also notes—*Zanoni*'s *moral* lesson was that it is *not*
by withdrawal into the serene isolation that Bulwer praises
in Gibson (and, in the dedication, pretends to crave for himself although he detests it in Mejnour) that salvation and
eternal life are to be won; they are achieved by the abandonment of isolation (and in Zanoni's case earthly immortality),
by participation, by sacrifice, and by death. Ironically enough,
this whole moral lesson was now negated by the new emphasis
of the new dedication.

But the dedication to Gibson left Bulwer still dissatisfied,
still unsure that the public would get the various complicated
messages of *Zanoni*, "this well-loved work of my matured
manhood," this "vent for what I long wished to symbolise and
typify." In July 1842, only a few months after the novel's first
appearance, Harriet Martineau had written to Bulwer from her
sickbed in Tynemouth to tell him not only that *Zanoni* had
given her "noble ideas" and roused her "best emotions," but
that it had surprised her—

> not only because all the reviews I have seen seem perfectly
> insensible to the very nature of the book, unaware, even,
> that it contains any doctrine—but because, although not one
> of the least admiring readers of your former works, I own I
> did not anticipate from you a gift so inestimable as this book.
> I did not expect to see, in our own language in this year /42
> a book worthy of Schiller's meditations, and such as his dis-
> ciples can joyfully take to their hearts. . . . If, for some long
> time to come, you find the world preferring your earlier
> works, or a hundred reading St. Leon [by William Godwin,
> 1799] for one that takes new life from *Zanoni*, you will be
> satisfied with the earnest of recompense you must already
> have had—certain moments and hours spent in conceiving
> and working out such a problem of sacred philosophy. Nor
> will it, I trust, be either a brief or trifling satisfaction to see

some who think now that they have read it awakening to its full reality; and some few more who appreciate it now growing more attached to it continually.... Without specifying ... clearly wherein particularly my personal obligation for it lies, I assure you I deeply felt it.

Now this was the kind of appreciation for which Bulwer thirsted, and the reference to the obtuseness of the reviewers must have been especially gratifying. No doubt he responded gratefully. On August 8, 1842, five weeks after her first letter about *Zanoni*, Miss Martineau wrote him a second. Ever since she had read the book herself, she told him, it had

much occupied the friends about me. Seeing that they were not habituated to the sort of contemplation necessary to the full enjoyment of the book, and not being satisfied that they should admire it only for its portions, missing the coherence, I made out, partly for their guidance, partly for my own pleasure, a very brief analysis—an epitome of its doctrine. This was after a hasty circulating-library reading. I have since read it leisurely, with increased pleasure and confidence in my interpretation. But certain of my friends would like to test it by your own, and I really do rate so highly the importance of the book that I should be glad if you could tell me that there exists anywhere—in any review or analysis that I may not have seen—a statement of your doctrines which you yourself would not object to endorse. If it surprises you that your full meaning should not appear plain to all (I confess that to me it seems perfectly clear) you will remember how new this sort of poem is to English readers, who are not conversant with the Germans, and to whom the language of the Ideal region may be more unfamiliar than its thoughts. A single line of reference to any interpretation which you can authorize may so much deepen the impression of your book that I think it is worth while to trouble you so far. The noble moral of the whole, no one can miss; but I wish that the steps to it should be as clear to all as the conclusion. I do adore Schiller, and have worshipped him from my girlhood. I shall never forget the day that I lighted on Die Künstler....

With her air of being the cleverest little girl in the classroom ("I confess that to me it seems perfectly clear"), who just the same would like a message from the master himself recommending some statement of his doctrines, Harriet Martineau was almost the ideal fan for Bulwer. Needless to say, nobody *had* published a statement of the kind she asked for, and we assume that Bulwer told Miss Martineau as much, and asked her to send him a copy of the one she had prepared for her slower-witted friends.

She did so, with an unconvincing modesty:

> I send you what you ask for. I cannot say "with pleasure," for there is no pleasure in sending an author a mockery of his own work; but you will remember that my object was not to elaborate your whole subject but to supply leading hints to unpractised readers. I trust you to tell me if I have misinterpreted you in any material point. I own the argument is, on the whole, as plain to me as that a map of Norfolk is meant for Norfolk, and not Cornwall. . . .[35]

Perhaps it was not altogether flattering to be told that *Zanoni*'s elaborate and half-veiled structure was as obvious to Miss Martineau as the map of Norfolk, but it must have been soothing to find so formidable a bluestocking sustaining her original interest in the novel, and emerging with that typically Martineau-like product, "leading hints to unpractised readers." Indeed, Bulwer liked what she had written so much that he published it too—as by a "distinguished writer (one of the most eminent our time has produced)"—prefaced by a further note of his own, at the end of all editions of *Zanoni* after 1853. Thus, any post-1853 edition of the novel is found complete (at the beginning) with the new dedication to Gibson emphasizing the aesthetic side of the author's purpose, and (at the end) with a new note by Bulwer himself and Harriet Martineau's key.

"The curiosity which *Zanoni* has excited," Bulwer begins his new *Note*, among those who think it worth while to dive into the subtler meanings they believe it intended to convey," has led him not to explain its mysteries, but to set forth the principles which permit them:

> *Zanoni* is not, as some have supposed, an allegory; but beneath the narrative ... *typical* meanings are concealed. ... No typical meanings (which, in plain terms, are but moral suggestions, more or less humorous, more or less subtle), can afford just excuse to a writer of fiction, for the errors he should avoid in the most ordinary novel. We have no right to expect the most ingenious reader to search for the inner meaning, if the obvious course of the narrative be tedious and displeasing. It is, on the contrary, in proportion as we are satisfied with the objective sense of a work of imagination, that we are inclined to search into its depths for the more secret intentions of the author. Were we not so divinely charmed with *Faust*, and *Hamlet*, and *Prometheus* ... we should trouble ourselves little with the types in each which all of us can detect—none of us can elucidate; —none elucidate, for the essence of type is mystery. We behold the figure, we cannot lift the veil. The Author himself is not called upon to explain what he designed. ... To have asked Goethe to explain the *Faust* would have entailed as complex and puzzling an answer as to have asked Mephistopheles to explain what is beneath the earth we tread on. The stores beneath may differ for every passenger; each step may require a new description; and what is treasure to the geologist may be rubbish to the miner. Six worlds may lie under a sod, but to the common eye they are but six layers of stone.
>
> Art in itself, if not necessarily typical, is essentially a suggester of something subtler than that which it embodies to the sense. What Pliny tells us of a great painter of old, is true of most great painters; "their works express something beyond the works"—"more felt than understood." This belongs to the concentration of intellect which high Art demands, and which, of all the Arts, Sculpture best illustrates. ...
>
> We of the humbler race not unreasonably shelter ourselves under the authority of the Masters on whom the world's judgment is pronounced; and great names are cited,

not with the arrogance of equals, but with the humility of inferiors. [This, one imagines, is included to avert a charge that Bulwer is comparing himself—as in fact he is, however —with Goethe, Shakespeare, and Aeschylus.]

The author of *Zanoni* gives, then, no key to mysteries, be they trivial or important, which may be found in the secret chambers by those who lift the tapestry from the wall; but out of the many solutions of the main enigma—if enigma, indeed, there be—which have been sent to him [one wonders: were many solutions to *Zanoni's* puzzles in truth submitted by readers? I doubt it], he ventures to select the one which he subjoins, from the ingenuity and thought which it displays, and from respect for the distinguished writer (one of the most eminent our time has produced) who deemed him worthy of an honour he is proud to display. He leaves it to the reader to agree with, or dissent from, the explanation. "A hundred men," says the old Platonist, "may read the book by the help of the same lamp, yet all may differ on the text; for the lamp only lights the characters— the mind must divine the meaning." The object of a Parable is not that of a Problem; it does not seek to convince, but to suggest. It takes the thought below the surface of the understanding to the deeper intelligence which the world rarely tasks. It is not sunlight on the water, it is a hymn chanted to the Nymph who hearkens and awakes below.

This note of Bulwer's strikes the present reader as disingenu-ous, defensive, and rather adding to the mystification of *Za-noni* than elucidating it. He has left the explanation to Harriet Martineau, while declining to say how far it represents his own intentions; and his claim that her solution was but one of many rings, rather hollow. Yet, of course, it was part of the fun not only to keep the mystery alive but to freshen and deepen it, while apparently seizing a good opportunity to offer at least a partial key. Here, then, without further com-ment, is Harriet Martineau's confident solution of the riddle.

" *'Zanoni'* Explained.
by ———."

Mejnour—Contemplation of the Actual—SCIENCE. Always old, and must last as long as the Actual. Less fallible than Idealism, but less practically potent, from its ignorance of the human heart.

Zanoni—Contemplation of the Ideal—IDEALISM. Always necessarily sympathetic; lives by enjoyment; and is therefore typified by eternal youth.* Idealism is the potent Interpreter and Prophet of the Real; but its powers are impaired in proportion to their exposure to human passion.

Viola—Human INSTINCT. (Hardly worthy to be called LOVE, as Love would not forsake its object at the bidding of Superstition.) Resorts, first, in its aspiration after the Ideal, to tinsel shows; then relinquishes these for a higher love; but is still, from the conditions of its nature, inadequate to this, and liable to suspicion and mistrust. Its greatest force (Maternal Instinct) has power to penetrate some secrets, to trace some movements of the Ideal, but, too feeble to command them, yields to Superstition, —sees sin where there is none, while committing sin, under a false guidance, —weakly seeking refuge amidst the very tumults of the warring passions of the Actual, while deserting the serene Ideal, and expiring (not perishing, but becoming transmuted) in the aspiration after having the laws of the two natures reconciled.

(It might best suit popular apprehension to call these three the Understanding, the Imagination, and the Heart.)

Child—NEW-BORN INSTINCT, while trained and informed by Idealism, promises a preter-human result by its early, in-

---

* "I do not understand the making Idealism less undying (on this scene of existence) than Science."—COMMENTATOR [i.e., Harriet Martineau]. —Because, granting the above premises, Idealism is more subjected than Science to the Affections, or to Instinct, because the Affections, sooner or later, force Idealism into the Actual, and in the Actual its immortality departs. The only absolutely Actual portion of the work is found in the concluding scenes that depict the Reign of Terror. The introduction of this part was objected to by some as out of keeping with the fanciful portions that preceded it. But if the writer of the solution has rightly shown or suggested the intention of the author, the most strongly and rudely actual scene of the age in which the story is cast was the necessary and harmonious completion of the whole. The excesses and crimes of Humanity are the grave of the Ideal.—AUTHOR.

communicable vigilance and intelligence, but is compelled, by inevitable orphanhood, and the one-half of the laws of its existence, to lapse into ordinary conditions.

Aidon-Ai [sic]—FAITH, which manifests its splendour, and delivers its oracles, and imparts its marvels, only to the higher moods of the soul, and whose directed antagonism is with FEAR; so that those who employ the resources of Fear must dispense with those of Faith. Yet aspiration holds open a way of restoration, and may summon Faith, even when the cry issues from beneath the yoke of Fear.

Dweller of the Threshold—FEAR (or HORROR), from whose ghastliness men are protected by the opacity of the region of Prescription and Custom. The moment this protection is relinquished, and the human spirit pierces the cloud, and enters alone on the unexplored regions of Nature, this Natural Horror haunts it, and is to be successfully encountered only by defiance, —by aspiration towards, and reliance on, the Former and Director of Nature, whose Messenger and Instrument of reassurance is Faith.

Mervale—CONVENTIONALISM.

Nicot—Base, grovelling, malignant PASSION.

Glyndon—UNSUSTAINED ASPIRATION: —Would follow Instinct, but is deterred by Conventionalism: —is overawed by Idealism, yet attracted, and transiently inspired; but has not steadiness for the initiatory contemplation of the Actual. He conjoins its snatched privileges with a besetting sensualism, and suffers at once from the horror of the one, and the disgust of the other, involving the innocent in the fatal conflict of his spirit. When on the point of perishing, he is rescued by Idealism; and, unable to rise to that species of existence, is grateful to be replunged into the region of the Familiar, and takes up his rest henceforth in Custom. (Mirror of Young Manhood.)

Argument

HUMAN existence, subject to, and exempt from, ordinary conditions—(Sickness, Poverty, Ignorance, Death).

Science is ever striving to carry the most gifted beyond ordinary conditions—the result being as many victims as efforts, and the striver being finally left a solitary—for his object is unsuitable to the natures he has to deal with.

The pursuit of the Ideal involves so much emotion as to render the Idealist vulnerable by human passion—however long and well guarded, still vulnerable—liable, at last, to a union with Instinct. Passion obscures both insight and Forecast. All effort to elevate Instinct to Idealism is abortive, the laws of their being not coinciding (in the early stage of existence of the one). Instinct is either alarmed, and takes refuge in Superstition or Custom, or is left helpless to human charity, or given over to providential care.

Idealism, stripped of insight and forecast, loses its serenity, becomes subject once more to the horror from which it had escaped, and by accepting its aids, forfeits the higher help of Faith: —aspiration, however, remaining still possible; and, thereby, slow restoration; and also SOMETHING BETTER.

Summoned by aspiration, Faith extorts from Fear itself the saving truth to which Science continues blind, and which Idealism itself hails as its crowning acquisition, —the inestimable PROOF wrought out by all labours and all conflicts.

Pending the elaboration of this proof,

Conventionalism plods on, safe and complacent:

Selfish passion perishes, grovelling and hopeless:

Instinct sleeps, in order to a loftier waking: and

Idealism learns, as its ultimate lesson, that self-sacrifice is true redemption; that the region beyond the grave is the fitting one for exemption from mortal conditions; and that Death is the everlasting portal, indicated by the finger of God, —the broad avenue, through which man does not issue, solitary and stealthy, into the region of Free Existence, but enters triumphant, hailed by a hierarchy of immortal natures.

The result is (in other words), THAT THE UNIVERSAL HUMAN LOT IS, AFTER ALL, THAT OF THE HIGHEST PRIVILEGE.[36]

No doubt Harriet Martineau's identification of the *types* intended by the characters was essentially correct as far as it went. Bulwer was certainly typifying rather than portraying. It was a practice he warmly defended, for example in his essay on "Certain Principles of Art in Works of Imagination":

> . . . the more forcibly the characters interest the generalities of mankind which compose an audience . . . the more they will be types and the less they will be portraits. Some critics have supposed that, in the delineation of types, the artist would fall into the frigid error of representing mere philosophical abstractions. [Harriet Martineau's soluton to *Zanoni*'s puzzles indeed was suggesting that Bulwer had done precisely that. But the artist] secures the individuality required, and avoids the lifeless pedantry of an allegorised abstraction, by reconciling passion, character, and situation with each other; so that it is always a living being in whom we sympathize. . . . the rarer and more unfamiliar the situation of life in which the poet places his imagined character, the more . . . we must recognise [qualities] akin to our flesh and blood, in order to feel interest in its fate. Thus, in the hands of great masters of fiction, whether dramatists or novelists, we become unconsciously reconciled, not only to unfamiliar, but to improbable, nay, to impossible, situations, by recognising some marvellous truthfulness to human nature in the thoughts, feelings, and actions of the character represented, granting that such a character *could* be placed in such a situation.[37]

The illustrations Bulwer immediately supplies are from Shakespeare, LeSage, and Cervantes; but the paragraph is instantly applicable to *Zanoni*. Indeed, his characters were intended to be types; the situations into which he had put them were deliberately designed as to be "improbable, nay, impossible," and he surely thought he had avoided the error with which Harriet Martineau's bloodless dissection tacitly charges him —the representation of "mere philosophical abstractions." Anthony Trollope once said of Bulwer, "I do not think he knew his own personages, nor do we know them." [38] But Bulwer certainly was aware of the problem, and he thought he had solved it. He did not hesitate to compare himself with

Shakespeare, Goethe, and Aeschylus, and he believed he too had avoided the "lifeless pedantry of an allegorised abstraction."

And indeed, a modern reader can see more in *Zanoni* than Harriet Martineau saw. Once we have accepted her identification of Bulwer's types, we are still only at the beginning. Despite his insistence that the supernatural was only the natural one did not yet understand, we have found much occult paraphernalia, a large parade of occult learning, and many mysterious names and references in *Zanoni*. These are effective only because they are not explained away. They harmonize entirely with Bulwer's straightforward acceptance of the occult. The Dweller of the Threshold may be identified by Miss Martineau as "FEAR OR HORROR," but in the novel it is an evil spirit. And the reason for its appearance is carefully and convincingly set forth: if one wishes to imbibe the elixir of life and achieve immunity from earthly disease—the elixir itself being a simple formula, a scientifically compounded substance —one must be "trained by degrees to endure the phantoms and subdue their malice," because the mere partaking of the elixir will make these "larvae of the air become ... audible and apparent." At the allegorical level, Bulwer may be saying that to live on earth forever, one must harden oneself to the terrors of life, or immortality would be intolerable. But at the narrative level, he is surely giving only occult explanations for occult phenomena. Glyndon's entire apprenticeship—from his first passionate desire to know the secrets, down to his failure and dismissal by Mejnour—is a convincing occult romance, deliberately set, as Bulwer set it, in a historic period when, as he carefully tells us, credulity was even more general than the prevalent revolutionary zeal.

Glyndon himself, in his old age, describing the manuscript which, deciphered, would become *Zanoni*, called it "a romance for those who can understand it, an extravagance for those who cannot." This is perhaps the moment to emphasize how thoroughly romantic a romance it is. Glyndon's master Mejnour tells him that his serious training will begin with trance: "In dreams commences all human knowledge; in dreams hovers over measureless space the first faint bridge between spirit and spirit—this world and the worlds beyond." Here is the pure romantic view of dreams, the view that Novalis championed when his youthful hero Heinrich von Ofterdingen challenged his father's warning that "dreams are mere froth" ("Träume sind Schäume"), and when he wrote that "Our life is no dream but it ought to become one, and perhaps it will," the view that E. T. A. Hoffmann took from Novalis and made a guiding principle of his own art. Trance and dream: only for the dedicated romantic are they the beginning of wisdom.

It was Novalis's blue flower, too, that Zanoni put into his bosom, the blue flower of love, mystery, and the feelings which led Heinrich von Ofterdingen to a dream of death and would later have led him to a welcome death itself, had Novalis himself not died first. The blue flower took Zanoni along the same path; only by means of death could he attain true life: the apparent immortality that he enjoyed on earth was a delusion. Conversely, Mejnour, who has the prize of illusory earthly immortality and is to the very end seen "at work with his numbers and his cabala," may indeed be the typification of science as Harriet Martineau pointed out; but he also reminds one at once of the intensely romantic personification of Intellect in Klingsohr's *Märchen* in Heinrich von Ofterdingen, a mere scribe, who writes perpetually, but most of whose writings disappear in a bowl of tears (truth). Whenever a few drops of this poetic truth touch the scribe, ciphers and geometric figures drop from him, and these he hangs around his neck as ornaments. In dying, Zanoni lives; in living, Mejnour is dead. Not the intellect but the emotions—the romantics' choice—is the choice Bulwer made in *Zanoni*.

Schiller's romantic idealizing principle and his concept of art we have heard Zanoni defending against the merely photographic "Dutch" principles of the villainous Nicot, just as Glyndon in his old age opened the novel with the same defense; and we have later observed Bulwer reemphasizing these values in the dedication to Gibson. But the romanticism of *Zanoni* lies far deeper than any set of aesthetic principles, important though they are. The influence and imagery of Novalis emerge at the key moments in the story. This is not in fact a Victorian novel, but a romantic one.

And with its occult and romantic aspects its political message is inextricably bound up. Those readers who had objected to the introduction of the French Revolution on the grounds that it spoiled the illusion of the supernatural had indeed missed the point. As Bulwer well knew and specifically proclaimed—and as modern scholars are only now fully realizing—there was an intimate association between the fashion for the occult and revolutionary politics, no doubt stimulated by the actual advances of science, which raised the hope of an early discovery of the formulae for universal happiness and seemed to put Utopia within reach. Not so, said Bulwer, explicitly pointing the moral in Zanoni's letter to Mejnour, from Paris under the Terror: "these would-be builders of a new world, like the students who have vainly struggled after our supreme science. ...have vainly attempted what is beyond their powers...." Glyndon's failure as a postulant forecasts the failures of the revolutionaries as reformers, and the explicit parallel forces us to reconsider the entire occult romance of Glyndon's apprenticeship: when we do, it emerges as a political parable. Glyndon's passionate eagerness to learn, his unwillingness to wait and acquire learning slowly and through proper preparation at each stage, and his final premature, overconfident experiment that produces the ghastly Dweller of the Threshold specifically betoken the French theorists' passion for political reform and social change, their dogmatic certainty that freedom is within their grasp and that equality is a valid principle, and the ghastly retribution of the Terror. Once the revolutionaries abandoned "this solid earth of usages and forms," they had "passed into the land of shadow, and its loathsome keeper had seized them as its prey." Here is the poetical and allegorical statement of the principles that Bulwer prosaically and straightforwardly enunciated in his essay on the Terror: the revolutionaries would have come closer to achieving true freedom for France if they had proceeded by the route of gradual reform and avoided violence. Once their impatience had led them too soon to imbibe the heady elixir, the Terror, like the Dweller of the Threshold, was in their midst.

Trollope, whose adverse criticism of Bulwer's powers of characterization we have already noted, remarked in the same paragraph of his *Autobiography* that Bulwer "thoroughly understood the political status of his own country, a subject on which, I think, Dickens was marvellously ignorant and which Thackeray had never studied." Having left Parliament in 1841 after ten years in the House of Commons, Bulwer was, at the moment when he wrote *Zanoni*, very close indeed to political affairs. Apprehensive of the social and political unrest which in fact would pervade the forties, both on the Continent and in England, Bulwer, in *Zanoni*, was issuing a warning against the temptation to try to achieve reform by violence.

So the occult themes are successfully made to carry the aesthetic, romantic, and political messages of the author. And because Glyndon has so well worked out his narrative's "Platonic" structure and has moved our souls upward—as he told us he would do—along the ascending path of enthusiasms successively through music, mysticism, and prophecy to the climax where it is the enthusiasm of love that triumphs and brings death and resurrection with it (we now remember the conclusion of his solemn invocation to the Brotherhood: "I scarcely know which of you dictate to me—O Love! O Death!"), we find *Zanoni* not an extravagance (like those readers who do not understand it), nor even merely a romance (like those who do), but something very like the deep and mature work that Bulwer declared it to be.

What does *Zanoni* owe to other writing, what are its sources or analogues if any, and how greatly did Bulwer allow himself to be influenced by them? Apart from his far-ranging reading

in the Neoplatonists, Neopythagoreans, alchemists, and romantics, which we have already tried to elucidate, were there
other writers working in the same vein by whom he was influenced? Our reading of Schiller's *Geisterseher* has, for example, furnished us with a few suggestive parallels to *Zanoni*.
Did any of the more important elements derive from other
artists' work?

Take, for example, the notion of earthly immortality, and
the closely related one of an elixir of life by which it is
attained. Both were commonplaces of romantic fiction. Perhaps the most celebrated and influential novel about a being
who lives forever was C. R. Maturin's *Melmoth the Wanderer*
(1820), which Bulwer, like everybody else, had certainly read.
Though Melmoth possesses eternal life, he is condemned to use
it for the wickedest of purposes, appearing to human beings
at the most painful moments of their lives, when they are
undergoing horrible suffering of one kind or another, and
appealing to them—never successfully—to sell out to the devil
in exchange for respite. As an immortal being he is as different
as possible from Zanoni or Mejnour. Nonetheless, among his
many adventures, told in a long series of stories within stories,
he does fall in love and enter into a "marriage" with a beautiful and innocent maiden named Immalee, and for a time they
share an idyllic life on an uninhabited island during the intervals between his crimes elsewhere. The island romance between
the immortal Melmoth and his Immalee may have contributed
in some measure to Bulwer's account of Zanoni's life with
Viola in its happy early stages on the Ionian island. The portrait of Melmoth is preserved in his descendants' house in
Ireland, and is burned early in the novel; however, any parallel
between its role in the story and that of Glyndon's ancestor's
portrait in *Zanoni* would seem forced indeed, as ancestral portraits naturally form part of the stock furnishings of almost
any novel. *Melmoth*, then, despite its enormous influence on
other writers, including Balzac, hardly seems to have affected
Bulwer at all.

We should, however, note that Balzac's early novel *Le Centénaire ou les deux Béringheld*, published in 1822 under the pseudonym of Horace de Saint-Aubin, which was itself enormously indebted to *Melmoth*, does include a single speech that brings us close to *Zanoni*. "Sir," says Béringheld—himself more than three hundred years old—to a *"rentier"* in a café who has made fun of the Rosicrucians and of alchemy,

> you have spoken of the Rosicrucians as well as of a science [alchemy] which is scorned in our day, and you have spoken of them with a disdain of the sort that people use who have learned nothing about them; is it nothing to run risks for a knowledge that has as its purpose the lengthening of the life of man, and making it virtually eternal? to search for what is called the vital fluid? What a glory for a man to discover it, and by using certain precautions to obtain a life that will last as long as the world itself. Do you see him, treasuring his knowledge, holding fast to everything learned by individual discoveries, resolutely, ceaselessly, always pursuing his researches into nature, acquiring every sort of power, traveling all over the world, knowing it in its smallest details, becoming all by himself the archives of nature and of humanity: avoiding all investigation, taking refuge in any country, free as the air, eluding all pursuit because of his exact knowledge of the underground areas upon which cities are built. Sometimes he wears the rags of misery; the next day he takes the title of an extinct noble family and travels in a magnificent coach; he saves the lives of the good and allows the wicked to die. Such a man is a substitute for Fate, he is almost God. He has in his hands all the secrets of the arts of government, and the secrets of every nation.... He looks at all the useless debates of this earth as if from the loftiness of a cloud, he wanders like a sun amidst the living, and, finally, he passes through the centuries without dying.

This does indeed suggest Zanoni and Mejnour, and Bulwer had probably read it, but *Le Centénaire* is on the whole a shoddy and derivative work showing little of Balzac's future promise.

Like *Melmoth* and *Le Centénaire,* all the fiction on the theme of the wandering Jew also introduces an immortal protagonist. But of the two chief examples that were surely familiar to Bulwer, the Reverend George Croly's *Salathiel* (1828) offers no suggestive resemblances to *Zanoni,* and Eugène Sue's famous *Juif Errant* belongs to 1844–1845, a few years after *Zanoni,* and so raises rather the question of possible influence coming from Bulwer. Similarly, Cagliostro of course was immortal, and appears under his own name, Joseph Balsamo, in Dumas's novel *Mémoires d'un Médecin* of 1846–1848, in which I think it would not be difficult to show the influence of *Zanoni.*

As for elixirs, the vital fluid in *Le Centénaire* is stolen from living victims, and so is most unlike that in *Zanoni.* For other elixirs one thinks of E. T. A. Hoffmann's *Die Elixiere des Teufels* (1814–1815) and of Balzac's *L'Élixir de longue vie* (1830–1831), which drew at least some suggestions from Hoffmann although it depended chiefly on an anecdote of Richard Steele. Hoffmann himself had been inspired by "Monk" Lewis, Grosse's *Genius,* and Mozart's *Don Juan.* It can be assumed that Bulwer was familiar with both Hoffmann and Balzac, and with their own sources and analogues, but the elixir in *Zanoni* plays a wholly different role, and I can see no possible influence.

When we turn, on the other hand, to Glyndon's passionate desire for occult knowledge, so notable a feature of *Zanoni* (as of "Kosem Kosamim, the Magician"), we can easily find several analogues. In addition to Schiller's young man at Saïs, and the prince in the *Geisterseher,* whose *Lieblingsschwärmerei* it was to get into touch with the spirits, we have the young Spanish guardsman, Alvare, the hero of Cazotte's *Le Diable amoureux,* who is possessed by a similar passion, "*plein de curiosité et affamé d'idées nouvelles....je mourrais d'impatience.... Vous ne pouvez concever la vivacité du désir que vous avez créé en moi: il me brûle....*" Like Glyndon too, Alvare must pass through the ordeal without showing fear, and, incidentally, the scene of his incantation and raising of the Devil is Naples, as in *Zanoni*. Bulwer, we know, had read Cazotte as well as Schiller. But the passionate eagerness for knowledge is a commonplace of the literature about alchemy. For example, in Balzac's *La Recherche de l'absolu* (1834), far removed in scene and theme from *Zanoni*, Balthasar Claës of Douai, though loving his wife and children and proud of his family fortunes and traditions, nonetheless ruins himself and those he loves several times over because of his passion for chemical experimentation, which preoccupies him so totally that he hardly notices when his beloved wife dies. But all that Glyndon has in common with Balthasar Claës is this eagerness. Claës is engaged in chemical (or alchemical) research, with all the paraphernalia of the laboratory—ovens, retorts, crucibles, expensive chemicals, and the like; while Zanoni and Mejnour have long since passed that stage, and no longer even need books—a few herbs and their products suffice.

But the wild passion for occult knowledge is ancient indeed. In a text, apparently of the first century A.D., a certain Thessalos, perhaps from Tralles in Asia Minor, tells an emperor (probably Nero) how he had thrown himself on the ground, weeping, and embraced the feet of a priest at Thebes, declaring that "it was absolutely necessary for me to converse with a god, and that, if this desire was not satisfied I was ready to give up living." Three days of impatient fasting precede the magic evocation of Asklepios, who reveals to Thessalos that the essential secrets of healing lie in plants, which must be gathered at the precise moments indicated by the stars. Glyndon's eagerness, then, is a commonplace of theurgic literature from earliest times, and so, incidentally, is Zanoni's herbalism.

And as for herbalism, in Balzac's mystic novel *Séraphîta* (1834–1835), when the androgynous protagonist is playing his rôle as Séraphîtüs, he gives to Minna, doomed to love him in vain, a single flower plucked from an almost inaccessible place on a mountain meadow, a hybrid plant that seems to symbolize his own double yet sterile sexual nature. The scene reminds us of Zanoni's blue flower, but the underlying meaning appears to be wholly different.

But perhaps more rewarding and suggestive than further search of particular analogues to *Zanoni* or its various and multiple themes, might be a general comparison between Bulwer's devotion to and use of the occult and that of Goethe, whom Bulwer regarded as the greatest genius of his age, and whose works he had read and reread. From Goethe's early laboratory experiments in alchemy during his university days, in his botanical writings on the metamorphosis of plants with his hypothesis of the *Urpflanze,* in his optical study on the theory of colors with its proclamation of the supremacy of red, in the *Märchen,* in *Faust* part II, and in the *Wanderjahre* of Wilhelm Meister, his entire life and work and his attitudes toward his own development were permeated by the theories and outlook of the alchemists. The paradox was that together with Goethe's "confidence in the wisdom of the alchemists" went a "mistrust and dislike of their methods and conclusions." He "rarely spoke of the occult, and when he did, it was almost always in terms of disparagement." In his writing he often repressed his driving interest in the irrational, but he allowed it to appear beneath the surface to those who read him with an eye to a second meaning. Goethe's devotion to an occult science, his occasional open use of it and more frequent hidden allusion to its symbolism in his fiction, and his ambivalent attitude toward its meaning for his own existence offer a suggestive and interesting parallel to Bulwer's use of the occult—a parallel that will, I hope, become more striking as our study advances.[39]

Bulwer's critics with much justice accused him of making himself the hero of each of his successive novels before *Zanoni.* Once we have grasped the fact that the manuscript was written by the elderly Glyndon as a memoir of the younger Glyndon's adventurous education, and have realized that *Zanoni*—in addition to all the other things it is—is therefore a

Bildungsroman as well, we can see, as we half expected, that
Bulwer put much of himself into the character of Glyndon.
Glyndon is a painter, Bulwer a writer: we have heard him
saying to Gibson, "I, Artist in words, dedicate, then, to you,
Artist . . . in marble." It is only a small step from the artist in
marble to the artist on canvas, and back to the artist in words.
Glyndon's Idealizing aesthetic principles, which he preached
in old age and, we find, learned in youth from Zanoni, in
opposition to Nicot the revolutionary and pupil of David,
were Bulwer's own artistic principles. Even the large picture
that Glyndon painted on the walls of Mejnour's castle after
the failure of his initiation was a painting of an ancient Egyptian religious ceremony, and so perhaps comparable to Bulwer's own *Last Days of Pompeii,* a youthful effort of which he
was very proud, and which bore an intimate relationship, we
know, to contemporary painting. Both the author, then, and
the protagonist are artists, and Idealizers, and successful.

Moreover, in Glyndon's relationship to Viola, whom he
loves but not enough to marry, we may without being too
fanciful find something of Bulwer's characteristic attitude
toward the women to whom he was attracted. We need not
here rehearse his early love affairs; but we may remind ourselves that he coolly and apparently without many pangs gave
up his wish to marry a beautiful and highborn French girl
only because his mother disapproved of his marrying a Catholic,
and that he entered upon his disastrous marriage to Rosina
chiefly out of a sense of duty because she had become his mistress some time before. The portrayal of Viola, far from being
the enchanting and convincing achievement that the *Literary
Gazette* critic found it, is—at least after the earliest phase in
which she performs her father's opera—one of the chief failures
of *Zanoni*. It is hard to believe that the immortal sage, despite
his romantic heart, would have fallen in love with her. In the
affairs of the heart, then, too, there is at least something of
Bulwer in Glyndon.

But there is more: in his determination "not to resemble

but to surpass my kind" and to acquire "preternatural knowledge and unearthly power" the young Glyndon was a self-
portrait of Bulwer. Despite his public tone of urbane scepticism, despite his convincing efforts to make the occultism of
Zanoni only a branch of science, it is true to an extent not
yet fully appreciated that Bulwer—like a later Goethe, with a
wider choice of subjects—for many years made himself a
determined student of all the contemporary efforts to acquire
preternatural knowledge and unearthly power. No doubt much
of this enterprise was pursued secretly, and all trace of it is
forever lost. But a surprising amount is still discoverable.
Zanoni, the first of his occult romances, stands near the beginning of his apprenticeship. It would be twenty years before
the second specimen appeared. Most of our evidence of Bulwer's explorations of the occult belongs to that interval. In
his Introduction to the 1845 edition of *Night and Morning* (in
which the criminal is the only virtuous man, the ostensibly
virtuous men mostly criminals), he did write a few words
that seem to refer back to *Zanoni* and forward to the work he
would later do:

> Long since, in searching for new regions in the Art to which
> I am servant, it seemed to me that they might be found lying
> far, and rarely trodden, beyond the range of conventional
> morality in which Novelist after Novelist had entrenched
> himself—amongst those subtle recesses in the ethics of human
> life in which Truth and Falsehood dwell undisturbed and
> unseparated. The vast and dark poetry around us—the Poetry
> of Modern Civilisation and Daily Existence, is shut out from
> us in much, by the shadowy giants of Prejudice and Fear.
> He who would arrive at the Fairy Land must face the
> Phantoms.[40]

Before we turn to *A Strange Story*, then, it may be appropriate to chronicle what can be retrieved of Bulwer's own efforts,
without a Zanoni or even a Mejnour, to guide him, to penetrate
the barriers, cross the threshold, and face the phantoms.

4 / *The Years Between: Bulwer as a Practicing Occultist* (*1842–1862*)

Among Bulwer's occult activities it is particularly difficult to assess his membership in the revived Rosicrucian Brotherhood, whose early history—or rather nonhistory—we have briefly summarized. His grandson says flatly:

> He was himself a member of the Society of Rosicrucians and Grand Patron of the Order. As this was a secret Society, it is not surprising that among Bulwer's papers there should be no documents which throw any light upon it, nor any mention of it in his correspondence.

On July 3, 1870, less than three years before his death, Bulwer wrote a letter of thanks to Hargrave Jennings, who had sent him his book on the Rosicrucians, saying:

> There are reasons why I cannot enter into the subject of the "Rosicrucian Brotherhood," a Society still existing, but not under any name by which it can be recognized by those without its pale. But you have with much learning and much acuteness traced its connection with early and symbolical religions, and no better book upon such a theme has been written, or indeed, could be written, unless a member of the Fraternity were to break the vow which enjoins them to secrecy. Some time ago a sect pretending to style itself 'Rosicrucians' and arrogating full knowledge of the mysteries of the craft, communicated with me, and in reply, I sent them the cipher sign of the "Initiate,"—not one of them could construe it.

An examination of Jennings's books not surprisingly reveals that it has little value either as scholarship or as "key" to any hypothetical mysteries.

Indeed, except for the significant hint that the "real" Rosicrucians no longer used the name, and that those who used the name were not real Rosicrucians, which in itself only provides an additional typical Bulweream mystification, we are no further. And if we find that people calling themselves Rosicrucians claim Bulwer as one of them, we must view their claim with scepticism. As a sample of such literature we may examine a largely fanciful biographical sketch of Bulwar in a recent publication calling itself "Rosicruciae." Bulwer, it says, was "Highest *Arcane* Initiate; Member of the *Great* or *World Council;* Order of the *Rose; L'Ordre du Lis;* Count de L., Hierophant of the World, *Fraternitas Rosae Crucis*," and Supreme Grand Master "by the time he was fifty," which would be in 1853. He was elevated to the "highest position of the August Fraternity, that of *Hierophant* (unknown) of the world, and was the *Count de L.*, who in 1856–1858 was present at the induction" of the French occultist Éliphas Lévi (Alphonse Constant, of whom much more later) and of an American named Randolph into their high office at the meeting of the Supreme *Grand Dome* in Paris. He also was, according to this account, the "instructor and guide of Hargrave Jennings," who became Supreme Grand Master of the Brotherhood in England. If this is so, then Bulwer's letter to Jennings, just quoted, was simply a case of one brother's scratching another brother's back. Bulwer was the "third supreme Hierophant following Saint Germain."

Zanoni, we are told,

> reveals, yet conceals to all but the *Initiate*, the entire mystery of *Philosophic Initiation*. If all books but *Zanoni* were destroyed, those with eyes to see, perception to understand, would easily be able to reconstruct the entire system of *Arcane* or Occult training.

For Bulwer himself, the mere "accomplishment of supreme initiation" was its own reward. Like Saint Germain, the first of the supreme hierophants, Bulwer lived up to the command, "Learn to know all things, but thyself remain unknown." The remainder of the article devoted to him consists of quotations from *Zanoni* and unidentified and largely unintelligible or trivial general precepts. This is what one would expect after the invocation of Saint Germain, self-styled Count, self-styled Transylvanian, one of those mysterious charlatans who flourished contemporaneously with Cagliostro, perhaps a Spaniard or Portuguese, a man of many aliases, expert in the manufacture of silk, fabricator of diamonds, who lived to be ninety-two and so passed for immortal. He had allegedly been present at the Passion of Christ, and his followers declared that he was alive and well in 1790, though in fact he had by then long since passed to his somewhat uncertain reward.[41] Saint Germain was precisely the kind of faker that the fastidious Zanoni (and the Bulwer that proclaimed the true science as against the false alchemy of Paracelsus and the others) would have repudiated out of hand.

We move out of the world of pure conjecture and undiluted mumbo-jumbo when we turn to Bulwer's long association with the revival of the interconnected phenomena of phrenology, animal magnetism, and clairvoyance in England. In the paper immediately preceeding this, we gave a preliminary sketch of this subject in connection with the mesmeric cure of Harriet Martineau in 1844, and noted that it was Bulwer himself who first suggested that she try mesmerism. He was indeed an admirer of Dr. John Elliotson, whom we have encountered as the leader of the revival, and a friend also of Dr. John Ashburner and the Reverend Chauncey Hare Townshend, Elliotson's fellow advocates of the new science. As early as February 29, 1840, Townshend gave Bulwer a copy of his new pamphlet, *Facts on Mesmerism,* and wrote him: "The subject on which I have written is unpopular, and terribly connected, in persons' imaginations, with quackery and humbug. But I have ventured to think, and to enquire for myself, and, as I cannot possibly be moved by filthy lucre [he was very rich], perhaps I may be believed—or at any rate only viewed as a mistaken enthusiast, but not as a calculating deceiver." He asked Bulwer to "speak conscientiously well" of the book amongst his friends, so that the subject might have "the support of an influential man. But all shrink from this task which requires much boldness. I do think you will not fear to advocate even Mesmerism, if convinced—and should I gain your suffrage, how much I shall rejoice." Urging Bulwer to consider mesmerism as a subject for fiction, Townshend wrote that he saw in him "a German *depth* . . . peculiarly calculated to invest the mysteries of mesmerism with solemnity and grandeur." [42] Although Glyndon's first trance is induced by Mejnour through something remarkably like mesmerism, as is Viola's extraordinary vision in Venice, *Zanoni* is not a novel of mesmerism properly speaking, but of many other subjects, as we have seen. Yet it is entirely possible that Townshend's suggestion may have helped encourage Bulwer to write *Zanoni*, which surely is satisfactorily deep in the German way.

In 1843 appeared the first number of *The Zoist*, "A Journal of Cerebral Physiology and Mesmerism," a quarterly to which for the next thirteen years all the leading serious advocates of the new treatment—with Elliotson foremost—would contribute case histories of mesmeric cures and episodes of clairvoyance, with vigorous polemics against their often equally violent opponents in and out of the medical profession. Elliotson was also a phrenologist—he had founded the Phrenological Society as early as 1824—and phrenology is largely what is meant by the term "cerebral physiology" in the journal's subtitle. If one believed in both, it meant that one could direct the mesmeric influence to that region of the patient's brain which phrenology indicated needed to be magnetized. In 1846, smitten by a fit of bad conscience at the harsh professional usage to which Elliotson's espousal of mesmerism had exposed him, the Royal Society of Medicine invited him to give the annual Latin Harveian Oration, in honor of the great William Harvey, then two centuries dead. Boldly Elliotson addressed his audience on the still enormously controversial subject of mesmerism, and even more boldly he delivered the oration (for the first time) in English, although he prepared printed editions of it in both languages. Of course he was attacked for both the form and content of his message, which likened mesmerism to earlier great medical discoveries rejected at first by obscurantists.

Touched to the quick (not very difficult with Elliotson) by one onslaught in *The Chirurgical Journal* for October 1, 1846, which impugned his mastery of Latin, Elliotson replied with his usual vigor in the pages of the *Zoist*, and in his own defense printed "the following letter from a highly educated and most distinguished man":

> My dear Dr. Elliotson,—
> I have had great pleasure in reading your very admirable oration, which I have done in both the languages in which it is written, and am much charmed with the ingenious elegance of the Latin, and the simple boldness with which you have surmounted many technical difficulties in your subject, in that very classical piece of scholarship; and still more pleased, as well as instructed, by the more important essentials in the matter and argument.
> I think the manliness of your appeal one of your finest efforts on behalf of the only true mode of following science, viz., experiment of what is before the eyes, with that proper mixture of faith and diffidence which teaches us both the illimitable resources of nature and the little knowledge we have yet acquired of her secrets. Most obediently yours,
> E. Bulwer Lytton.[43]

The letter is in many respects typical. While it certainly gave Elliotson both classical and scientific ammunition, it virtually took away with one hand what it gave with the other, by its final emphasis on the depth of our ignorance and by its avoidance of anything like an all-out endorsement of mesmerism as such. It did urge scientists not to ignore what lay before them, and to that degree supported the proponents of mesmerism, who vociferously argued that all they wanted was not to have mesmeric data dismissed unstudied. Bulwer's attitude in this letter (which Elliotson published in 1850 but which probably belongs to 1846, the year of the Harveian Oration) exactly corresponds with his views as later expressed in fiction in *A Strange Story*, where mesmerism and, as we shall see, the attitude of doctors toward it would play an important role.

In his later essay, "On the Normal Clairvoyance of the Imagination," Bulwer paid public tribute to Elliotson: "No man," he wrote

> has sacrificed more for the cause of mesmerism than Dr. Elliotson, and perhaps no man would more earnestly warn a neophyte—startled by his first glimpses of phenomena, which, developed to the utmost by the priesthood of Delphi, once awed to subjection the luminous intellect of Greece— not to accept the lucky guesses of the Pythian for the infallible response of Apollo.

Wrapped up in the tribute once more is the scepticism, this time not of mesmerism in general but of its clairvoyant aspects in particular. Indeed the entire thrust of the essay is to belittle mesmeric clairvoyance, of which, as Bulwer says, "most men are sceptical."

> "I concede," says the cautious physiologist, "that you may produce a kind of catalepsy upon a highly nervous subject; that in the state of quasi-catalepsy there may pass through the brain a dream, which the dreamer is able to repeat, and which in repeating, he may colour or exaggerate according to an unconscious sympathy (called *rapport* by the mesmerists) with the will of the person who has cast him into sleep, or according to a bias of his own mind, of which at the moment he may not be aware. But to conceive that a person in this abnormal state can penetrate into the most secret thoughts of another—traverse, in spirit, the region of time and space—describe to me in London what is being done by my son in Bombay— ... is to contradict all we know of the organization of man, and of the agencies established by nature. ..."

Even if you jettison this hypothetical cautious physiologist, and instead ask "the most ardent believer in the gift of mesmeric clairvoyance," he will admit that

> the powers it bestows are extremely capricious and uncertain—that although a somnambulist tells you accurately today the cause of an intricate disease or the movements of your son in Bombay, he may not be able tomorrow to detect a cold in your head or tell you what is done by your next-door neighbour. So uncertain, indeed, so unreliable, are the higher phenomena ascribed to mesmeric clairvoyance, that experiments of such phenomena almost invariably fail when subjected to those tests which the incredulous not unreasonably demand.

And even when everything goes as well as possible, an experienced mesmerist would take great care in using for practical purposes what he learned from his somnambule, and would not count on his getting such information regularly. Somnambules have occasionally told the police where to find a murderer and have predicted the winner of the Derby; but one cannot count on their doing so frequently.

The indictment continues:

> How little has mesmeric clairvoyance realized the hopes that were based on the early experiences of Puységur! With all its assumptions of intelligence more than mortal, it has not solved one doubtful problem in science. It professes to range creation on the wings of a spirit, but it can no more explain to us what is "spirit," than it can tell us what is heat or electricity. It assumes to diagnosticate in cases that have baffled the Fergusons and the Brodies—it cannot tell us the cause of an epidemic. It has a cure for all diseases— it has not added to the pharmacopeia a single new remedy. It can read the thoughts hoarded close in your heart, the letter buttoned-up in your pocket, —but when it has done so, *cui bono!* you start, you are astonished, you cry "Miraculous!" but the miracle makes you no wiser than if you had seen the trick of a conjuror.

Nor does a clairvoyant improve with practice; indeed, often the "connoisseurs in mesmerism prefer as the most truthful the youngest and rawest Pythoness they can obtain, and are inclined to view with distrust all sibyls in lengthened professional practice." How much more reliable, and how much more marvelous is the "normal clairvoyance which imagination bestows upon healthful brains." [44]

Of course, the purpose of this particular essay was to describe and extol the clairvoyant feats that the poetic imagination quite normally performs. But the judgment of mesmeric clairvoyance, with which Bulwer is contrasting that of the imagination, is a particularly cool and measured judgment, a judgment which, as Bulwer himself emphasizes, came from long experience. In the *Zoist*, for example, one may read a whole series of articles appearing year after year about the remarkable clairvoyant performances of a young French somnambule named Alexis Didier, whose mesmerist was a certain M. Marcillet, and who convinced Dr. Elliotson and the leading English proponents of mesmerism of the genuineness of his accomplishments. Alexis would read pages of text from a closed book given him in a parcel; he could accurately describe for those present at one of his séances the interiors of their houses, although he had never seen them, down to the last detail of the signature upon a painting over the drawing room fireplace. Although Bulwer's name, as it happens, never does appear on the *Zoist*'s lists of those present during one of these evenings with Alexis, it is highly probable that he did indeed witness the performance: it was the sort of thing he never missed; his friends Lady Blessington and the Count d'Orsay are noted on one occasion; Chauncey Hare Townshend on another; and of course the *Zoist* recorded only a few of the many performances Alexis put on.[45] Whether Bulwer ever saw him hardly matters, however: Alexis was the best somnambule the forties and fifties provided, and the response of a modern reader of the *Zoist*'s record of his performance is exactly like Bulwer's own judgment—after twenty years—upon mesmeric clairvoyance as a whole: miraculous, but *cui bono;* extraordinary, but so what?

Even the phrenological side of the *Zoist*'s interests, however, enlisted Bulwer's attention. Dr. John Ashburner reported that Mr. Holme of Highgate made two casts of Coleridge's head at intervals of some years, and that the later cast, when measured with calipers, distinctly showed a shrinkage in size. This Ashburner attributed to Coleridge's increased use of opium. Holme did the same for Ashburner himself, but instead of adding to his vices after the first cast, as Coleridge had done, Ashburner gave up wine, "acquired improved power of self-control, and exercised the intellectual faculties," so that when the second cast was made Ashburner's improved habits had "created a magnetic accession of mental forces" and increased the size of his head, and so naturally of the cast. And Ashburner records that "Sir E. Bulwer-Lytton was with me when Holme took the second cast of my head, and he then witnessed Holme's application of his calipers to Coleridge's two casts." [46]

As for Braid of Manchester—whom we have mentioned in an earlier essay as one of the key transitional therapists between the mesmerists and the Freudians—Bulwer had also observed in person "the curious effects . . . produced by what is called 'hypnotism,' from *hypnos* (sleep)."

Mr. Braid rejected the theories of the mesmerizer and phrenologist, and maintained that he could produce, by action on the muscles, phenomena analogous to those with which the phrenological mesmerist startles the spectators. I saw him thus fascinate to sleep a circle of miscellaneous patients by making each patient fix successively his (or her) eyes upon a lancet-case that the operator held between finger and thumb. And when slumber had been thus induced, without aid of magnetic passes, and merely by the concentration of sight and mind on a single object, Mr. Braid said to me, "Now observe, I will draw into play the facial muscles which are set in movement by laughter, and ludicrous images will immediately present themselves to the sleeper."

This sleeper, of course, laughs; another is made to pray as if in church; and even to think that she has gone to heaven and sees the angels. "I believe," Bulwer goes on,

> that Mr. Braid has in one respect been more fortunate than his fellow Thaumaturgists, the mesmerisers. He has not been derided as a dupe, nor denounced as an impostor by sceptical physiologists. His experiments, dating from 1842, have attracted considerable attention in England, and a still more severely critical attention abroad. In France they appear to have been confirmed and extended by the experiments of very eminent and cautious philosophers and physicians.

Here, in a footnote, Bulwer cites the chapter on hypnotism in Maury's "comprehensive and enlightened book," *Le Sommeil et les rêves*. And he concludes:

> Taking it for granted that no deception was practised, either by himself or his patients, the hypnotism exhibited by Mr. Braid conveys a striking illustration of the instantaneous and involuntary sympathy between the ideas presented to our inward intelligence and the slightest threads of that external web-work behind which sits the soul vigilant and unseen.[47]

Once again, it is only by accident that we know of Bulwer's presence at a demonstration: indeed, it seems as if this particular one had been conducted especially for him ("Mr. Braid said to me 'Now observe. . . .' "). The essay from which we have been quoting is one on the distinction between active thought and reverie, and the material observed at Braid's demonstration is brought in only by way of illustration. But it shows once more how thoroughly up to date—and not only in a superficial way—Bulwer kept with the progress of all scientific (as well as all pseudo-scientific) experiment in the realms of human psychology. He had gone to see Braid not merely as a curiosity-seeker; he knew that Braid's work was highly regarded in France (where it would soon be influencing Charcot and then Freud); he not only knew this, but he had read Maury on sleep and dreams, and Maury's book was only a year old when Bulwer wrote his essay.

And in another essay in the 1863 series (this time on "Essay-Writing in General and These Essays in Particular"), Bulwer comments as if half in fun on Sir William Hamilton's "grave enthusiasm" for continued progress in science and philosophy, "never attaining, but ever approximating to, perfection." How about periodical *retro*gression, instead of progression? asks Bulwer. And his illustration once again is chosen directly from our own present field of investigation:

> Perplexed by the phenomena of hypnotism, mesmerism, and the like thaumaturgia, physiology (at least in the more progressive schools of the Continent) has recurred for its most valuable hints to the mysticism of Alexandrian Platonists, who are again taken down from their shelves to corroborate "a system." Van Helmont has become once more an authority; and there is scarcely a new work treating of psychology which the inquirers of France and Germany have lately put forth, wherein the great discoverer of gas is not quoted with respect. M. Maury, accounting rationally for the phenomena ascribed to magic, vulgarly confounded with conjuring or imposture, says, with simple truth, "The secret of magic is to be sought in physiology"—viz., it is centred in rare effects, producible on certain constitutions. But that is no discovery; it had been said before by the sages of antiquity, and the illuminati of the middle ages.[48]

And, Bulwer might have added, twenty-one years ago, I said it myself, speaking through Zanoni and Mejnour.

Aristotle, he says cheerfully, is on his way out; the mystics are on their way back. Soon, he is clearly predicting, the psychologists will be genuinely coming to grips with the irrational. Meanwhile, as a sensitive and prescient observer, Bulwer himself, as he had systematically done for many years, kept his eye firmly on the "rare effects producible on certain constitutions," the physiological manifestations around him that most approximated magic. During the two decades that separated *Zanoni* from *A Strange Story*, the most generally notorious of such phenomena in Europe and America were those associated with spiritualism. Having observed Bulwer's activities among the mesmerists, clairvoyants, phrenologists, and hypnotists, and his attitudes toward their experiments, we turn now to the spiritualists.

The most important popularizer of spiritualism in the mid-century, especially in fashionable and literary circles in England and on the Continent, was Daniel Dunglas Home, born in Scotland in 1833, perhaps an illegitimate grandson of the tenth Earl of Home. Brought up since childhood in Connecticut, Home reached maturity at the height of the American spirit-rapping craze of the early fifties, rocketed to celebrity as a successful medium, and made his first visit to England in 1855. Thackeray had already seen him perform in New York; Mrs. Browning knew all about him and was awaiting him eagerly; nine years later Browning himself would confer an unwanted immortality upon him by a head-on attack in the famous poem, "Mr. Sludge, the Medium" (although Home always said that nobody who knew him had ever been able to discover one point of resemblance). As we would expect, Bulwer was deeply interested in Home's performances.

At Ealing in 1855, Home reports,

> a distinguished novelist, accompanied by his son, attended a séance, at which some very remarkable manifestations occurred that were chiefly directed to him. The rappings on the table suddenly became unusually firm and loud. He asked "What spirit is present?" The Alphabet was called over, and the response was, "I am the spirit who influenced you to write Z———." "Indeed," said he, "I wish you would give me some tangible proof of your presence." "What proof? Will you take my hand?" "Yes,"—and putting his hand beneath the surface of the table, it was immediately seized by a powerful grasp, which made him start to his feet in evident trepidation, exhibiting a momentary sus-

picion that a trick had been played upon him. Seeing, however, that all the persons around him were sitting with their hands quietly reposing on the table, he recovered his composure, and offering an apology for the uncontrollable excitement caused by such an unexpected demonstration, he resumed his seat.[49]

Even if this were all, we should unhesitatingly guess that the distinguished novelist must have been Bulwer, since it is hard to think of anyone else who had written a novel called Z_____ and who went to séances. But we are spared the necessity of any conjecture, since the second Mrs. Home, in the first of the two books she wrote about her husband after both he and Bulwer had died, reprints the story, and names Bulwer:

> At Ealing, Sir E. B. Lytton took part in at least one séance at the house of the Rymers. During the life-time of that celebrated man, Mr. Home published in his first volume of "Incidents" [a] description of what occurred, and as Lytton remained silent, though the press at once called on him either to deny or affirm—it may be presumed that the account was substantially correct. In a matter of this sort to be silent was to affirm, and that Lord Lytton could not but know.

In fact, the spirit who had inspired *Zanoni* did not limit itself to a firm handshake under the table, but immediately afterward produced "another equally remarkable phenomenon;"

> "We wish you to believe in the _____" was spelled out, and there the message stopped. "In what am I to believe," asked Lytton, "in the medium?" "No." "In the manifestations?" "No." As this second negative was returned Sir Edward felt himself gently touched on the knee, and on putting down his hand a cross was placed in it, by way of finishing the sentence. The cross, which was of cardboard, had been lying with some other articles on a table at the end of the large room in which the party were seated. Lytton, apparently much impressed, turned to Mrs. Rymer,

and asked her permission to retain the cross as a souvenir. She assented.[50]

Madame Home cherished against Bulwer a deep and genuine anger. No doubt this reflected her late husband's feelings, since she herself never had met Bulwer, and married Home only in 1871. Soon afterward, Home retired, and in 1873 Bulwer died. "Lord Lytton," she assures us,

> was perfectly convinced of the genuineness of the phe-nomena he witnessed in Mr. Home's presence, and even of their spiritual origin, but too timid to avow his conviction publicly. Mr. Home was his guest for a short time at Kneb-worth in 1855; and several séances took place there, no record of which is available. Home never himself wrote down the record of a séance, but left it to others to speak; and when, from fear of the world or from fear of ridicule, they preferred to remain silent, he acquiesced in their si-lence with the easy good nature that characterised him. His mission, as he understood it, was to convince people of the facts; if they were bold and honest enough afterwards to declare what they had witnessed, that was as it should be; if not, it was their affair, not his. . . . Home collected noth-ing, published in his two volumes of "incidents" such séances as friends chose to give him, or had already made public; and let the memory of the rest perish. . . . These facts ex-plain why nothing can be said here of the séances at Kneb-worth. Mr. Home kept no record of them; and Lord Lytton, though he probably preserved one, never published it. In the years 1860 and 1861, Lord Lytton was again present at many séances with Mr. Home, both at Knebworth and in London. . . .

Weakness and fear of ridicule: Madame Home returns again and again to these accusations against Bulwer. "In public he was an investigator of Spiritualism, in private a believer." He wrote many friendly letters to Mr. Home, condoling with him over the loss of his first wife. When a friend had just lost a relative, and wanted to try to get into touch with him through a medium, Bulwer wrote to S. C. Hall to ask him to recommend

a suitable one. With the Halls, Bulwer attended another of
Home's séances in 1861, at which bells were rung, and other
spirit phenomena recorded. Madame Home cannot reconcile
herself to Bulwer's unwillingness to commit himself publicly
to a belief in spiritualism.[51] In her second book, she tries another explanation:

> long before he met Home his mind—or rather his imagi-
> nation, had been coloured by superstitions derived from
> the mediaeval and mystical authors in whom he delighted.
> He saw the facts of Spiritualism through a haze of fancies
> concerning sylphs, gnomes, "Dwellers on (sic) the Thresh-
> old," fiendish or angelic creatures compounded of fire or
> air, and capable, under imperfectly known conditions, of
> manifesting themselves to human beings. Mingled with these
> fancies were others more vague and shapeless of magical
> effects that might be wrought on objects both animate and
> inanimate by the force of human will.[52]

Here Madame Home comes far closer to the Bulwer we know.
Not weakness or fear of ridicule, but scientific curiosity com-
bined with a set of superstitions of his own prevented Bulwer
from publicly committing himself to Home any more
thoroughly than he had been willing to commit himself to
Elliotson: these phenomena, he felt, were interesting indeed;
but one must not assume that the spirits were behind them,
and this he would have had to avow publicly before he could
have satisfied Home.

In undated letters to his son, which his grandson and biographer tentatively dated 1853, but which I believe properly
belong to 1855 after the first séances with Home, Bulwer
comments on his own reaction to the spiritualist phenomena:

> I have had the American rappers and Media with the spirit
> world, as they call themselves, here. It is very curious, and
> if there be a trick, it is hard to conceive it. There are dis-
> tinct raps given to a table at which they sit, and by rapping
> at the letters of the alphabet which the supposed spirits
> select, they hold distinct dialogues, you merely thinking or

writing your questions on slips of paper which you hold
concealed in your hand. They profess to be spirits of the
dead, but I much doubt, supposing they are spirits at all,
whether they are not rather brownies or fairies. They are
never to be relied on for accurate answers, tho' sometimes
they were wonderfully so, just like clairvoyants. Altogether
it was startling. A spirit promised to communicate with me
alone, and named day and place, but never did so. It does
not inspire awe, but rather heightens the spirits and produces a gay humour.

Here, in a private letter, we have evidence that indeed Bulwer
did believe in "brownies or fairies," whom he was willing to
consider responsible for the manifestations rather than the
spirits of the dead. Madame Home was not so far off. Moreover, the accuracy of the answers to his questions left Bulwer
somewhat shaken:

I have been interested in the spirit manifestations. They are
astounding, but the wonder is that they go so far and no
farther. To judge by them, even the highest departed spirits
discovered seem to have made no visible progress—to be as
uncertain and contradicting as ourselves or more so—still
with answers that take away one's breath with wonder.
There is no trick, but I doubt much whether all be more
than some strange clairvoyance passing from one human
brain to another, or if spirits, something analogous to fairies
or genii. Emily [his daughter who had died in 1848 in tragic
circumstances, neglected and yet persecuted by both her
warring parents] comes often, generally most incoherent,
as when, poor thing, she died, but I asked her the last name
she thought of, and she answered Carl Ritter [the name of
a young German with whom she had thought herself in
love]. No Medium can know that, and the question was
only put in thought. Shakespeare has come to me, and gave
me most thrilling advice as to the future and other predictions. Afterwards he came again and flatly contradicted
himself; yet I asked him to prove that he was a good spirit
sent by God, by telling me the closest secret I have, and
he gave it instantly! Still, whatever these communicants be,

as yet they "palter with us in a double sense," do not enlarge our knowledge, and I doubt if any practical end can be gained. I shall now in all probability dismiss for ever these researches. Their interest is too absorbing for human life and true wisdom.[53]

Far from "dismissing for ever" the experiments with spiritualism, Bulwer returned to them again and again. But preserved in this letter are apparently some of the events of the séances whose records—according to Madame Home—Home did not keep and Bulwer did not publish. Despite his fascination and the strong challenge to his doubts, we find him saying in effect exactly what he had said about the clairvoyants: miraculous, but *cui bono?* Just as the somnambules were unable to solve a single scientific problem, so the spirits "palter" with us, "do not enlarge our knowledge," and serve no practical end. He had struck a similar note of scepticism in a letter of 1854 (before he had met Home) to Lady Combermere, one of the leading fashionable amateurs of the occult, and later one of Home's patrons. To the "childish" question, what can be causing the phenomena if not spirits?, the only answer can be the one "a sensible savage" would give about the electric telegraph, "We don't know yet." And if they are spirits, "or beings of material tho' invisible form—such as animalcules, with which Creation abounds," they need not necessarily be wicked, nor yet necessarily benign.

There may be intermediate beings of mixed nature, not deliberately evil, nor steadily benevolent—capricious, uncertain, and only able to get at crude and imperfect *rapport* with humanity. They may amuse themselves with taking feigned names, and sporting with mortal credulity, and be delusive and erring advisers without any settled motive. . . . I believe that . . . whatever they be, they serve no useful purpose nor will conduce to any higher knowledge. They may be very injurious to ordinary understandings and very disappointing to the highest.

If they appeared to "persons of powerful will and moral

courage" perhaps they might be controlled, and so help "to increase our powers over nature," and also incidentally help us find out what they really were. But they never do appear to such people, only "to sensitive or timid persons whose reason they disorder; or to calm lethargic persons like the ordinary Media, whom they don't influence at all," or to people who give up the whole effort because they are frightened at the first communication. There are obviously "agencies of communication which no philosophy has yet solved, but which bear out the universal and immemorial traditions of mankind, and are analogous to the boasted powers which the philosophical magician of old assumed; and some of them, such as the later Platonists—Agrippa, Albertus Magnus &c.—with a degree of earnest detail which the gravity of their characters and their general observation of science and nature do not permit candid inquirers to dismiss as invented lies." Here we find the affection for medieval authorities of which Madame Home complains, together with the strong doubts as to the value of the spiritualist operation, and some sort of effort to generalize about the physiology of the sensitive.

Madame Home tells us that an account of the Ealing séance mentioning Bulwer by name was sent "by Mr. Benjamin Coleman to a Spiritualist Journal." This I have not traced, but at a later date Bulwer did write a stiff letter to Mr. Coleman, who was clearly a believer in spiritualism and who had wanted to quote in print part of a previous communication from Bulwer that would have suggested that Bulwer too accepted the manifestations. Coleman was absolutely restricted now to expressing Bulwer's views—if at all—only in the following words, expressly sent him for the purpose:

> I volunteer no opinion as to the phenomena exhibited by professional exhibitors receiving money [Note: this would not include Home, who never took money]. . . . Some of the phenomena produced, where the person called a Medium is a person of well-known probity and honor [Note: this would probably represent Bulwer's view of Home] and

those present are of equally high character, I believe to be genuine. All such phenomena, when submitted to the same laws of rational evidence, which are adopted in Courts of Law as scientific investigation, are found to disprove the wild notion that they are produced by the spirits of the dead or by any cause whatever, to be called spiritual in the proper meaning of the word. Tho' the persons producing such phenomena may not be deceivers, the phenomena are eminently deceptive; they may have interest to a physiologist or philosopher beyond the gratification of curiosity. But the intellectual results of any careful examination of them are so poor and meagre, and they so belong to abnormal and exceptional physical organisation that the man who is best fitted to investigate their nature would probably be much better occupied in other pursuits; and the credulous and indiscriminate temper with which persons even of good education and ability gather round these revivals of the ancient magic which has in former ages duped the human mind, is likely to do much harm, unsettle rational beliefs, engender senseless superstition; and my advice to anyone who is not of philosophical mind and habits, would be to trouble his head as little as possible about the matter.[54]

There was precious little comfort here for the convinced spiritualist, and none for the Homes.

In 1869, the London Dialectical Society conducted a formal investigation into spiritualism, and, in addition to appointing subcommittees to look into the phenomena, solicited correspondence from individuals supposed to be knowledgeable on the subject. Bulwer, now an old man, replied (February 28, 1869) in a way that shows how unchanged his views remained down to within a few years of his death:

I am unable to offer any suggestions as to a scientific examination of the phenomena which you classify under the name of "Spiritualism," for the data requisite to science are not yet attainable. So far as my experience goes, the phenomena, when freed from the imposture with which their exhibition abounds, and examined rationally, are traceable to material influences, of the nature of which we are ignorant. They require certain physical organisations or temperaments to produce them, and vary according to these organizations or temperaments. Hence, Albertus Magnus says that a man must be born a magician, i.e., born with certain physical idiosyncrasies, which no study can acquire.

In those constitutional idiosyncrasies, whether the phenomena exhibited through or by them be classed under the name of clairvoyance, spirit manifestation, or witchcraft, I have invariably found a marked comparative preponderance of the electric fluid; and the phenomena are more or less striking in proportion to the electricity of the atmosphere. Hence the most notable exhibitions appear to have been obtained in the dry winter nights of New York.

I should say that if any number of sound thinking persons wish to investigate these phenomena, they should commence by dismissing all preconceived judgments, and in a temper utterly free from credulity; and, above all, be very careful not to jump to the conclusions that spirits of another world are concerned in the matter! They who adopt that opinion stop all genuine scientific inquiry, and are apt to be led into very dangerous and mischievous errors of conduct. They are deceived into believing that they hear predictions and receive counsels from beings wiser than themselves, and, acting accordingly, may readily be duped into disgrace and ruin. I have known such instances.

It is now as in the days of Mediaeval witchcraft, in which the supposed fiends juggled and betrayed the invoker; where one truth is announced through these abnormal media, 100 lies are uttered; people are, as in dreams, apt to remember the truth and forget the lies. And as to the responses obtained, emanating from wiser intellects than are vouchsafed to the living, it is noticeable that triviality and inanity are the prevalent characteristics of the revelations, and not one thought has been put forth by them which was not in the world before.

To those who believe that they are conferring with the spirits of the dead, I would only say, "Let them be as rigid in their cross-examination of these pretended souls departed as they would be in that of a claimant of their property on the ground of identity with some heir-at-law long missing," and the communicants will soon break down, and be condemned as impostors by any practical jury.

The word "Spiritualism" should not be admitted in rational inquiry. Natural agencies are apparent in all the phenomena (at least so far as I have witnessed them) ascribed to spirits.

If matter be moved from one end of the room to the other, it must be by a material agency—though it may be as invisible as an electric or odic fluid—and the matter of a human brain is always needed to convey any impression to the auditor or spectator.

If an inquiry were instituted in the rational spirit with which metaphysics, mechanics, and physiology are studied, it is possible that some useful discoveries may be made; in any other mode of inquiry my persuasion is, that the result will be disappointment to real philosophers, and only conducive to the increase of profitless and mischievous superstition.

We have quoted the letter in full because it so thoroughly expressed the disillusionment that Bulwer wished the public to believe he felt after all the time and energy he had devoted to the occult: "triviality and inanity" were all the spirits —or whatever else they might be—had to offer. It is little wonder that even Madame Home, determined to keep up her attack on Bulwer, found herself forced to quote (without admitting that she was abbreviating) only the less devastating passages from this letter, in the hope that her readers would not refer to its original publication, but would instead, as she urged them to do, "read between the lines of Lord Lytton's cautious admissions" to see that after all he really did believe in the spirits, and was merely displaying "all the reticence of a man who throughout his life dreaded nothing so much as ridicule." [55]

Before leaving the topic of Bulwer's interest in spiritualism, we should note one more of Madame Home's claims, this time with regard to his short story, "The Haunters and the Haunted," which first appeared anonymously in *Blackwood's* in 1859. Calling it "singular" and "powerful," Madame Home declares that in it

> Lytton has unintentionally furnished evidence, both of the extent to which he had been impressed by his séances with Home, and of the wild conjectures with which his romantic imagination busied itself concerning the agencies at work to produce the wonders he had witnessed. Half the phenomena described by the solitary watcher in the haunted house—the luminous form collapsing gradually into a vivid globule, the loud measured knocks at the bed-head, the vibrations of the floor, the grasp of an unseen hand, the hand emerging from under the table to seize the letters on it, the multitude of fiery sparks that flitted through the darkness —read like a transcript of Lord Lytton's records of his séances with Home at Knebworth and in London. . . . the material phenomena of those séances have never been more graphically and powerfully described than in "The Haunters and the Haunted." But, even as a fiction, the Blackwood story was spoiled by the incoherent and unsatisfactory pages with which it closed. Lytton did wisely, in republishing it, to cut out the figure of the mesmerist-magician, and to leave the reader in the company of the haunted house and its sights and sounds, without attempting to set forth the extraordinary theory that phenomena similar to many which he had witnessed at the séances of Home might be produced by such an inadequate agent as the human will.[56]

Poor Madame Home. Indeed "The Haunters and the Haunted"—which was published with the subtitle "Or, The House and the Brain," and which has always been regarded as one of the best Victorian stories of the supernatural—does contain a whole battery of phenomena similar to those which Home commonly produced. They had impressed Bulwer, as we have seen: the firm handshake from the spirit that had inspired *Zanoni* had brought him to his feet with a start, and who can wonder?—but Home had no patent on such manifestations. Alas, they were all or almost all part of the regular bag of tricks of all mediums, and they were equally part of the necessary frightening accompaniment for ghost stories. Bulwer cheerfully admitted that he could not understand how they were done; but he hardly owed Home an acknowledgment when he used them in fiction. "The Haunters and the Haunted" is a straightforward story—therein lies its effectiveness—of a dreadful night in a house alleged to be haunted. A bold man, his dog, and his brave and faithful servant are terrified at the manifestations, the servant fleeing, the dog dying, and the narrator barely surviving to tell the tale, despite his long experience of the marvelous and his announced theory—which we have learned in *Zanoni*—that "the Supernatural is the Impossible, and that what is called supernatural is only a something in the laws of nature of which we have hitherto been ignorant."

On the Continent, the narrator declares, "you will still find magicians who assert that they can raise spirits." Even if they can, the magician himself is always present, and the phenomena come through him, as they come through a medium in spiritualism and a mesmerist in mesmerism. But the appearance in the haunted house, in the *absence* of human beings, of a "Darkness" (very like the Dweller of the Threshold) and of other manifestations brings terror even to this sophisticated theorizer. He eventually puts a stop to them by sheer will power, and is sure that if he could get to the bottom of the matter a human agency would prove to have been involved: "...there may be a power akin to mesmerism, and superior to it—the power that in the old days was called Magic....a rare power...which might be given to constitutions with certain peculiarities, and cultivated by practice to an extraordinary degree." It might even extend over the dead, and "compel...a phantom" not of the soul, but "of what has been most earth-stained on earth," to appear. Still it would not be supernatural. It would be but the eidolon of the dead form. Hence, like the best-attested stories of ghosts or spirits, the thing that most strikes us is the absence of what we hold to be soul—that is, of superior emancipated intelligence. They come for little or no object—they seldom speak, if they do come; they utter no ideas above that of an ordinary person on earth.

The volumes that the American spirit-seers have published, purporting to be what Shakespeare and other great men have said as spirits, are "wondrously inferior" to what the great men said when alive and never "contain an idea that was not on earth before." The phenomena

> are but ideas conveyed somehow or other (we have not yet discovered the means) from one mortal brain to another. Whether in so doing, tables walk of their own accord, or fiend-like shapes appear in a magic circle, or bodyless hands rise and remove material objects, or a Thing of Darkness, such as presented itself to me, freeze our blood—still I am persuaded that these are but agencies conveyed, as by electric wires, to my own brain from the brain of another.... But ... the chemical wonders ... the electric wonders ... are alike objectless, puerile, purposeless, frivolous. They lead on to no grand results; and therefore the world does not heed, and true sages have not cultivated them.

So the narrator insists that a powerful, malignant, and destructive brain had set loose the terror that had killed the dog, and might have killed a man without the will to resist the terror. Ten years before Bulwer wrote to the Dialectical Society, then, he had set forth in a short story, often in identical words, the same theory of supernatural manifestation that he would later formulate in his public letter.

Investigation in the haunted house reveals that, some thirty-five years before, a wicked woman and her wicked husband had murdered her brother there, and later caused the death of his child in the house by brutal mistreatment. The male murderer had later died at sea, and the female had lost the money for which she had committed the crime and had returned to live at its scene, where she had recently died. The new owner of the house naturally decides to destroy the room from which the manifestations had emanated. Below it he and the narrator find a hidden room with a safe containing crystal bottles of "colourless volatile essences, of what nature I shall say no more than that they were not poisons. . . . There were also some very curious glass tubes, and a small pointed rod of iron, with a large lump of rock-crystal, and another of amber—also a loadstone of great power." In one of the drawers is a miniature portrait of a man, with a serpentlike face, ruthless and powerful.

At this point in the original (*Blackwood's*) version, the narrator recognizes the portrait as representing a rich, noble, and profligate sixteenth-century occultist who had died accused of capital crimes before the law had caught up with him. The proprietor of the haunted house also recognizes the portrait, but as that of a man he himself had known a few years before in India as the wicked adviser of a Rajah. But the portrait contains an inscription dated 1765, signed with the name of "a dazzling charlatan, who had made a great sensation in London for a year or so, and had fled the country on the charge of a double murder within his own house— that of his mistress and his rival." So the sixteenth-century profligate had not died, but had survived as an eighteenth-century charlatan and a nineteenth-century adventurer in India. As Bulwer first wrote "The Haunters and the Haunted," then, the source of the villainy was to have been a man with a Zanoni-like (or Cagliostro-like) gift of immortality.

In another drawer of the safe is discovered a

very singular apparatus in the nicest order. Upon a small thin book, or rather tablet, was placed a saucer of crystal . . . filled with a clear liquid—on that liquid floated a kind of compass, with a needle shifting rapidly round, but instead of the usual points of the compass were seven strange characters, not very unlike those used by astrologers to denote the planets. A very peculiar, but not strong or dis-

pleasing odour came from the drawer, which was lined with
... hazel.... It produced ... a creeping tingling sensation
from the tips of the fingers to the roots of the hair.

When the narrator takes hold of the saucer to remove it so
that he may examine the tablet, he has a shock, drops the
saucer, spills the liquid, breaks the saucer. The walls shake.
The tablet proves to contain a single sheet of thick vellum
with a Latin inscription within a double pentacle, cursing the
house and all the dwellers therein. The curse is now ended,
and thereafter people can live in the house undisturbed. Here
the story ends, in all published versions but the first.

The *Blackwood's* version continued past this point with a
long additional episode in which the original of the portrait
actually appears in London. He is an Orientalist and a great
mesmerist, whose will can make a piece of paper follow his
directions and who can affect the weather. As an amateur of
the occult, the narrator knows a password to which this mysterious figure must respond. So the narrator puts to him his
theory that intense malignity may be magically transmitted by
a powerful will to haunt a house with the memory of all the
evil deeds ever done within its walls. The stranger assents.
The narrator produces once more Bulwer's favorite statement
of Albertus Magnus: that a man must be born a magician before he can summon up spirits. Such people have highly
developed powers of will, but are often twisted or perverse,
or sensualists. Could not such a hypothetical magician successfully obtain for himself the power to survive for very
long periods by using his will to arrest the decay of parts of
his body? Could he not then arrange to seem to die occasionally, and then reappear? Charged with having changed
his own identity several times in this way over the centuries,
the stranger puts the narrator into a trance, in which he
thinks he sees a vision of the stranger's eventual death. When
he awakes, the stranger has vanished, leaving the narrator under a magic ban to keep the story secret for three months
thereafter.[57]

In revising the story for publication Bulwer later cut this episode. So he also had to remove both the sixteenth-century and the nineteenth-century incarnations of the villainous figure of the portrait, leaving only the "dazzling charlatan" of the eighteenth century. Thus the element of immortality vanished from the final version, which is the one everybody reads, and "The Haunters and the Haunted" *is* in fact still widely read, in anthologies of ghost stories. One must agree with Madame Home that the story is better without it. But one may conjecture that the real reason for dropping it after the first magazine publication in 1859 was that in 1861 Bulwer began to publish his new novel, *A Strange Story*. In *A Strange Story* this obsessive notion of immortality would crop up again, not this time the immortality of two sages, one benevolent and idealistic and the other learned and dispassionate, but the immortality—as in the first version of "The Haunters and the Haunted"—of a wicked and profligate man. Thriftily excised from the short story, these materials were made to do double duty in the novel.

What we have been dealing with in "The Haunters" is not mere mesmerism or spiritualism, though some of the external phenomena have a strong resemblance, but, as Bulwer has told us, magic. All the equipment found in the safe in the hidden room under the floor is magic equipment. The spirits that walk unquiet are spirits raised by magical means, a powerful will exerting a malignant influence, in this case through a written curse and the machinery to make it effective. On the Continent, as the narrator declares, "you will find magicians who assert that they can raise spirits." And this was no mere bit of atmospheric window-dressing intended to make the effect of "The Haunters" more powerful. One could indeed find such men on the Continent, and they could find one in England. We do not know—and we would not expect to know—all about Bulwer's dealings with magicians, but by good fortune there survives at least the partial record of his relations with one magician, the extraordinary Frenchman who called himself Éliphas Lévi, though that was not his real name.

Alphonse-Louis Constant (1810–1875), born of a working-class family and educated for the priesthood at St.-Sulpice, took sub-deacon's orders, but early fell into irregular habits, became one of the adepts of the Mapah (discussed above in connection with Laurence Oliphant and T. L. Harris), and by the early 1840s found himself in jail for his generally socialist *Bible de la Liberté*, and again in 1847 for *La Voix de la famine*. Having read Swedenborg in prison, and having encountered the notable Polish occultist Hoëné-Wronski (builder of a machine for predicting the future, known as the Prognometer), Constant went completely over to occult studies after the revolution of 1848. He changed his name to Éliphas Lévi, became a well-known magician, and in 1854 made his first visit to London.

Here he was on the whole disappointed with the students of the occult whom he met. "I had letters of introduction," he later wrote,

> for important people who were curious about revelations of the supernatural world. I saw several of them, and found in them, together with a great deal of courtesy, a basic indifference or lack of seriousness. At first, everybody asked prodigies of me, as if I were a charlatan. I was a little discouraged, for, to tell the truth, far from being inclined to initiate others into the mysteries of ceremonial magic, I always was afraid, for myself, of its illusions and tiring aspects. Moreover, these ceremonies require apparatus that is expensive and difficult to assemble. So I shut myself up and studied the high Cabala....

However, there were two Englishmen whom he found friendly and knowledgeable. They were Dr. John Ashburner, whom we have met as a mesmerist and spiritualist, and Sir E. Bulwer Lytton, author of *Zanoni*. Lévi's biographer, himself an occultist, adds that "the great novelist knew how to appreciate the vast knowledge of the Master, and became his friend," and tells us also that Lévi himself for the first time received the "baptism of Light" in London. Precise details of this ceremony are naturally not communicated to us.

But another impressive one is fortunately preserved intact in the words of the Master himself. One day a note was brought to him at his hotel, containing half of a card diagonally cut in two and bearing the seal of Solomon, together with a small piece of paper saying, "Tomorrow at three o'clock, in front of Westminster Abbey, you will receive the other half of this card." At the appointed time and place, Lévi found a carriage waiting, and when he responded to the footman's invitation to enter it, he saw a lady in black with a long thick veil, who produced the other half of the card. They drove off; she unveiled, and proved to be an elderly woman with gray eyebrows and "bright black eyes of a strange fixed gaze." She had heard, she said, from a lady who was a friend of Sir B***** L*****, that Lévi had been refusing to perform experiments: perhaps he would change his mind upon seeing her completely equipped magic room. Recognizing her as a lady of high rank, and solemnly promising to maintain the strictest secrecy, Lévi found that she did indeed have a good collection of the necessary equipment and was soon persuaded to try, at her house, a "complete evocation." The preparations, all of which we know in full detail, occupied three full weeks, and on the fateful day Lévi actually prepared to evoke the spirit of none other than Apollonius of Tyana, who was to be asked two questions—one for himself, and the other for Bulwer's friend's friend, the noble lady with the piercing black eyes.

Between July 20 and 26, 1854, Lévi successfully conducted various preliminary evocations: during one of them the spirit of Apollonius sent him a message telling where in London to find the manuscript of a Greek ritual written by Apollonius that should be read aloud at the major ceremony (Lévi later published the text). And on July 26, with the white marble altar properly engraved with a gilded pentagram and covered with a new lamb's fleece, and with the proper mixture of ingredients burning in two copper chafing dishes on tripods, Lévi in his magician's robes, amid the smoke and flame, uttered the proper chant, and—after the floor had duly trembled—the shape appeared, a man "wrapped in a sort of shroud." At first offended by the drawn naked sword of the necromancer, the spirit vanished, but it came back when Lévi put the sword down. But the effort had been too great: with sore and swollen arm, Lévi fainted away before he could put the questions to the spirit, although he thought he had been given the answers silently: the lady's friend, about whom she had wished information, was dead; and the possibility of a reconciliation between Lévi and his wife, about which he had planned to inquire, was dead too.

As for Lévi, he felt dreadful. Nonetheless, he summoned Apollonius twice more and obtained "the revelation of two cabalistic secrets, which if they were known to the general public could in a short time change the bases and laws of society as a whole." Yet, Lévi declares, he could not positively affirm that he had actually evoked, seen, and touched the great Apollonius. His efforts, he says, may have intoxicated his imagination: he had always been impressionable. The practice of evocations, however, is surely dangerous and harmful, and bad for the health if indulged in too often. As for the elderly lady, she gave Lévi a lot of trouble afterward, and sometimes seemed not quite right in her head.

Though Bulwer was not present on this occasion, it has seemed appropriate to describe it summarily, because the lady who persuaded Lévi to undertake it was a friend of a friend of Bulwer's (Sir B***** L*****), and also because when Lévi paid a second visit to England, in May 1861, he attempted another evocation despite his professed reluctance, this time on the roof of the Pantheon, a large shop in Regent Street. We have no details of this performance, but we do know that Bulwer was present; so we must perforce imagine that it was something like the earlier ceremony, whose details we do know so precisely. The interval between the two visits to England Lévi had spent in producing large and learned books on magic and witchcraft; on his visit to Knebworth, he gave Bulwer inscribed presentation copies of these. With Lévi was one of his Polish associates from Paris, Count Alexander Branicki, who had already visited Knebworth in 1856 with Daniel Dunglas Home. Lévi's biographer suggests that there was a connection between Lévi's visit there in May 1861 and the appearance the next year of *A Strange Story*.

Indeed, we shall find much magic in that novel, which may well owe something to Lévi's alleged experiments with Bulwer in Regent Street, and to the full descriptions of magic rites in Lévi's books, which we now know that Bulwer had in his possession while the novel was appearing serially. In the magical rites Bulwer describes in *A Strange Story* we find much to remind us of Éliphas Lévi's own account of his evocation of Apollonius of Tyana. And once, apropos of the desirability of having a multiple of three persons present at a magical ceremony (what authorities on the occult call *"le ternaire"*), Bulwer in a footnote quotes Lévi directly but without naming him:

> ... the author of Dogme et rituel de la Haute Magie ... a book less remarkable for its learning than for the earnest belief of a scholar of our own day in the reality of the art of which he records the history—insists much on the necessity of rigidly observing Le Ternaire in the number of persons who assist in an enchanter's experiments.

Once again we note the typical Bulwerian ambivalence: he has gone to the top of the Pantheon with a man to evoke Apollonius of Tyana (whom he had mocked thirty years before), and he has read the man's books with great care; but in published comment he will indicate only his scorn for a learned chap who can take such things seriously. Like Elliotson or Home, Lévi could count on Bulwer's patronage only in private.[58]

The suggestion that Bulwer was the leader of a London Club founded in 1861 for the practical teaching of magic, which included "the most ardent and enterprising as well as some of the most advanced scholars in mesmerism and 'ceremonial magic," must alas, be rejected, since its purported source, the Mahatma K. H. (Kut Humi), seems in fact never to have existed, and the whole idea to be simply a final posthumous tribute paid to Bulwer by that determined and imaginative admirer, Madame Blavatsky.[59]

5 / A Strange Story (*1862*): *a Commentary*

In 1860 Bulwer began to write *A Strange Story*. Like *Zanoni*, it was inspired by a dream, which Bulwer's son called "even more interesting and striking than the longer story which was afterwards founded upon it." While Bulwer was writing it, Dickens pressingly invited him to contribute a novel to *All the Year Round*, and by December 1860 had enthusiastically agreed to publish *A Strange Story* on most generous terms. It appeared in *All the Year Round* from August 10, 1861, to March 8, 1862, and was published in two volumes by Blackwood early in 1862. In recent years it has received more critical attention than *Zanoni*, but even its most sympathetic student has misunderstood or only partly understood what Bulwer was trying to say.[60] The vogue for supplying each chapter with an epigraph, still strong in the days of *Zanoni*, had by now disappeared; but Bulwer did provide a motto for the title page, which was intended to set the tone for the novel:

> To doubt and to be astonished is to recognize our ignorance.
> Hence it is that the lover of wisdom is in a certain sort a
> lover of mythi (*philomythos pōs*) for the subject of mythi
> is the astonishing and marvellous.
> Sir W. Hamilton (after Aristotle) *Lectures on Meta-*
> *physics*. Vol. I, p. 78.

The narrator, Allen Fenwick, a young doctor of good family and position, comes to the country town of L_____ to take up the practice of an elderly colleague Julius Faber, who is retiring to travel abroad. In L_____, where those of birth and privilege live in a tight social circle centering on Abbey Hill, Fenwick's chief medical competitor is the much older Dr. Lloyd, who enjoys the patronage of the Hill. Not only does Fenwick find Lloyd inadequate in medical consul-

tations, but he also scorns him for being a follower of
Puységur, "not only an enthusiastic advocate of mesmerism,
as a curative process, but an ardent believer of the reality of
somnambular clairvoyance as an invaluable gift of certain
privileged organizations." For his own part, Fenwick is a
pupil of Broussais in medicine and of Condillac in metaphysics,
accepting nothing without evidential proof, including specifically the existence of the human soul, which can be deduced
only from revelation, not from science. To Fenwick, death
means the end of body and mind, and as for the soul, he dis-
believes in its existence. Proud of his medical successes and
his physical good health, Fenwick engages in pamphlet controversy with Lloyd, and has the best of it. Abbey Hill, obey-
ing its social leader, Mrs. Colonel Poyntz, shifts its patronage
to Fenwick, and Lloyd, sinking into illness and poverty, summons Fenwick finally to his deathbed, where he denounces
him and predicts his punishment: "In those spaces which
your sight has disdained to explore, you shall yourself be a
lost and bewildered straggler. . . . The gibbering phantoms are
gathering round you."

Though shaken, Fenwick salves his conscience by contributing generously to help Lloyd's orphaned children. But a
local magistrate, Vigors, Lloyd's cousin and himself an ex-
perimenter in "electric biology," continues to blame Fenwick
for Lloyd's ruin and death. And Vigors is related also to Mrs.
Gilbert Ashleigh, who soon moves in to Lloyd's former
house, with her beautiful eighteen-year-old daughter Lilian,
an heiress, whom Fenwick—now hoping to find a wife—first
glimpses deep in reverie amid the ruins of the Abbey in the
garden of her new home. He falls in love with her at once:
she reminds him of "The Maiden from Abroad," a famous
German poem he has read in his youth, "variously supposed
to be an allegory of Spring, or of Poetry," which is of course
by Schiller, and which Bulwer had translated. But Lilian is
frail: Fenwick is summoned to her bedside, in the very room
in which Dr. Lloyd had died. He finds her hysterical but

physically sound, nervously impressionable but not consumptive. He attributes her illness to perfume from rank flowers and to fatigue, and prescribes matter-of-fact remedies. But Lilian is deeply moved by "objects in nature, rural sounds, by music, by the books she reads," and since childhood she has had visions during her reveries although she had never been permitted to talk about them. She is "one of the elfin people." Soon Fenwick's enemy, Vigors, persuades Mrs. Ashleigh to have another doctor and they consult a clairvoyant, who fears Lilian is consumptive.

Fenwick's punishment has begun. We are by now familiar enough with Bulwer's ideas to recognize in Lilian one of those natures he believed to be peculiarly susceptible to occult influences of all kinds. Through the influence of Mrs. Poyntz Fenwick is taken back as Lilian's doctor, but he finds his patient unaccountably feeble at times, mysterious, childlike, innocent, self-absorbed, inconsiderate. He looks forward to the day when her "intellect and heart will ultimately . . . blend in . . . the perfection of union." She tells him that at the moment he first saw her she was having a vision in which her dead father told her that she and Fenwick "would have need of one another," and that her subsequent illness had been caused by the appearance between her and Fenwick of

> a vague dusky vapour, undulous and coiling like a serpent, nothing of its shape and figure definite, but of its face one abrupt glare, a flash from two dread luminous eyes, and a young head like the Medusa's, changing . . . into a grinning skull.

The down-to-earth Fenwick declines to listen to her talk of such apparitions—familiar to all acquaintances of Glyndon —and continues to work on his book, *Inquiry into Organic Life,* which will include a chapter on "Cheats of the Senses and Spectral Phantasms." Death turns us all to dust, he insists, and he so stoutly believes it that even when he hears a sigh and sees something like a phantom of Lilian at the very moment he says it, he plans only to include the anecdote in his book.

Even while Lilian is away on a visit arranged by Vigors in the hope that she will fall in love with a rival suitor, Fenwick cannot steer clear of the supernatural. The steward of a neighboring absentee landlord, Sir Philip Derval, has a stroke after seeing what he takes to be his master's apparition; Fenwick declares it epilepsy. At Mrs. Poyntz's, Fenwick learns that Derval—who has lived abroad for years—has recently been in Syria inquiring into the murder there of a noted benevolent sage, Haroun of Aleppo, and into the subsequent disappearance from Haroun's house of an Englishman, Louis Grayle, an elderly, rich, but wicked amateur of the occult, who had been socially ostracized and legally exiled after a murder more than forty years before.

And soon Fenwick meets the new arrival in L_____, a certain Margrave, of quite unusual attractions:

> Never have I seen human face so radiant as that young man's.... an indefinable something that simply dazzles.... In the features themselves there was no faultless regularity ... stature ... about the middle height. But the effect of the whole was not less transcendent. Large eyes, unspeakably lustrous; a most harmonious colouring; and the form itself so critically fine that the welded structure of its sinews was best shown in the lightness and grace of its movements. His vein of talk ... peculiar, off-hand, careless, shifting from topic to topic with a bright rapidity.... In one sentence he showed that he had mastered some late discovery by Faraday or Liebig; in the next ... he was talking the wild fallacies of Cardan or Van Helmont.

In fact, Margrave wants Fenwick to perform experiments in order to "replenish or preserve to each special constitution the special substance" that it needs to keep its health in balance. There must be a single vital principle, and a way of discovering the secret of supplying it. When Fenwick rejects the notion as "the old illusion of the mediaeval empirics,"

Margrave reverts to Van Helmont, who discovered gases: the vital principle must surely be a gas.

But he breaks off the discussion to greet the sun in a strange chant, a Persian fire-worshipper's hymn he had learned in the East. Then he rushes up a tree in pursuit of a squirrel; it bites him, and he furiously wrings its neck and tramples on its corpse. He shows as little concern when he carelessly drops and hurts a child he has been carrying on his shoulders. Healthier than the savages, he likes to dive into streams like an otter and catch fish. "Man! Man!" he says to Fenwick; "Could you live one hour of my life you would know how horrible a thing it is to die." And he bursts into tears. Exerting extraordinary charm, he is rich, fascinating, and fickle. He is eagerly seeking a rare discovery (the local clairvoyants are no good), someone "in whom the gift of the Pythoness is stored, unknown to the possessor, undetected by the common observer, but the signs of which should be as apparent to the modern physiologist as they were to the ancient priest." In such a person, with the perfect gift of "unveiled, lucent sight,"

> he who knows how to direct and profit by it should be able to discover all that he desires to know for the guidance and preservation of his own life. He will be forewarned of every danger, forearmed in the means by which danger is avoided. For the eye of the true Pythoness has no obstruction, space no confines, time no measurement.

Fenwick would just as soon search for a unicorn.[61]

Trained Bulwerians as we are, we can now see what his dramatic plan for the novel is to be: Margrave—whom we already suspect of being the aged Louis Grayle, murderer of the Arab sage Haroun, rejuvenated by some elixir—is animal vigor and conscienceless selfishness incarnate, and is determined to remain immortal. When he fails to get Fenwick's help as a chemist, he describes exactly the clairvoyant Pythoness (oracle of the Pythian Apollo, speaking in a trance) he needs in order to gain for himself the powers that Zanoni and Mejnour possessed. And the characteristics he seeks—familiar from our explorations of clairvoyance with Bulwer—are all possessed by Lilian, the innocent visionary girl, whom Margrave has not yet met. In his stubborn refusal to see anything not supported by hard scientific evidence, in his inability to search for unicorns and Pythonesses, the able Fenwick is bringing upon himself the punishment that his defeated and dying mesmerist rival, Dr. Lloyd, had foretold.

Whereas heat, following the ancient tradition, was the vital principle of the sages in *Zanoni*, gas (etymologically derived from "chaos") had been proclaimed by Jean Baptiste Van Helmont (1579–1644) in a sharp break from his predecessors and contemporaries, and is here put forward by Margrave. *A Strange Story* is thus putting into fictional terms what Bulwer would soon assert in the essay "On Essay-Writing," which we have already cited: that modern scientists were again quoting Van Helmont with respect, and that they were gradually recognizing the wisdom of the ancient mystics whom they had hitherto treated with contempt. In a long footnote in *A Strange Story*, Bulwer quotes a passage from Liebig's *Organic Chemistry*, in which Liebig ironically indicates that to accept certain contemporary views would be to agree with Van Helmont—which of course Liebig himself does not. And Bulwer adds that Van Helmont, in announcing the importance of gas, also rejected materialism and proclaimed the necessity of profound Christian faith. We find Bulwer's view confirmed in the words of the leading modern authority on Van Helmont:

> ...he regards Life as a direct emanation from God and therefore not only the noblest but also the only subject which opens the way to scientific and at the same time to eternal truth. Van Helmont's biological bent is due to his religious zeal, and his scientific achievement is the fruit of his religious conviction.

A Strange Story, then, taking place in Bulwer's own day, is to be a novel of the occult set in the framework of nineteenth-century science and religion, as contrasted with *Zanoni*, set in the framework of eighteenth-century illuminism and revolution.[62]

At the house of the absent Sir Philip Derval—last heard of investigating Haroun's murder—Margrave persuades the housekeeper to let him in; and she reports to Fenwick that Margrave has carefully examined the books in Derval's library. These are "Iamblichus and Plotinus; Swedenborg and Behmen [i.e., Jacob Boehme]; Sandivogius, Van Helmont, Paracelsus, Cardan." A small study nearby has an inscription recording the discoveries there of a seventeenth-century astrologer and soothsayer, Simon Forman. Still unsuspecting, Fenwick jokingly asks Margrave if "the Rosicrucians" have "bequeathed him an elixir of life," and once again Margrave—who denies it, but believes the secret is a gas (Phosoxygen)—vainly tries to bribe Fenwick into performing experiments under direction, and turns "sinister, wrathful, menacing" when Fenwick refuses.

At a great ball given by the Mayor of L_____ to celebrate the opening of a museum of specimens collected by the late Dr. Lloyd, Fenwick encounters Sir Philip Derval in person. Himself learned in the occult, Derval tries to persuade Fenwick that the study of mesmerism

> may enable you to perceive the truth that lies hid in the powers ascribed to witchcraft; benevolence is but a weak agency compared to malignancy; magnetism perverted to evil may solve [i.e., lie at the root of] half the riddles of sorcery.

Fenwick has been too hasty in deriding clairvoyant phenomena: "trance is as essential a condition of being as sleep or waking.... [it] is producible in every human being however unimpressionable to mere mesmerism."

And Derval distinguishes three kinds of trance: the ordinary mesmeric state, to which animals are susceptible; the mental trance, in which the mind, with the force of a projectile, sends forth its emanation intensely and over great distances, just as the waking imagination travels, but more intensely (Bulwer's own theory, as we have seen, in "The Clairvoyance of the Imagination"); and the spiritual trance, in which the soul entirely supersedes the action of the mind. Fenwick refuses to believe that he could be put into a trance, or to make a distinction between the mind and the soul; but Derval insists that the threefold distinction between human animal, mental, and spiritual existence is exactly parallel to that between the solid, liquid, and gaseous states of matter. And just as it is *heat* that changes matter from one to another form, so heat ("the occult agency of the whole natural world") determines which of the three human states prevails.

Derval is in England to pursue a monster—Margrave. An Arab girl *clairvoyante* has shown him where Margrave is, and revealed that Fenwick will help in the pursuit. Astonished, Fenwick brings Margrave to Derval, who puts them both into a trance. Fenwick sees Margrave-Grayle as he had been three years earlier in Haroun's house in Aleppo—aged, withered, vicious. Fenwick's vision extends to the inside of Margrave's brain, and in it he beholds flashes of light in three colors: red signifying the animal nature, pale azure the intellectual nature, and a silvery color the spiritual nature. All about him in the museum he can see that even the stuffed animals have the red and azure but not the silvery flashes. And, while Fenwick watches the flashes in Margrave's brain, he actually sees Margrave's soul depart: "I knew that it was imploring release.... And suddenly the starry spark rose... into space and vanished." The red light burns still, ever more vividly. Margrave's body has been restored to youth by his murder of Haroun and his theft of the elixir, but his soul, unable to bear the crime, has left him. And the azure light of the mind, though still present, has "lost its faculty of continued and concentrated power."

Margrave is then truly what Fenwick has observed, a being with superb animal strength and a good though capricious mind, but with no soul at all. If we were to put it in Freudian terms, we would say that Margrave had retained id and ego but that he had lost his superego. This is a particularly important point for us to stress, since Professor Fradin, a serious modern student of *A Strange Story*, has got it wrong. One of Bulwer's central purposes here (as usual he had several) was to portray a human being who had lost his soul. We have actually seen Margrave's soul leave him: there can be no doubt of what has happened. Not only does the soul *not* remain "inviolate in Margrave, even when surrounded by evil," as Fradin writes: it does not remain at all. The silver spark ascends and disappears. Margrave is soulless now. Fenwick is at last convinced that there is a human soul, as distinct from the human mind.

Apropos of Margrave, Madame Home reports that Bulwer had told her husband that at first he had intended to put a portrait of him into *A Strange Story*, but had later abandoned the plan, and

> substituted for it the fantastic conception of Margrave, ... adding that the original plan [of the novel] differed almost as materially from the course the story actually took as Home's portrait would have differed from that of Margrave.

But the lady goes on to say that

> In forsaking his design of attempting to picture Home, Lytton took from him a single hint—not for the character of Margrave, but for the impression that abnormal being is represented as making on the ordinary mortals who encountered him. All who knew Home were struck by the joyousness of his temper that no wrong could embitter and no sufferings sour.... Home's gaiety and cheerfulness ... exercised an irresistible spell on all around him.... Lytton, like others, had remarked this trait, and he attached it to the outward man of Margrave in "A Strange Story." "Never," he makes Fenwick say ... "have I seen a human face so radiant.... transcendent." The charm of Margrave's conversation is represented as equalling the charm of his

appearance; and here the description is even more closely applicable to Home. "... his vein of talk was peculiar, off-hand, careless, shifting from topic to topic with a bright rapidity." Later in "A Strange Story," we find that Margrave's joyousness is born of his union of splendid health with perfect soullessness, which certainly was not the source of the similar fascination exercised by Home. But Margrave is not Home, nor was meant to be; he is the embodiment of a fancy that takes shape in more than one work of Lytton's —the alchemist's dream of the Elixir of Life. Margrave has renewed his youth with it, and those who read between the lines of "A Strange Story" and "Zanoni" will suspect a fact familiar to some who knew the author of those romances— that Lytton was half-persuaded of the possibility of youth being thus renewed, and had a half-hope that he might one day revive his own.

Naturally enough, Madame Home wishes to claim for her late husband all Margrave's attractive features and none of the sinister ones, and we cannot know to what degree, if any, Bulwer intended Margrave as a portrait of Home. But we can be certain that *if* Bulwer *had* intended to portray Home as Margrave, he would have forestalled reproaches—and, who knows, a suit for libel—by telling Home exactly what Madame Home here reports: that he had planned to try to portray Home, but had given it up. In this way, if Home saw any flattering resemblance to himself in Margrave's external attractions, he would be pleased; and he would not suspect that he himself might also have suggested some of Margrave's sinister qualities. If Home then had suggested animal charm, intellectual febrility, and soullessness to Bulwer, Bulwer would have been free to try to portray them. Leaving out of account Browning's passionate hatred for Home, which was perhaps understandable, we have to reckon also with the fact that Home did arouse strong dislike in many men who had no ostensible reason for it. Dickens, for example, who was by no means a disbeliever in the spirits, and who had himself practiced mesmerism (curing his female patient but arousing his wife's jealousy), once abused Home roundly at a dinner party in Boston (November 7, 1867), using "all the hard names he could lay his tongue to, 'ruffian' and 'scoundrel' being two which I particularly remember." [63] In any case, I think we may safely say that Margrave's portrait contains some of Bulwer's notions of Home.

After his experience in trance, Fenwick agrees to assist Derval in attempting to bring Margrave to justice, but before they can begin to act in concert Derval is murdered, and a casket of medicines that he had obtained in Aleppo is stolen. Derval's heir, an old friend of Fenwick's, invites him to read and edit an autobiographical manuscript that Derval has left. And when Fenwick goes to Derval Court to examine the manuscript, alone in the chamber of Forman, the astrologer, cabalist, and magician, he reads that Derval, in his youth, had read Forman's manuscripts, had continued his apprenticeship in the occult by traveling in the East, and had concluded that

> there does exist an art of magic, distinct from the guile of the conjurer, and applying to certain latent powers and affinities in nature a philosophy akin to that which we receive in our acknowledged schools.

Indeed, Haroun of Aleppo had been the "master of every secret in nature which the nobler or theurgic mind seeks to fathom," and knew the great "Principle of Animal Life" by which all disease can be cured if the organs are not destroyed. Haroun had already three times renewed his own life, but did not intend to do so a fourth time. Alone and melancholy, he had worn out his time on earth. The only man who could

> feel continued joy in continued existence [would be one] who could preserve in perfection the sensual part of man, with such mind or reason as may be independent of the spiritual essence, but whom soul itself has quitted.

This hypothetical being was precisely Margrave, as we have seen, and we have also witnessed his passionate eagerness, in his new youthful state, not to age for a second time. The mythology has changed somewhat from *Zanoni*, where Mejnour, purely intellectual, had indeed been prepared to live to eternity. But *Zanoni* was far more allegorical than *A Strange Story*, and Mejnour was Science incarnate.

Fenwick now comes to the place in Derval's manuscript where Louis Grayle had arrived at Haroun's house at the point of death. From Haroun Grayle had received a drop of elixir in a cup of water, which gave him a brief reprieve. Grayle had talked of his power over evil spirits; had he obtained it soon enough, he would have ruled the world.

> He spoke of means by which his influence could work undetected on the minds of others, control agencies that could never betray, and baffle the justice that could never discover. He spoke vaguely of a power by which a spectral reflection of the material body could be cast, like a shadow, to a distance; glide through the walls of a prison, elude the sentinels of a camp—a power that he asserted to be . . . almost infallible in its effect to seduce or to appal.

Haroun had then told Grayle that "this was the meanest of all abuses of knowledge, rightly abandoned, in all ages, to the vilest natures," and had flatly refused to save Grayle's life. He had also told Derval of instances where the human soul had departed:

> The human animal without soul . . . might ravage and destroy . . . and the moment after would sport in the sunlight harmless and rejoicing because like the serpent and the tiger it is incapable of remorse.

And so we have seen Margrave kill the squirrel and injure the child, and rejoice a moment afterwards.

That Grayle would try to kill Haroun to get the secret elixir Derval had learned from Haroun himself. And indeed, when Derval had left with his casket of medicines (but no elixir) to help sufferers from the plague at Damascus, Haroun had been strangled, and Grayle had disappeared with his two servants, a beautiful Arab woman, and a Hindu member of "that murderous sect of fanatics ... who strangle their unsuspecting victim in the firm belief that they thereby propitiate the favour of the goddess they serve." Derval had concluded that Grayle was Haroun's murderer, and that he still lived, now transformed into a soulless animal, but with the secrets of his black magic as well. Just as Fenwick is about to read further details of "the terrible fate of an Armenian family with three daughters," at the hands of the revived and frightful Grayle, he sees a spectral figure of Margrave, exactly like those Grayle had boasted of being able to produce, and loses consciousness. When Fenwick comes to some hours later, the manuscript has been stolen, but he cannot account for it. And the next morning he is arrested for Derval's murder: the missing casket and the knife have been found in his house. In prison the spectral form of Margrave offers to save Fenwick on conditions unspecified, but Fenwick refuses. And the real Margrave has now obtained familiar entrée to the Ashleighs' house, where Lilian has returned.[64]

The apparition of Margrave which has twice appeared to Fenwick—and which reminds him of the shining corpse, or Scin-Laeca, of Scandinavian legend—now appears for the third time, in Fenwick's prison cell. All Margrave asks is that Fenwick say nothing against him and meet him freely. He does not demand that Fenwick give up Lilian or do anything criminal. Fenwick accepts, and is soon released: Margrave has led the police to Derval's murderer, an escaped homicidal maniac who maintains that he was urged to commit the crime by the Devil in the form of an apparition like that which appeared to Fenwick. The reader realizes that Margrave has managed the murder, obtained the casket, and planted the weapon and the knife in Fenwick's house. When Fenwick emerges from prison, his name cleared, he finds Lilian listless and willing to end their engagement: her peculiar state also is attributable to Margrave's sinister influence. Even the lost autobiographical manuscript by Sir Philip Derval turns up, but with the passages about the murder of Haroun now burned away: the housekeeper, directed by the same apparition of Margrave-Grayle, had stolen it. Baffled and reluctant to believe in the magical aspects of the happenings, Fenwick is cheered by the return to L——— of his old mentor, Dr. Julius Faber.

The fast-moving narrative is now interrupted by the first of several lengthy philosophical dialogues between Fenwick and Faber. Long before the end of the novel—we are at this point about halfway through—these conversations will weary the modern reader, but they are essential to an understanding of Bulwer's own ambivalences about religion, science, and the occult. And this first one succeeds also as a literary device. When it begins, Fenwick's tragic experiences have convinced him against his will that supernatural forces are at work. But Faber successfully argues that "there is nothing here which your own study of morbid idiosyncrasies should not suffice to solve." Fenwick is not insane, but he is under an illusion. With many references to learned books—Beattie's *Essay on Truth*, Müller's *Physiology of the Senses*, Abercrombie on *The Intellectual Powers*, Sir David Brewster's *Letters on Natural Magic*, Newton's letter to Locke on his midnight vision of the spectrum of the sun—Faber succeeds in reawakening Fenwick's natural inclination to accept only rational scientific explanation and to unlearn even his own painful lessons. As with Fenwick, so with the reader, who once again doubts even whether Margrave can be Grayle. At a later stage, when Fenwick and the reader must finally accept the supernatural truth, the horror of it will seem so much the worse.

But Faber is himself puzzlingly inconsistent. So long as the supernatural is evil, he explains it away. On the other hand, he is a "believer in the main divisions of phrenology," and diagnoses Lilian's case in those terms: in Lilian, he says, "ideality, wonder, veneration loom large . . . but they are balanced by other organs, now perhaps dormant, which will come into play as life passes from romance into duty." And Faber is deeply religious: he cannot approve Fenwick's rationalistic book on physiology because Fenwick has left God out of nature, as—in his interpretation of Margrave—he has left the soul out of man. Giving him a Bible and urging him to pray, Faber tells Fenwick he has not enough imagination, while Lilian has too much.

Because he had promised the apparition never to refuse an invitation to meet Margrave, Fenwick now must go to Derval's former house, where Margrave is staying. Margrave has a strange Egyptian cane, with a dark blue unpolished stone in its head, which will cure snakebite; holding it gives Fenwick a singular thrill, and makes him feel lighter. At Margrave's request, Fenwick copies from a book a woodcut fascimile of Solomon's seal, the pentacle in the circle. He need not, says Margrave, "add the astrological characters, they are the senseless superfluous accessories of the dreamer [Éliphas Lévi, perhaps] who wrote the book." And having thus touched the magic wand, and himself traced the mystic figure, Fenwick is summoned once more at two in the morning by the Scin-Laeca, the apparition of Margrave, which proceeds to force him to perform a magical evocation almost exactly like the one that Éliphas Lévi performed, of which we have already examined an account.

Out of the Egyptian cane Margrave's apparition takes a lump of "dark bituminous substance" and a wand of polished steel tipped with a crystal. With the bitumen it draws the pentacle in a nine-foot circle on the floor, and this is set alight; then Fenwick standing in the fiery circle is made to repeat words in an unknown tongue, which he would now not set down again if he could remember them. Dogs howl, the ground trembles, shadows are glimpsed thronging. Terrified and unwilling to continue, Fenwick is just about to be forced to do so by the apparition when he hears Lilian's voice saying "Hold!" and sees her. He throws the wand to the ground and escapes to bed, convinced that it is all an hallucination. In the morning, Margrave has gone away, but the pentacle is still visible on the floor where he had drawn it: it was no dream. The ostensibly passive and indifferent Lilian does love Fenwick; she called out the warning to him in her sleep.

But Lilian now vanishes from L_____, and Fenwick slowly traces her flight on foot to a remote seaside village, to which she is being impelled by suggestion from Margrave, who is planning to escape with her aboard his yacht. Before the two can meet, Fenwick finds and grapples with Margrave, and seizes from his hand the magic wand which had figured in the effort to evoke the spirits and is now being used to draw Lilian to her destination. Its possession gives Fenwick instant power over Margrave, who is compelled to reveal that he has not intended to seduce Lilian, but only to make use of her gifts in trance to force her to discover the secret by which he might have "defied the grave and lived on." She would soon have died. Margrave warns Fenwick that "the fluid which emanates from that wand in the hand of one who envenoms the fluid with his own hatred and rage will prove fatal to my life." So, rather than murder Margrave on the spot, Fenwick does not push his questioning about the magical evocation. He leaves Margrave in a swoon, finds Lilian where she had stopped nearby at the moment Margrave dropped the wand, and takes her home. When she recovers from a three-day illness she loves Fenwick again, and can remember nothing of Margrave, not even his existence.

The whole episode, however, becomes known at L_____, where the gossips have heard of Margrave and his yacht waiting for Lilian, and of course cannot know the true nature of Fenwick's intervention or Lilian's rescue. Unable to persuade the socially powerful Mrs. Poyntz to help him defy the World's disfavor, Fenwick determines to marry Lilian quickly, before she hears the rumors about herself. The night before they are to be married Fenwick uses the wand, whose sexual symbolism in this context is surely inescapable: he has seized it from Margrave, obtained the lady as a result, and thinks of its uses only immediately before his marriage. It is hollow, containing a wire whose unattached end touches the wielder's hand and gives him "an increased consciousness of vital power." By its use Fenwick summons up Margrave's Scin-Laeca, which tells him that Margrave will not remember their conversation when he wakes. It predicts that in the future Margrave will be able to work through Lilian to subdue Fenwick. The apparition will not tell him how "to invoke intelligences higher than mine," and warns him that "in the hands of him who has learned not the art, the wand has its dangers." Remembering *Zanoni*, we surmise that its use by an inexperienced theurgist will bring down upon him a sinister Dweller of the Threshold. Fenwick is no Glyndon; he has not the passionate urge for occult power. When he merely contemplates summoning up a spirit, with the wand in hand, the floors tremble and a mist rises outside the window. And when he hears Lilian singing a "simple sacred song," he does not use the wand further, but drops it carefully into the middle of a nearby lake.[65]

Immediately after the wedding, Lilian receives a poison-pen letter from an anonymous gossipmonger at L_____, warning her not to return. She faints, falls ill, and loses her mind. Though she is gentle and calm, she almost never talks, but does draw pictures like Blake's, and once at least seems to remember the night of the magic evocation by mentioning circles of fire and a veiled woman in black. In the hope that her health may improve, Fenwick and she migrate to Australia, where Faber has already settled. Though Fenwick has defied the spirits, a malicious anonymous letter has ruined his life; it turns out, however, that the sender was directed by Margrave's apparition. Comparing Lilian's disorder to the effect produced on Sir Humphrey Davy by nitrous oxide ("laughing gas"), Faber expects her to recover her mental stability in the future, but to undergo a severe physical illness as a result. The very loss of her faculties of imagination—which Faber praises, just as Bulwer would do in his essay on clairvoyance—has made her physically stronger: when she recovers them, she will be correspondingly weaker.

But Fenwick now positively demands that Faber account

for "facts which you cannot resolve into illusions": Margrave's influence over Lilian, the adventures with the magic wand. To Fenwick's (and our) surprise, Faber answers:

> ... here we approach a ground which few physicians have dared to examine. Honour to those, who, like our bold contemporary Elliotson, have braved scoff and sacrificed dross in seeking to extract what is practical in uses, what can be tested by experiment, from those exceptional phenomena on which magic sought to found a philosophy, and to which philosophy traces the origins of magic.

Though he has not himself experienced the wonders "ascribed to animal magnetism and electrical biology," mankind has always thought that "in some peculiar and rare temperaments [there is] a power over forms of animated organisation, with which they establish some unaccountable affinity; and even ... over inanimate matter." Referring to Descartes, to Sir William Hamilton's *Lectures on Metaphysics and Logic*, and again to Müller's *Physiology of the Senses*, to Chauncey Hare Townshend's *Facts on Mesmerism*, to Maury's *La Magie et l'astrologie dans l'antiquité et au moyen-âge*, to Lord Bacon, Spinoza, Aristotle, Sir David Brewster, and Éliphas Lévi himself, Faber—beginning with the open praise for Elliotson—now voices all the theories we have found Bulwer himself espousing as the result of his own occult investigations: the peculiar sensitivity of certain temperaments, the relationship of the phenomena to electricity, the ability of magicians to provoke hallucinations in other brains, the importance of Van Helmont ("of all the mediaeval mystics ... the most suggestive to the disciplined reasoners of our day") and his emphasis on the independent power of the imagination (Phantasy) to create independently of the senses.

Fenwick properly observes that Faber is now willing to depart from his former insistence on purely naturalistic explanation: Margrave must be one of those "persons endowed with a rare and peculiar temperament," who can "exceed even the powers ascribed to the practitioners of magnetism and electric biology." Perhaps the wand had been dipped in hallucinogenic drugs? Or perhaps iron and crystal have special properties, as yet uninvestigated, that have always made them favorite substances of mystics...? Neither denying nor admitting his obvious shift in position since their last long debate, Faber ends this one by insisting on the necessity of religious faith.

Soon Faber's prediction with regard to Lilian begins to prove true. She slowly recovers her mental powers, but falls alarmingly ill with a chronic fever that nothing seems to cure. Regretting that he had not long ago accepted Margrave's invitation to perform chemical experiments looking for the "one primary essence, one master substance, in which is stored the specific nutriment of life," the desperate Fenwick is ready for any expedient when Margrave appears, emaciated and feeble, having come to Australia in his own ship. From a dervish former pupil of Haroun in Arabia, he has half-forced, half-purchased the secret of the substance from which the elixir is extracted, but he has been unable to obtain any of the elixir itself. The process of making it is an awful one, but it can be done in a single night; if Fenwick will assist, and if the experiment is successful, he will have the substance which may save Lilian's life as well as prolong Margrave's (who is dying of heart disease). Any lingering doubts are removed when Fenwick learns that Lilian, in her illness, has been having trances and recommending to Dr. Faber for her own treatment herbs, of which he and she have hitherto known nothing, but which have proved effective. Fenwick does question Margrave about the two murders he has committed: Derval was killed in self-defense, and Margrave remembers only hearing from his Arab servant-woman, Ayesha, that Haroun was dead. She had also told him that Grayle was dead; and, although Fenwick cannot believe this after all the evidence he has had that Margrave *is* Grayle, he decides to go ahead with the great experiment.

All that is necessary is a natural substance, found near natural gold deposits (there is one on Fenwick's estate) which must be cooked in a cauldron for six hours, mixed with other ingredients already in Margrave's possession. To protect themselves against the "invisible tribes that abhor men," who appear when the borders of knowledge are crossed—our old acquaintances the Dwellers of the Threshold, from *Zanoni*—Margrave will employ magic, and Fenwick his native courage. Near the gold, the substance is soon found; the cauldron is set up within a wide circle traced on the ground; within it are four interlaced triangles. About the circle twelve lamps are placed, and four more mark the points of the triangles. These Fenwick must constantly feed with a special fluid, of which there is only a limited supply. In the tense and climactic scene of magic, the ground trembles, as it did for Éliphas Lévi or Martines de Pasqually, or the Egyptian practicing theurgy for Plotinus in the Temple of Isis, or even Margrave and the unwilling Fenwick in the earlier evocation at Sir Philip Derval's house. The spirits gather and manifest themselves: a great eye is seen in the distance, and other eyes appear; some of the fuel for the lamps is spilled; Ayesha's chant temporarily quiets the aggressive spirits, but a giant foot, belonging to one of the demons, crosses into the circle and is only temporarily halted by Ayesha's and Fenwick's courage. Then a great fire in the bush behind them precipitates a stampede of cattle. At the last moment, when the six hours are almost over, the fire-maddened beasts overrun the magic circle and tip over the cauldron. Margrave dies trying to lap up the elixir that has been spilled on the ground. Foiling the ambush planned for him by Margrave—who had never intended to abide by their agreement, but had stationed the Thug strangler to kill him—Fenwick wins his way back to his house through the burning forest. With Margrave's death, Lilian has completely recovered.

This dramatic "cauldron scene" is of course magical. The circle and triangles on the ground and the protection against the gathering demons provided by the strategically placed lamps differ little from the apparatus used at Derval Court during Margrave's earlier efforts at evocation, blocked by Lilian's warning. Both scenes remind us of Éliphas Lévi and Apollonius of Tyana: indeed, Fenwick's arm, briefly and inadvertently thrust outside the magic circle, receives a violent numbing shock just like the one that Lévi received when Apollonius made his first appearance. But here in Australia the main purpose of the effort is not theurgy or evocation, but alchemy. The process taking place in the cauldron is the manufacture of the elixir of life, which, we know, is one form of the Philosopher's Stone, the *lapis* of the alchemist. For Zanoni and Mejnour the elixir had been an easy substance to make, once one knew the secret herbal formula: in *Zanoni* alchemy is openly despised. In *A Strange Story* it is explicitly relied upon.

After four of the necessary six hours have passed, Margrave says, "See how the Grand Work advances! how the hues in the cauldron are glowing blood-red through the film on the surface!" The alchemists generally referred to their experimentation as the "opus," or work; and in the alchemical order of values the *rubedo*, or turning red, was the climactic final color change, signifying rebirth and the development of a new life. The *rubedo* followed upon the *nigredo*, or turning black with death and decay of the substances that one began with, and the subsequent *albedo*, or turning white with purity in preparation for the new substance. Bulwer has omitted these two earlier stages; he has not described the boiling contents of the cauldron until the red color had begun to appear, but as alchemical amateurs we may assume that the *nigredo* and *albedo* had already taken place. Because there are still two more hours to go, the red color is still seen only "through the film on the surface." During the fifth hour Margrave says, "the sparkles at last begin to arise, and the rose-hues to deepen— signs that we near the last process."

As the surrounding bushfire spreads, Margrave is oblivious to the animals desperately advancing on the magic circle, and sees only "the bubbles of life, how they sparkle and dance—I shall live, I shall live!" Just before the catastrophe Margrave exclaims, " 'behold how the Rose of the alchemist's dream enlarges its blooms from the folds of its petals! I shall live, I I shall live!' " And when Fenwick looks, after the six hours have passed,

> the liquid . . . had now taken a splendour that mocked all comparisons borrowed from the lustre of gems. In its prevalent colour it had, indeed, the dazzle and flash of the ruby; but, out from the mass of the molten red, broke coruscations of all prismal hues, shooting, shifting, in a play that made the wavelets themselves seem living things, sensible of their joy. No longer was there scum or film upon the surface; only ever and anon a light rosy vapour floating up. . . . And these coruscations formed, on the surface of the molten ruby, literally the shape of a Rose, its leaves made distinct in their outlines by sparks of emerald and diamond, and sapphire.

Just before the cauldron is irretrievably spilled, then, Bulwer the Rosicrucian pays his final tribute to the mystic society: the elixir of life shows upon its bubbling surface their emblem, the rose, symbol on earth of the face of the sun in the heavens, betokening for humanity the victory over pain and death and the achievement of peace and immortality.

And when Fenwick has won his way home, and Faber tells him that Lilian will be restored to him, "heart to heart, mind to mind," Fenwick himself cries, " 'And soul to soul. . . . Above as below, soul to soul!' " The words "above as below" are the occult words implying to the initiate all the age-old doctrines of correspondences between the macrocosm of the universe and the microcosm of the individual human being elaborated by the medieval alchemists. But here they have lost their primarily occult meaning. The whole passage says that Fenwick and Lilian will enjoy physical communion "heart to heart," intellectual communion "mind to mind," and spiritual communion "soul to soul," climaxing the novel's doctrinal theme of the triple nature of man. Fenwick now has undergone his ordeal. He believes in the human soul and in eternal salvation. In this context, then, "above as below" seems to mean only that Lilian's soul and Fenwick's will commune in heaven above after death as during life they commune here on earth. The last occult note has been struck faintly and only implicitly: the message is Christian.

In one of his many suggestive studies of alchemy, Jung declares that "... the psychic nature of the arcane substance did not escape the alchemists; indeed, they actually defined it as 'spirit' and 'soul.'" May we then conjecture that, whereas the wicked Margrave was denied his triumph and lost his life as the elixir spilled irrevocably despite the successful completion of the "opus," Fenwick had literally found the soul or spirit which his scepticism and hubris had so long denied him? His new belief assured him of immortality beyond the grave. So the "opus" had conferred immortality after all, though not earthly immortality, not upon Margrave, and not through the elixir. Like Zanoni, Fenwick would enjoy a heavenly reward.[66]

Throughout the writing and publication of *A Strange Story*, Dickens kept constantly encouraging and reassuring the temperamental Bulwer. The men had always been friends; it is possible that the memory of Zanoni's self-sacrifice at the guillotine lingered in Dickens's mind when in 1859 he sent Sydney Carton to so similar a death, and it was surely Bulwer who persuaded Dickens to change the ending he had planned for his own *Great Expectations*, which preceeded *A Strange Story* as the chief serial in *All the Year Round*. On January 23, 1861, months before he had seen a single word of Bulwer's novel, Dickens wrote:

> I have never been so pleased at heart in all my literary life, as I am in the proud thought of standing side by side with you before this great audience. . . . I have perfect faith in such a master hand as yours; and I know that what such an artist feels to be terrible and original is unmistakably so. You whet my interest by what you write of it to the greatest extent.

Bulwer was sure to be pleased at the prospect of *All the Year Round*'s huge circulation ("several thousands more than the Times newspaper") and at Dickens's reiterated expressions of faith in the story. By May 12, still three months before publication would begin, when Bulwer had followed Dickens's suggestion and had the earlier portion of the novel printed, Dickens had read the proofs, and wrote:

> I COULD NOT lay them aside, but was obliged to go on with them in my bedroom until I had got into a very ghostly state indeed. This morning I have taken them again and have gone through them with the utmost attention.

> Of the beauty and power of the writing I say not a word, or of its originality and boldness, or of its quite extraor-

dinary constructive skill. I confine myself solely to your misgiving, and to the question whether there is any sufficient foundation for it.

On the last head, I say, without the faintest hesitation, most decidedly there is NOT sufficient foundation for it. I do not share it in the least. I believe that the readers who have never given their minds (or perhaps had any to give) to those strange psychological mysteries in ourselves, of which we are all more or less conscious, will accept your wonders as curious weapons in the armoury of fiction, and will submit themselves to the Art with which said weapons are used. Even to that class of intelligence the marvellous addresses itself from a strong position; and that class of intelligence is not accustomed to find the marvellous in such very powerful hands as yours. On more imaginative readers, the tale will fall (or I am greatly mistaken) like a spell. By readers who combine some imagination, some scepticism, and some knowledge and learning, I hope it will be regarded as full of strange fancy and curious study, startling reflections of their own thoughts and speculations at odd times, and wonders which a master has the right to evoke. In the last point lies, to my thinking, the whole case. If you were the Magician's servant instead of the Magician, these potent spirits would get the better of you; but you *are* the Magician; and they don't, and you make them serve your purpose.

Having duly provided this warm praise, Dickens continued with the utmost tact to make certain editorial suggestions. It is clear from what we have just read that Bulwer had been worrying about the public reception of his treatment of the supernatural: would he meet with ridicule or disbelief? No, Dickens had roundly said, because of Bulwer's masterly handling of his material. But

Occasionally in the dialogue I see an expression here and there which might—always solely with a reference to your misgivings—be better away; and I think that the vision, to use the word for want of a better—in the museum, should be made a little less abstruse.

Dickens proposed that the story be given the subtitle, "A Romance," and suggested no fewer than seven possible titles: *The Steel Casket, The Lost Manuscript, Derval Court, Perpetual Youth, Magic, Dr. Fenwick,* and *Life and Death,* of which he said he preferred the last four. He urged that a final decision as to the title be reached soon, and made various "mechanical" suggestions about subdividing the book to suit weekly publication. Even this tiny pill he thoroughly sugarcoated:

> Be sure that I am perfectly frank and open in all I have said . . . and that I have not a grain of reservation in my mind. I think the story a very fine one, one that no other man could write, and that there is no strength in your misgiving for the two reasons: firstly, that the work is professedly a work of Fancy and Fiction, in which the reader is not required to take anything for Fact; secondly, that it is written by the man who can write it. The Magician's servant does not know what to do with the ghost, and has, consequently, no business with him. The Magician does know what to do with him, and has all the business with him that he can transact.

Give up all your doubts, Dickens urges: if he were at Knebworth, he "would swarm up the flagpole as nimbly as Margrave and nail the Fenwick colours to the top."

And now the letters came thick and fast, always supremely considerate and cunningly designed for their recipient. On May 15, Dickens writes that others too liked the proofs: "a woman whom I could implicitly trust, and in whom I have frequently observed (in the case of my own proofs) an intuitive sense and discretion"; also Wills, the managing editor of *All the Year Round,* who "is in literary matters, sufficiently commonplace to represent a very large proportion of our readers. He too was enchanted by the story, and obliged to go on. He has no fears of the story, and thinks it will certainly make a sensation. His suggestion to me was, 'If Sir Edward should lengthen it, don't you think he would point the mysterious and supernatural parts more, by getting in among them some new touches of character and ordinary life.' That was all." Wilkie Collins would also be reading the proofs. And in personal conferences the author and editor dealt with detail. It is clear that at this stage Lilian was called Isabel, and that Bulwer intended that she should die and Fenwick grow old, to which Dickens answered only that "whatever the meaning of the story tends to, is the proper end." By now (May 16) they were considering *Margrave, a Tale of Mystery* (or "*of Wonder*") as a title. In early June Dickens begged Bulwer not to publish the story anonymously, and by early July both Forster and Collins were receiving enthusiastic notes from Dickens. Bulwer himself, Dickens told Forster on July 1, was "in a better state than I have ever seen him in all these years, a little weird occasionally regarding magic and spirits, but perfectly fair and frank under opposition." And on July 12, Collins heard from Dickens that he would be amazed at

> what [Bulwer] has done with his first four numbers—all I have read—and with what curious patience, study, and skill he has gone into the art of the Weekly No. There is a remarkably skillfully done woman, one Mrs. Colonel Poyntz. The whole idea of the story turned in a masterly way to the safe point of the compass.

Such comments to Forster and Collins, of course, clearly show that there was nothing feigned in Dickens's expressions in his letters to Bulwer himself.

And these continued after publication began in August. Sales were keeping up well. Bulwer "seems so far to succeed capitally" (to Wills, on August 31). And on September 17 Dickens told Bulwer that "Not one dissentient voice has reached me. ...Forster...really was more impressed than I can tell you by what he had seen of it. Just what you say you think it will turn out to be, *he* was saying...." And Dickens is "delighted with the addition to the length of the story—delighted with your account of it, and your interest in it—and even more than

delighted by what you say of our working in company." Moreover, he has been "fairly staggered" by "the exquisite art with
which you have changed it, and have overcome the difficulties
of the mode of publication. . . . there is no other man who
could have done it, I swear." Dickens had not yet seen the
rest of the story: on September 29—after the first eight weekly
numbers had already appeared—we find him not only dealing
authoritatively with a legal question that Bulwer had raised
(*"Fenwick would not be taken before the coroner at all*. But
would be taken before a bench of magistrates—or a magistrate
—and remanded until the result of the coroner's inquest was
known. . . . Fenwick would have to go to jail in the meanwhile"), but repeating once more "I am burning to get at the
whole story—and you inflame me in the maddest manner by
your reference to what I don't know." This kind of editorial
attention continued: on November 20 Dickens was praising
numbers 19 and 20, complimenting Bulwer on "the introduced
matter . . . for its policy, its beauty, or its wise bearing on the
story," but tactfully urging the avoidance of footnotes where
possible. And two days later: "I have gone over the proof and
have not touched a single word—simply because it could not,
I think, stand better. And it is much more terrible notwith-
standing than it was before." This letter was written from
Newcastle. Even on his strenuous reading tours, Dickens the
friend and editor never ceased to hold Bulwer's hand.

Up to this point, Bulwer's side of the correspondence has
not been published. Indeed, it was probably destroyed when
Dickens burned all available letters to him. But it is reasonably
clear that—as in the case of *Zanoni*—Bulwer was doubtful
whether the public would understand what he was trying to
do, and anxious lest he be misunderstood. In a letter which his
grandson published and dated late 1861 or early 1862, and
which, judging from the available Dickens letters, I think may
safely be assigned to mid-December 1861, Bulwer returned
to this subject:

No doubt every story should contain in itself all that is essential to its own explanation—and to a thinker I hope mine does. The question is only how far it is necessary to anticipate the objections of those who don't think. I had already thought how far it would be possible to effect this in the body of the work by adding something to one of the later conversations between Faber and Fenwick, and can do so to a limited extent, viz: —why the supernatural is a legitimate province of fiction. But also, how the supernatural resolves itself into the natural when faced and sifted. But that does not meet the case *in toto*. Because the parts which would seem most to require explanation are the concluding scenes, which appear those of demonology, and the previous conversation must anticipate these, or the effect would be lost, and vanish in philosophical unreality.

Now, in truth, it is in the latter science that for the first time the interior or symbolic meaning, that contains the true philosophical explanation, is carried out. Margrave is the sensuous material principle of Nature, Ayesha, with her black veil, unknown song, and skeleton attendant, Death, is Nature as a materialist, like Fenwick, sees her.

Fenwick is the type of intellect that divorces itself from the spiritual, and disdaining to acknowledge the first cause, and the beliefs that spring from it, is cheated by the senses themselves, and falls into all kinds of visionary illusions, similar to those of great reasoners, like Hume, La Place and La Marck.

Lilian is the type of the spiritual divorcing itself from the intellectual, and indulging in mystic ecstasies which end in the loss of reason. Each has need of the other, and their union is really brought thro' the heart—Fenwick recognising soul and God, thro' love and sorrow, tho, he never recognised them till the mysterious prodigies, which puzzled him, had passed away. Lilian struggling back to reason and life, thro' her love and her desire to live for the belov'd one's sake.

But all this could only be implied, either by something supplementary or by a preface. But if in a preface, the interest of the book would be gone. Now there is a course that has just occurred to me. Zanoni was symbolical, and Miss Martineau divined the key to it, which she gave and which is appended to the popular editions of the book.

2dly, whether some such key, as if suggested by a third person, a friend, might be added to the story (very short). If you thought this desirable then return me this letter with any comment on it you desire.

I don't see how Mrs. Poyntz can be reintroduced to the story. How could she come to Australia? She could only come into a supplementary chapter, as talking over the book, Mr. Vigors arguing for the supernatural, she pooh-poohing, and some third person, a friendly critic, giving the key suggested above. This might be done in a half-humorous vein around Mrs. Poyntz's tea-table.

This important letter proves beyond question that Bulwer, here as in *Zanoni*, intended each of his chief characters to portray an ideal type, according to the Schillerian theories he had adopted so long ago and still defended. But it also illustrates his continuing fear that he would have to labor his point to get it across, and would himself have to do for *A Strange Story* what Harriet Martineau had done for *Zanoni*. His proposals distressed Dickens, whose reply (December 18, 1861) reiterated his praise for the story as it stood:

> most masterly and most admirable! It is impossible to lay the sheets down without finishing them. I showed them to Georgina [Hogarth] and Mary [Boyle], and they read and read and never stirred until they had read all. There cannot be a doubt of the beauty, power, and artistic excellence of the whole.

But Dickens went on to urge, bringing to bear more pressure than he had yet done, that Bulwer follow none of the courses he had been proposing:

I counsel you most strongly NOT to append the proposed dialogue between Fenwick and Faber, and NOT to enter upon any explanation beyond the title-page and the motto, unless it be in some very brief preface [which, of course, would appear only in a later book-edition, and not in the pages of *All the Year Round*]. Decidedly I would not help the reader, if it were only for the reason that that antici-pates his being in need of help, and his feeling objections and difficulties that require solution. Let the book explain itself. It speaks *for* itself with a noble eloquence.

It is clear that even this was not enough for Bulwer, who now seems to have urged Dickens to confer with Forster about the proposed additional explanatory material. On December 20 Dickens promised to do so, but reiterated his advice:

I have no doubt, and do not think I shall have any doubt, that if anything be done, *it must be done as a part of the book*—must involve the resumption and disposal of some-body—must, in short, have that connexion with the story which will force the reader of the story also to read what you so desire to be read. Otherwise it will not be read by one person in fifty—not by one in a hundred. Could Mrs. Poyntz as the representative of The World be brought into it? I fancy I see a loophole of light in that direction.

And, on December 26, having re-examined the proofs and dis-cussed the question with Forster, Dickens stuck to his guns: it had to be Mrs. Poyntz's tea-table or nothing, he wrote, as the public would surely not read a preface or "anything in the way of an essay or treatise about the book." This disposed of any suggested "key" to *A Strange Story*, like Harriet Mar-tineau's key to *Zanoni*.

The ever-touchy Bulwer apparently thought that because Dickens had suggested "softening" the "scene where Nature and Death are," he was recommending some omission from the final scene of the incantation. Not at all, wrote Dickens in the last letter of the series on *A Strange Story*, dated January 18, 1862: all he had meant was that

if the explanation were rendered particularly necessary by
that part of the story ... then it might be worth while to
consider whether that scene, not being yet published, might
not be so re-considered and re-touched as to explain itself.
I could not suggest the omission of any passage, as it stands,
because I recognise in it extraordinary care, purpose, art,
and knowledge.

So, over a period of an entire year, the indefatigable and
patient Dickens dealt affectionately with his prickly contribu-
tor, and incidentally gave him excellent literary advice.[67]

As with *Zanoni*, Bulwer spoke in glowing terms of *A Strange
Story* while he was writing it. An "original and a psychological
curiosity" he called it in a letter to Forster, and, writing to his
son Robert, "my best work of imagination. ... it deals with
mysteries within and without us wholly untouched as yet by
poets. ... not my widest work, but ... perhaps the highest and
deepest." And, again to Forster, as the final instalments were
completed:

I don't think the ending ... is too fantastic—it is written
with too much power for that, and is, I imagine, the finest
thing in point of interior meaning I ever wrote. Margrave
at the close comes out with a certain pathos, and even, perhaps, mental (not spiritual) grandeur. I leave the whole to
be solved either way, viz: —entirely by physiological causes,
or by the admission of causes that may be in Nature, but
[that] physiology as yet rejects as natural.

But when it came to publishing the novel in book form, Bulwer
could not in the end bring himself to take Dickens's advice.
He did not let the story speak for itself, even with all its ex-
position in the Faber-Fenwick dialogues, but wrote the preface
he had so long been threatening, which restated his position
once again, just in case the public was too obtuse to understand it.

Dickens was certainly right from the literary point of view
in believing the preface unnecessary, because any intelligent

reader would have got the point of *A Strange Story* from the story itself. But we can be grateful to Bulwer for having written the preface, since it identifies one of his most important inspirations for the novel, something it would otherwise have been virtually impossible to discover. The most accomplished philosopher of France in our time, he says, Victor Cousin, has called Maine de Biran the most original. And Maine de Biran, who began his career with blind faith in Condillac and materialism, was induced by the observation of certain phenomena, inexplicable in terms of the senses alone, to add to Condillac's animal life of man, the "second or human life, from which Free-will and Self-consciousness emerge," thus uniting mind and matter. But, even then, "a something is wanted—some key to the marvels which neither of these conditions of vital being suffices to explain." And this third life would make it clear that beyond the greatest "human" happiness, the highest "human" wisdom, and the loftiest "human" intellectual and moral perfection there is a further happiness, a further wisdom, a further perfection. So, in this "Strange Story . . . Romance conducts the bewildered hero [Fenwick] toward the same goal [belief in the soul] to which Philosophy leads its luminous student [Maine de Biran]."

Pierre François Gonthier Maine de Biran (1766–1824), the founding father of the science of psychology, and a philosophical link between Pascal on the one hand and Bergson and Freud on the other, published very little during his lifetime compared to the vast amount of manuscript work left at his death in various stages of completion. This legacy suffered severe vicissitudes at the hands of his literary heirs. Some of it is still unpublished, and much has appeared in mutilated or badly edited versions. Bulwer had been using the three-volume edition of materials by Maine de Biran published in 1859 by Ernest Naville as *Oeuvres Inédites*. The first citation is from Naville's introduction, in which the editor declares that when Maine de Biran was planning a last work, which death would force him to leave unfinished, he "grouped all the facts which human nature had successively revealed to his observation, into the three following classes, which he called *lives*."

> Animal life, which is characterized by impressions, appetites, and movements, organic in their origin, and ruled by the law of necessity. Human life, which results from the appearance of free will and of self-consciousness. The Life of the spirit, which begins at the moment when the soul, set free from the yoke of its lower attractions, turns toward God, and finds in God its power and its rest.

These three lives, Naville goes on, were actually the three successive stages by which Maine de Biran himself had gradually arrived at his grasp of the truth. Bulwer follows Naville here, and proceeds to quote two further passages, from materials published by Naville as *Nouveaux Essais d'anthropologie*, in the third volume of these previously unpublished works. This—Maine de Biran's last work—has a subtitle: "concerning the science of the inner man." It is ascribed to 1823 or 1824, and is divided into three sections, one each on the animal life, the human life, and the life of the spirit. It is in this last section on the life of the spirit that Bulwer found his two additional passages, one reiterating the existence of the third life, and the other avowing that, in contrast to Stoicism, which "makes abstraction of the animal nature, and absolutely fails to recognize all which belongs to the life of the spirit, . . . Christianity alone [as Fenwick will learn] embraces the whole Man." These passages, Bulwer declares, indicate one main purpose of his story, and he cites them in order to acknowledge a "priceless obligation." So at the very outset of the book publication of *A Strange Story* Bulwer put himself under the banner of Maine de Biran.

In conveying this message, Bulwer will, he says, avail himself of the machinery of the supernatural, indispensable in the Epic, used by Shakespeare and Goethe, and in the prose romance ever since Apuleius: by Fénélon, de la Motte Fouqué,

Swift, Horace Walpole. Moreover, since everybody wants to account scientifically for the supernatural, there will also be a good deal of science in the story. Its purpose will be made manifest. The reader will see

> through all the haze of Romance.... the image of sensuous, soulless Nature, such as the materialist had conceived it. [i.e., Margrave.] Secondly, the image of Intellect, obstinately separating all its inquiries from the belief in the spiritual essence of man, and incurring all kinds of perplexity and resorting to all kinds of visionary speculation before it settles at last into the simple faith which unites the philosopher and the infant. [i.e., Fenwick.] And Thirdly, the image of the erring, but pure-thoughted, visionary seeking overmuch on this earth to separate soul from mind, till innocence itself is led astray by a phantom, and reason is lost in the space between earth and the stars. [i.e., Lilian.][68]

Robert Lytton, who wrote his father an enthusiastic letter praising *A Strange Story* just after its publication in book form, received an answer showing that Bulwer was himself apprehensive about the Faber-Fenwick dialogues:

> in poetry they would be inexcusable. I am not sure that in prose they are justified. But still they are essential...1st because they do not explain tho' they use all the best known arguments in physiology and metaphysics. The supernatural in man is inexplicable by the natural sense of man. 2dly. They show that philosophers getting rid of soul and 1st cause indulge in more romance and fantastic chimera than any novels can do. Margrave is a trifle compared to Lornosch's [sic, for Lamarck?] and Laplace's theories of man and creation. It is clear that Goethe thought (as an artist) that prose narrative might include these dissertations which partially belong to essay.... But an artistic narrative demands that these dissertations should be strictly pertinent to the main conception for which the characters are created; that they should be as necessary to the moral or intellectual narrative as the incidents are to the external; that they are not episodical but essential.... If you strike out those con-

versations you strike out all that part of the story for which Fenwick and Margrave and Lilian are created. They carry on the history of the soul.

One senses instantly the defensiveness of the author, even in writing to his own son, who had admired the novel extravagantly.

"It is said," Bulwer continues, that the Fenwick-Faber conversations "will be skipped."

> True that they may be skipped by the first rush of novel readers; but if the book lives, they will not and cannot be skipped. They will be read first by a few, then the few will communicate them to the many.

Goethe's criticisms of art in *Wilhelm Meister* were skipped at first, but the book now lives and is studied because of them. Bulwer's arguments for the immortality of the soul are not "old hashes-up," and they are directed against "the most popular and modern objections now current." Indeed "the argument which rests our immortality on our special capacities to comprehend abstract ideas connected with immortality" is "a great advance on metaphysical science." To Forster too, Bulwer reiterated this particular claim:

> I have built out a theory, not wholly new but I think never so plainly put before, viz: —that the evidence of man's soul is not in his mind, i.e. not in his ideas as received thro' the senses, but in his inherent capacity to receive ideas of God, Soul, etc. which capacity is not given to the brutes.

And to Robert, still in defense of the "attempted explanations of Faber," Bulwer added that they

> serve to bring together a great variety of ideas of all schools of physiology and in reality do not explain the phenomena of marvel—no philosophy yet formed does—but they still tend to show that a thing is not inexplicable because men can't explain it.

He emphasized that the "true moral . . . is in Faber's final conclusion after the catastrophe, viz: —that what signified whether these magic marvels are true or not—how small is their marvel compared to the growth of a blade of grass." And the final climactic episode of the book, the "cauldron scene,"

> can only be thoroughly understood by those who are made to perceive that it is there the story obtains its diaeresis in summing up all the symbolical truths of the work. There in the ... new world ... man seeks to renew his own youth, and there the magician, long estranged from Nature, finds her (Ayesha). . . . Vulgar critics say I dismiss Mrs. Poyntz too soon. So I do if the novel is only a novel. But if you look into its deeper meanings, Mrs. Poyntz (the polite world) vanishes exactly where the polite world does vanish to ... Fenwick ... for he escapes to ... Nature; but Nature cannot enlighten him so long as he ignores Nature's God.[69]

To Robert at the same time, Bulwer sent a copy of the criticism published by the *Eclectic Review*, a serious nonconformist periodical, which had pleased him as the "most favourable I have seen." Here the anonymous critic reviewed *A Strange Story* together with the Reverend James M'Cosh's book on *The Supernatural in Relation to the Natural*. Asserting that the supernatural had now found its way into the general public interest, and that Christian teaching itself rests upon a supernatural basis, while the Bible, practical though it is, also provides "visions of worlds beyond the ... terrestrial ... far beyond those of any poet or clairvoyant," the reviewer refers to the power of an intense, corrupting, mendacious will— a devilish will, like that of the fiend himself—over weaker human wills. "Not to perceive that which is above nature is to miss altogether its intentions and design." And so he approves Bulwer's position that the supernatural is indispensable for "the highest form of romantic narrative," and remarks that whereas M'Cosh has not dealt with the limits of man's relationship to the supernatural, Bulwer has done so. In *A Strange Story*, the critic sees "a protest against the intrusion of man into hidden mysteries." Paying tribute to Bulwer's artistry and his learning, and noting that neither sceptic nor spiritualist will like the book, he remarks on Bulwer's own acquaintance with "the strange feats of superstition in our own day." At séances "in the rich and wealthy homes of Belgravia and Norwood, . . . cunning Yankees" are paid to summon up the spirits. If the reviewer was referring to Home, he was, as we know, being unfair, since Home did not take money for his performances; but, also as we know, he was right in acknowledging Bulwer's expertise in these matters and in surmising that spiritualists did not much like Bulwer.

So, for the *Eclectic* reviewer, *A Strange Story* reduces "to a dramatic order" the "various characters" of an "age . . . as superstitious as any age which has gone before it." Fenwick, Vigors, Margrave, Faber, each receives a crisp and appreciative descriptive sentence; Sir Philip Derval is "a kind of Sir Kenelm Digby —a believer in the possibility of acquaintance with occult . . . things," and Lilian is "a portrait of the modern Medium." Bulwer's opponents accuse him of having "read up" his materials: what is wrong with that? asks the critic. The tendency of the book is healthy; it administers a proper rebuke to those who spend their time "loitering around the tables and listening for the rappings. . . ." The critic quotes Bulwer's introduction with approval and, for good measure, comes to the defense of Bulwer's *Lucretia*, which detractors had called immoral. Fenwick's vision of Margrave's brain, seen in trance at the museum, is quoted in full—four whole pages of it—and so is one of Faber's long speeches to Fenwick in favor of the Bible and of prayer.

Broadening his subject matter from *A Strange Story* to a general estimate of Bulwer's literary achievement, and completely losing sight of poor M'Cosh in the process, the critic acknowledges that Bulwer has always worked "too consciously . . . by the rules of art"; but then, so did Goethe. The possible pernicious influence of Bulwer's early works on the young does not animate his recent novels. Because "the orbit in which he travels is larger than that attempted by any other writer of fiction," he has a "licentiousness of imagination, the daring innovation of an unbridled and unregulated fancy into the domain of moral order and completeness." But *A Strange Story* illustrates a "healthy change" from his earlier writings. Though not as witty as they, it is full of brilliant aphorisms, which the reviewer quotes, and it is sublimely conceived. While the *Last of the Barons* is better than Scott, and *The Last Days of Pompeii* the most vivid historical epic imaginable, *A Strange Story* is the epic of the soul, and, finally, it is absurd to say that it is made up of "odds and ends" left over from *Zanoni*. "The world has made some advances since the day when *Zanoni* was published; nor is Sir Edward's mind where it was then." No wonder Bulwer liked this review: detailed, understanding, and wholly laudatory. "This, from a religious quarter," he wrote Robert, "will do the book much good." [70]

But the other critics notably failed to measure up. The *Athenaeum* reviewer said that "magic and science, poetry and prose, meet here in a sort of witch-dance. The tale will be a torment for any bystander who has not 'eaten of the insane root.' " Derval's murder is "too summary"; Fenwick's behavior when he releases Margrave instead of punishing him to the full with the magic wand or when he falls in love with Lilian is "strange and aimless ... unbefitting an acute and enterprising man of science." Bulwer's dialogue is unconvincing; the "didactic matter" interferes with the story. Only Mrs. Poyntz meets with approval. The rest is too stagey, too contrived. Quoting long passages of the cauldron scene, and sneering at the apparition of the Eyes and the colossal Foot, the critic grudgingly concedes at the end that the other evocation, at Sir Philip Derval's, had been "managed like a true magician." But, on the whole, the work had been a mistake.

The critic of *The Saturday Review* wondered petulantly that Bulwer should have returned to the supernatural so many years after *Zanoni*, and after succeeding in a naturalistic novel like *The Caxtons*: "... we have ... supped so full of horrors that our powers of digestion are seriously endangered. ..." The preface obtrudes itself clamorously "upon the reader's notice," and must be read, though it is too hard (even after three readings) for the average intellect, and although the story itself is extremely ugly. Fixing upon the motto (". . . the lover of wisdom is in some sort of a lover of mythi. . . .") from Aristotle and Sir William Hamilton, the reviewer declares that most novel-readers do not love wisdom, and myth-lovers prefer to choose their own. Thoroughly philistine, this reviewer too liked nothing about *A Strange Story* except Mrs. Poyntz.

Even *The Examiner*—which had been kind to *Zanoni* twenty years earlier—seems somewhat lukewarm in its review of *A Strange Story*. Accepting the validity of Bulwer's arguments for the legitimacy of the supernatural as a subject in fiction, and referring, as he had done, to Goethe and Swift as his predecessors in its use, warning the reader not to think of Bulwer as a "dupe" of such a man as Home, and showing an understanding of the preface, the *Examiner*'s critic concedes the "perfect originality" of Margrave, and praises the cauldron scene without spoiling the story by summarizing it or quoting it at length. He accepts the reality of Fenwick's conversion, approves the Fenwick-Faber conversations as necessary, understands what Lilian represents, and likes Mrs. Poyntz. Even the footnotes are recommended, and the "new" argument for ascribing a soul to man—the argument that Bulwer was so proud of—receives due appreciation. So faithfully does the reviewer accept Bulwer's own view of *A Strange Story* that one is tempted to identify him once more as Forster, whom Bulwer had briefed at every stage of the novel's preparation. But somehow the review, though dutiful, is so unenthusiastic that one wonders if any reader would have been tempted to go on to read the novel, and it may be that Forster did not himself write the review.[71]

In any case, Bulwer was deeply disappointed. "I am at present," he wrote to Robert probably sometime in April 1862,

> under the damp of the general critical outcry against my . . . *Strange Story*, and . . . the dislike of our practical public to

Bulwer's letter to Mrs. Maxwell (M. E. Braddon, the celebrated novelist), with comment on his own *A Strange Story*.

mysticism and allegory.... Even with my long authorship, if I had my time over again, I would not have published *A Strange Story*, nor do I think if I had shown it ... to an anxious friend, that he would have counselled me to publish it. Yet I have no doubt in my own mind that it is my highest, though not my broadest work, of prose fiction.

He did, he added later, want "some aid from the critics, to explain and vindicate it to the Public. But the critics seem to attack it ruthlessly, even one's friends among the reviewers seem shy of praising it." This may be a reference to the understanding but limp review in the *Examiner*.

The Public don't know exactly what to make of it, whether to admire or condemn. A powerful review by a great critic, such as a German might write, would at once decide the public in its favour, but none such is likely to appear. It sells well, is discussed much, has a few earnest admirers, but generally I should think it has hurt my reputation, and I have not seen so many impertinent personalities in the reviewers for many years as blossom out now. But I am not so thin-skinned as I was.

Ten years or so later, however, the reception of *A Strange Story* still rankled. To his old friend and protegée, Mrs. Maxwell (the celebrated novelist M. E. Braddon), Bulwer wrote, in an unpublished letter in my collection:

I am delighted with ... your too partial liking to the Strange Story. I always thought it had received scanty justice at the hands of the reviewers—I don't call them critics, and thanks to them, by the ordinary public. And few seem to me to have recognised the purport of the book. The originality of a character like Margrave and the application of modern superstitions or beliefs into the agencies of terror—which Poets in a former age took from the superstitions of their time—yet all blending themselves into a philosophical argument for the immortality of the soul—However I am not going to prose further about my own book....

Chauncey Hare Townshend, at least, who had in 1850 tactfully and firmly saved Bulwer's son Robert from a threatened nervous breakdown, and had attained new intimacy with both father and son as a result, admired *A Strange Story* wholeheartedly, and wrote Bulwer while it was still appearing serially that he had been "sending you a brain-message by mesmeric post," but now would write and express his "debt of gratitude for the great and beautiful story with which you are enriching the world and elevating our literature." The book had cast a "charm of freshness and novelty over" his existence:

To strike at once the diapason of life which includes the two extremes of the Ideal and the Real was, in itself, a grand idea. To idealize the Real, and to make the Ideal seem Real, is a triumph of art in the execution of your Idea. Mrs. Poyntz & Lilian! Wonderful both! The woman who says "I am the World—the girl who feels she has mysterious & immeasurable Nature within her breast. With what a sharp touch you have struck off and distinguished, as eternal types of character, Adam Fenwick & Julius Faber; to say nothing of other types revolving round them! But the most marvellous thing is that you make us accept Margrave as a man though beside Nature, not out of Nature. I vow I almost accept the soulless being as a truth! Never was I more impressed by anything than by the scene in the Museum of Natural History. In reading it the spell was not so much upon Fenwick as myself. I seemed to see that all must be as you described it. To have treated that difficult part of the subject so eloquently, yet so simply & with such essential truth, is indeed your triumph. The dropping of the Wand into the lake is a fine part of the story, and, like all the other grand shadows with which you have ennobled this story of your imagination, has substantial truth in it. Fenwick's meetings with facts beyond philosophy, Faber's, even Faber's, inadequate measuring-rod for the Infinite in the Soul-World: the obstinate recurrence of facts that upset in a moment the card-houses built by reasoning (not Reason); depict most

admirably our innate tendency to cut Nature down to our
own conceptions, while every day she startles us with new
marvels "beyond the reaches" of our comprehension. Then,
the necessity of a Soul—a God—the soul's relation to God,
are sublime truths, which seem to grow incidentally out of
the story, but are, in fact, the very staple of it, the unin-
tended, yet ever-persuasive moral. . . . Perfect art, too, there
is in the light & shade, in the distribution of action & repose,
in the balance between thought & incident, in your work.

Ecstatically selecting his favorite passages, Townshend was
rather hoping that in the end Lilian would be cured by Mesmerism, so that the beneficial would triumph over evil magic:
"I am far from saying that Magic (defining it as the baneful
use of Will) is not a (dreadful) truth: but I would keep it
asunder as the poles from mesmerism which *purely practiced*
is holiness and healing," he wrote, and added, when he found
his own name mentioned with that of Elliotson, "I look upon
it as a very grand thing of you, that you have never shrunk
from bearing testimony to (Mesmeric) truth." Indeed, said
Townshend, rating *A Strange Story* as the best of Bulwer's
books ("and that is saying a great deal"), "Methinks you wield
the magic you describe." Two weeks later, when Margrave
has reappeared and Lilian is "in a critical moment," Townshend protested that "I cannot help becoming breathless at
these things as if they were real."
    And, when he had at last received the conclusion, he felt
that it had been the only possible one, "simple, yet altogether
unexpected," and actually rejoiced that Mesmerism played
no part in the denouement:

I think the scene on the rocky platform, and all that per-
tains to the making of the Elixir, magnificent, and the
Natural, wrapping round and veiling the Ideal—the Conflagration, the rush of wild cattle—superbly imagined and
executed.

Jumma and Ayesha he called "fine . . . grand . . . superb." Such praise from a good and wholly disinterested critic must have given Bulwer great pleasure.[72]

As the *Eclectic* reviewer had noted, "the world [in 1862] had made some advances since the day when *Zanoni* was published [in 1842], nor is Sir Edward's mind where it was then." True indeed: Bulwer had put himself through a wide-ranging course of experimentation in the practical investigation of the occult, leaving unexamined not even the most outré practices of the magicians, and simultaneously he had systematically educated himself in the latest works of physiologists, philosophers, and students of the supernatural as they appeared. In the 1860s, revolution no longer seemed to threaten; therefore, unlike *Zanoni*, *A Strange Story* contains no political message. Nor, having made his case for the Ideal, did Bulwer need to argue in his fiction for his preferred aesthetic doctrines—that message too is absent from *A Strange Story*, although he continued to "typify" in his characters as he had in *Zanoni*, and took upon himself the task of providing a key for *A Strange Story* as Harriet Martineau had done for *Zanoni*. Gone from *A Strange Story* too are the influence and ambience of the German romantics. Here death is no longer explicitly the way to life (Zanoni) or continued life the way to death (Mejnour). Margrave is wicked, unlike either Mejnour or Zanoni. He wants to live forever simply to enjoy the world's pleasures, which Mejnour had long since abandoned and Zanoni sought only in order to sacrifice himself. Though Dickens had suggested that Bulwer give his novel the subtitle, "a Romance," Bulwer did not take his advice, and he was right. For all its supernatural features, *A Strange Story* is not a romantic novel in the way that *Zanoni* had been.

The two novels, of course, share a supernatural theme and some of the same supernatural machinery. The elixir of life haunts the desperate Margrave-Grayle as it had tempted the young Glyndon. Magical evocation brings with it the same danger of intrusion by hostile spirits; but the Dweller of the Threshold, who personifies fear in *Zanoni*, has been partially replaced in *A Strange Story* by the folklore figure of the Scin-Laeca and, in the end, by whatever the spirits were to whom the great eyes and the monstrous foot belonged. Firm refusal to be afraid still conquers a demon. The magic in *Zanoni* is beneficent theurgy gone wrong because of Glyndon's undue haste and lack of preparation. In *A Strange Story*, at Derval Court and in Australia, the magic is that of Éliphas Lévi. Chaldaeans, Platonists, Pythagoreans, Rosicrucians, Elect Cohens, all the mystic brotherhoods characteristic of the period before and during the French Revolution, who thronged the pages of *Zanoni*, have given way in *A Strange Story* to the preoccupations of Bulwer's own period with clairvoyance and mesmerism (Fenwick's opposition to Lloyd, the proper selection of a medium, the dreamy character of the sensitive Pythoness, Lilian), and with magic (Margrave's virtuoso performances with his wand), and—unexpectedly—to alchemy (the cauldron scene). But by and large, Sir William Hamilton, Sir Humphry Davy, and their like have replaced Iamblichus and the Chaldaean Oracles in the footnotes. *Zanoni* is the novel of the learned neophyte; *A Strange Story* is the novel of the adept.

But as we saw, *A Strange Story* carries with it, as *Zanoni* did not, an important religious message. It attempts to demonstrate scientifically and to illustrate graphically—in Fenwick's trance-vision in the Museum—the existence and immortality of the human soul, and to inculcate Faber's teaching that Christianity is the only true belief and that the Bible and prayer point the way to human salvation. No wonder the Congregationalist *Eclectic Review* hailed it so enthusiastically. The parade of scientific authorities is marshaled only in the service of religion. Even the final occult words, "above as below," point only toward a Christian future life. No Christian could fail to applaud such a message, if he could understand that indeed this was the message.

But the religious message was delivered at a particularly opportune time and in a particularly timely way. Bulwer's philosophical proof—not entirely original, he admitted, but better argued, he believed, than by anybody previously: that man alone in creation has an immortal soul because alone in creation man can apprehend ideas of God is in itself a vigorous argument against the Darwinian view of human evolution. During Fenwick's trance in the Museum, the silvery spark that betokens soul can be seen only in the brain of Margrave, the human being—which it promptly abandons for reasons of the story, it is true. But the beasts which surround Fenwick and Derval and Margrave at the time, the collection of Dr. Lloyd ranged on their stands and in their cases, exhibit only the red and azure lights that mark their physical and intellectual natures, their animal and mental selves: the beasts have no souls; only man has a soul. Therefore—although no contemporary critic seems to have noted it, and although even Dickens and Forster seem not to have picked up the point, and although Bulwer himself did not, even in his preface, come right out and say so—man cannot have evolved in the way that Darwin was suggesting, since man's possession of soul differentiates him totally from all the rest of animal life. Within two years of the publication of *The Origin of Species*, Bulwer was arguing subtly but mightily against its thesis. Since no powerful critic of the German sort for whom he had wished actually did appear to analyse his meanings, he determined to hold his fire for a time, and on the next occasion to attack Darwinism so frontally and obviously that nobody could miss the point. This we shall find him doing in *The Coming Race*.

The ambivalence in Bulwer's feelings about the supernatural, which we have so often noted in the course of our efforts to retrace some of his own explorations, found its subtlest expression in *A Strange Story*. We have already quoted the letter to Forster of November 19, 1861, in which Bulwer, with apparent satisfaction, seems almost to triumph in the ambivalence. Does the answer lie "in physiological causes" or in "causes that may be in Nature, but [which contemporary] physiology as yet rejects as natural"—that is, in causes that modern science still refuses to accept, causes that others regard as supernatural, which, we know, has always been to Bulwer only the natural that is not yet understood? Where does the answer lie, in *A Strange Story*? Bulwer himself says complacently to Forster, "I leave the whole to be solved either way." Hence the delicate balance of the story, the shifts in point of view: even Faber is inconsistent, as we have seen. Hence, what one modern critic regards as Bulwer's unsureness, his hedging, his maddening inarticulateness, we can recognize as deliberate, challenging, subtle. Why should he come right out and say that the apparently supernatural was actually supernatural, when this would not only destroy the delicate tensions of the novel, but commit him to a position he was not ready to defend? And why, on the other hand, should he give perfectly natural explanations of phenomena that in fact the scientists could not explain, although they often sneered at them? To deprive the apparently supernatural of its apparent supernaturalness before the scientists had truly investigated it would have been as unscientific as they, and as damaging to the novelist's purpose as it would be to proclaim it truly supernatural.[73]

Only about two weeks later—December 3, 1861—writing once more to Forster, Bulwer put on record his own view of the supernatural in a form we may regard as definitive. Without taking up mesmerism and spirit manifestation, he declared:

> what I really wish to imply is . . . that in their recorded marvels which are attested by hundreds and believed by many thousands, things yet more incredible than those which perplex Fenwick are related, and philosophers de-

clining thoroughly to probe these marvels, they have been abandoned for the most part to persons who know little or nothing of philosophy or metaphysics, and remain insoluble.

I wish to make philosophers inquire into them as I think Bacon, Newton, and Davy would have inquired. There must be a natural cause for them ... even if that natural cause be the admission of a spirit world around us. ... I do believe in the substance of what used to be called Magic, that is I believe that there are persons of a peculiar temperament who can affect extraordinary things not accounted for satisfactorily by any existent philosophy. ... the constitution or temperament is always more or less the same in these magicians, whether they are clairvoyants or media ... it is only persons who are highly susceptible of electricity who have it, and their power is influenced according as the atmosphere is more or less charged with electricity. This all Media and Mesmerists will acknowledge.

But here we get a commencement for philosophical inquiry. Electricity is in inanimate objects as well as animals; hence the power of media over inanimate objects. In my final scene I suppose the atmosphere extremely electrical—there is a spontaneous combustion in the bush, the soil is volcanic, there is trembling of the earth. I observe that all the newest phenomena in spirit manifestation resemble markedly in character the best attested phenomena in witchcraft. For instance, Hume [this spelling represents the proper and usual pronunciation of D. D. Home's family name in Scotland and England] floats in the air—this was said of the old magicians. Now I find that the Seeress of Provorst [sic] whose story is told by a physician and a very learned man, and who lived in a state of catalepsy, was at times so light that her body floated on water, and could not be kept down; that she would also rise in the air as if she would fly out of the window. There again philosophy is on its own ground. There is a cataleptic disease in which abnormal phenomena occur. But all Media and clairvoyants are more or less cataleptic. You will judge by these remarks of my own idea. Abnormal phenomena may solve some great problems in real science. Thus common reasoners reject a good, well-authenticated ghost story altogether. But real philosophers delight in one; and some of the most interesting chapters in the works of physicians are upon spectral illusions founded on these very ghost stories. The mystery of dreaming is the vexed question to this day between materialists and immaterialists. Spectral phenomena are dreams turned inside out. . . .[74]

Although this letter contains some echoes familiar to us from other letters and essays of Bulwer's—the peculiar temperaments, the electrical constitutions, and the like—it relates them in an illuminating way to his own intentions in the cauldron scene of *A Strange Story*, and it makes certain wholly new comparisons. That between spirit manifestation and witchcraft, between Home and the witches, is fresh, and so is the mention of the celebrated seeress of Prevorst (the proper spelling), Friedrike Hauffe, née Wanner (1801–1829), whose tragic story was first published in 1829 by Dr. Justinus Kerner (1786–1862), the town physician of Weinsberg not far from Heilbron, who was her medical attendant in the last years of her illness, and who was also an important romantic poet. In her cataleptic states the seeress spoke and wrote a secret language and had prophetic visions. She also worked at least one miraculous cure.[75] Bulwer's recognition that dreams lay close to the center of scientific interest in the supernatural is a particularly perceptive one.

Taken altogether, the record of Bulwer's active interest in the supernatural and his literary use of occult themes is probably unique among English writers of the period. Some few others dabbled in mesmerism, like Dickens himself, or went in for mysticism like George MacDonald. But, so far as I know, no other English writer embarked on such active investigation as Bulwer or displayed such an open mind and such commitment in this field. Does this prove Bulwer an eccentric or even a madman? In his lifetime many poked fun at him, especially as he grew older—lonely, looking like a sorcerer, smoking a pipe six feet long whose bowl rested on the floor, likely to make an unexpected appearance at the breakfast table in an old dressing gown, fresh from who knew what imaginary sinister labors in his (nonexistent) laboratory. Perhaps it is superfluous in these days, when general interest in the occult has once again risen so high, even to try to defend his activities. On the other hand, unless one tries to put them into perspective, lovers of the irrational may accept them too readily and praise him too highly, just as lovers of the rational may deprecate them overmuch.

Perhaps the most effective way of estimating Bulwer's achievement is to remind oneself how deeply addicted to the occult—in contrast to the English—were many of the novelists of the Continent. Leaving aside Goethe and Schiller, who influenced Bulwer directly, and Dumas, Gautier, and those later French adepts of the supernatural treated by John Senior in his *The Way Down and Out*, let us limit ourselves to Balzac and Victor Hugo, who resemble Bulwer both in their devotion to the occult, and in their literary versatility: like him, they sometimes wrote of the occult, and more often they did not. But, as with him, it played a very great part in their lives. And the parallels in their writings and in their attitudes are sometimes astonishingly close.

Balzac's mother showed a deep interest in Swedenborg, Saint-Martin, Boehme, and other mystics, and we know that he too read these authors extensively. He probably used, for the most part at least, the 1788 *Abrégé* of Swedenborg published at Stockholm and Strasbourg by Daillant de la Touche, but he also had access to the difficult and cumbersome originals. From Swedenborg he got, as he once said, "the rational explanation of phenomena ordinarily called supernatural," precisely the view that Bulwer put into the mouths of Zanoni and Mejnour. Like Bulwer, Balzac was early and deeply interested in mesmerism (magnetism), with which he later said he had been familiar as early as 1820. In the novel *Louis Lambert* (1834–1835), whose hero Balzac drew in part as a self-portrait, Madame de Staël finds fourteen-year-old Louis reading Swedenborg's *Heaven and Earth* and sends him off to school, but promptly forgets him. At school, defying the authorities, Lambert makes a deep study of magnetism, "seeking to collect all the facts and then proceed by analysis, the only torch that can guide us through the darkness." Louis becomes convinced of the enormous importance of the human will, and believes it can be trained as a mighty force that can accomplish almost any deed. As Balzac himself may have done as a schoolboy, Louis Lambert writes a treatise on the will—*Traité sur la volonté*—which the school authorities confiscate: the will is a physical force like the "odic" or "odyllic" fluid postulated by Mesmer and his followers. So is human thought.

Both are physical realities, and the inner man, the *être actionnel,* can project them into the outer world so as to learn the past, foretell the future, and see things taking place at great distances. One might be reading a more dramatic and excitably French and youthful version of Bulwer's "Normal Clairvoyance of the Imagination." In his preface to *La Peau de chagrin* (1839) Balzac remarks that "the warmest and most exact painter of Florence has never been to Florence," just as Bulwer would say, "I am not sure that I could not give a more truthful picture of the Nile, which I have never beheld except in my own dreams, than I could of the little lake at the bottom of my own park, on the banks of which I loitered out my school boy holidays. . . ." The deadly power of the will we have seen defined and operating in Balzacian terms in Bulwer's "The Haunters and the Haunted," especially in the unrevised version. "Thought," says an aged doctor in Balzac's *Les Martyrs ignorés* (1837), "is the most powerful of all agents of destruction, the real destroying angel of humanity." In *A Strange Story,* Sir Philip Derval compares it to a projectile.

But this is not all. After Louis Lambert's death, the narrator recovers fragments of Lambert's written *Pensées.* Here Lambert distinguishes three levels of humanity. The first are the *Instinctives,* "who are born, work, and die without ever rising to the second degree of human intelligence, that of *Abstraction*." The second are those who do reach the level of Abstraction, which "compared to the Instinct is an almost divine power.... from it are born laws, the arts, interests, and social ideas.... Man judges everything by his abstractions, good, evil, virtue, crime." Naturally, there are human beings who combine the power of instinct and that of abstraction in all sorts of proportional combinations.

The third and highest sphere, as far above Abstraction as Abstraction is above Instinct, is the sphere of "*la Spécialité*," which alone can explain God, and to which the far too intellectualized abstraction often bars the way.

> The *Spécialité* consists in seeing the things of the material world, as well as those of the spiritual world, in their original and consequential ramifications. The greatest human geniuses are those who have left behind the darkness of Abstraction to reach the light of the *Spécialité*. (*Spécialité*, *species*, sight, to speculate, to see everything and all at once; *speculum*, the mirror or means of appreciating a thing by seeing it whole.) Jesus was a *Spécialist*, he saw a deed in its origins and in its results, in the past that had given rise to it, in the present where it was happening, and in the future when [its consequences] were developing; his sight penetrated the understanding of everybody else. The perfection of inner sight gives birth to the gift of *Spécialité*. *Spécialité* brings intuition with it. Intuition is one of the abilities of the HOMME INTÉRIEUR of whom the *Spécialisme* is an attribute. It operates by a sensation not perceptible to the man who obeys it: Napoleon instinctively moving from his position just before a bullet reaches it.

And of course, just as there are human beings who combine their instinctiveness with their powers of abstraction, so there are those who combine their powers of abstraction with the *Spécialité*. These are men of genius.

Louis Lambert's fragmentary *Pensées* provide us with further triplets corresponding to these three levels of humanity:

the natural world, the spiritual world, and the divine world; action, the spoken word, and prayer; fact, understanding, and love. But we have already discovered enough to realize the striking parallel with the lesson of *A Strange Story*, with its division between the worlds of the body, the mind, and the soul; the animal, the intellectual, and the spiritual; Margrave, Fenwick, and Lilian. At first glance no two novels seem less alike than *Louis Lambert,* in which virtually nothing happens and there is no magic or sensationalism, and *A Strange Story*, with its complicated series of events and its wild supernatural manifestations. Yet the underlying philosophy is the same.

And our interest is the more whetted when we discover that the very same Maine de Biran, to whom Bulwer attributed his inspiration for the ideas underlying *A Strange Story,* actually has been singled out by Henri Evans, the chief authority on Balzac's novel, as providing the closest contemporary parallel imaginable to the fictional Louis Lambert. "Biran and Lambert, were temperamentally brothers, and their philosophical development was parallel, down to, but excluding the final phase." And from Maine de Biran's *Journal* of December 18, 1818, Evans quotes passages which, as he says, instantly bring to mind the instinct, the abstraction, and the "spécialité" of *Louis Lambert*. But while Maine de Biran, and Bulwer in his footsteps, drew from his analysis the necessity of belief in orthodox Christianity, Louis Lambert did not take the last step and "remained to the last attached to a mystical and occultist naturalism." As we know, Bulwer had read Maine de Biran, while Balzac, in whose lifetime Biran's *Journal* and the *Nouveaux Essais d'anthropologie* were still unpublished, may have been introduced to his ideas by Victor Cousin himself, Biran's admirer and later editor, and Balzac's own instructor in philosophy.

We shall perhaps find no other parallels as startling as those between Louis Lambert's view of the power of the will and that expressed in "The Haunters and the Haunted," between the thesis of Louis Lambert's *Pensées* and the thesis of *A*

Strange Story, or between the views that Balzac and Bulwer both proclaimed on the power of the clairvoyant imagination. But let us look at the fragmentary sketch called *Les Martyrs ignorés*, already cited, which probably reproduces conversations at the Café Voltaire in which Balzac himself had participated ten years earlier with several other amateurs of the occult, including the Prussian mesmerist Dr. Koreff, and the extraordinary Polish mathematician and mystic Hoëné-Wronski, whose sale for an enormous sum of his secret of the Absolute to a credulous millionaire had created a scandal and suggested in part *La Recherche de l'absolu.* Here we find one of the company, Physidor, a young doctor whose specialities are phrenology and madness, quoting with full approval the advice an aged doctor has given him:

> Believe in the occult sciences! Most people deny their truth, nothing more natural than that; they are known only by men scattered here and there among the human race, like the trees in a forest that stay green when the other have lost their leaves. Becher, Stahl, Paracelsus, Agrippa are men who are not understood, misunderstood like the alchemists who are all accused of trying to make gold. Making gold was their point of departure; but believe the testimony of an aged scholar, they were looking for something better than that, they wanted to find the basic molecule, they were seeking for the primal substance. In things that were infinitely small they sought to surprise the secret of that universal Life whose game they were observing. The combination of all these sciences constitutes Magism, do not confuse it with Magic. Magism is the lofty science which seeks to find the intimate meaning of things, and looks to see to what loose threads natural consequences are truly attached.

Zanoni and Mejnour would have agreed, but would have entered the caveat that these later alchemists had been deprived of the true Chaldaean secrets. But in *Falthurne*, written in 1820 but never published until 1950—so we can be sure that Bulwer never read it—Balzac's female magus gets her secret

knowledge from a patriarch, who himself had obtained it
from Moses, the priests of Egypt, the Brahmans of India, and
the mysteries of Isis, quite the proper pedigree.

A recent student of Balzac says of his interest in the occult
that he was in love with the invisible, with magnetism and
somnambulism, but that he also kept right on studying the
scientists of his epoch. While feeding himself on occultism,
he sought at the same time in the science of his period a more
solid groundwork for his mind. With few reservations one
might say the same of Bulwer, a more learned adept than
Balzac, but one who was, like him, unwilling to abandon the
writing of novels of daily life. So from Balzac and Bulwer
we have both excursions into the occult and many many works
totally without occult elements.

As for Victor Hugo, it was Balzac who first introduced
him to Saint-Martin. At some time before 1840 it is believed
that Hugo successfully mesmerized his young son, and cured
him of attacks of insomnia that had left the doctors helpless.
In the forties he went to séances with *somnambules,* and with
the famous clairvoyant Alexis Didier, who successfully read
the word *"politique"* which Hugo had written on a pale green
slip of paper and wrapped up in a parcel. The drowning of
Hugo's young daughter and her husband in 1843 brought him
great grief, and his failure to win political preferment from
Louis Napoleon, which led to his exile in Guernsey, also contributed to his becoming a devotee of the occult. Hugo's house
was haunted: there were strange beings, "impalpable and mysterious creatures that floated in the atmosphere," and one
day while taking notes in his garden he saw the diaphanous
shadow of their wings trembling on his pages.

In the craze for spiritualism that struck France in the early
1850s—by then Balzac, of course, was dead—Hugo was instantly caught up. As his old friend Madame de Girardin
introduced him to the new fad and his son Charles usually
acted as medium, all sorts of spirits manifested themselves
while the table tipped: Tyrtaeus, the Spartan military poet,

Hannibal, Dante, Racine, André Chenier, the spirits of Tragedy and of Criticism, and even Androcles's lion made their
presence known and gave messages. No such parade had ever
rewarded Bulwer's researches: so far as we know, only Shakespeare had come, except for Bulwer's daughter Emily and the
single manifestation of the spirit that had inspired *Zanoni*.
The madness of Hugo's friend Hennequin made him begin
to fear for his own reason, and he gave up active investigation
of the occult. But he had been deeply affected by it, and was
perhaps a more convinced believer than either Balzac or Bulwer had ever been. And more than either, he took upon
himself the rôle of magus, of intermediary between the human
race and God: here we need not follow him.

But it is arresting to discover that Hugo, Balzac, and Bulwer in the end all reached identical conclusions with regard
to occult manifestations. "All these things," Hugo wrote in
his *Post-Scriptum de ma vie*,

> spiritualism, somnambulism, catalepsy, those with convul-
> sions, second sight, tables that tip and speak, invisible rappers,
> ... fire-eaters, snake-charmers, etc. so easy to make fun of,
> require to be examined from the point of view of reality.
> ... If you give up these facts, watch out; charlatans will
> take over and imbeciles too. Where Laplace refuses to deal
> with the situation, Cagliostro makes his appearance. . . . What
> would have been astronomy becomes astrology, what would
> have been chemistry becomes alchemy. As Lavoisier gets
> smaller, Hermes gets bigger. Thaumaturgy, the philosopher's
> stone, potable gold, Mesmer's tub, all that false science per-
> haps is asking only to be true science. You have not wished
> to see man's face, and so you shall see his mask.

And in a note for *Les Misérables*, written August 12, 1860,
Hugo says:

> Science was frightened by chloroform, by biological phe-
> nomena, by the strange question of the [tipping and speak-
> ing] tables, by Mesmer, by Deleuze, by Puységur, by mag-
> netic ecstasy, by artificial catalepsy, by sight that passed

through obstacles, by homeopathy, by hypnotism. Science, under the pretext that such things are "marvels," abandoned its scientific duty. To the great profit of the charlatans she left the mass of the people a prey to visions mingled with reality. She stumbled and lost her footing, and where she should have advanced she retreated.

As for Balzac, in *Le Cousin Pons* (1847), one of his latest novels, with nothing of the supernatural about it, he interpolated an entire chapter called "Treatise on the Occult Sciences," simply on the pretext that one of his characters was about to consult a fortune-teller. The élite of society, he says, have for about two centuries simply abandoned the occult, and nowadays those who insist on hard physical or chemical evidence scorn it. It is absurd to tell men's fortunes by reading cards or palms, but at one time travel by steam and photography were also regarded as absurd, and aerial navigation still is. The occult sciences do in fact exist, and so many verified and authentic facts have emerged from them that there ought to be an endowed chair for teaching them at the Sorbonne. In the absence of such serious study, they have fallen into the hands of frauds.[76] So, with respect to the occult, both our French novelists sound a note identical to that sounded by Bulwer in the letter to Forster with which we concluded our account of *A Strange Story*: scientists (he calls them "philosophers") are unwilling to give the supernatural serious consideration, and he would like to force them to do so.

In *The Coming Race* (1871), Bulwer returned for the last time—and in a very limited way—to the occult. This short, fast-moving novel finds its closest past analogues in Swift's accounts of Lilliput, Brobdignag, Laputa, and the land of the Houyhnhnms. Like them it describes in convincing detail an imaginary civilization, while cleverly and effectively satirizing certain major social developments of the author's own time. But it also clearly belongs to the school of science fiction often considered to have been invented by H. G. Wells some twenty years after Bulwer's death, and it anticipates in an uncanny way major scientific advances that would not in fact take place for several generations. The portentousness of *Zanoni*, the philosophy of *A Strange Story* have altogether disappeared, and very little indeed is left of the occult machinery that gave them their characteristic mystery. Yet *The Coming Race* is nonetheless at once the climax and the summing up of Bulwer's long love affair with the supernatural.

As the result of an accident in a mine he is exploring, the narrator, an unnamed American, finds himself dropped into an underground country, one of many that he learns exist beneath the surface of the earth. Its people have detachable wings, live altogether by artificial light, easily learn to communicate with him, and prove to enjoy a tranquil, harmonious existence, from which war and armies have been totally banished and, with them, police, crime, corruption, poverty, discontent and government by force. Machines do most of the work, and the little assistance that they require is cheerfully supplied by children under sixteen. All enjoy freedom, and all accept a simple religion of a single creator, about which nobody argues or debates. Luxurious living, flowers, singing birds, perfumes, massive architecture, personal comeliness are everywhere. People rarely die before they reach the age of a hundred, they eat temperately, there is no alcoholic drink, and there are no tensions. For diversions, they have flying games and boring theatrical productions performed by the children and attended by the mothers and sisters. They trade with other peoples. They have newspapers and journals devoted to mechanical science, but no literature, which is regarded as "incompatible with . . . perfection of social or political felicity." The public libraries contain all the best books. Science provides a congenial occupation. Music flourishes, but art less than it once did. In fact, to the visitor the paintings are a puzzle: the rules of perspective seem to be new and different, and the effect is "vague, scattered, confused, bewildering—heterogeneous fragments of a dream of art." One could almost believe Bulwer had seen an early Picasso, if one did not know that to be impossible.

The chief target of Bulwer's satire is the concept of equality, so fully realized in this imaginary society. Among its actual manifestations that he disapproved of in his own world, he took aim especially at the Darwinian theory of evolution, at the Americans, and at the "new" woman. Long ago Zanoni had vainly attempted to prove to Nicot the utter impossibility of the French revolutionaries' dream of equality, and how undesirable such a society would be if ever it could be realized. Here, in *The Coming Race*, Bulwer has painstakingly and credibly portrayed such a society, with its many delightful features. But its American discoverer, at first full of admiration, soon finds things dull. He decides that if

> you could take a thousand of the best and most philosophical of human beings you could find in London, Paris, Berlin, New York or even [!] Boston and place them as citizens in this beatified community, . . . in less than a year they would either die of *ennui* or attempt some revolution by which they would militate against the good of the community. . . . Where there are no wars there can be no Hannibal, no Jackson, no Sheridan—where states are so happy that they

fear no danger and desire no change, they cannot give birth to a Demosthenes, a Webster, a Sumner, a Wendel [sic] Holmes, or a [Ben] Butler. . . . no Shakespeare, Molière, or Mrs. Beecher Stowe.

The fun poked at American national pride here is incidental only: the chief message is the intolerable boredom to which the attainment of Utopian equality would condemn ordinary mortals.

As for evolution—against which, we remember, *A Strange Story* had too subtly protested—in *The Coming Race* Bulwer now attacks it head on. Here underground, the archaeological section of the museum contains a great collection of historic portraits of the people's leaders, extending back some 7,000 years. At the beginning of the series stand three "pre-historical" portraits, painted at the order of a hero-sage, a mythical philosopher, the ancestor of the entire race. These show the philosopher himself, his grandfather, and his great-grandfather:

> The philosopher is attired in a long tunic which seems to form a loose suit of scaly armour, borrowed, perhaps, from some fish or reptile, but the feet and hands are exposed: the digits in both are wonderfully long and webbed. He has little or no perceptible throat, and a low receding forehead . . . bright brown prominent eyes, a very wide mouth, and high cheek-bones, and a muddy complexion. . . . the grandfather had the features of the philosopher, only much more exaggerated: he was not dressed, and the colour of his body was singular; the breast and stomach yellow, the shoulders and legs of a dull bronze hue: the great-grandfather was a magnificent specimen of the Batrachian genus, a Giant Frog, *pur et simple*.

Tradition records—just to drive the point home—that in their "Wrangling or Philosophical Period of History,"

> a distinguished naturalist . . . proved to the satisfaction of numerous disciples such analogical and anatomical agreements in structure between an An [the "coming race's" own

name for itself] and a Frog as to show that out of the one must have developed the other. Others argued that the reverse was true.

But nobody any longer cares for such disputes. And no reader could miss Bulwer's point this time. Indeed he even quotes Louis Agassiz's famous remark that only the "direct intervention of a reflective mind" could ever have called into existence an "organized being."

It is the American narrator himself who supplies much of the anti-American satire, often both funny and well-taken. His father had once run for Congress, but was signally defeated by his tailor, and was regarded as disqualified for public life by his opulence. Americans prefer "for the exercise of power and the acquisition of honours, the lowliest citizens in the point of property, education, and character." That, at least, has changed during the last century. In telling his new subterranean friends about the world from which he had come, the narrator

> Naturally. . . . touched but slightly, though indulgently, on the antiquated and decaying institutions of Europe, in order to expatiate on the present grandeur and prospective pre-eminence of that glorious American Republic, in which Europe enviously seeks its model and tremblingly foresees its doom.

This exaggeration of the *Martin Chuzzlewit* type he follows by quoting the peroration from a speech by an American Senator (who has just accepted a large bribe to vote for a railway appropriation). The Senator looks forward to that happy day

> when the flag of freedom should float over an entire continent, and two hundred millions of intelligent citizens, accustomed from infancy to the daily use of revolvers, should apply to a cowering universe the doctrine of the patriot Monroe.

In 1971 this passage stings harder than it could possibly have done in 1871. One of the other underground states is still a democracy, evidently much like America. There,

> the evil passions are never in repose—vying for power, for wealth, for eminence of some kind; and in this rivalry it is horrible to hear the vituperation, the slanders, and calumnies which even the best and mildest among them heap on each other without remorse. . . . their misery and degradation are the more appalling because they are always boasting of their felicity and grandeur. . . . They desire to enlarge their dominions more and more. . . .

The "new woman," or "girl of the period," with her increasingly independent attitudes and her participation—to what seems to us a ludicrously small degree—in activities Victorian England normally regarded as masculine, had in the 1860s aroused in England some conservative alarm that women were becoming unsexed. Heavy-handedly Bulwer strikes out at such women: the females of "the coming race" are taller and larger than the males, wear longer wings, do better in the study of abstruse and mystical subjects, and perform all the wooing. They have "perseverance, ardour, and persuasive power," and usually get the men they want, since after all it matters more to a woman to have the proper mate. Once married, they are "amiable, conciliatory, and submissive wives." The narrator is vigorously (and comically) courted by Zee, the kind and handsome but terrifyingly Amazonian daughter of his host; this puts him in an embarrassing and even a dangerous position. Another girl too, the daughter of the chief magistrate, seems to be in love with him. For a time this brings out the worst American traits in him: the love for titles (he thinks of the girl as a prince's daughter) and his determination to change everything once he comes to power—he will introduce whiskey and opera and ballet with girls one does not have to marry, invade the lands of other people, and generally "bestow on the people of the nether world the blessings of . . . the upper." But the impossibility of his marriage with a woman of their race soon becomes clear, and he manages to escape.

The agency that has enabled the coming race to reach their extraordinary level of social advancement is a single substance, which is called vril: one identifies the Latin root that means man, and implies manhood, virility. And it is with the all-important and all-pervasive vril that we rejoin the occult tradition, and discern a direct development from Bulwer's earlier work. The narrator is first introduced to vril as a force that can make people forget anything they may have been told—in this case any disturbing facts that he himself might reveal to them about the frightening forms of behavior still fashionable in the world above, about which it is preferred that they remain ignorant. What is vril exactly?

> I should call it electricity, except that it comprehends in its manifold branches other forms of nature, to which in our scientific nomenclature, differing names are assigned, such as magnetism, galvanism, &c. These people consider that in vril they have arrived at the unity in natural energic agencies, which has been conjectured by philosophers above ground, and which Faraday thus intimates under the more cautious term of correlation: "I have long held an opinion," says that illustrious experimentalist, "almost amounting to a conviction. . . . that the various forms under which the forces of matter are made manifest, have one common origin: or, in other words, are so directly related and mutually dependent that they are convertible, as it were, into one another, and possess equivalents of power in their action."

With his unerring eye for the latest and soundest scientific speculation, Bulwer has jumped to a passage in Faraday that hypothesizes something very like what we would call atomic energy.

With vril the members of the coming race (who call themselves Vril-ya, because of the very importance of their discovery) can influence the weather and regulate the temperature.

By other operations, akin to those ascribed to mesmerism, electro-biology, odic force &c. but applied scientifically through vril-conductors, they can exercise influence over minds, and bodies animal and vegetable to an extent not surpassed in the romances of our mystics.

Was it not known in his world, he is asked, that

all the faculties of the mind could be quickened to a degree unknown in the waking state, by trance or vision, in which the thoughts of one brain could be transmitted to another, and knowledge rapidly interchanged?

Yes, he says, he had heard tales of mesmeric clairvoyance in the world he came from, but imposture, and the unreliability even of genuine manifestations, had led to its abandonment. Similar abuses had accompanied the earliest stages of Vril-ya's researches as well, before vril itself had been properly understood. It was vril, rightly used, however, the narrator now learns, that enabled him while in trance to learn the language of the Vril-ya.

But vril, which was only discovered after long researches, during which the race had gone through a period of democracy, class struggle, and war, could also

destroy like a flash of lightning; yet, differently applied, it can replenish or invigorate life, heal, and preserve, and on it they chiefly rely for the cure of disease, or rather for enabling the physical organization to re-establish the due equilibrium of natural powers, and thereby to cure itself. By this agency they rend their way through the most solid substances, and open valleys for culture through the rocks of their subterranean wilderness. From it they extract the light which supplies their lamps, finding it steadier, softer, and healthier than the other inflammable materials they had formerly used.

Since its force was so terrible,

war between the Vril-discoverers ceased, for they brought the art of destruction to such perfection as to annul all superiority in numbers, discipline, or military skill. The fire lodged in the hollow of a rod directed by the hand of a child could shatter the strongest fortress or cleave its way from the van to the rear of an embattled host. If army met army, and both had command of this agency, it could be but the annihilation of each. The age of war was therefore gone . . . all notions of government by force gradually vanished from political systems and forms of law.

In vril we can see the fluctuating and uncertain power of the earthly mesmerist and the clairvoyant and Braid, the hypnotist, transformed into a sure triumph: viewed in this aspect, vril is Louis Lambert's *Spécialité* or Margrave's mighty power to govern people's minds and behavior at a distance, but what happens in the world above only in trance and with irregular and disappointing results has now been made dependable and brought within the regulating grasp of the coming race that dwells below. At the same time, vril's curative powers properly exercised are precisely like those of Zanoni's and Mejnour's elixir of life: by natural means vril permits the restoration to the human physiology of whatever it needs to combat disease or to continue life. The immortality that had preoccupied Bulwer in his later thirities, that Glyndon in *Zanoni* had so eagerly sought, and that still haunted Bulwer in his late fifties, when the used-up Margrave-Grayle committed two murders and planned a third to secure it, had now, in Bulwer's late sixties, reduced itself simply to a life of a century or more, passed in excellent health through the power of vril. And the principle of the saving substance had moved from the simple but dangerous mystic command of herbalism in *Zanoni*; through Margrave's elaborate magic and alchemy, heat, Van Helmont's primal gas, or Phosoxygen, in *A Strange Story*; to vril, the essential substance that meets Faraday's conjecture with respect to the convertibility of the forces of matter.

Only a man extremely well-read in the sciences, however, could have then gone on to make the connection between matter and energy, and to realize that if one ever could make vril it might be turned into a completely effective agent of destruction. Like atomic energy, vril, in its peacetime uses, supplies power for public lighting, and its blast cuts through underground rock to open paths into inaccessible areas of the subterranean world. Used for war, it has made war impossible. And Bulwer has stated our own theory of the deterrent so well that in the 1970s one might fail to realize what original imaginative genius this must have required: "if army met army, and both had command of the agency, it could be but the annihilation of each." On the other hand, it is only the *mutual* possession of vril that acts as a deterrent: if necessary, the Vril-ya use it quite cold-bloodedly against the less developed subterraneans who have not got it. A distant barbarian democratic underground state of 30,000,000 people that is threatening a neighboring Vril-ya tribe of 50,000 will be wiped out by a few Vril-ya children. The children also use vril freely to destroy the terrifying monsters which would otherwise threaten the lives of the Vril-ya.

The machine for using vril is an all-purpose vril staff, which the narrator is never allowed to handle for fear of a terrible accident.

It is hollow, and has in the handle several stops, keys, or springs by which its force can be altered, modified, or directed—so that by one process it destroys, by another it heals—by one it can rend the rock, by another disperse the vapour—by one it affects bodies, by another it can exercise a certain influence over minds. It is usually carried in the convenient size of a walking-staff, but it has slides by which it can be lengthened or shortened at will. . . . its power . . . was proportioned to the amount of certain vril properties in the wearer, in affinity or *rapport* with the purpose to be effected. Some were more potent to destroy, others to heal, &c; much also depended on the scale and steadiness of volition in the manipulator. . . . the full exercise of vril-power can only be acquired by constitutional temperament—i.e. by hereditarily transmitted organization . . . a female infant of four years old belonging to the Vril-ya . . . can accomplish feats with the wand placed for the first time in her hand, which a life spent in its practice would not enable the strongest and most skilled mechanician, born out of the pale of the Vril-ya, to achieve.

Children have simpler vril-staffs than adults, but also the most destructive, since it is they who are entrusted with the duty of monster-hunting and killing. Wives and mothers have the most healing instruments: the destructive power is usually altogether removed from theirs. Special tubes can shoot vril an indefinite distance, with range finding unerringly assisted by an observer in an airboat, to destroy in a flash if necessary a city twice as large as London.

Zee, the magnificent but terrifying lover of the narrator, demonstrates her own extraordinary skill with the vril-staff in the museum's department of vril-mechanisms. Her thumb is bigger, and her palm thicker and of a finer texture than that of human beings, and a special nerve that circles her wrist around the ball of the thumb physiologically equips her, and her fellow Vril-ya, for the precise control of a vril-staff that no human being (all of whom of course lack this special nerve, which had developed in the Vril-ya over the course of many generations) could ever develop even with practice. Zee can stir apparently lifeless mechanisms into action by the vril-staff. She explains that this is possible because

> no form of matter is motionless and inert; every particle is constantly in motion and constantly acted upon by agencies, of which heat is the most apparent and rapid, but vril the most subtle, and, when skilfully wielded, the most powerful.

Vril "animates" the targets toward which it is directed, and has thus enabled the Vril-ya to construct a whole range of automata that serve them. So, like the power that emanates from Margrave's wand, vril, with its enormously wider and more effective scope of activities, emanates from a staff. And again as in regard to Margrave's wand, the reader of *The Coming Race* can decide for himself to what extent he wishes to recognize male genital imagery in the vril-staff that dispenses the force deliberately named to recall virility, and to what extent the parallel, if any, was intentional with Bulwer.

Published anonymously, *The Coming Race* had a great success and was praised, Bulwer wrote, by "precisely the reviewers who would have been most uncivil to the author if they had guessed him." He enjoyed what he called his book's "solemn quiz on Darwin and on Radical politics," but once again, for the last time, did not "think people have caught or are likely to catch the leading idea of the book": that if

> all the various ideas of philosophical reformers could be united and practically realised, the result would be firstly, a race that must be fatal to ourselves; our society could not amalgamate with it; it would be deadly to us, not from its vices but its virtues. Secondly, the realisation of these ideas would produce a society which we should find extremely dull, and in which the current equality would prohibit all greatness.[77]

True indeed: these are the ideas that motivate *The Coming Race*.

Yet for us the most impressive thing about it must be the skill, originality, imagination, and perception with which Bulwer handles his old preoccupations. Besides its social and political purposes, *The Coming Race* stands as his culminating effort to deal with nonpolitical and nonsocial topics that had engaged his attention for more than thirty years—with the occult, the supernatural, the mystic, the basic forces that might be imagined to underly the world of matter, of energy, of human survival, and of communication between mind and mind. Having accompanied Bulwer through the decades since these matters had first attracted him, and having observed his experiments and his growth as he three times used fiction to translate his views into art, we must, I think, agree with Dickens: he was not the Magician's servant, but the Magician.

NOTES

1 Michael Sadleir, *XIX Century Fiction* (Berkeley and Los Angeles: University of California Press, 1951) Vol. I, p. xix. All that Sadleir published on Bulwer was *Bulwer: A Panorama. I. Edward and Rosina 1803–1836* (Boston: Little Brown, 1931), which, as we have noted, breaks off in 1836. Bulwer's name was Edward George Earle Lytton Bulwer, but he usually left out the George and the Earle. On Queen Victoria's coronation in 1838 he was made a Baronet, and so prefixed "Sir" and added "Bart." When he inherited his mother's estates in 1843, he hyphenated his last name to Bulwer-Lytton, and was usually called "Sir Edward Bulwer-Lytton," although the full name was now Sir Edward George Earle Lytton Bulwer-Lytton. When he was raised to the peerage in 1866 as first Baron Lytton of Knebworth, he became even more resoundingly Edward George Earle Lytton Bulwer-Lytton, Lord Lytton. This increasingly pompous orchestration contributed to the irritation of his enemies, who were many and articulate. Long before the peerage, in April 1847, Thackeray signed his *Punch* magazine parody of Bulwer's Newgate novels as by "Sir E.L.B.L.BB.LL.BBB.LLL., Bart." Fortunately Thackeray died before Bulwer became a lord. Despite the fact that this present study deals chiefly with writings produced after the conferring of the Baronetcy in 1838, it seems simplest to call our man simply "Bulwer." Confusion is compounded because Bulwer's son, the second Lord Lytton, became an Earl (First Earl of Lytton), and both he and *his* son, Bulwer's grandson, the second Earl of Lytton, wrote biographies of Bulwer. In fact, the second Earl wrote two. These three works are all useful, the second listed is indispensable. They are *The Life, Letters, and Literary Remains of Edward Bulwer, Lord Lytton*, by his son [Robert Lytton, First Earl of Lytton, "Owen Meredith"] (2 vols.; London:

Kegan Paul, Trench and Co., 1883); The Earl of Lytton
[Victor A. G. R. Lytton, Second Earl of Lytton], *The
Life of Edward Bulwer, First Lord Lytton, By his Grand-
son* (2 vols.; London: Macmillan, 1913)—hereafter cited
as *Life* (1913); and The Earl of Lytton, K. G. [Victor
A. G. R. Lytton, Second Earl of Lytton], *Bulwer Lytton*
(London: Home and Van Thal Ltd., 1948), The English
Novelists, hereafter cited as *Bulwer-Lytton*. Sadleir's *XIX
Century Fiction* includes the most useful bibliography of
Bulwer's writings yet available. For an interesting essay on
Bulwer as a politician, see Keith Feiling, *Sketches in Nine-
teenth-Century Biography* (London, New York, Toronto:
Longmans Green, 1930), pp. 121–136.

For a useful bibliographical introduction to the litera-
ture about Bulwer, see Curtis Dahl, "Edward Bulwer-
Lytton," *Victorian Fiction: A Guide to Research*, Lionel
Stevenson, ed. (Cambridge, Massachusetts: Harvard University Press, 1964). In reviewing this book in *Nineteenth-
Century Fiction* 19, 4 (March 1965), p. 407, the Professors
Tillotson remark that it is not surprising that little work
has been done on Bulwer because Bulwer is "third-rate in
his fiction." Disraeli and Bulwer, treated together in
Dahl's bibliographical essay, are often linked. See for example, Lionel Stevenson's early essay, "Stepfathers of Vic-
torianism," *Virginia Quarterly Review* 6, 2 (April, 1930),
pp. 251–267. For Bulwer's plays, Charles H. Shattuck,
*Bulwer and Macready, A Chronicle of the Early Vic-
torian Theatre* (Urbana: University of Illinois Press,
1958). For an entertaining "sequel" to *The Lady of Lyons*,
written in sham Bulwerese, see St. John Hankin, *Dramatic
Sequels* (New York: Minton Balch, 1926), pp. 89–104.
England and the English has been recently re-published,
edited by Standish Meacham (Chicago and London: University of Chicago Press, 1970), Classics of British Historical Literature, John Clive, ed. For *Pelham* and dandy-
ism, most recently, see Ellen Moers, *The Dandy: Brummell
to Beerbohm* (London: Secker & Warburg, 1960), pp.
68–83. For the Newgate novel, see the excellent study by
Keith Hollingsworth, *The Newgate Novel, 1830–1847:*

Bulwer, Ainsworth, Dickens and Thackeray (Detroit: Wayne State University Press, 1963) with a good account of Thackeray's hostility to Bulwer, which almost (but not quite) goaded Bulwer to challenge Thackeray to a duel, and with full references to all earlier scholarship. For the historical novels, see Curtis Dahl, "History on the Hustings: Bulwer Lytton's Historical Novels of Politics," *From Jane Austen to Joseph Conrad. Essays Collected in Memory of James T. Hillhouse,* edited by Robert C. Rathburn and Martin Steinmann, jr. (Minneapolis: University of Minnesota Press, 1958), pp. 60–71.

2 The only study known to me on our subject is a thoroughly amateurish brief little book by a practicing Theosophist and occultist, C. Nelson Stewart, *Bulwer Lytton as Occultist* (London: The Theosophical Publishing House, 1927). It deals to some degree with Bulwer's own occult investigations and associations but hardly at all with his fiction. Even within his own subject the author has missed most of the interesting sources. The occult themes in *Godolphin* are chiefly to be found in Chapters XXVI–XXX, XLI, LXIII. Quotations from XXVI and LXIII. For two good essays on *The Last Days of Pompeii,* see Curtis Dahl, "Bulwer-Lytton and the School of Catastrophe," *Philological Quarterly* XXXII, 4 (October, 1953), pp. 428–442, and "Recreators of Pompeii," *Archaeology* 9, 3 (Autumn, 1956), 185–191. J. C. Simmons, "Bulwer and Vesuvius: the Topicality of *The Last Days of Pompeii,*" *Nineteenth-Century Fiction* 24, 1 (June, 1969), pp. 103–105, points out that Vesuvius obligingly erupted in 1834, and that the news reached England just before the novel was published, thus enhancing its success. Quotations from *The Last Days of Pompeii* (3 vols.; London: Bentley, 1834), Vol. I, pp. 283–284, 285; Vol. II, p. 149ff. "The Tale of Kosem Kosamim the Magician," first published in *The Student* (1832), is here cited from the reprint in *Miscellaneous Prose Works* (London: Bentley, 1868), Vol. II, pp. 211–228; quotation from p. 215. For the alchemists and fire, see for example, C. G. Jung, "The Spirit Mercurius," *Alchemical Studies,* The Collected Works of

C. G. Jung, 13, Bollingen Series XX (Princeton University Press, 1967), pp. 209–210. Although it is not truly an occult short story, we may make brief mention here of "Arasmenes the Seeker," which also first appeared in *The Student* and was reprinted in *Miscellaneous Prose Works*, Vol. II, pp. 112–145. It deals wtih the search of a young Chaldaean for the Garden of Eden. Though he enjoys both sensual and married love, and achieves wealth and military and political power, paradise eludes him. The story is a parable of human life without the introduction of occult machinery. Nor shall we consider the much later short story, called "A Dream of the Dead," and published under the pseudonym of "Hermides" in Blackwood's *Edinburgh Magazine* 49, 3 (September, 1859), pp. 358–363. It tells of the unhappy bafflement of a man who dreams that he has died, and who finds that the dead are impatient, unwilling to answer his questions, poor, mean, and suspicious; in fact death is a sort of caricature of life. This is effective as dream-narrative, but we need not include it in the canon of Bulwer's occult fiction.

3 Bulwer has Pelham say of himself that when he left Eton he "could make twenty Latin verses in half an hour; . . . could construe without an English translation all the easy Latin authors, and many of the difficult ones *with it;* . . . could *read* Greek fluently and even translate it through the medium of a Latin version at the bottom of the page." *Pelham* (London: Colburn, 1828), Vol. I, p. 11. But it would be wrong to take this literally of Bulwer, especially in his maturity. On foreign-language tags note the harsh and unfair criticism of Walter Frewen Lord, "Lord Lytton's Novels," *The Nineteenth-Century* 50 (No. 295, September 1901), pp. 449–458, reprinted in Lord's *The Mirror of the Century* (London and New York: John Lane, 1906), pp. 172–189: ". . . we do not expect to find a practised writer allowing himself to write 'Diavolo!' or 'tout Paris' or 'auf Wiedersehen!' when the rest of the page purports to be in English. . . . Lytton . . . was addressing ignorant readers who had a few shillings to spare. He fooled their taste to the top of its bent. The odd little

tags in Greek, Latin, French, German, and Italian with
which he filled his pages were found to be very acceptable."
For a celebrated parody of the "silver fork" school's habit
of using French tags, see the passage from Chapter XXVIII
of *Nicholas Nickleby* cited and quoted by Kathleen Tillotson, *Novels of the Eighteen-Forties* (Oxford: Clarendon
Press, 1954), pp. 73–74. For "Bulwer-Lytton and the
Religion of Schiller," see Chapter VIII, pp. 197–206, of
Frederic Ewen, *The Prestige of Schiller in England, 1788–
1859* (New York: Columbia University Press, 1932). On
Goethe and Bulwer, see H. Goldhan, "Über die Einwir-
kung des Goethischen Werthers und Wilhelm Meisters
auf die Entwicklung Edward Bulwers," *Anglia* 16 (1894),
pp. 297–369, and Susanne Howe, *Wilhelm Meister and his
English Kinsmen* (New York: Columbia University Press,
1930), Chapter VI, pp. 126–177. We shall be dealing below with the influence on Bulwer of Goethe's views on
alchemy, of Novalis, and of the mystical and alchemical
writers. For the scientists, see the references in the footnotes of Bulwer's volumes of essays published as *Caxtoniana* (2 vols.; Edinburgh and London: Blackwood, 1863);
quotation from "On Essay-Writing in General and These
Essays in Particular," Vol. II, pp. 243–244.

4   Lord in *loc. cit.*, note 3 above, Aytoun's verses published
under the pseudonym of Bon Gualtier in "Lays of the
Would-Be Laureates," Tait's *Edinburgh Magazine* 10
(May, 1843), p. 276, as part of "A Midnight Meditation
by Sir E. L. Bulwer." For another spoof of *Zanoni*, famous
at the time, see Bret Harte, "The Dweller of the Threshold.
By Sir Ed—d L-tt-n B-lw-r," *Condensed Novels and
Other Papers* (New York: F. W. Carleton, 1867), pp. 49–
55. For the Psychical Research Society comparison, and
the Rosicrucians, *Life* (1913), Vol. II, p. 41.

5   For a short useful introduction to the mysteries of alchemy,
see R. Bernouilli, "Spiritual Development as Reflected in
Alchemy and Related Disciplines," *Spiritual Disciplines.
Papers from the Eranos Yearbooks* (New York: Pantheon
Books, 1960), Bollingen Series XXX, 4, pp. 305–340. *Zicci*
appeared in Harrison Ainsworth's *The Monthly Chronicle*

during 1838. It is occasionally reprinted in collected editions. *Zanoni* appeared in 3 vols. (London: Saunders and Otley, 1842). Unless otherwise specified all references are to this first edition. *Le Comte de Gabalis* is a novel, by the Abbé N. de Montfaucon de Villars, first published in 1670. Its sub-title . . . *ou entretiens sur les sciences sécrètes* suggests its occult content, but not its flippant and mocking tone. The Abbé Villars, as Bulwer elsewhere simply calls him (*Zanoni*, p. xii), introduced Paracelsus's elemental spirits, salamander, sylph, goblin, and undine (see note 7 below) into his story. There were two English translations in 1680, one by A. L[ovel] for R. Harford, and the other by P[hilip] A[yres] for B. M. "Printer to the Royal Society of the Sages at the Sign of the Rosy Crusion." More available is the most recent translation, *Comte de Gabalis by the Abbé N. de Montfaucon de Villars, Rendered out of French into English with a Commentary* (New York and London: The Brothers [i.e. of the Rosy Cross], 1914). It is interesting that self-styled Rosicrucians should publish this novel, which, it was rumored, so angered their seventeenth-century forerunners by revealing their secrets that they arranged for the death of its author, who was indeed mysteriously murdered. The novel had a long-lasting and powerful influence on later writers, not still fully studied. See Constantin Bila, *La Croyance à la magie au XVIIIe siècle en France dans les contes, romans, et traités* (Paris: J. Gamber, 1925); P. Sucher, *Les Sources du merveilleux chez E. T. A. Hoffmann* (Paris: Félix Alcan, 1912); M. Milner, *Le Diable dans la littérature française* (Paris: Librairie José Corti, 1960), Vol. I, pp. 69ff. especially p. 70, n. 1.

6 *Zanoni*, Vol. I, pp. iv, xi, xiii, xvii, xx.

7 *Phaedrus*, 265; B. Jowett, tr., *The Dialogues of Plato* (Oxford University Press, 1892), Vol. I, p. 473; *Iamblichus on the Mysteries of the Egyptians, Chaldaeans, and Assyrians*, T. Taylor, tr. (Chiswick: C. Whittingham, for the Author, 1821), pp. 350ff. For "pagan" Taylor, friend of Blake and Peacock, whose works influenced Coleridge, Shelley and other Romantics, see now the prefaces to K.

Raine and G. M. Harper, eds., *Thomas Taylor the Platonist, Selected Writings* (Princeton: University Press, 1969), Bollingen series LXXXVIII. For Taylor's influence on Bulwer, see below, note 17. This has not been previously noticed.

So far we need a word of identification of each of the following:

Averroes (1126–1198) the Spanish Muslim philosopher, Ibn Rushd, was an astronomer, physician, and commentator on Aristotle.

Paracelsus (1495–1541), Theophrastus Bombast von Hohenheim, was the German physician, alchemist, and magician, popularizer in his day of the Neoplatonic and Byzantine lore of the "elemental spirits." Each of the four elements had its own indwelling form of elemental spirit: earth the goblins or gnomes, air the sylphs, water the undines, and fire the salamanders. Paracelsus' treatise on this subject conveniently translated into English in Henry E. Sigerist, ed., *Four Treatises of Theophrastus von Hohenheim Called Paracelsus* (Baltimore: Publications of the Institute of the History of Medicine, The Johns Hopkins University, 1941), second series, Texts and Documents, Vol. I, pp. 215–253. The Abbé de Montfaucon de Villars (see above, note 5) took his elemental spirits direct from Paracelsus.

"Bringaret," see below, end of note 8.

Apollonius is Apollonius of Tyana (or Tyaneus), the sage of the first century A.D., who died in the reign of Nerva (96–98), and whose life-history, written in Greek by Philostratus (born c. 172), was published sometime after the year 217. It was allegedly based in part on a memoir (long since lost) composed by a disciple of Apollonius, named Damis of Nineveh, which was given to Philostratus by the Empress Julia Domna, wife of Septimius Severus (193–211). Philostratus also used Apollonius's own letters, which were circulating in his day, and many of which survive in our own. Philostratus' chief purpose was to prove that his hero was no mere magician, but a true sage and prophet. The life declares that Apollonius was a neo-Pythagorean ascetic, following the rules of Pythagoras for the simple life and performing miraculous cures. Though he kept a rigid vow of silence for five years, Apollonius knew all languages without having learned them, could converse with birds and animals, had power over the spirits, and could predict the future. He traveled widely, reforming the pagan cults wherever he went, especially urging the end of animal sacrifice; went to India, where he grew to know the Brahmans, and to Egypt, where he took the voyage up the Nile to visit the Gymnosophists (naked philosophers) of Ethiopia. Though often in difficulties with the Roman authorities, he ended his days at an advanced age as a favorite of Nerva. Apollonius was believed to have ascended bodily into heaven, and later to have appeared to the living to reassure them about survival after death. Temples were set up to him, and in the third century pagan opponents of Christianity sometimes put Apollonius forth as a rival to Christ—Hierocles, a Roman provincial governor under Diocletian (284–305), writing a book to prove it. This was answered by Eusebius of Caesarea, the Christian historian, who dismissed Apollonius as a charlatan who owed whatever success he might have had to his use of evil spirits. Philostratus' *Life of Apollonius,* together with the surviving letters and Eusebius' treatise, are available in a translation by F. C. Conybeare, in the Loeb Classical Library (2 vols.; London: Heinemann, and New York: G. P. Putnam's Sons, 1926). Apollonius's life and deeds and reputation made him a natural hero for later amateurs of the occult, as we shall soon see. In *The Last Days of Pompeii* (Vol. I, p. 314) Bulwer has a Pelham-like flippant note: "Apollonius knew the language of birds, read men's thoughts in their bosoms, and walked about with a familiar spirit. He was a devil of a fellow with a devil, and induced a mob to stone a poor demon of venerable and mendicant appearance, who ... changed into a huge dog. He raised the dead, passed a night with Achilles, and when Domitian was murdered, he called out aloud (though in Ephesus at the time) 'Strike

the tyrant!' The end of so honest and great a man was
worthy his life. It would seem that he ascended into
heaven. What less could be expected of one who had
stoned the devil?" In *Zanoni*, "Platonists," as elsewhere
among the occultists, means what we would call Neoplatonists.

Apollonius of Tyana is the leading character in the
late novel *Agathodämon* (1799) by Christoph Martin
Wieland (1733–1813), which Bulwer no doubt knew. It
is most conveniently found in C. M. Wieland, *Aus-
gewählte Werke*, ed., Friedrich Beissner, Vol. III, *Erzäh-
lende Prosa und andere Schriften* (Munich: Winkler, n.d.
[1965]), pp. 5–237. Wieland's own favorite among his
many writings, it has close relationships with the myth of
the magus in general and of the Faustian tradition in particular, as well as with Wieland's own view of Christianity.
See the dissertation of Johanna Mellinger, *Wieland's
Auffassung vom Urchristentum mit hauptsächlicher Be-
rücksichtigung seines Romans Agathodämon* (Marbach
a.N.: A. Remppis, 1911).

8 The views in the text are largely those of Paul Arnold,
*Histoire des Rose-Croix et les origines de la Franc-Maçon-
nerie* (Paris: Mercure de France, 1955), the only truly
scholarly and dispassionate approach to the subject known
to me, with a most useful bibliography of sources and
secondary writings. Even so able a scholar as John Senior
went badly astray on the Rosicrucians in *The Way Down
and Out: The Occult in Symbolist Literature* (Ithaca:
Cornell University Press, 1959) because he did not know
Arnold's book. Also useful is R. Kienast, "Johann Valentin
Andreae und die vier echten Rosenkreutzer Schriften,"
Palestra 152 (Leipzig, 1926), pp. 1–284. For a view hostile
to Arnold, see the note by Walter Weber to his new High
German translation of Johann Valentin Andreae, *Die
Chymische Hochzeit des Christian Rosenkreuz Anno 1459*
(Stuttgart: Verlag Freies Geistesleben, 1957), pp. 179ff.,
which contains also a convenient version of the *Fama
Fraternitatis*, and an essay by Rudolf Steiner, originally
written in 1917–1918. For alchemical comment on rose

and cross, see C. G. Jung *Psychology and Alchemy*, 2nd edition (Princeton University Press, 1968), Collected Works 12, Bollingen Series XX, p. 76. In addition to Andreae, the Tübingen collaborators almost surely included his friend Christoph Besold, a scholar of Greek and Hebrew, and perhaps of Arabic, who had studied the Neoplatonists, the Pythagoreans, and the Hermetic writings, and who believed that the Greeks owed much of their wisdom to Hebrew and to Egyptian traditions. A mystic and ascetic, Besold wrote of man's duty to cultivate his soul, and thus to attain the ecstatic union with the divine that the Neoplatonists had taught was possible. After his conversion to Catholicism in 1620, he broke with Andreae. Others included a Saxon nobleman, Wilhelm Wense, a disciple of Johann Arndt (1555–1621), who in turn, like the mystic cobbler Jacob Boehme (1575–1624: *Aurora*, or *Morgenroth im Aufgang*, 1612), had gone to school to Valentin Weigel (1533–1588), founder of the "Enthusiasts." There were probably several other collaborators on the Rosicrucian treatises besides Andreae, Besold, and Wense, but in any case it is not possible to allot any part of any treatise (except the *Chymische Hochzeit*) to any individual author.

The Tübingen group, then, had intimate connections with the most flourishing school of contemporary German mysticism. To their thinking Tommaso Campanella (1568–1639), the Calabrian Dominican turned social reformer who languished for 27 years in Neapolitan prisons, made his contribution; his *City of the Sun* was brought in manuscript to Tübingen in 1611. Behind the contemporary mystics the tradition and the borrowings stretched back to Joachim of Fiore (1145–1202), whose own life as a pilgrim, an *illuminatus*, and a recluse probably provided the model for the biographers of the mythical Rosenkreutz, and whose division of human history into the age of the Father (Adam to Uzziah), the age of the Son (Uzziah to Joachim's own lifetime, c. 1160), and the age of the Holy Spirit (which was about to begin in catastrophe) gave rise to all the many later triadic divisions of history, and was directly echoed in the *Fama's* announcement of the imminent arrival of the third age. Joachim's prediction of the Fall of the New Babylon was widely interpreted in his own day as meaning the papacy; and the Lutheran authors of the *Fama* made it specific. The authors of the Rosicrucian message inherited also the Neoplatonic current of thought that passed from the fifth-century writings of Pseudo-Dionysus the Areopagite, via the Belgian Jean Ruysbroek (1293–1381) and other fourteenth-century mystics, who wrote of the truly illuminated, the "hidden sons of God," those who would find their names written in the Book of Life. Indeed, the actual birth and death dates of Thomas à Kempis himself (1380–1471) approximate those assigned to Rosenkreutz by his inventors, one of whom took the pseudonym "a Campis" deliberately. And everybody, it seems—certainly both Paracelsus and Luther himself—echoed these voices in predicting the imminent end of the world. So there was nothing new in the *Fama* except Rosenkreutz's life and tomb.

Maier's defense of the Order in *Silentium post Clamores* (1617), the disappearance to India and Tibet in Heinrich Neuhaus, *Pia et ultissima admonestatio de Fratribus Rosae Crucis* (1618). All details in Arnold. Goethe's *Geheimnisse*, in *Werke* (Weimar, 1887–1918), Vol. XVI, p. 173.

Bulwer's "Bringaret," whom he later in *Zanoni* once (Vol. I, p. 173) calls "Bringeret," was clearly Johann Bringeren, a Frankfort publisher, who issued the 1615 edition of the *Fama* (II in Arnold's bibliography) and a collection of documents defending the Rosicrucians in 1616 (*Judicia clarissimorum aliquot virorum.* ... XXIV in Arnold's bibliography), as well as a collective demand for admission to the order (Arnold, p. 153). The fact that Bulwer misspells his name and refers to him as if he had *written* books about the Order instead of merely publishing them suggests two things: Bulwer had never himself seen one of these books or he would have got the name right; and whoever had furnished him with the garbled name— perhaps the occult bookseller in *Zanoni* (who actually existed; his name was Dendy; see *Life*, 1913, Vol. II, p.

39)—had taken it for the name of the author, not merely
the publisher, since the treatises were anonymous, and
Bringeren's the only name on the title-pages. In a nineteenth-century (undated) edition of *Biographie Univer-
selle*, Vol. V, p. 540, there is a short notice identifying
Bringeren as the publisher of the *Fama* of 1615; the book
is "introuvable." B. de Telepnef, "Paracelsus und die Fama
Fraternitatis. . . ." *Nova Acta Paracelsica, Jahrbuch der
Schweizerischen Paracelsus-Gesellschaft*, Vol. IV (1947),
pp. 30–36, who used a copy in Basel, refers to it as
"aüsserst selten."

9   *Zanoni*, Vol. I, pp. 17, 48, 53–54, 54–55, 62, 63, 64. Cagliostro (1743– ?) born Joseph Balsamo, the celebrated adventurer, healer, magician, freemason, died in the papal prison
at an unknown date. During his lifetime he allowed it to
be understood that he was immortal.

10 John Ashburner, M.D., *Notes and Studies in the Philosophy of Animal Magnetism and Spiritualism* (London: H.
Baillière, 1867), pp. 282ff. For a summary of the various
theories of the prophecy, see E. P. Shaw, *Jacques Cazotte
(1719–1792)* (Cambridge, Massachusetts: Harvard University Press, 1942), pp. 90–94, who takes a middle position
on its historicity: it probably did not happen quite the way
La Harpe reported it, but *some* prophecy was voiced.
Shaw's view accepted by Max Milner, *Le Diable dans la
littérature française de Cazotte à Baudelaire* (Paris: Librarie
José Corti, 1960), Vol. I, p. 105, n. 4 ("une bonne mise au
point.") My own brief statement in the text reflects the
formulation of A. Viatte, *Les sources occultes du roman-
tisme, 1770–1820* (Paris: Honoré Champion, 1928), Vol. I,
pp. 195–200. For Cazotte's initiation into Martines' de Pasqually's sect, which was a historic fact, and its later legend-
ary accretions, see the same authorities. Cazotte remained
deeply imbued with Martinism, though he broke with its
leaders over the Revolution, and continued to support the
monarchy.

11 For Martines de Pasqually, see G. Van Rijnberk, *Un
Thaumaturge au XVIIIe siècle, Martines de Pasqually* (2
vols.; Paris: Alcan, 1935 and Lyon: Raclet, 1938); R. Le

Forestier, *La Franc-maçonnerie occultiste au XVIIIe siècle et l'Ordre des Élus Coëns* (Paris: Dorban-Ainé, 1928). For Saint-Martin, Mieczyslawa Sekrecka, *Louis-Claude de Saint-Martin. Le philosophe inconnu* (Wroclaw: Acta Universitatis Wratislavensis Nr. 65. Romanica Wratislavensia II, 1968). Martines de pasqually, *Traité de la Réintegration de êtres* (Paris: Bibliothèque Rosicrucienne, 1899); [Louis Claude de Saint-Martin] Un ph(ilosophe) in (connu), *Des Erreurs et de la Vérité* (Edinburgh, 1775). More generally, Viatte, *Sources*, Vol. I, pp. 45–71, 188–195, now a trifle outdated. For the confusions involved in the term "Martinism," which is best avoided, see R. Amadou, "Balzac et Saint-Martin," *Année Balzacienne* (1965), pp. 45ff.

12 *Zanoni*, Vol. I, pp. 123, 108–109, 111, 124–125, 173, 176, 127, 132. Agrippa is Heinrich Cornelius Agrippa of Nettesheim (1487–1536) alchemist, cabalist, healer, astrologer, author of the influential *De Occulta Philosophia*, vague and derivative but much admired.

13 *Zanoni*, Vol. I, pp. 129, 130. For Goethe and plants, see Chapters III and IV of R. D. Gray, *Goethe the Alchemist* (Cambridge: University Press, 1952). For the blue flower see Bruce Haywood, *Novalis: The Veil of Imagery* (Cambridge, Massachusetts: Harvard University Press, 1959), *passim*, but especially pp. 140–142. Jung's most interesting comments in *Psychology and Alchemy*, *op. cit.* note 8 above, p. 76. He also suggests (pp. 79–80, n. 33) a connection with the "sapphire-blue flower of the hermaphrodite," referred to in the *Epistola ad Hermannum*, Archbishop of Cologne, concerning the Philosopher's Stone. One wonders if Novalis may have encountered this text in his mineralogical studies.

14 *Zanoni*, Vol. I, pp. 150, 166, 262, 173–174, 191–192; Vol. II, p. 19.

15 *Zanoni*, Vol. I, p. 292; Vol. II, p. 93. Nicot has already played a large part in some of the less important episodes of the novel, which I have omitted here, and we shall encounter him later in Paris as a leading revolutionary and friend of Robespierre. I have not been able to find any

pupil of David's who would fit this description, but it applies perfectly to David himself. D. L. Dowd, *Pageant-Master of the Republic, Jacques-Louis David and the French Revolution,* University of Nebraska Studies, New Series No. 3. (Lincoln: The University, June, 1948), shows how David's reputation has fluctuated with the acceptability of his politics, and in the "Bibliographical Essay" points out (p. 150) that Sir Walter Scott had "pictured David as a bloodthirsty terrorist and disparaged his artistic genius," while (p. 152) Carlyle in his French Revolution (1837) had "execrated 'gross David with the swoln cheek.' " Bulwer of course knew these references of Scott and Carlyle to David, and besides was deeply read in the French works on the Revolution. Being thoroughly anti-revolutionary, and disliking the realistic neoclassical school of painting which David had founded, Bulwer could combine his political and his aesthetic dislikes by caricaturing David as Nicot, and making him an unconscionable villain. David, who died in exile in Brussels late in 1825— only seventeen years before *Zanoni* was published—was loathed and feared as a dangerous revolutionary by all who viewed the revolution as Bulwer did, both on the continent and in England. In fact, he *had* voted for the death of Louis XVI, and always defended the Terror, as befitted an unrepentant ex-president of the Jacobin Club, and member of the Committee of General Security, which, with the Committee of Public Safety and the Revolutionary Tribunal, exercised dictatorial authority during the Terror. The commission on which David sat controlled the police and decided who should be tried by the Tribunal. See also Dowd's article "Jacques-Louis David, Artist Member of the Committee of General Security," *American Historical Review* LVII, 4 (July, 1952), pp. 871–892, and L. Hautecoeur, *Louis David* (Paris: La Table Ronde, 1954), who depends on Dowd.

16   *Zanoni,* Vol. II, pp. 58, 60, 61.

17   *Zanoni,* Vol. I, pp. 155, 157, 170; Vol. II, pp. 46–47; Vol. I, pp. 189, 265–267. For "shemaia" see Alexandre Safran, *La Cabale* (Paris: Payot, 1960), pp. 103ff. For modern

scholarship on the Chaldaean Oracles and their tradition, see E. R. Dodds, "Theurgy," Appendix II of *The Greeks and the Irrational* (Berkeley and Los Angeles: University of California Press, sixth printing, 1968), pp. 283–311, reprinted from *The Journal of Roman Studies* 37 (1947), pp. 55–69. Quotations in text from pp. 284, 285, 287, 288. Fuller and more recent discussion in Hans Lewy, *Chaldaean Oracles and Theurgy, Mysticism, Magic, and Platonism in the Later Roman Empire*, Publications de l'Institut Français d'Archéologie Orientale, 19, Recherches d'Archéologie, de Philosophie et d'Histoire, 13 (Cairo: Imprimerie de l'Institut, 1956), where the oracle used by Bulwer is cited and discussed pp. 133–134, n. 256. As Lewy points out, it comes from Proclus' commentary on the *Cratylus*, G. Pasquali, ed. (Berlin: Teubner, 1908), 29. Lewy renders it "The sublime name leaps in tireless revolution into the worlds at the mighty command of the Father," and explains that the tireless revolution (akoimeto strophalingi) refers to the magical tops (*Iynges*) spun by Chaldaean theurgists as part of the ceremonies in summoning up the gods. Bulwer could not have known of this meaning of *Iynx*. Lewy's book critically reviewed by E. R. Dodds, "New Light on the Chaldaean Oracles," *Harvard Theological Review* 54 (October, 1961), pp. 263–273. For a general recent discussion of theurgy see P. Boyancé, "Théurgie et Telestique néoplatoniciennes," *Revue de l'Histoire des Religions* 148 (1955), pp. 189–209. Most recently see F. W. Cremer, *Die chaldäischen Orakel und Jamblich de mysteriis* (Meisenheim am Glan: Anton Hain, 1969) Beiträge zur klassischen Philologie, R. Merkelbach, ed., Heft 26. Our oracle on pp. 72, 73, and notes 281, 288. For texts of Psellus see J. Bidez, *Catalogue des Manuscrits alchémiques grecs*, Vol. VI (Brussels, 1928); J. M. Hussey, *Church and Learning in the Byzantine Empire 867–1185* (Oxford: University Press, 1947), pp. 73–88; and K. Svoboda, *La Démonologie de Michel Psellus* (Brno, 1927), Spisy Fakultety Masarykovy Universitety v Brne, no. 22. For Bulwer's probable immediate source see Thomas

Taylor, "Collection of the Chaldaean Oracles," *The Classical Journal* 16 (1817), pp. 333–344; 17 (1818), pp. 128–133, 243–264, with our oracle on p. 255. Modern scholars no longer refer to this extraordinary learned effort. For Paracelsus and iliastrum, see Walter Pagel, *Paracelsus. An Introduction to Philosophical Medicine in the . . . Renaissance* (Basel and New York: Karger, 1958), pp. 89ff, 112, 227ff, with much information on his precursors. For animal heat, see Everett Mendelsohn, *Heat and Life. The Development of the Theory of Animal Heat* (Cambridge, Massachusetts: Harvard University Press, 1964); quotation from p. 14. *The illuminati* and their eagerness for death in Viatte, *Sources,* Vol. I, p. 40, n. 5. While we wait for the blessed moment when we shall be joined to the creator, let us try to get into touch with angels and other spirits; death itself is the great enlightenment. With Novalis especially, the nobility of the view degenerates into morbidity.

18   *Zanoni,* Vol. II, p. 107. *The Poems and Ballads of Schiller.* Translated by Sir Edward Bulwer Lytton Bart. (Edinburgh and London: Blackwood, 1844), Vol. I, p. 68; *Zanoni,* Vol. II, p. 104. For Hyacinth and Rosebud, see Novalis, *Schriften,* Paul Kluckhohn, ed. (Leipzig: Bibliographisches Institut, 1928), Vol. I, pp. 23–27. In *The Last Days of Pompeii* (Vol. I, pp. 104ff.) the wicked Egyptian wizard Arbaces tells the disillusioned priest of Isis, Apaecides, that "Isis is a fable. . . . that for which Isis is a type is a reality, an immortal being; Isis is nothing; Nature, which she represents, is the mother of all things—dark, ancient, inscrutable, save to the gifted few. 'None among mortals hath ever taken off my veil,' so saith the Isis that you adore; but to the wise that veil hath been removed, and we have stood face to face with the solemn loveliness of Nature." And later (Vol. I, p. 309), during the fight between Glaucus and Arbaces in Arbaces's house, the Egyptian calls upon his statue of Isis to help him, and the machinery responds: ". . . the still and vast features of the goddess seemed suddenly to glow with life; through the

black marble, as through a transparent veil, flushed lumi-
nously a crimson and burning hue—around the head played
and darted coruscations of livid lightning—the eyes became like balls of livid fire, and seemed fixed in withering
and intolerable warmth." Bulwer with his Neoplatonic
learning probably knew of the séance in the temple of Isis
(the only place pure enough) in Rome, to which Porphyry
reports that his master Plotinus (205–270) was invited
by an Egyptian priest, and at which a god in fact manifested himself. Dodds, *op. cit.*, (note 17 above), pp. 289ff.
For Madame Blavatsky's plagiarisms from Bulwer, see
S. B. Liljegren, "Quelques Romans anglais source partielle
d'une religion moderne," *Mélanges d'Histoire générale et
comparée offerts à Fernand Baldensperger* (Paris, 1930),
Vol. II, pp. 60–67, and again in *Bulwer Lytton's Novels
and Isis Unveiled*, Essays and Studies in English Language
and Literature XVII (Upsala; Copenhagen; Cambridge,
Massachusetts, 1957).

19 *Zanoni*, Vol. II, pp. 146, 149, 150, 151, 151–152, 153, 154,
159–160, 160, 167, 168. Albertus Magnus (1193–1280), is
the prolific scholar, scientist, and theologian, student of
Aristotle. He experienced a revival in the nineteenth century, was hailed in 1836–1837 by Ernst Meyer as the
greatest botanist of his age, was long regarded as a magician, and was surely a believer in magic and in demons.
He distinguished between good and bad magic, and was
much interested in dreams and in alchemy. In one of the
treatises ascribed to him, perhaps wrongly, he argues for
the power of the human mind to control or alter objects
through love or hate. See L. Thorndike, *A History of
Magic and Experimental Science*, fifth printing (New
York: Columbia University Press, 1958), Vol. II, pp. 517–
576 and 720–750. To Hermes Trismegistus (associated
with the Egyptian god, Thoth) was ascribed a great mass
of mystical writing of the early Roman period of which
the surviving fragments are largely astrological. See A. D.
Nock and A. Festugière, eds., *Corpus Hermeticum* (4 vols.,
Paris: Les Belles Lettres, 1945–54).

20 *Zanoni*, Vol. II, pp. 172, 173, 175, 175–176, 188, 210, 212, 265, 267. "Burri" is Giuseppe Francisco Borri (c. 1625–1695), alchemist, physician, medical attendant to Queen Christina of Sweden, born in Milan, died in the papal prisons. For the alchemists' view of the elixir, with special reference to Goethe, see R. D. Gray, *Goethe the Alchemist, op. cit.*, note 13 above, pp. 118–119, 168–169, 226ff., 266. The treatise falsely ascribed to Ramon Lull quoted in C. G. Jung, *Psychology and Alchemy, op. cit.*, note 8 above, p. 250.

21 *Zanoni*, Vol. II, p. 294; Vol. III, pp. 15, 16, 28, 73, 79–80, 83, 86.

22 *Zanoni*, Vol. III, pp. 145, 147. *The Jerusalem Delivered of Torquato Tasso. Translated into English Spenserian Verse With a Life of the Author*, by J. H. Wiffen, fifth edition (London: Bohn, 1857), pp. 328–330. *Zanoni*, Vol. III, pp. 212, 227. For Goethe, *Wilhelm Meister*, and Tasso, see R. D. Gray, *Goethe the Alchemist, op. cit.*, p. 224. It is of some interest also that at the end of *Le Diable amoureux*, Cazotte, in a whimsical epilogue, says that the tale has been inspired by "an infinitely respectable author" who had discussed the ruses that the devil might adopt when he wished to seduce people, and adds that he will not explain further, because he has always remembered how as a young man he had refused to read a book explaining the allegory in Tasso's *Jerusalem Delivered*: let us not explain the allegory away lest the beautiful allegorical females lose their charms as females. Perhaps Tasso's Armida, mortal daughter of a magician in league with Satan, may have inspired Cazotte. (See E. P. Shaw, *op. cit.*, note 10, p. 59). And perhaps Bulwer, conscious that he too was writing an allegory, may have been thinking not only of Tasso here, but of Cazotte's use of Tasso. We shall find Schiller too using Tasso in an occult story. Below, text and note 25.

23 See, for example, the excellent article by Michael Lloyd, "Bulwer-Lytton and the Idealising Principle," *English Miscellany* 7 (Rome, 1956), pp. 25–39. See also E. Drou-

gard, *Villiers de l'Isle-Adam, Les Trois premiers contes* (Paris: "Les Belles Lettres," 1931), Vol. II, p. 66, n. 1, where Zanoni and Mejnour are called "les deux derniers Rose-Croix."

24 *Zanoni*, Vol. III, pp. 261, 266.

25 The "poor fribble" quoted from Francis Espinasse's *Literary Recollections* in Susanne Howe, *Wilhelm Meister ...*, *op. cit.*, note 3 above, p. 49. Carlyle's letter on *Zanoni* in *Life* (1913), Vol. II, p. 39; Anne Thackeray Ritchie, *Chapters from some Unwritten Memories* (London: Macmillan, 1894), p. 178. *The Athenaeum* 748 (Saturday, February 26, 1842), pp. 181–183. I cite *Der Geisterseher* from Friedrich Schiller, *Sämtliche Werke* (Munich: Winkler, 1968), edited by Perfahl and Koopmann, Vol. III, pp. 529ff. See Friedrich Burschell, *Schiller* (Hamburg: Rohwolt, 1968), pp. 215ff., 239. Bulwer "The Art of Fiction," *Monthly Chronicle*, 1826 reprinted in *Critical and Miscellaneous Writings* (Philadelphia: Lea and Carey, 1841), Vol. I, p. 81. *Life of Schiller, op. cit.*, n. 18 above, Vol. I, p. xciv. For the influence of *The Ghost-Seer* in England, F. Ewen, *The Prestige of Schiller, op. cit.*, n. 3 above, *passim*. "Lieblingsschwärmerei," *Geisterseher*, p. 539.

26 *The Literary Gazette* 1310 (Saturday, February 26, 1842), pp. 137–138.

27 *Life* (1913), Vol. II, pp. 33, 34.

28 *The Examiner* (Saturday, February 26, 1842), pp. 132–133. The two Lucianic satires conveniently in the Loeb Classical Library edition, Vol. II, A. M. Harmon, ed. (London and New York: Heinemann and Macmillan, 1915), pp. 451ff. (*Philosophies for Sale—Bion Prasis*) and Vol. III (London and New York: Heinemann and G. P. Putnam, 1922), pp. 319ff. (*The Lover of Lies, or the Doubter—Philopseudos e Apiston*).

29 *Life* (1913), Vol. II, p. 35.

30 "The Reign of Terror: Its Causes and Results," here cited from the reprint twenty-six years after the original publication, in *Miscellaneous Prose Works by Edward Bulwer, Lord Lytton* (London: Richard Bentley, 1868), Vol. I,

pp. 1–48. Quotations from pp. 4–5, 42–43, 45, 46. Letter
to Forster about the essay in *Life* (1913), Vol. II, pp. 51–
52. Twenty years later, Bulwer repeated with additions
his *Zanoni* portrait of Robespierre in an essay on "The
Sympathetic Temperament," *Caxtoniana* (Edinburgh and
London: Blackwood, 1863), Vol. I, pp. 286–289.

31 This dedication is to be found prefixed to all editions of
Zanoni, beginning with that of 1845.

32 *Life* (1913), Vol. I, p. 441. For Gibson, see the fine article
by Jörgen B. Hartmann, "Canova, Thorvaldsen, and Gibson," *English Miscellany* 6 (Rome, 1955), pp. 204–235,
and the works there cited. The plates illustrating Hartmann's article include a photograph of Gibson's tombstone with Bulwer's epitaph (Plate 51).

33 Michael Lloyd, "Bulwer-Lytton and the Idealising Principle," *English Miscellany* 7 (Rome, 1956), pp. 25–39.

34 See Curtis Dahl's articles, cited in note 2 above.

35 Miss Martineau's letters printed in *Life* (1913), Vol. II,
pp. 35–38. R. K. Webb, *Harriet Martineau, A Radical
Victorian* (London: Heinemann, 1960), pp. 199–200 has
a brief summary of the correspondence.

36 Here quoted from the 1853 reprint published by George
Routledge and Son, the new postscript by Bulwer and
Miss Martineau's "key" to *Zanoni* can be found appended
to any edition of the novel after that date.

37 *Caxtoniana* (Edinburgh and London: Blackwood, 1863),
Vol. II, pp. 148–149.

38 *Autobiography*, ch. XIII.

39 C. R. Maturin, *Melmoth the Wanderer* (4 vols.; Edinburgh: Constable, 1820), Vol. III, pp. 151–224 for the
idyll between Melmoth and Immalee. For *Melmoth* and
Balzac, see most recently M. Le Yaouanc, "Présence de
'Melmoth' dans 'La Comédie humaine,'" *l'Année Balzacienne* (1970), pp. 103–128, the second portion of an
article of which the first, on the earlier novels of Balzac,
was scheduled to appear in the *Mélanges* [Herbert J. ?]
Hunt; other bibliography in Le Yaouanc's first footnote.
The passage from *Le Centénaire* here I translate from the
1962 facsimile reprint by Les Bibliophiles de l'Original of

the first edition of 1822 (Paris: Pollet, 1822), Vol. IV, pp. 76–79. On Hoffmann's sources for *Die Elixiere des Teufels*, P. Sucher *op. cit.*, n. 4 above, pp. 196ff.

Balzac and Hoffmann's *Elixiere*, see R. Guise, "Balzac lecteur des '*Élixirs du diable*,'" *L'Année Balzacienne* (1970), pp. 57–68, and the bibliography there cited. Quotation from J. Cazotte, *Le Diable amoureux* (Paris: Grasset, 1921), pp. 6, 7 (first publication in 1772). Has anybody ever noticed that the androgynous devil in Cazotte's novel takes the form of the servant Biondetto–Biondetta, while the servant in Schiller's *Geisterseher* (first publication in 1786–1789)—who may be the devil—is named Biondello? On *La Recherche de l'absolu*, see now the extraordinarily detailed monograph of M. Fargeaud, *Balzac et La Recherche de l'absolu* (Paris: Hachette, 1968) with much information on Balzac and the occult. See also below, text and note 76. For Thessalos, see Jack Lindsay, *The Origins of Alchemy in Graeco-Roman Egypt* (London: Frederick Muller, 1970), pp. 204ff, and the authorities he cites. Similarly Apuleius, in *The Golden Ass*, II, 2 was "attonitus, immo vero cruciabili desiderio stupidus" in his wish for marvels. *Séraphîta* in H. Balzac, *Oeuvres Complètes* (Paris: Club de l'Honnête homme, 1956), Vol. XVI, pp. 611ff.

40 The passage, to be found in any edition of *Night and Morning* after 1845, is quoted also in the interesting and suggestive article by Jack Lindsay, "Clairvoyance of the Normal. The Aesthetic Theory of Bulwer-Lytton," *The Nineteenth Century and After* 145 (January, 1949), pp. 29–38.

41 *Life* (1913), Vol. II, pp. 41–42. Hargrave Jennings, *The Rosicrucians. Their Rites and Mysteries* (London: John Camden Holten, 1870). On the other hand our harsh judgment of Jennings simply shows that we are uninitiated. As the Rosicrucian book we are quoting declares (Vol. II, p. 51, n. 1), "To the profane the things he has written is (sic!) but *jargon;* to the Initiate, the mysteries of life, of death, and of the Soul. In it will be found the *Arcanum* of

The *Light behind the Shadow*
in the
Innermost Centre of the Centre of the Triangle."

R. Swineburne Clymer, M.D., *The Book of Rosicruciae* (sic!) (Quakertown, Pennsylvania: The Philosophical Publishing Company, 1949), Vol. III, pp. 48–59. The biographical entry on Hargrave Jennings follows immediately after Bulwer's, pp. 60ff. The fact seems to be that Clymer knew very little about Bulwer or about the Rosicrucians. A long letter from Hargrave Jennings to Bulwer dated July 1, 1870 and preserved among the Lytton mss, Hertfordshire County Record Office (D/EK C18/36) shows plainly that the two men had never met. Jennings sends Bulwer a copy of the book on the Rosicrucians, mentions his own poverty, *Zanoni,* and a single note of appreciation that Bulwer had written him twenty-eight years previously for an anonymous poem. He also asks Bulwer to help find him employment. For the Comte de St. Germain, Viatte, *Sources Occultes,* Vol. I, pp. 200–203, and G. van Rijnberk, *Episodes de la Vie esotérique 1780–1824* (Lyon: Paul Derain, 1948), pp. 195–224. Even the learned scholar E. M. Butler, *The Myth of the Magus* (Cambridge: University Press; New York: The Macmillan Company, 1948) pp. 244ff., goes astray when she asserts that Zanoni was modeled on Saint-Germain. Quite the contrary. But then she also seems to accept as genuine the "Mahatma Letters" and their reference to Bulwer's club of magicians: see below, text and note 59.

42 Lytton Mss, Hertfordshire County Record Office D/EK C6/11. The last sentence only is quoted from the Lytton Manuscripts in the footnote to a letter from Dickens to Dr. Elliotson accepting an invitation to meet Townshend, in Madeline House and Graham Storey ed., *The Letters of Charles Dickens,* Vol. II: 1840–1841 (Oxford: Clarendon Press, 1969), p. 110, n. 1.

43 John Elliotson, "On Medical Anti-Mesmerists," *The Zoist* 7 (No. XXVIII, January, 1850), p. 382, footnote with double-dagger, continued on p. 383.

44 *Caxtoniana*, Vol. I, pp. 43–45.

45 *The Zoist* 2 (January, 1845), p. 512; 9 (October, 1851), p. 402ff.

46 John Ashburner, *Notes and Studies in the Philosophy of Animal Magnetism and Spiritualism* (London: H. Baillière, 1867), p. 64.

47 "On the Distinction Between Active Thought and Reverie," *Caxtoniana*, Vol. I, pp. 207–208. L. F. Alfred Maury, *Le Sommeil et les rêves* (Paris: Didier, 1861).

48 "On Essay Writing in General and These Essays in Particular," *Caxtoniana*, Vol. I, pp. 240–241.

49 For Home in general, see the lively and popular book by Jean Burton, *Heyday of a Wizard, Daniel Home, the Medium* (New York: Knopf, 1944). For the séance at Ealing, D.D. Home, *Incidents in My Life* (London: Longman, Green, Longman, Roberts and Green, 1863), p. 65. His other works do not include any mention of Bulwer.

50 Mme. Dunglas Home, *D.D. Home, His Life and Mission* (London: Trübner, 1888), pp. 50–52 (hereafter *Life and Mission*); and *The Gift of D.D. Home* (London: Kegan Paul, Trench, Trübner, 1890), p. 81 (hereafter *Gift*).

51 Mme. Home, *Life and Mission*, pp. 50, 178, 179. The Lytton Mss. in the Hertfordshire Country Record Office contain only three letters from Home (D/EK C6/25, 26 and D/EK C17/132) from 1861, 1862, and 1867, but none indicates anything but amicable feelings toward Bulwer.

52 Mme. Home, *Gift*, p. 35.

53 *Life* (1913), Vol. II, pp. 42–44.

54 *Life* (1913), Vol. II, pp. 44–47; Mme. Home, *Gift*, p. 81; *Life* (1913), Vol. II, pp. 49–50.

55 Full text of the letter here taken from *Report on Spiritualism of the Committee of the London Dialectical Society* (London: J. Burns, 1873), pp. 240–242. This is a cheap edition printed by permission from the original plates for the first edition, published by Longmans in 1870, where the page-references should therefore be the same. Mme. Home, *Gift*, p. 36 prints excerpts as if she

were giving the full text, which indeed is more damaging
to her cause than anything from Bulwer's pen.

56   Mme. Home, *Gift*, pp. 35–36.

57   "The Haunters and the Haunted," Blackwood's *Edin-burgh Magazine* XLIX, 2 (August, 1859), pp. 224–245.
All quotations in the text are from this first version. All
subsequent versions have been revised as indicated, and
there are as well, less important changes in wording. The
story is to be found in any complete edition of Bulwer's
works, sometimes in a volume with *A Strange Story*,
sometimes with other fiction.

58   Though still comparatively new to the game, Lévi receives attention as early as Alexandre Erdan (pseudonym
of Alexandre Jacob), *La France Mistique* (Paris: Coulon-
Pineau, 1854), Vol. I, pp. 288–292. The second edition,
less rare (Amsterdam: R. C. Meijer, 1860), Vol. I, pp.
213–217, reprints the essay unchanged. A. Viatte, *Victor
Hugo et les illuminés de son temps* (Montreal: Les Editions de l'Arbre, 1942), pp. 91–101, has a brief discussion
of Lévi's early days, all the more important because the
only full-length biography is by an uncritical follower.
This is Paul Chacornac, *Éliphas Lévi. Rénovateur de
l'Occultisme en France (1810–1875)* (Paris: Chacornac
Frères, 1926). See now also the Preface to F. P. Bowman,
Éliphas Lévi Visionnaire romantique (Paris: Presses Universitaires de France, 1969) "À La Découverte" Publications du Départment de Langues Romanes de l'Université
de Princeton. Chacornac, pp. 149ff. for Lévi's first English visit. The evocation of Apollonius is reprinted from
Lévi's own *Dogme et Rituel de la haute magie* (Paris:
Germer Baillière, 1861), Vol. I (*Dogme*), pp. 265ff. The
fuller description of the necessary preparations for evocation are in Vol. II (*Rituel*) of the same work, pp. 175ff.
For the second London visit, Chacornac, pp. 194ff. Lévi's
other books given to Bulwer were *Histoire de la magie*
(Paris: Baillière, 1860) and *La Clef des grands mystères*
(Paris: Baillière, 1861). Bulwer's reference to Lévi's
Dogme et Rituel without naming Lévi in *A Strange Story*

(Edinburgh and London: Blackwood, 1862), Vol. II, p. 220, footnote.

59   The statement about Bulwer's magic club comes from *The Mahatma Letters to A. T. Sinnett* (London: T. Fisher Unwin, 1923), pp. 209–210, in a letter purportedly written by Mahatma K. H. to A. O. Hume in 1881. It is taken at face value by C. Nelson Stewart, *Bulwer Lytton as Occultist* (see above, note 2), pp. 57–58. But see H. E. Hare and W. L. Hare, *Who Wrote the Mahatma Letters?* (London: Williams and Norgate, 1936), in which it is demonstrated to my satisfaction that Madame Blavatsky wrote them. I have also read several anguished defenses of the letters: H. R. W. Cox, *Who Wrote the March-Hare Attack on the Mahatma Letters?* (Victoria, British Columbia, H.P.B. Library [which is Helena P. Blavatsky], n.d. [1936]); Beatrice Hastings, *Defence of Madame Blavatsky, Section 1, Madame Blavatsky and the Mahatma Letters* (Worthing, Sussex: The Hastings Press, 1937); Irene Bastow Hudson, *"Who Wrote the Mahatma Letters?" Answered* (Victoria, British Columbia: The Author, 1936). None of these is convincing. For Madame Blavatsky's plagiaristic passion for Bulwer see the works of Liljegren cited above in note 18. To imagine a club of magicians including Lévi, Regazzoni and the Copt "Zergvan Bey" with Bulwer as its impressario would have been easy and natural for Madame B., if indeed she wrote the Mahatma Letters.

60   Bulwer's dream and Dickens's invitation, *Life* (1913), Vol. II, pp. 340–344. All references will be to the first edition: (2 vols.; Edinburgh and London: Blackwood, 1862). Recent criticism, notably Joseph I. Fradin, " 'The Absorbing Tyranny of Every-day Life,' Bulwer-Lytton's *A Strange Story*," *Nineteenth-Century Fiction* 16 (June, 1961), pp. 1–16, hereafter cited as "Fradin."

61   *A Strange Story*, Vol. I, pp. 14, 21, 68, 88, 118, 125, 126, 159, 168, 170, 178, 194. Cardan is Geronimo Cardano (1501–1576), physician, mathematician, astrologer, alchemist, and autobiographer. For Van Helmont see next note.

62 Bulwer's footnote on Liebig and Van Helmont, in *A Strange Story*, Vol. I, pp. 170–172. Walter W. Pagel, *The Religious and Philosophical Aspects of Van Helmont's Science and Medicine*, Supplements to the "Bulletin of the History of Medicine," no. 2 (Baltimore: Johns Hopkins University Press, 1944), p. 44. See especially pp. 16ff. for gas. And for a salutary warning *not* to see in Van Helmont's gas theory a mere outgrowth of Paracelsus's views of chaos, Walter Pagel, *Das medizinische Weltbild des Paracelsus. Seine Zusammenhänge mit Neuplatonismus und Gnosis* (Wiesbaden: Steiner, 1962), Kosmosophie.... edited by K. Goldhammer, Vol. I, pp. 50–51 and especially p. 50, note 5, where Pagel stresses that Paracelsian Chaos is merely an etymological not a conceptual forerunner of Van Helmontian Gas.

63 *A Strange Story*, Vol. I, pp. 212, 222, 237, 238, 239, 240, 253. Sandivogius is the Pole, Michael Sendivogius [Sędziwój] (1566–1636), author of many alchemical works including the *Novum lumen chemicum*, a treatise on sulphur, and a dialogue between Mercury, an alchemist, and nature. Quotation on Margrave's soul from Fradin, p. 6. Madame Dunglas Home, *Life and Mission*, pp. 183–184. Jean Burton, *Heyday of a Wizard*, p. 150. John Bigelow, *Retrospections of an Active Life* (Garden City, New York: Doubleday, Page, 1913), Vol. IV, pp. 121, 123. When Dickens was asked why Bulwer seemed to trust Home, he answered "... you see Bulwer is deaf and he does not like to have it remarked; so Home would say, 'Do you hear those raps?' And Bulwer would say, 'Oh yes, I heard them per-fect-ly.' And this Dickens pronounced so exactly as Bulwer since his deafness pronounced, as to convulse the whole table with laughter."

64 *A Strange Story*, Vol. I, pp. 311, 313, 314, 321, 328, 330, 332. The actual murderer is then one of the Thugs, "whose existence as a community has only recently been made known in Europe," and for whose goddess Kali the murders were committed. It was Captain Philip Meadows Taylor, long in the service of the Nizam of Hyderabad, who had introduced the Thug to the Eng-

lish drawing-room in his famous novel of 1839, *Confessions of a Thug* (3 vols.; London: Bentley, 1839), and it had been Bulwer himself, who in 1833 had read an article by Taylor on Thuggee and had urged Meadows Taylor to write a romance on the subject. See the late Colonel Meadows Taylor, *The Story of My Life* (Edinburgh and London: Blackwood, 1877), Vol. I, p. 113. Quite possibly Bulwer felt that Taylor owed him the use of a Thug in his own fiction. The whole concept of Thuggee fascinated the English novelists, and Dickens later introduced a Thug into *Edwin Drood,* left unfinished at his death.

65   *A Strange Story,* Vol. II, pp. 48, 60, 86, 123, 154. The word "scinlaeca" means wizard in Anglo-Saxon, and so appears in the Old English dictionaries. "scinn" or "scinna" means a spectre. Apparently there is no such word in Old Norse, nor have I been able to find a plausible source for Bulwer's use of the term.

66   *A Strange Story,* Vol. II, pp. 211, 213, 218, 222, 359, 362, 364, 366, 367, 383. Dr. Elliotson was so pleased to find this tribute to himself that he wrote to Bulwer (unpublished manuscript, Lytton Mss, Hertfordshire County Record Office D/EK C4/2) from Conduit Street, February 8, 1862, "My dear Sir Edward, Mr. Dallas has pointed out to me a passage in your *Strange Story* for which I return my heartfelt thanks. It is exceedly kind and handsome of you to write of me thus. May I take the liberty of adding that the manner and style of the passage are exquisitely elegant. Believe me, My dear Sir Edward, Ever yrs sincerely, J. Elliotson."

The stages of the alchemical *opus* are found conveniently described in Gray, *Goethe the Alchemist, op. cit.,* pp. 17ff.; for its relationship with Neoplatonism, p. 49: "a practical attempt to prove the truth of neoplatonist doctrines . . ."; for its impact upon Goethe's work in optics and his theory of colors, with red as the ultimate in beauty, pp. 114ff. The "rosy" or "ruby" tints demanded by the alchemists might alone have suggested to Bulwer the appearance of the rose on the surface of the liquid;

so might their frequent comparison between the final red color and the flaming sun, whose face above corresponds to the rose below. See also, C. G. Jung, *Psychology and Alchemy*, *op. cit.*, pp. 227–242; *Alchemical Studies* (Princeton: University Press, 1967), Collected Works, 13, Bollingen Series, XX, p. 294ff; quotation from p. 211. I have not attempted to theorize on the psychological meaning for Bulwer of his preoccupation with the elixir of life, which in its occult significance required the successful completion of the alchemist's *opus* for discovery. I believe, although I cannot demonstrate it, that Bulwer read the extraordinary book by Mary Anne Atwood, *A Suggestive Inquiry into the Hermetic Mystery, with a Dissertation on the More Celebrated of the Alchemical Philosophers* (London: Trelawney Saunders, 1850). It was published eight years later than *Zanoni*, of course, and its author, then a Miss South, lived with her father, a wealthy scholar and recluse who specialized in the occult, and had a splendid library. Soon after its publication, father and daughter bought back the unsold copies, and for years thereafter bought up all other copies that could be found, and burned them. Despite the fact that it must have been hard to get, Bulwer would probably have obtained it; he must have known the Souths, who were "mixed up," as she put it, with Dr. Elliotson and the others publishing the *Zoist*. She had already published anonymously a little book on *Early Magnetism in Its Higher Relations to Humanity* (London: H. Baillière, 1846). The *Suggestive Inquiry* was reissued only after her death (Belfast, William Tait, 1918), with an introduction by W. L. Wilmshurst, from which I take the details above.

67 *The Letters of Charles Dickens*, edited by Walter Dexter (Bloomsbury: Nonesuch Press, 1938), Vol. III, quotations from pp. 207, 218–220, 221, 226, 229, 232, 236–237, 241, 255, 256, 268, 269, 270, 280. Bulwer's letter in *Life* (1913), Vol. II, pp. 345–347. For Sydney Carton and Zanoni see Jack Lindsay, *Charles Dickens* (London: Andrew Dakers, 1950), pp. 364ff., who also argues for the in-

362   *Strange Stories: The Occult Fiction of*

fluence of *Paul Clifford* on *Oliver Twist* and for the influence of *A Strange Story* on *Edwin Drood.* See also, E. M. Eigner and J. I. Fradin, "Bulwer-Lytton and Dickens' Jo," *Nineteenth-Century Fiction* 24, Vol. 1 (June, 1969), pp. 98–102, and E. M. Eigner, "Bulwer-Lytton and the Changed Ending of *Great Expectations*," *ibid.* 25, 1 (June, 1970), pp. 104–108.

68 *Life* (1913), Vol. II, pp. 344, 345, 401. *A Strange Story*, Vol. I, pp. iv–v, x. Maine de Biran, *Oeuvres Inédites*, Ernest Naville, ed., avec la collaboration de Marc Debrit (3 vols.; Paris: Bezobry, E. Magdeleine et Cie, 1859), the three citations in Bulwer's Preface from Vol. I, p. v; Vol. III, p. 546; Vol. III, p. 524. The *Nouveaux Essias d'anthropologie* were re-published as Volume XIV of the *Oeuvres*, P. Tisserand, ed., this volume edited by H. Gouhier (Paris: Presses Universitaires de France, 1949). Two good very recent studies of Maine de Biran as a psychologist are F. C. T. Moore, *The Psychology of Maine de Biran* (Oxford: Clarendon Press, 1970) and D. Voutsinas, *La Psychologie de Maine de Biran (1766–1824)* (Paris: S.I.P.E., 1964), neither of whom makes more than passing reference to the *Nouveaux Essais d'anthropologie.* The best available discussion of this uncompleted and sometimes incoherent text and of the passages that appealed to Bulwer is, so far as I know, the perceptive treatment in H. Gouhier, *Les Conversions de Maine de Biran* (Paris: Vrin, 1947), especially pp. 316ff., 352ff., 360ff., 411ff., with references to the earlier literature and to suitable parallel passages in Maine de Biran's own *Journal Intime*, which Gouhier later edited, as *Journal* (3 vols.; Neuchatel: La Baconnière, 1954, 1955, 1957). The "Avertissement" to Volume II is also important in emphasizing the imperfections of Naville's text: but this imperfect text is all that was available to Bulwer.

69 *Life* (1913), Vol. II, pp. 347–350 (to Robert Lytton, April 15, 1862); p. 401 (to Forster, November 19, 1861).

70 "The Literature of the Supernatural," *The Eclectic Review* 115—New Series 2—(April, 1862), pp. 302–326; *Life* (1913), Vol. II, p. 350.

71 *The Athenaeum* No. 1790 (February 15, 1862), pp. 219–221; *The Saturday Review* (March 8, 1862), pp. 273–275; *The Examiner* (March 22, 1862), pp. 180–181.

72 *Life* (1913) Vol. II, p. 351. The previously unpublished and unused letters from C. H. Townshend are among the Lytton Mss in the Hertfordshire County Record Office, no.'s D/EK C6/33–35, 36–37, 38–39, dated respectively 26 January and 11 and 23 February, 1862.

73 *Life* (1913), Vol. II, p. 401; is "Fradin," p. 13.

74 *Life* (1913), Vol. II, pp. 47–49 (printed far out of sequence, as is indeed—but in the other direction—the letter just quoted, which precedes it).

75 The text of Kerner's work conveniently in J. Kerner, *Die Seherin von Prevorst* (Leipzig: Philipp Reclam jun., n.d., c. 1938) with introduction by Carl du Prel and text of the 1846 revised edition; an early partial English translation by Mrs. (Caroline) Crowe was published both in London and in New York (Harper, 1845); two good essays in Erich Sopp and Karl Spiesberger, *Auf den Spuren der Seherin* (Sersheim—Württ.: Osiris, 1953), the second, on Kerner's seeress in the framework of esoteric tradition and in the light of modern physical research, being especially interesting in connection with the letter of Bulwer here quoted; more generally on Kerner, see H. Büttiker, *Justinus Kerner, Ein Beitrag zur Geschichte der Spätromantik* (Zürich: Emil Rüegg, 1952); O. Ackermann, *Schwabentum und Romantik* (Breslau: Priebatsch, 1939), Sprache und Kultur de Germanischen und Romanischen Völker, edited by W. Horn, Paul Meihner, P. Merker, F. Neubert, and F. Ranke. B. Germanistische Reihe, Vol. XXXI; more popular, F. Kretschmar, *Die Seherin von Prevorst und die Botschaft Justinus Kerner* (Weinsberg: Justinus-Kerner-Verein e. B. und Frauenverein, 1929); more specialized, H. Straumann, *Justinus Kerner und der Okkultismus in der deutschen Romantik* (Horgen-Zürich/Leipzig: Munster-Presse, 1928), "Wege zur Dichtung," ed. E. Ermatiker, Vol. IV.

76 For Balzac and Swedenborg, see most recently the article by M. Fargeaud, "Mme Balzac, son mysticisme et ses en-

fants," *L'Année Balzacienne* (1965), pp. 3–33, and the reply by K. E. Sjödén, "Remarques sur le 'Swedenborgisme' balzacienne," *ibid.* (1966), pp. 33–45, to which Mlle. Fargeaud provided a brief rejoinder, pp. 47–48. Sjödén insists on the imperfection of Balzac's knowledge of Swedenborg: earlier bibliography in these articles. *Séraphîta, op. cit.*, n. 39 above, contains a long disquisition on Swedenborg's life and work, but apparently owes more to Boehme and Saint-Martin. See J. Borel, *Séraphîta et le Mysticisme Balzacien* (Paris: J. Corti, 1967). (For Balzac and Saint-Martin, see R. Amadou, *L'Année Balzacienne* (1965), pp. 35–60, who shows that Balzac's acquaintance with him was inexact, though admiring. Bulwer in *Caxtoniana, op. cit.*, Vol. I, p. 60. In "Les Proscrits" (1831) [*Oeuvres Complètes* (Paris: Club de l'Honnête Homme, 1956), Vol. XVI, p. 431] Balzac mentions Boehme, Swedenborg, Martines de Pasqually, Saint-Martin, and others as the chief mystic theologians, and gives a kind of preliminary sketch of what would soon be *la Spécialité*. I quote Louis Lambert from the same volume, pp. 558–559. Louis Lambert even refers to Apollonius of Tyana's feat of reporting from Asia Domitian's death in Rome, which Bulwer had used in *The Last Days of Pompeii*. On Maine de Biran and Louis Lambert see H. Evans, "Louis Lambert, Victor Cousin, et l'eclectisme," *Les Études Balzaciennes*, Nouvelle Série 1 (March–June, 1951), pp. 3–10, quotations from pp. 8 and 9; and the same author's *Louis Lambert et la philosophie de Balzac* (Paris: Corti, 1951), pp. 105–106, 176–178. For Balzac's use of Bichat and the phrenologist Gall, also cited by Bulwer, *ibid.*, pp. 140ff. The December 18, 1818 entry in Biran's journal now in *Journal*, ed. H. Gouhier, *op. cit.*, n. 68 above, Vol. II, p. 188. For Victor Morillon in the *Avertissement* for *Le Gars* (1828) as a self-portrait of Balzac preliminary to that of Louis Lambert and having much in common with it, including the practice of "la Spécialité," and for the gift of the same Spécialité in *Séraphîta* (1835), see also S. Bérard, "Une Énigme Balzacienne: 'la Spécialité.'" *L'Année Balzacienne* (1965), pp. 61–82, who mentions Leibniz and

Swedenborg (without carrying much conviction) and Deleuze and du Potet, the leading theorists of magnetism in the wake of Mesmer, from whom came the notion of the magnetic fluid, which lay behind the theory of *la Spécialité*. But Mlle. Bérard, surprisingly enough, has missed the key contribution of Maine de Biran. I cite *Les Martyrs ignorés* from the *Oeuvres Complètes* (Paris: Les Bibliophiles de l'Originale, 1968), Vol. XIX, quotations from pp. 465 and 466. For Dr. Koreff, the old friend of Hoffman and a celebrated "magnétiseur," and his relations with Balzac, with whom he quarreled in 1837, see F. Baldensperger, *Orientations Étrangères chez Honoré de Balzac* (Paris: Champion, 1927), pp. 101–104, 117–119; for Hoëné-Wronski who "before 1826 spoke of atomic chemistry, of tanks, and of the League of Nations under names which need only to be shifted slightly to produce their equivalent today," *ibid.*, pp. 237–259. A generally useful survey of the appearances in Balzac's works of the homicidal power of thought in M. Le Yaouanc, *Nosographie de l'Humanité Balzacienne* (Paris: Maloine, 1959), pp. 53ff.; for the will, pp. 131ff.; for magnetism, pp. 158ff. The book is a mine of information on Balzac's ideas about illness, medicine, pathology, and psychology as expressed in his fiction, and on their sources in contemporary scientific writings. For a recent general essay—helpful despite its somewhat outdated bibliography—see Mieczyslawa Sekrecka, "Balzac et l'Occultisme," *Romanica Wratislaviensia* III (Wroclaw, 1968), Acta Universitatis Wratislavensis, no. 82, pp. 3–25. Quotation from p. 8. *Falthurne*, edited by P. G. Castex (Paris: José Corti, 1950). The Besançon thesis of S. R. B. Smith, *Balzac et l'Angleterre* (London: Williams, Lac & Co., 1953) points out (p. 124) that Balzac read *Zanoni*, but makes no claim that Bulwer had an influence upon him, and does not deal with the reverse question. For Victor Hugo, see A. Viatte, *Victor Hugo et les illuminés* (Montreal: Éditions de l'Arbre, 1842), *passim;* quotations from pp. 137–138 and 110–111; also Gustave Simon, *Chez Victor Hugo, les Tables tournantes de Guernsey* (Paris: L. Conard, 1923) and Paul

Stapfer, *Victor Hugo à Guernsey* (Paris: Société française d'imprimerie et de librairie, 1905). The chapter in Balzac's *Le Cousin Pons* is now numbered XXXII. See, for example, pp. 119–125 in the edition edited by Maurice Allem (Paris: Garnier, 1956).

77 *The Coming Race* (Edinburgh and London: Blackwood, 1871). It is worth noting here that Samuel Butler's *Erewhon* was written slightly later, and Butler denied having read *The Coming Race* until after he had finished *Erewhon*. See Geoffrey Wagner, "A Forgotten Satire: Bulwer-Lytton's *The Coming Race*," *Nineteenth-Century Fiction* 19 (1964–1965), pp. 379–385. Quotations here from the above-cited first edition, pp. 153, 29, 269–270, 136–137, 138, 105, 44, 43–44, 123, 76, 79, 253, 47, 48, 49, 58, 59, 125–126, 132. See three letters to Forster about *The Coming Race* in *Life* (1913), Vol. II, pp. 464–467, which seem to show that, as usual with Bulwer's excursions into the supernatural, Forster had doubts about the manuscript of the new novel; quotations from *ibid.*, pp. 469, 468. Those interested in Bulwer's anti-radical politics in his last years should also note that in *Kenelm Chillingley*, (3 vols.; Edinburgh: Blackwood, 1873) and in *The Parisians*, (4 vols.; Edinburgh: Blackwood, 1873), left incomplete at his death, Bulwer conveyed the same message as in *The Coming Race* but in two books as different from each other as they are from the one we are considering. The Franco-Prussian War and especially the Commune of 1871 once again brought to the fore all his anti-mob sentiments of the early 1840s expressed in the picture of the French Revolution in *Zanoni*.

INDEX

Agassiz, Louis, 154, 326
Agrippa, Heinrich Cornelius, of Nettesheim, 154, 175, 190, 250, 319, 346n
Ainsworth, W. Harrison, viii, 8; the copy of his *Rookwood*, 22–31; his *Jack Sheppard*, 24–26, 65n, 338n
Albertus Magnus, 180, 188, 250, 252, 258, 350n
Alchemy, 153, 159, 165, 166, 189, 285–288, 336n, 338–339n, 360–361n. *See also* Occult
All the Year Round (magazine), 265, 288, 295
Andreae, Johann Valentin, 165–166. *See also* Rosicrucian Brotherhood
Apollonius of Tyana, 160, 261–263, 285, 340–342n, 364n
Apuleius, Lucius, 298, 354n
"Arasmenes the Seeker" (Bulwer), 337n
Armstrong, T., 54
Arnold, Thomas, the elder, 46
Arnold, Thomas, the younger, 46
Arnold, William Delafield: his *Oakfield*, 11–12, 46, 63n
Ashburner, Dr. John, 169, 170, 235, 241, 260, 345n, 356n
Astrology, in *Godolphin*, 149–150, 171–173. *See also* Occult
Athenaeum, 41, 202–204, 303
Atwood, Mary Anne, 361n
Averroes, 159, 190, 340n
Aytoun, W. E., 26, 65n, 156–157, 338n

Balsamo, Joseph, *see* Cagliostro
Balzac, Honoré de, 226; his *Le Centénaire ou les deux Béringheld*, 227; influences upon, 227, 228, 315–316, 318; and Bulwer-Lytton, vii, 227, 316–320; his *L'Elixir de longue vie*, 228; his *La Recherche de l'absolu*, 229, 319; his *Séraphîta*, 229, 364n; and

the occult, 315–321; his *La Peau de chagrin*, 316; his *Louis Lambert* and *la Spécialité*, 315, 318; his *Les Martyrs ignorés*, 316, 319; his *Falthurne*, 319–320; and Victor Hugo, 320, 322; his *Le Cousin Pons*, 322, 353–354n, 363–365n
Banim brothers ("O'Hara Family"), 15
Banks, Mrs. G. Linnaeus, her *The Manchester Man*, 14, 64n
Barrie, J. M., 58–60, 67n
Bartley, Mrs. H. P., *see* Graves, Lizzie
Benson, E. F., 31, 32, 66n
Bérard, Mlle S., 364–365n
Bernheim, Dr., 123–124
Besant, Walter, 65n
Besold, Christoph, 343n. *See also* Rosicrucian Brotherhood
Biran, Maine de, *see* Maine de Biran
Blackwood, publisher, 135n, 265
Blackwood's Magazine, 131n, 135n, 254, 257, 258
Blake, William, 126
Blavatsky, Madame Elena Petrovna, 186, 264, 358n; her *Isis Unveiled*, 186, 350n
Blue flower, 175. *See also* Herbalism and Novalis
Boccalini, Traiano, 163
Boehme, Jakob, 126, 128, 271, 315, 343n
Boldrewood, Rolf, *see* Brown, T. A.
Borri, G. F., 190, 351n
Bowen, Elizabeth, 31
Braddon, Mary Elizabeth (Mrs. Maxwell), 306
Braid, Dr. James, 123, 241–242, 356n. *See also* Hypnotism
Bray, Anna Eliza, 15
Bringeren, Johann (Bringaret), 159, 344–345n
Brontë family, 22, 71

Brotherhood of the New Life, 102, 105, 111
Broussais, François, 266
Brown, Catherine (Hueffer), 38
Brown, Ford Madox, 37–38
Brown, Lucy Madox (Mrs. W. M. Rossetti), 38, 42
Brown, Norman O., 128–129, 141n
Brown, Oliver Madox, 38, 41–42; *the* copy of his *Gabriel Denver*, 22–23, 37–43; his *The Black Swan*, 38–39, 40, 42; his *The Dwale Bluth*, 42–43, 66n
Brown, T. A. (Rolf Boldrewood): his *Robbery Under Arms*, 18, 64n
Browning, Elizabeth Barrett, 124, 244; her "Bertha in the Lane," 87, 133n
Browning, Robert, 244, 274
Bulwer, Edward George Earl (Bulwer-Lytton, First Lord Lytton, Bulwer), viii, 23; variety of works, 145; and politics, 145, 148, 210, 225; his plays, 145; *Pelham*, first novel, 146, 337n; *Paul Clifford*, first "Newgate" novel, 23, 146; and sociology (*England and the English*), 146, 209–210; *Night and Morning*, 146, 232, 354n; *Eugene Aram*, 23, 146; *Ernest Maltravers*, 146, 153; crime fictionalized, 146; *Rienzi*, 146; *Harold, the Last of the Saxon Kings*, 148; historical romances, 146, 148; *The Last of the Barons*, 148, 303; *The Caxtons*, 148; "The Tale of Kosem Kosamim the Magician," 152–153, 185, 288; his translations of Schiller, 146, 153, 266; his learning, 153–156; influence of Schiller, Goethe and Novalis upon, 153–154, 186, 203, 223; and the Neoplatonists, 154; and science, 154; his Byronism, 154; character of, 154-156; collapse of marriage, 156; as Rosicrucian, 158, 200, 233–234, 286, 333; and

Thomas Taylor, 161, 184; and Cazotte, 170; and Saint-Martin, 173; use of footnotes in novels, 173; and Chaldaean Oracles, 182, 184; influence of Van Helmont upon, 185, 243, 270; and primordial principle, 185; and Tasso, 198; his *Life of Schiller*, 203; and John Forster, 205–206, 296, 300; view of French Revolution, 207–210; review of Duval, 208–210; and John Gibson, 211-213; and Harriet Martineau, 213, 235; his "Certain Principles of Art in Works of Imagination," 221; and Balzac, 228–230, 315–322; as a practicing occultist, 233–264; and mesmerism, clairvoyance, and phrenology, 235–241; letter in *The Zoist*, 237; his "On the Normal Clairvoyance of the Imagination," 238–240, 270–272; and mesmerism, 238–240; at Didier's seance, 240; and phrenology, 241, 356n; and Maury, 242; and hypnotism, 241–243; and spiritualism, 244–253; and Daniel D. Home, 244–247, 273–274; correspondence with London Dialectical Society, 251–253; and magic, 259–263, 270–280, 298; and Éliphas Lévi, 259–263; and Mahatma letters, 264; "Essay-Writing in General and These Essays in Particular," 270; and Charles Dickens, 265, 288, 292–296; influence of Maine de Biran upon, 298; his *Lucretia*, 302; his opposition to Darwin's theory of evolution, 311–312; letter to Hargrave Jennings, 333. *See also The Coming Race, Godolphin,* "The Haunters and the Haunted," *The Last Days of Pompeii, A Strange Story, Zanoni*
Burton, Jean, 356n, 359n
Bulwer, Emily, 248, 321
Bulwer, Rosina, 156, 231, 248
Burri, *see* Borri

Cagliostro, (Joseph Balsamo), 168, 203, 228, 257, 321, 345n
Campanella, Tommaso, 166, 343n
Cardano (Cardan), Geronimo, 268, 271, 358n
Carleton, William, 15
Carlyle, Thomas, 202, 352n
Caxtoniana, 338n, 353n, 356n
Cazotte, Jacques: and Martines de Pasqually, 168; his prophecy, 169; his *Le Diable amoureux*, 169, 228–229; and French Revolution, 345n, 351n. *See also Zanoni*
Chaldaean Oracles, 181–184; Shemaia, ordination rite of, 182; as "earliest oracles," 182; "akoimeto strophalingi," 183; and Iamblichus, 183; and Michael Psellus, 183; and theurgy, 183; and Bulwer, 184; and Thomas Taylor, 184, 310, 347–349n. *See also Zanoni*
Charcot, Dr. Jean Martin, 123–124, 242. *See also* Hypnotism
Chesney, General George, his *The Dilemma* and *The Battle of Dorking*, 11, 62–63n
Christians, *see* Rosicrucian Brotherhood
Clairvoyance: and mesmerism, 88; and Bulwer, 149–150, 238–241, 271–272; and the oracle of the Pythian Apollo, 269; in *A Strange Story*, 267, 269–272
Clarke, Marcus, his *His Natural Life*, 18, 64n
Coleridge, Samuel Taylor: casts of his head, 241
Collins, Mortimer, his *Sweet Anne Page*, 5, 61n
Collins, Wilkie: his *The Moonstone*, 4, 19, 61n; his *Armadale*, 19; his *No Name*, 19; his *The Woman in White*, 19; his *Man and Wife*, and Scottish marriage laws, 19–21; and Caroline Graves, 20; and Lizzie Graves Bartley, 20–21; his *New Magdalen*, 21; and Georgina Hogarth, 21; his *The Evil Genius*

and Holman Hunt, 21; his *Blind Love*, 21, 65n; and Bulwer's *Strange Story*, 291
Coming Race, The (Bulwer), 148, 323–333; Darwin's theory attacked, 311, 325–326; and Jonathan Swift, 323; and H. G. Wells, 323; supernatural in, 323; and equality, 324–325; Americans target in, 325–327; "new" woman attacked, 327; vril as primordial principle, 328–331, 333; published anonymously, 333
Comte de Gabalis, Le, see Zanoni (Bulwer)
Condillac, Etienne Bonnot de, 154; influence on *A Strange Story*, 266
Constant, Alphonse-Louis, *see* Lévi, Éliphas
Cousin, Victor, 297, 318
Cowper, Mrs. (Lady Mount-Temple), 106
Creighton, Mandell, 48
Croly, George, his *Salathiel*, 228
Croker, Bertha M., 12, 63n
Cruikshank, George, 27, 30–31

Darwin, Charles: and Bulwer, 154, 311–312, 325–326
David, Jacques-Louis, 178, 347n
Davies, Arthur Llewellyn, 58
Davies, Sylvia du Maurier, *see* Du Maurier, Sylvia
Davis, Andrew Jackson, 101, 136n
Davy, Sir Humphrey, 154, 281, 310, 313
Deerbrook (Martineau), 74–79; and author's neurosis, 73, 74, 92; Hester, 74, 77, 80; Margaret, 74, 77–79, 84; men in, 74, 76, 79, 84; Maria Young, 74, 76, 79, 85; Mrs. Rowland, 74, 80, 86; as novel of middle-class life, 79; and women, 84–85, 87; source of plot, 86–87, 133n; and Catherine Sedgwick, 86–87; compared to *Masollam*, 122–123; and neuroses of Martineau and Oliphant, 125

Descartes, René, 154, 166, 282
Dickens, Charles, 8; *Oliver Twist*,
26, 61n, 71, 88, 134n, 139; editor
of *All the Year Round*, 265; and
D. D. Home, 274–275, 359n;
and Bulwer, 288, 292; and
Great Expectations, 288; let-
ters to Bulwer about *A Strange
Story*, 288–294, 311; and mes-
merism, 314, 333, 360n, 361–362n
Didier, Alexis, 240, 320
Disraeli, Benjamin, 114, 145
Dowd, D. L., cited, 347n
Doyle, Sir Arthur Conan, 9, 61n
"Dream of the Dead" (Bulwer),
337n
Dublin University Magazine, 31
Dumas, Alexandre, 228
Du Maurier, George (Louis Pal-
mella Busson), 50, 54; his illus-
trations, 8, 50; *the* copy of his
Peter Ibbetson, 22–23, 50–60;
his novels, 51; Thackeray's in-
fluence upon, 51; his *Trilby*, 51,
54–55; and F. W. H. Myers, 55,
58, 67n
Du Maurier, Sylvia, 58–60, 67n
Duval, Georges, 208–209; Bul-
wer's review of, 208–210

Eclectic Review, 301–303, 309–310
Eden, Charles H.: his *George
Donnington, or, In the Bear's
Grip*, 13, 64n
Edward, Prince of Wales, 103–
104, 114
Eliot, George, 71, 125, 139n
Elixir of Life: and Philosopher's
Stone, 159, 188, 189, 228, 285–
288, 330. *See also* Occult
Elliotson, Dr. John, 90, 235–238,
282, 351n, 361n
Examiner, The, 206–208, 304

Faith, problem of, *see* Ward, Mrs.
Humphry
Fama Fraternitatis, 163–165, 187,
201. *See also* Rosicrucian
Brotherhood
Faraday, Michael, 154, 268, 328,
330
Fire, 153, 185, 272. *See also* Pri-
mordial principle

Ford, Ford Madox, *see* Hueffer,
Ford Madox
Foreign Quarterly Review, 208
Forster, John, 205–208, 209, 211,
291, 296, 300, 304, 311, 312–313,
322, 366n
Fradin, Joseph I., 273, 359, 362n,
363n
Fraser, James Baillie, 12, 63n
Fraser's Magazine, 23, 156
Freud, Sigmund, 71, 124, 129,
139n, 242

Gabriel Denver, the copy of, *see*
Brown, Oliver Madox
Gallaher, Fanny, 15
Ganneau, 127–128
Gas (Phosoxygen), 243, 268–269,
271, 330. *See also* Primordial
principle
Gaskell, Elizabeth Cleghorn, Mrs.,
14, 51, 64n
Gerard, E. D. (Emily and Doro-
thea), their *Beggar My Neigh-
bour*, 13, 63–64n
Gibson, John R. A., 211–213, 231.
See also Zanoni
Gissing, Algernon, 61n
Gladstone, William E., 48, 67n
God, bisexual (androgynous),
101, 126–129; and Thomas Harris, 101, 126; and Boehme, 126,
128; and Calvinists, 126; and
MacDonald, 126–127; and Swedenborg, 126; as Victorian
phenomenon, 126–129; and
Tom Brown's School Days
(Hughes), 127; the Mapah, 127–
128; and Brown, 128–129
Godolphin (Bulwer), 146, 149–
150; as novel of high society,
146, 150; astrology and prophecy in, 149–150; as forerunner
of occult fiction, 149, 151; Chaldaeans in, 150
Goethe, Johann W., vii; his *Werther*, 154; his *Wilhelm Meister*,
154, 189, 230; and Bulwer, 154,
230, 298; and Rosicrucian symbolism, 167; his *Die Geheimnisse*, 167; and Saint-Martin,
172; and herbalism, 176, 189,

198, 230; and alchemy, 189, 230, 231, 315; and his *Märchen*, 189; his *Weissagungen des Bakis*, 189; and Tasso, 198, 338n, 345n, 351n, 360n
Graves, Caroline, 20, 65n
Graves, Lizzie (Mrs. H. P. Bartley), 20–21, 65n
Gray, R. D., on Goethe, 346n, 351n, 360n
Griffin, Gerald, 15
Gymnosophists, 166

Haggard, H. Rider, 9, 61n
Hall, Anne (Mrs. Samuel Carter), 87, 133n, 134n, 246–247
Hamilton, Sir William, 282, 243, 265, 282, 310
Harper's Magazine: and *Trilby*, 51, 54
Harris, Thomas Lake, viii; early life, 101–103; and A. J. Davis, 101; and bisexual God, 101, 111–112, 126; as Swedenborgian, 101–102; his *Arcana of Christianity*, 102; and internal respiration, 102; and Brotherhood of the New Life, 102; and Laurence Oliphant, 104–115; and Lady Oliphant, 104–115; in *Piccadilly*, 105, 137–138n; and Alice Oliphant, 109–115; in Amenia, New York, 105; in Santa Rosa, California, 111, 124; in Brocton, New York, 111
Harte, Francis Bret, 338n
Hartley, Mary Laffan, 15
"Haunters and the Haunted, The" (Bulwer), 148, 254–259; supernatural in, 254, 258; magic in, 259, 316, 318
Heat, animal, caloric, 185, 187
Hennigsen, C. F., 13, 64n
Henty, G. A., 3–4, 61n
Herbalism: as occult science, 175–176, 187; and blue flower (blaue Blume), 176; and Novalis, 176; and Tasso, 198; and Goethe, 198; and Balzac, 229–230
Hermes Trismegistus, 188, 190, 321, 350n

Hermias, 161
Heydon, John, 167
Hockley, W. B., 11, 62n
Höene-Wronski, 260, 319, 364n
Hoffmann, E. T. A., 126, 223, 228, 354n
Hogarth, Catherine, 21
Hogarth, Georgina, 21
Home, Daniel Dunglas, 244–247, 248–251, 273–274; and Bulwer, 244–247; and Robert Browning, 244, 274; and "The Haunters and the Haunted," 254–259; and *A Strange Story*, 273–275; and Dickens, 274–275, 313
Home, Madame D. D., and Bulwer, 245–254, 273–274, 356n, 357n
Heuffer, Ford Madox (Ford Madox Ford), 38
Hueffer, Francis, 42
Hughes, Arthur, 8
Hughes, Thomas, 127
Hugo, Charles, 320
Hugo, Victor, vii; and the Mapah, 128; parallels with Balzac, 320; and the occult, 320–322; parallels in Bulwer, 321–322, 365–366n
Hunt, Holman, 21
Huxley, Thomas Henry, 48
Hypnotism: and Braid, 123, 241–242; and Bernheim, 123–124; and Charcot, 123–124; and Liebault, 123; and Freud, 124; and Bulwer, 241–242; and Maury, 242

Iamblichus, 154; his *On the Mysteries*, 161, 183; and Chaldaean Oracles, 183; and demons, 183, 271, 339n
Isis, veiled image of: as used by Bulwer, 151, 185–186, 349–350; as used by Madame Blavatsky, 186; as used by Novalis, 186; as used by Schiller, 186

James, Henry, 31, 48, 51, 67n, 71
James, Henry, the elder, 102
James, M. R., 31–32, 65n
Jennings, Hargrave, 233, 354–355n

Jerrold, Douglas, 72
Joyce, James, and Le Fanu, 32, 65–66
Jung, Carl Gustaf, 176, 287, 336–337n, 343n, 346n, 351n, 360n

Kaye, J. W.: his *Story of Basil Bouverie*, 12, 63n
Kay-Shuttleworth, James: his *Scarsdale* and *Ribblesdale*, 14–15, 64n
Keene, Charles, 8
Kerner, Dr. Justinus, 314, 363n
Kingsley, Charles, 15, 20
Kingsley, Henry, 10, 15, 18, 62n, 64n
Kingston, William H. G., 14, 64n
Kipling, Rudyard, 11; his *Brushwood Boy* and *Peter Ibbetson*, 55, 63n

La Harpe, 168–170
Lamont, T. R., 54
Landor, Walter Savage, 125
Last Days of Pompeii, The (Bulwer), 151–152, 303
Lavater, 172
Lawless, Lady Emily, 15
Lear, Edward, 12, 63n
Le Fanu, Joseph Sheridan, viii, 31–32; the copy of his *Uncle Silas*, 22, 31–37; his *Green Tea*, 31; his *Carmilla*, 31; his *House by the Churchyard*, 32; his *Wylder's Hand*, 32; his *Guy Deverell*, 65–66n
Leibniz, Gottfried, 166, 364n
Lévi, Éliphas (Alphonse Constant), 234, 260–263; as magician, 259–260; and Ashburner, 260; and Bulwer, 260, 262–263; and Apollonius of Tyana, 261–263; and Bulwer's *A Strange Story*, 263, 279, 282, 310, 357n
Liebault, Dr., 123
Liebig, Justus von, 268, 359n, 270
Liesching, Louis, 135n
Linton, Mrs. Eliza Lynn, 125–126, 139–140n
Linton, W. J., 125
Literary Gazette, 205, 231

London Dialectical Society, 251–253, 356n
Lord, Walter Frewen, 156
Lucian of Samosata, 206, 352n
Lucretia (Bulwer), 146, 302
Lull, Ramon, 191
Lytton, Lord, *see* Bulwer, Edward George Earle Lytton, first Lord
Lytton, Robert, first Earl of Lytton, 247, 296, 299, 300, 301, 304, 307, 337n
Lytton, Victor A. G. R., second Earl of Lytton, 335n

MacDonald, George, viii, 10, 106, 126–127, 140n, 314
Magic, 298; and Lévi, 259–260; "The Haunted and the Haunters," 259; *A Strange Story*, 279–280, 283–286, 298
Mahatma, K. H. (Kut Humi), 264, 358n
Maier, Michael, 166, 344n
Maine de Biran, Pierre François Gontheir Marie, 297; and Bulwer, 154, 297–298; father of psychology, 297; and Condillac, 297; *Oeuvres Inédites*, 297–298; his *Nouveaux Essais d' anthropologie*, 298; parallels in Balzac, 318, 362n
Maison, Marguerite, 46, 66–67n
Mapah, the, 127–128, 210. *See also* Ganneau
Marcillet, M., 240
Martin, Theodore, 25–26, 65n
Martineau, Harriet, viii, 72, 80–91; as pamphleteer and popularizer of socio-economic issues, 72; as historian, 72; and religion, 72; and science, 72; her neurotic "adventure," 73, 84, 92; her *Autobiography*, 80–84; childhood, 80–81; and jealousy, 81; and older sister, Rachel, 81–82; and her mother, 82, 84–85; her brother, James, 83; her views on marriage, 83–84; engagement to Worthington, 83–84; and Catherine Sedgwick, 86; Amer-

ica, 86; bed-ridden, 87; and mesmerism, 88, 90–91; her *Life in
the Sickroom*, 88; her *Letters
on Mesmerism*, 90; and Greenhow, 90; and Bulwer, 90, 235;
and Mrs. Wynyard, 90; un-
published letter on her mesmeric cure, 91; and submission,
123; her neurosis compared with
Oliphant's, 123–125; latent
homosexuality in, 124–125, 130n;
and Bulwer's *Zanoni*, 213–215,
218–222, 294, 295, 309. *See also
Deerbrook*
Martineau, James, 83, 133n
Martines de Pasqually, 168, 170;
and Order of the Knights Elect
Cohens of the Universe, 170–
172; and Réau-Croix, 170; and
astrology, 171; and theurgy,
171; his *Treatise on the Reintegration of Beings*, 172, 345–
346n
Masollam (Laurence Oliphant),
92–100; and Oliphant's career,
74, 107–122, 125; and T. L. Harris, 101, 106, 109; aspects of Oliphant in, 104–105, 107, 123; and
Alice Oliphant, 112–113; Santalba as self-portrait, 115–116;
and breathing together and
sympneumata, 117–121; Oliphant doctrines stated in, 118–
121; men in, 122–123; compared
with *Deerbrook*, 122–123
Maturin, C. R., his *Melmoth the
Wanderer*, 226, 227, 228, 353n
Maury, L. F. Alfred, 242, 243,
282
Mesmer, Franz Anton, 88, 321
Mesmerism, 88–92; and Harriet
Martineau, 88, 91, 235; and the
medical profession, 88; and radical politics, 88, 90; theory of,
88; and hypnotism, 88; treatment in, 88; and Mrs. Wynyard,
90; and Elliotson, 90, 236–238;
and psychotherapy, 123; and
Ashburner, 235; and Townshend, 235; and Bulwer, 235–240.
See also A Strange Story
Milnes, Monckton, 66n, 105

Montfaucon de Villars, Abbé N.
de, 159, 202, 203, 204, 339n
Morgan, J. P., 54
Morier, David, his *Photo the
Suliote*, 12, 63n
Morier, James, his *Hajji Baba*, 12,
63n
Myers, F. W. H., 55–58

National Vigilance Association,
125
Neoplatonists, 154, 343n. *See also*
Iamblichus, Proclus
Neuhaus, Heinrich, 166, 344n
"Newgate" novels, 24, 26, 146
Novalis (Friedrich von Harden-
berg), 126, 154, 176, 223; his
Lehrlinge zu Saïs, 186; his *Hein-
rich von Ofterdingen*, 176, 223,
346n, 349n

Occult, the: astrology, 149–150,
171–173; alchemy, 153, 159,
165, 166, 189; and Bulwer, 158,
244–253, 311–314; and Martines
de Pasqually, 168–172; and
herbalism, 175–176; and revolutionary politics, 224; and Home,
244; and London Dialectical
Society, 251–253; and magic,
259–260, 298; and loss of soul,
272, 273
"O'Hara Family," *see* Banim
brothers
Oliphant, Alice: and Laurence
Oliphant, 109–112, 114, 116–118;
and T. L. Harris, 109–113
Oliphant, Sir Anthony, 103
Oliphant, Laurence, viii; career,
72–73, 103; travels in youth, 72–
73; his neurotic "adventure," 73;
and Parliament, 73; *Piccadilly*,
73, 104–105, 108, 137–138n; and
Masollam, 74; and Edward,
Prince of Wales, 103–104, 114;
and his mother, 103, 106, 115;
and T. L. Harris, 104–115; pur-
ification in his neurosis, 107–
108; and Alice LeStrange, 109–
111; last years in Palestine, 116–
121; and his *Sympneumata*, 117–
118; *Scientific Religion*, 118,

120–121; and Rosamond Dale Owen, 121; submission in his neurosis, 123–124; his neurosis compared with Harriet Martineau's, 123–125; latent homosexuality in, 125; his *Altiora Peto* and *Traits and Travesties*, 136n. See also *Masollam*

Oliphant, Mrs. Margaret, 10, 73, 108–109, 130n, 135n, 137n, 138n

Oliphant, Mary, Lady (née Campbell), mother of Laurence, 103, 105–115

Owen, Rosamond Dale (Oliphant), 121, 128, 130n

Paganini, 167

Pagel, Walter W., 270, 349n, 359n

Paracelsus (Theophrastus Bombast von Hohenheim), 154, 159, 175, 184, 188, 271, 319, 340n

Pasqually, Martines de, see Martines de Pasqually

Peter Ibbetson, the copy of, *see* Du Maurier, George

Peter Pan, see Barrie, J. M.

Phrenology, 235, 241, 356n

Phrenological Society, 236

Piccadilly (Laurence Oliphant), 73, 104–105, 108, 137–138n

Plato, Phaedrus, and *Timaeus,* 161–162; and Thomas Taylor, 161, 184, 339–340n

Powell, George, of Nant-Eos, 36–37, 66n

Praed, Mrs. Campbell, her *Policy and Passion* and *Mrs. Tregaskiss,* 18, 64n

Pre-Raphaelites, 37–43, 66n

Prevorst, Seeress of (Friedrike Hauffe), 313–314, 363n

Primordial principle (of life), in alchemy, 153; heat (fire), 153, 185, 272; and Rosicrucians, 184; and Bulwer, 185; heat (animal), 185; heat (caloric), 187; as gas, 268–269; in *A Strange Story,* 269; as vril in *The Coming Race,* 328, 330–331

Pritchett, V. S., 31

Proclus, 154, 161, 182–184, 191, 348n

Psellus, Michael, 154, 182–183, 348n

Psychical Research Society, The, 157

Punch, 50, 334n

Puységur, 88, 239, 266

Pythagoreans, 160, 166, 269

Redding, Cyrus: and *Pandurang Hari,* 11

Reid, Captain Mayne, 9, 61n

Respiration, internal, 102, 117–121. See also *Sympneumata*

Rilke, Rainer Marie, 129

Ritchie, Lady, see Thackeray, Anne

Robert Elsmere, the copy of, *see* Ward, Mrs. Humphry

Rookwood, the copy of, *see* Ainsworth, W. Harrison

Ros, Amanda McKittrick, 135n

Rosenkreutz, Christian, 163–166, 187. See also Rosicrucian Brotherhood

Rosicrucian Brotherhood, 158, 159, 162, 163–167, 227; as true Christians, 159; and Andreae, 163–166; and the *Fama Fraternitatis,* 163–165; and Christian Rosenkreutz, 163–166; and Tübingen Lutheran group, 165, 343–344; *Chymische Hochzeit,* 165–166; revival of in England, 166–167; as Brothers of the Rose-Cross, 167; and *Zanoni,* 177; in Balzac, 227; and Bulwer, 233–234, 271, 285–288, 359n; and Besold, 343n; and Bringeren, 344n

Rossetti, Dante Gabriel, 41, 42, 66n

Rossetti, William Michael, 42, 43, 66n

Ruskin, John, 106

Russell, W. Clark, his *The Frozen Pirate,* 19, 64n

Sadleir, Michael, 4, 10, 60n, 62n, 130n, 140n, 145, 334n

Saint-Germain, Comte de, 234–235, 355n

Saint-Martin, Louis-Claude de,

168, 172; his *Book of Errors and of Truth* and a *Key*, 172; and Goethe, 172; and Bulwer, 173; and Balzac, 315, 320; and Victor Hugo, 320, 345–346n. *See also Zanoni*
Saturday Review, The, 41, 303–304
Schiller, Friederich, vii; and Bulwer, 146, 153; used in *Zanoni*, 185, 186, 203–204; influence in England, 153, 203–204; his *Ghost-Seer*, 203; and *Zanoni*, 203–204, 226, 228; and Romantic Ideal, 223
Schneider, Herbert, and George W. Lawton, 135n
Scott, Sir Walter, 146
Sedgwick, Catherine, 86, 133n; her *Tales and Sketches*, 338n, 349n, 351n, 352n
Sendivogius, Michael, 271, 359n
Smith & Elder (publishers), 37, 40, 41
Soul, loss of, 272–273. *See also* Occult
Spiritualism, 244–259. *See also* Occult
Stoker, Bram, 31
Strachey, Ray, 125, 131n, 135n
Strange Story, A (Bulwer), 148, 153, 231, 263, 265–322; religious message in, 249, 283, 287, 310; first publication of, 265; plot, 265, 269–270; published by Blackwood (2 vols.), 265; and Dickens, 265, 288–295; motto for, 265; scientific proof, 265–266; Schiller in, 266; Liebig used in, 266, 270; use of Condillac, 266; use of Puységur, 266; use of clairvoyance, 267, 269–272; Lilian as clairvoyant, 267, 270; and immortality, 268; Van Helmont's influence on, 269–270; framework of, 270–271; compared with *Zanoni*, 270–271, 276, 281, 309–310; primordial principle in, 270; existence in, 272; elixir of life in, 274–275, 283–286; Scinlaeca in, 277, 279, 281, 360n; ambiva-

lences expressed in, 278; and Lévi, 279, 310; magic in, 279–280, 283–286, 298, 310; sexual symbolism in, 280; use of Descartes in, 282; use of Sir William Hamilton, 282; use of Müller in, 282; and Rosicrucians, 286; Christian message in, 287; anxiety about, 296, 299–301; and Maine de Biran, 297–298; preface for book version, 297–299; *Eclectic Review*, 301–303, 310; and *Saturday Review*, 303–304; *Athenaeum* review of, 303; defense of, 304–306; and the *Examiner*, 304–306; and German romantics, 309; and Darwinian theory, 311–312, 330
Sue, Eugène, his *Juif Errant*, 228
Supernatural, *see* Occult
Swedenborg, Emanuel, 101–102; and bisexual God, 126; and Lévi, 260, 271; influence on Balzac, 315–316; his *Heaven and Earth*, 316, 364–365n
Swift, Jonathan, 298, 323
Swinburne, Algernon Charles, 19, 31, 32–33, 36, 37, 42, 66n, 125, 139–140n
Sympneumata (Oliphant), 117–118; and *Scientific Religion*, 118; modern parallels, 129. *See also Masollam*

Taine, Hippolyte, 48
Tasso, Torquato, 196–198, 204, 351n
Taylor, Captain Meadows: his *Confessions of a Thug*, 10–12, 62n; and Bulwer, 359–360n
Taylor, Thomas, 161–162, 184, 339n, 348–349n
Thackeray, Anne (Lady Ritchie), 202, 352n
Thackeray, William Makepeace, 8; and "Newgate" novel, 26–27; and du Maurier, 50–51, 90; and Bulwer, 156, 334n, 336n
Thayer, William Roscoe, 48–49
Thessalos of Tralles, 229, 345n
Theurgy, *see* Chaldaean Oracles, and *Zanoni*

Thorwaldsen, 149, 353n
Thug, 359–360n. *See also* Taylor, Captain Meadows
Tourreil, Louis du, 127
Toussaint l'Ouverture, Pierre, 72
Townshend, The Reverend Chauncey Hare, 235–236, 240, 282, 307–309, 355n
Trevelyan, Janet Penrose Ward, 48, 67n
Trollope, Anthony, 8, 63n, 221, 225, 353n

Van Helmont, Jean Baptiste, 154, 185, 243, 268–269, 270, 271, 282, 330
Vaughan, Thomas (Eugenius Philalethes), 167
Victoria, Queen, 117–118
Villiers de l'Isle Adam, 352n
Vril, *see Coming Race*

Ward, Mrs. Humphry: *the* copy of her *Robert Elsmere*, 22, 43–49; her *Unbelief and Sin*, 47, 66–67n
Webb, R. K., 124, 130n, 132–133n, 135n, 353n
Wells, H. G., 323
Whistler, James A. McNeill: and *Trilby*, 54
White Slave (Hennigsen), 13
Wieland, Christoph Martin, 342n
Wilkinson, Garth, 102
Williams, Harley (John Hargreaves), 134n, 139n
Wolff, R. L., 62n, 137n, 140n
Wordsworth, William, 126
Worthington, John, 83–84, 133n

Zanoni (Bulwer), 148, 159–232; astrology in, 151; and "Kosem

Kosamin," 152; Aytrun satirizes, 156–157; as romantic novel, 160, 176, 222–223; design of, 167; and *Zicci,* 159, 160, 203, 204; and Rosicrucians, 159, 163, 182, 185, 187, 199–200; and Platonic enthusiasms, 160–162, 167–191, 193–200; "Real" or "Dutch," 160, 162, 223; "Ideal" or "Greek," 160, 162, 223; and French Revolution, 167; and Mejnour, 168, 178, 180, 187, 194, 200, 206, 218; and Cazotte, 168–169, 193–196; Zanoni as magus, 170, 176; and Saint-Martin, 173; and herbalism, 175–176, 180, 186–187; Glyndon as neophyte, 173, 177–179; Zanoni no Rosicrucian, 177, 181–182, 185, 199, 207, 351–352n; and J. L. David, 178, 180, 347n; and *The Coming Race,* 180; as Chaldaean novel, 182, 185, 187, 200; and Isis, 186; and elixir of life, 188–191; comic relief in, 192; and Tasso, 197–198; and Iamblichus, 198; Glyndon as Bulwer, 200, 231–232; reception of, 202–206; and Schiller, 223; and political message, 209–211, 224–225; and Gibson, 211–213; moral lesson, 213; and Martineau's key, 213–215; 218–220, 222; Note to, 215–217; influence of Novalis, 223–224; other influences, 222–228; and Chauncey Hare Townshend, 235–236; in a seance, 245; compared with *A Strange Story,* 270–271, 274, 281, 284, 285, 294, 295, 296, 309–310, 319, 324
Zicci, see Zanoni
Zoist, The, 236–237, 240, 241, 356n, 361n